# The Oxbridge Formula

# The Oxbridge Formula

Paarul Shah
Jess Grindlay
Chris Parker

STEPMATHS'
OXBRIDGE
ACADEMY

ISBN (print) 978-1-8380031-0-4
ISBN (ebook) 978-1-8380031-1-1



Published by STEPMaths Publishing (UniPrepCo Ltd.)
www.oxbridgeformula.co.uk
info@oxbridgeformula.co.uk
Tel: 020 7459 4139


Typeset by A. Manikanndaprabhu, Madurai

# Foreword

I love this book.

I wish *The Oxbridge Formula* was available years ago. It would have helped me support the many students I have worked with over the years with their Oxbridge applications. *The Oxbridge Formula* is ideal for any parent or teacher who is wanting to support their child through to Oxbridge or, frankly, any of the Russell Group universities. It is directed at the students themselves and, if you are one of them, take my word for it: this book is essential reading.

Students who don't have much experience with Oxbridge, who don't have friends or older family members who have been there, or don't have teachers who know the process, can often feel overwhelmed by the application process. This book demystifies that process, in particular for those students applying for a STEM subject.

I love the honesty and direct approach of *The Oxbridge Formula*. It tells it as it is. *The Oxbridge Formula* talks to students in an accessible way. You will feel as if someone is sitting next to you chatting away with lots of advice. Whatever questions you may have about the Oxbridge application process – the skills you need, the qualities of an ideal Oxbridge candidate, degree choice, the interview process, how to succeed with admissions tests or your personal statement – you will find answers in this book.

I have known too many young people from disadvantaged backgrounds who think Oxbridge 'isn't for them'. Often, this is because the process of applying is terrifying. It is daunting, not just for the students, but for the adults supporting them.

I consider myself relatively experienced in this world of Oxbridge applications. I went to Oxford, have spent decades supporting students with their applications, have given talks at Oxford on how to broaden their student body, and have advised teachers with the responsibility for supporting Oxbridge-potential students in their schools. Yet, I have learned so much from reading this book.

We will use *The Oxbridge Formula* with our Sixth Form students at Michaela Community School. Our students speak highly of the STEPMaths and Oxbridge Formula Academy resources that we have used with them and I know they will feel similarly about this book.

The three authors of The Oxbridge Formula, each highly successful in their own Oxbridge journeys, have combined their experience in mentoring Oxbridge candidates to put together all of these pearls of wisdom into one book. It is packed full of information and doesn't pull its punches.

As the Introduction says, 'Note: ability doesn't necessarily mean natural talent—you can improve your ability through *hard work*.' Reading this book and digesting its insights is part of that hard work. *The Oxbridge Formula* tells you what you have to do if you want to get into Oxbridge. Follow the advice in this book and you are several steps closer to getting there.

Katharine Birbalsingh

# Contents

# Part V: Next Steps

# Introduction

## Why did you pick up this book?

There are many reasons why you might have picked up this book. Perhaps it's because you're fascinated by one or more of the subjects on the front cover? Perhaps you're thinking of applying to Oxbridge (Oxford or Cambridge) or know someone who is? Or perhaps you're intrigued by the idea of a formula you can use to get in!

Whatever the case, we bet you already know one thing—**studying at Oxbridge has many advantages:** not least that it's a unique opportunity to learn directly from world-class academics[1] and be surrounded by the brightest minds in the form of your fellow students. What's more, once you graduate, just having Oxford or Cambridge on your CV will often put it straight to the top of the pile[2].

## Here's the problem

**The Oxbridge admissions process can feel like a mystery.** Compared with other universities, applying to Oxford or Cambridge involves a lot of extra moving parts (admissions tests and interviews, to name only two) and every stage is very demanding. Outdated stereotypes about the universities and their typical students don't help matters at all—and it can be hard to know where to turn for advice.

Unfortunately, the majority of the advice that's been written to guide Oxbridge applicants through this exacting process has been created by (and for!) arts and humanities graduates. It might be great advice, but it isn't necessarily suitable (or even relevant) for a STEM or Economics applicant.

The truth is: a strong grasp of current affairs might help you get an offer for an Oxbridge Geography degree, but it's unlikely to propel you into an

1 Through the unique tutorial/supervision system, where you'll often have an hour with a tutor and just one other student.

2 An Oxbridge degree requires dedication and hard work—and employers know it.

Oxbridge Computer Science course; crafting a beautiful personal statement for Engineering won't hurt, but it won't get you your place either. Whereas being able to tackle the toughest physics and maths problems—well, that might just get you through your admissions test, through your interview, and all the way to the final goal: an offer from Oxford or Cambridge.

## Our solution: this book, 'The Oxbridge Formula'

If you're applying for a quantitative subject at Oxford or Cambridge, this is the only book you'll need. It's a one-of-a-kind resource catering to the unique requirements of students who enjoy maths and science and want to apply for a subject with mathematical foundations.

Our team (consisting of Oxbridge-educated teachers and tutors, and current students) has compiled all the useful advice we were lucky enough to receive when we applied—as well as the advice we wish we'd been given! We want to give everyone the knowledge that some applicants might pick up from having friends, teachers, parents, etc. with personal experience of Oxbridge, or from their school sending many students to Oxbridge every year. Inside this book, you'll find not only *our* insights, but also those gleaned from countless interviews with other graduates, students, and academics about everything they learned before or after coming to Oxford or Cambridge.

And if you're a parent or teacher whose teenager or student is thinking of applying to Oxbridge, this book will also be a useful guide as to how you can support them. It includes example personal statements and mock interview scripts—plus plenty of specific, tangible pieces of advice to ace admissions tests.

## So, what is the Oxbridge Formula?

All universities use several pieces of data to decide whether to make you an offer. These include:

- Your GCSE grades
- Your predicted A-Level grades
- Your teacher reference
- Your personal statement.

Getting into Oxbridge is notoriously difficult compared to other universities. Why? Well, not only do Oxford and Cambridge expect very good grades and references—they also add two more especially important data points. These are:

- Your admissions test score
- Your interview score.

Although all uni applicants have to write a personal statement, as an Oxbridge applicant, your personal statement could be scrutinised in an additional way, in that it might be discussed at interview. The personal statement is also an opportunity for you to prove that you're ready for the immense challenge that an Oxbridge degree will present.

In other words: your personal statement, test score and interview score are the **three tangible factors** that ultimately determine whether you'll receive an offer from Oxbridge. If we were to write this out as a simple formula, it might look like this:

$$\text{Chance of Oxbridge success} = P + T + I$$

Where:
P = Personal statement quality
T = Test score
I = Interview score

However, each stage of the application process is designed to test for **three intangible factors: Ability, Passion and Potential**.

This means that in reality, your personal statement, test score and interview score can be thought of as *functions* of:

a = ability
$p_a$ = passion
$p_o$ = potential

**The Oxbridge Formula**

$$\text{Chance of Oxbridge success} = P(a, p_a, p_o) + T(a, p_a, p_o) + I(a, p_a, p_o)$$

Although it can be tempting to focus all of your attention on the tangible aspects of the selection process, it's important to always keep in mind the three intangible qualities that are being tested at every stage.

## Let's explore the qualities in a bit more detail:

Without **Ability**, **Passion** and **Potential**, it's highly unlikely that you will:

**a.** Get an offer
But even if you do, it will be almost impossible for you to:
**b.** Enjoy your Oxbridge degree
**c.** Succeed in it.

So, there's no point just *pretending* to have them. And you wouldn't succeed if you tried: admissions tutors aren't easily fooled. Throughout the admissions process, they can smell feigned passion or grandiose claims of academic achievement from a student who just wants the prestige of Oxbridge on their CV.

### Ability

'Ability' means having the necessary foundation for an Oxbridge degree in your subject. Not only does that include subject knowledge and related skills, but you'll also need a knack for tackling problems typical of your discipline. Note: ability doesn't necessarily mean natural talent—you can improve your ability through *hard work*.

If you are serious about applying to Oxbridge, you must make sure your A-level techniques are second nature to you. For the subjects we explore in this book, that means: knowing theory and equations by heart; understanding the connections between different parts of the syllabus; completing exam-style questions without using notes; and understanding where formulae come from so that you can derive them when needed. It also means never being content with *not understanding* something—and taking the initiative to find extra practice questions to boost your confidence and performance.

Ability **isn't about** asking teachers to bump up your predicted grades at the last minute so you meet the Oxbridge admissions criteria. It doesn't mean cramming for an admissions test the night before, or claiming on your personal statement to have won competitions while being unable to recall anything about them when asked.

### Passion

'Passion' is an intangible quality that can't be faked. A student who is passionate about their subject will get lost in exploring it, trying to understand new phenomena and puzzling over tough problems for hours on end. They will eat, breathe and dream their subject.

Without this enthusiasm, boredom will likely set in. Worse, when it comes to a tough Oxbridge degree (in which a single problem sheet may take three days to complete), your innate passion gives you the 'staying power' to push through when the work is challenging (which it will be, more often than not).

Remember: your admissions tutors are academics or professors who have dedicated their lives to their subject—and they want to teach students that share that passion.

Passion can be *displayed* in many forms. It could be that you *research* and *read* around your subject in great depth outside of the classroom. It could be that you participate in *competitions* and *contests*—getting lost in problems and exploring every avenue you can until you solve each one.

As you may have guessed, passion **isn't about** reading a book simply because it will make you look good on your personal statement.[3] It isn't about slogging through extra work just to impress your admissions tutors. It doesn't mean applying to a subject just because your parents want you to, or because your teachers think you are good enough.

Although passion on its own isn't enough to guarantee an offer, without that underlying interest, it's very difficult to succeed in the long run.

## Potential

'Potential' refers to having the skills needed to learn and grow in your discipline—and to engage with the teaching you'll receive at Oxford or Cambridge. That means personal traits such as curiosity, a capacity for critical reflection, and an open mind. It also means being able to absorb and apply new concepts, use familiar techniques in unfamiliar contexts, read and understand academic texts, and engage in academic discussions.

Potential correlates strongly with being a 'teachable' student, which is the number one quality tutors look for in an interview. It means being able to share your ideas and accept criticism or advice in the context of a tutorial or supervision. Tutors at Oxford and Cambridge look for potential because it's proof that you haven't reached your ceiling in your A Levels or the IB, but instead will be able to succeed in a difficult degree. Learning from others and using their different viewpoints to enhance your understanding is also a sign of potential.

---

3 We'll provide suggested reading lists throughout this book, and the same thing applies: read these books because you're interested in them, not because you think they're the key to getting in.

Potential **isn't the same as** current ability. Being the top student in your class doesn't necessarily mean having the potential to study the subject at Oxbridge. Neither does memorising a lot of facts or being stubborn in your views.

Having potential can also be linked to having a **growth mindset**. Having a growth mindset means that you value the process as much as the results and that you're not afraid to take on challenges to achieve greater heights. You'll be tested on your potential both in admissions tests and during your interviews, where you may be pushed outside the comfort zone of what you have learned at school and will have to apply what you know in unfamiliar situations.

## The rest of the Oxbridge Formula

Although ability, passion and potential form the intangible heart of your application, they aren't something you can improve *just* by reading this book. Instead, they will flourish as you work on the *tangible* parts of the application—so long as you approach those parts in the right way.

For instance, practising for your admissions test goes hand in hand with improving your problem-solving ability. Investing time in your subject requires passion, but also nurtures that passion. Applying the Oxbridge Formula means preparing the tangible parts of your application to both boost and reflect the intangibles.

Throughout this book, we will describe the application process in full detail, and we will show you where the Oxbridge Formula can be applied at every stage!

### Personal statements

When applying to Oxbridge, you will typically write your personal statement[4] over the summer for submission in early October. We won't touch too much on the *structure* of personal statement, but in general a good personal statement might look something like:

- **Paragraph 1:** Your interests and inspirations, and why they motivated you to apply for *this degree*. Passion

4 Cambridge applicants also complete a Supplementary Application Questionnaire (SAQ), containing an explanation as to why you are a good fit for the Cambridge course. What you should include in your SAQ depends heavily on the subject you apply for. It's most important if you're applying for something at Cambridge that's different from the rest of your UCAS choices. It's best to ask on an open day or by phone what the tutors are looking for for your subject.

- **Paragraphs 2 and 3:** How your reading, super-curricular[5] activities, work experience, and other actions show you're suited to the degree. Ability Passion Potential
- **Paragraph 4:** How you've gained other relevant skills (e.g. teamwork or communication) from extracurricular activities, and/or further sources of motivation (e.g. career plans). Passion Potential,
- **Concluding sentence:** Why you belong in this degree programme.

However, each degree has its own demands, so make sure to check out our advice for your particular subject. To help you put together an amazing personal statement, we'll provide you with tailored reading lists curated by current Oxbridge students—as well as subject-specific tips to make your personal statement stand out from the crowd. We've included an annotated selection of personal statements from successful Oxbridge candidates to give you an idea of what you're aiming for.

## Admissions tests

Most admissions tests covered in this book are taken in late October or early November as pre-interview tests. The exception is STEP, which you take at the same time as your A Levels or final IB exams.

To help you prepare effectively for your test, we've collected a range of preparation techniques – tried and tested by generations of Oxbridge students – and synthesised them into a series of structured exam techniques that will help you achieve that top mark on the day. But, as you will see time and again, there is no substitute for practice!

Where relevant, we will point you to the many useful resources we have created specifically for these tests.

## Interviews

Oxford and Cambridge typically interview applicants in early December before making offers in January. In this book, you'll find a range of tips to help you prepare for your interview. What's more, we have created sample Oxbridge interview questions with interview scripts to show you how a strong candidate is expected to approach the question and engage with the interviewer.

This book will also offer insight into what life as an Oxbridge student is really like. For each course, we present a picture of the typical workload, as well as a flavour of what each of your first-year subjects is really

5 Super-curricular activities are academic activities that go beyond what you study at school, such as extra reading, problem-solving, competitions, lectures, etc.

## Application timeline

| When? | What? |
|---|---|
| During Year 11 | Choose A Levels |
| Spring Year 12 | Start admissions test preparation |
| Summer before Year 13 | Work experience<br>Prepare/draft personal statement<br>Continue admissions test preparation<br>Summer schools<br>Early applications for organ/music scholars and some overseas applicants |
| October Year 13 | UCAS application (including personal statement)<br>SAQ (Cambridge)<br>Heavy admissions test preparation |
| End of October/Early November Year 13 | Admissions tests (excluding STEP, CSAT)<br>Start interview preparation |
| December Year 13 (can continue into January) | Interviews (including at-interview tests, CSAT) |
| Mid-January Year 13 | Offers made |
| Spring Year 13 | Heavy STEP preparation (Cambridge Maths) |
| May/June Year 13 | A Levels<br>STEP (Cambridge Maths) |
| Summer Year 13 | Results<br>Adjustment* (Cambridge)<br>Summer reading<br>Getting ready to start uni! |

*Cambridge makes additional offers to a few disadvantaged students with very good results.

about—so you can see if the reality of studying that subject at Oxbridge lives up to your expectations!

## How can you use this book?

We have tried to make the book as accessible and user-friendly as possible. It is split into five parts:

- **Part I: Mathematical and Computational Sciences**
- **Part II: Physical Sciences**
- **Part III: Economics**
- **Part IV: Philosophy (bonus part!)**
- **Part V: Next Steps**

The first three parts each consists of three divisions:

- **A: The Courses:** We'll give you an insight into the content you'll study in each degree and why the degree might be for you. We'll introduce new, undergraduate-level concepts, which we're hoping will spark your interest and act as a springboard for further research!
- **B: The Admissions Process:** We'll walk you through everything you need to know to put the Oxbridge Formula into practice in your personal statement, admissions tests and interviews.
- **C: Before Your Degree:** We'll discuss the work you can do after the end of Year 13 to make the best possible start at Oxbridge.

This book will help you at every stage of the application process. Use it as you decide what to apply for, review it the night before your interview, dive back in when you need advice preparing for STEP, and come back when you're using your summer to get ready for your degree!

Feel free to dip in and out of this book as needed—there's no right way to read it. You might want to:

- **Scan all the sections** to get an overview of all the subjects you're considering
- **Read in detail** all the information on applying for your chosen course to find out what will be expected of you
- **Re-read** the description of one particular stage of the admissions process as you prepare for it
- **Scan a section** to refresh your memory on a particular subject or tip as it becomes more relevant
- **Use the cross-references** to seek out further relevant information in other sections of the book

- **Check out the bonus chapter** on our website (scan the QR code below!) for even more tips, tricks and insights into nailing the Oxbridge Formula.[6]

Scan this QR code with your camera app to download the bonus chapter

## The Oxbridge System

Throughout this book, we'll assume some background knowledge about Oxford and Cambridge. The essential points are:

- **Degree length:** Your degree could last three or four years—the description of each course will say which.
- **Oxbridge year:** An Oxford/Cambridge year consists of three terms, which are each eight weeks long.
- **Teaching:** The teaching process is as follows:
  - **Lectures:** You attend lectures on multiple courses from your degree programme each week—see our course descriptions for examples
  - **Problem sheets/Example sheets:** For quantitative topics, you're assigned sets of questions called 'problem sheets' or 'example sheets' based on recent lectures
  - **Essays:** For qualitative topics, you're assigned essay questions, as well as reading to prepare for these
  - **Tutorials/Supervisions:** For each problem sheet or essay, you attend a 'tutorial' (Oxford) or 'supervision' (Cambridge), which is a small-group lesson (typically with one or two other students) in which you discuss the questions with a tutor[7]

6 See oxbridgeformula.co.uk/bonus-chapter—there are lots of things we wanted to add to the book but simply didn't have space for. So, our bonus chapter will link you to other useful resources and provide direct links when it wasn't practical to provide the whole URL in this book.

7 The ability to get such personal teaching from leading academics is one of the most attractive features of an Oxbridge degree.

   - **Labs and classes:** For some subjects, you may have other kinds of teaching, such as laboratory work ('labs'), or lessons in groups of five or more students ('classes' or 'seminars').
- **Exams:** You sit exams at the end of the first year to check your progress. However, your final result is based on your exams at the end of the second year (for some subjects) and the third year (for all subjects). For some degrees, other elements (such as labs) also count towards your final result. If you do a fourth year, it is usually examined separately.
- **Colleges:** Oxford and Cambridge are composed of different colleges that handle most of the admissions process for most subjects. You can either apply to a specific college or make an open application. A college is like a small community—it's where you'll live, eat, and have most of your tutorials/supervisions.[8] Although much of the process is standardised across colleges, there is variation, especially when it comes to interviews. For instance, only some colleges use at-interview written tests.
- **Winter and summer pool:** If you are a strong candidate who isn't made an offer by your original college or just misses their offer, you might be put into a 'pool' so that other colleges have the chance to take you. A similar process happens at Oxford in a less formal way. Both universities try to make sure that the strongest candidates end up with a place, even if not at their first-choice college.

## Before you read on

Bear in mind: all of the details in this book are correct at the time of writing (spring 2020). However, all details are subject to change[9]. Also, due to the collegiate system, some aspects of your application may be different from what is described here. You must check the official website to verify key details before choosing a subject, sitting your admissions test and preparing for your interview.

For the sake of brevity, we have written the book as if we were speaking to a student who is taking A Levels, though we have also included typical offers for the IB where relevant.

A word of caution before we get started—in fact, we can't say it enough! This book is a useful starting point for your application. It provides you with

8 There's a lot more that can be said about colleges, including how to choose a college, but that discussion is unfortunately beyond the scope of this book.

9 In particular, by the time you read this book, some admissions tests are likely to have been altered. At the time of printing, Cambridge has announced that the ECAA and NSAA will be changing, but has not released details. Please download the Bonus Chapter at oxbridgeformula.co.uk/bonus-chapter to read up on any changes.

all the vital information you need. However, simply reading this book will *not* guarantee you a place at your dream university. The real work begins once you've finished reading and get to work developing your ability, passion and potential so that you can ace your personal statement, admissions tests and interviews… and maximise your chances of getting an offer!

## Who are we?

### Paarul

After graduating with a first-class Maths degree from Oxford, Paarul qualified as a maths teacher and went on to teach in some of London's leading grammar and independent schools, taking responsibility for extracurricular teaching of critical thinking and for mentoring Oxbridge STEM applicants. She is the founder of the Oxbridge Formula (formerly STEPMaths).

*"My love of maths is rooted in the sense of satisfaction I get from having struggled over an impossibly difficult problem, and finally arriving at the solution. Problem-solving is at the heart of everything I love doing: maths, teaching, entrepreneurship… and more!*

*I've often heard it said that you can't prepare for admissions tests, but in my experience, that's not true. I suppose I took it as a personal challenge to seek out patterns among seemingly disparate questions, extract the problem-solving techniques needed to handle them, and share those ideas in a simple-to-understand way. This, combined with the realisation of how much I had gained from my own Oxbridge experience, is what led to the birth of the Oxbridge Formula Academy.*

*Our Oxbridge Academy has been more successful than I ever could have hoped at helping students secure places at Oxford and Cambridge. It has been a sincere pleasure to work alongside our dedicated and talented team of tutors, to watch our students have 'lightbulb moments', and to witness their successes at university and beyond.*

*This book is our latest effort to level the playing field for Oxbridge applicants. I am particularly proud that two women have co-authored this book, and I hope this encourages girls everywhere to explore and pursue STEM degrees!*

*A huge thank you to Jess, whose 'on the ground' journalism, talent, and clear, engaging writing style have allowed us to transform hundreds of accounts from current Cambridge and Oxford students into such a comprehensive and coherent book—as well as Chris, whose sheer breadth and depth of knowledge have added to it a level of detail that is unprecedented. I sincerely hope it helps you win a place at the university of your dreams!"* –Paarul

## Jess

Jess is a third-year Maths & Philosophy student at St Hilda's College, Oxford. Jess began with nothing but our ambition for this book, and with her industriousness and enthusiasm quickly turned it into a concrete reality.

*"I did Maths, Further Maths, Physics and English at A Level, and applied to Oxford when I was in Year 13. When preparing for the MAT, I attended Oxbridge Formula courses and also used their online resources. Both of these provided invaluable help with my application. I love reading and writing (skills thrust upon me by my mum, who is an English teacher!) and have also written blogs for Oxbridge Formula in the past.*

*University applications can be daunting—especially when you have to jump through as many hoops as you do for Oxford and Cambridge. Throughout this book, we have tried to give you the advice we would have loved to hear when we were applying. Think of this book as a buddy you can turn to when you need to overcome a hurdle!" –Jess*

## Chris

A multipotentialite with a talent for explaining tricky concepts with logic, clarity and insight— Chris is a professional tutor and holds a first-class master's degree in Maths & Philosophy from Oxford. He is the lead tutor at the Oxbridge Formula Academy.

*"I get a real sense of satisfaction in clarifying, explaining and expressing ideas 'just right', whether that's through a precise combination of words, condensing the outcome of a long calculation into a diagram, or finding the simplest possible proof. It's the same reason I love teaching and enjoyed writing this book.*

*I've been involved with the Oxbridge Formula Academy from the start, and I've had the pleasure of working face-to-face with hundreds of students, whose questions and concerns about the Oxbridge application process motivated the writing of this book.*

*I was never sure what degree I wanted to study. Although I ended up studying Maths & Philosophy at Oxford, I applied to Physics, Natural Sciences, Maths and Ancient History, and Philosophy at other universities in the same year (not a strategy I recommend!)—and I have an active interest in those subjects to this day.*

*If, like me, you have a variety of degree courses on your shortlist, I hope this book will help you decide between them. If you have no idea what you want to study, I hope you're inspired by the many subjects that we explore here. All three of us learnt so much in researching this book, and we were all intrigued by a number of degree courses we'd never considered before that we could genuinely picture ourselves pursuing." –Chris*

## What is the Oxbridge Formula Academy?

At the Oxbridge Formula Academy, we help students with the application process for any degree containing an element of mathematics—from Maths itself, to Physics and Engineering, to Computer Science, to Economics. We also help students with admissions tests when they contain a quantitative element, such as Geography, Psychology, and Medicine (BMAT).

You might previously have know us as 'STEPMaths', but we felt the name 'Oxbridge Formula' encapsulated how we help students to develop the intangibles in order to perfect their personal statements, ace their admissions tests, and nail their interviews.

For each admissions test covered in this book, we run courses that have helped hundreds of students get into their chosen university. To expand this opportunity to as many people as possible, we launched online courses with more than 5500 video tutorials—including worked video solutions to thousands of past paper questions, and videos packed with preparation tips. We also run mock-interview courses and one-to-one interview sessions. You can read more about what we offer from page 469.

If you'd like more information about how we can help you with your application, please visit: oxbridgeformula.co.uk.

We hope you'll find this book tremendously helpful, and we'd be very grateful if you'd consider leaving us a review on Amazon. For enquiries, please do contact us at *support@oxbridgeformula.co.uk*.

# Part I:

# Mathematical and Computational Sciences

# Part I A: The Courses

Part I will go through all the Maths, Computer Science and related courses offered at Oxbridge. We will outline what it's actually like to study these courses at university and will help you identify whether or not they are for you. The courses offered are:

- Maths
- Computer Science
- Maths & Computer Sciences
- Maths & Statistics
- Maths & Philosophy
- Computer Science & Philosophy
- Maths with Physics

# Chapter 1:
# Maths

## 1.1: Why Maths?

Maths is a difficult course, and not to be embarked upon lightly! If you've heard anything about university-level maths it's probably that it's ludicrously difficult, but that it can give you amazing prospects for the future. But how do you know if Maths is for you?

Here's a checklist of things that might make you suited to studying Maths at Oxbridge:

- ❑ **You enjoy problem-solving:** You enjoy the sort of questions that appear on UKMT Maths Challenge papers (if you've never seen these before, have a look at the standard of the Senior Kangaroo rounds on their website[10]) and other mathematical problems.
- ❑ **You're interested in the theory behind maths:** You love maths at A Level, but you want to dig deeper to understand *why* what you've learnt at school is true. For example, why do the product and chain rules work every time? How can we approximate functions or roots of functions—and do those approximations always work? Why do all polynomials have solutions in the complex numbers?
- ❑ **You're fluent with the skills required for A-Level Maths.** At university, the maths you do will presume understanding of all the core skills developed at A Level. Some of the most important skills include:
  - Integration
  - Differentiation
  - Manipulating polynomials (factorising, dividing, finding roots, sketching graphs)
  - Handling complex numbers
  - Calculating with matrices (multiplying, finding determinants and inverses, interpreting them as transformations).
- ❑ **You're committed and hard-working.** It goes without saying that pursuing any degree at Oxford or Cambridge will mean a lot of work. However, you have to be *especially* committed if you're going to succeed in

10 Please see oxbridgeformula.co.uk/bonus-chapter for more information.

Maths. In your first term, not everything will come immediately to you. You might feel in over your head: the teaching style is different to school and the concepts will take some time to get your head around. But with perseverance you will get there. It's just about sticking it out and being prepared to dedicate the time.

- ❑ **You have a knack for precision.** A big part of a Maths degree is proving propositions and theorems. This requires attention to detail and an eye for precision. In a proof, you must dot every *i* and cross every *t!*
- ❑ **You're creative and prepared to think about maths in a new way.** Whereas the maths you do at school can feel repetitive, maths at university is much more creative! It's about proving results, experimenting with ideas and trying multiple methods to see what takes you in the right direction. You'll meet more dead ends, but it's a lot more rewarding when you finally get to the result!
- ❑ **You love maths!** We can't stress this enough: it's *so* important that you're passionate about the subject you apply to study at university. A degree is a serious undertaking and you won't be able to find the motivation to study unless you really love the subject.

If you can tick off most of the items on the list, Maths could be the perfect course for you! Read on for more details about what is covered in the Maths courses at Oxford and Cambridge.

## Case studies

Why did students currently studying Maths at Oxford and Cambridge apply there?

> *"For A Levels, I took Maths, Further Maths, Physics and Chemistry. I knew from a very young age I wanted to do something science-related—and I've always loved the elegance of maths, with its logic and problem-solving. I thought I'd enjoy that about studying Maths at uni."*
> –Nick, Maths, Cambridge

> *"Trying out the Oxford and Cambridge admissions tests is what led me to apply. I found the problems interesting, and I liked the out-of-the-box thinking they need. They convinced me that maths at university would consist of similarly fascinating problems."* –Jack, Maths, Oxford

> *"Solving the hardest, most out-there problems, and discussing them with world experts—it sounded like a dream."* –Anna, Maths, Cambridge

> *"Maths has always intrigued me. I wanted to find out how everything we'd been taught in school actually worked and this course has allowed me to do that!"* –Sam, Maths, Cambridge

> *"I was thinking of applying to study physics. But then, when I did more research, I found the idea of proving and exploring the concepts I would be using in physics much more exciting than the idea of actually using them. So I thought Maths was for me, and I was absolutely right."* –Katie, Maths, Oxford

## 1.2: Maths: Oxford vs. Cambridge

So, you know that you want to study maths—and that you want to apply to either Oxford or Cambridge. Now you need to figure out: which blue are you?[11]

This table compares the Maths courses offered at Oxford and Cambridge so you can see which one would suit you best. For joint courses at either uni, most of the details are the same as in this table—but check out Chapter 3 on page 40 for the full details.

| OXFORD | CAMBRIDGE |
|---|---|
| **Entry requirements:** Generally, the offer is A*A*A (with A* in Maths and Further Maths) or 39 in the IB (including core points), with 7, 6, 6 at Higher Level and a 7 in Higher Level Maths. | **Entry requirements:** Generally, the offer is A*A*A (with A* in Maths and Further Maths) or 40–42 in the IB (including core points), with 7, 7, 6 at Higher Level and a 7 in Higher Level Maths. |

11 Traditionally, Oxford is dark blue, Cambridge light blue.

| OXFORD | CAMBRIDGE |
|---|---|
| **Admissions tests:** The MAT is the pre-interview maths test that is sat by all Oxford Maths applicants. | **Admissions tests:** There are 3 maths papers called STEP, which are sat in the summer of Year 13—STEP 1, 2 and 3. Cambridge does not hold a pre-interview test but will typically ask for a grade 1 in both in STEP 2 and 3 as part of your offer. Some colleges, such as Trinity and King's, may ask you to sit a test at interview. |
| **Applicants per place:** In 2018, there were 2281 applications to study Maths and 373 offers—or 1 offer for every 6 applicants. After results day, there's an overall success rate of 1 in 7 applicants. | **Applicants per place:** In 2017, 1456 students applied for Maths at Cambridge and 532 received offers—equivalent to 1 offer for every 3 applicants. After A-Level and STEP results, there were 257 successful students, which means an overall success rate of 1 in 6 applicants. |
| **Course length:** In your third year, you can choose to leave with a BA, or continue to the fourth year and leave with an MMath. You can choose to move into Maths and Theoretical Physics in your fourth year, in which case you leave with an MMathPhys. | **Course length:** In your third year, you can choose to leave with a BA, or continue to the fourth year (confusingly called 'Part III') and leave with an MMath. You can also apply to Part III as a 1-year master's degree—for instance, if you've left Oxford with a BA. |
| **First-year studies:** In your first year at Oxford you'll study linear algebra, analysis, geometry, dynamics, calculus and multivariable calculus, probability, Fourier series, constructive mathematics, statistics and data analysis, and groups. The next section has details of these courses. | **First-year studies:** In your first year at Cambridge you'll study abstract algebra, analysis, number theory, differential equations, mathematical methods, Newtonian dynamics, special relativity and probability. The next section has details of these courses. Maths at Cambridge has a greater emphasis on theoretical physics in all years than Maths at Oxford. |

| OXFORD | CAMBRIDGE |
|---|---|
| **Later years:** In your second and third year, Oxford and Cambridge offer very similar modules with a wide variety of choices. By your third year, you can select from up to 50 options, allowing you to specialise in areas of your choice. | |
| **Teaching style:** You'll have an average of 12 lectures per week in your first year and 3–4 tutorials per week. In second year at Oxford, you continue with tutorials in your colleges—but in third year, due to the wide range of options, you'll have classes on each of your modules at the Maths faculty with the professor, another tutor and another 5–20 students from other colleges. Oxford also offers computational maths, essay-based modules (in the third year), and a LaTeX[12] project. If you do the fourth year, you'll study a similar number of options to the third year, including a compulsory dissertation. | **Teaching style:** In your first year at Cambridge, you'll typically have 12 lectures and 2 supervisions per week.[13] In your second and third years, the number and frequency of supervisions and lectures fluctuate depending on the courses you choose. You also have optional computational projects in your second and third years. If you do Part III (the fourth year), you'll again have a wide choice of courses in both maths and theoretical physics. |

## Choosing between Oxford and Cambridge

As you can see from the table, the Oxford and Cambridge Maths courses cover a lot of the same material and are similar in structure. If you're still confused as to how to choose between them, here are some other factors you might consider:

- **Joint courses**: At Oxford, you can study Maths with Statistics, Computer Science or Philosophy. At Cambridge, you can study Maths with Physics. See Chapter 3 on page 40 for more details.
- **Physics crossover**: Even if you don't apply for Maths with Physics, the Cambridge Maths degree tends to touch on mathematical physics more than its Oxford counterpart. For example, at Oxford you need to choose the appropriate options after your first year to be exposed to special relativity or fields (such as electromagnetic fields and gravity),

12 A typesetting system that makes maths look pretty.

13 At Cambridge small group lessons are called supervisions, at Oxford they are called tutorials. They are essentially the same thing.

whereas at Cambridge they are studied by all students.

- **Careers**: Cambridge Maths graduates are more likely than their Oxford counterparts to go into further study (O: 30%, C: 40%) or IT and telecoms (O: 15%, C: 30%). On the other hand, Oxford graduates are more likely to go into business and administration (O: 15%, C: 6%) or teaching (O: 9%, C: approx. 0%). An explanation for this last stat might be that Oxford offers a module specifically for would-be teachers.
- **Size**: Cambridge's Maths intake is smaller, at around 250 compared to Oxford's 350 (plus another 80-100 from joint courses). Unusually, around a fifth of Cambridge maths students are at a single Cambridge college – Trinity – whereas Oxford students are more evenly distributed. If you like to be part of a small, tight-knit group, you might prefer Cambridge, whereas if you like to be part of a larger scene, you might prefer Oxford.
- **Saturday lectures**: Cambridge Maths students notoriously have lectures on Saturday mornings. If you can't bear the thought of working at the weekend, you might want to keep this in mind. On the other hand, it does mean your contact hours are more evenly spread across the week.
- **City and college**: If you can't choose between the courses themselves, that's completely natural. Many students find they actually base their decision on which city they prefer, or that they particularly want to live in a particular college. The best way to see if this might apply to you is to visit both cities, perhaps via an open day.
- **Maths department buildings**: You'll spend a lot of time in the Maths department at the university you choose, so you might also want to visit them and see which you prefer the feel of. Both have relatively modern buildings: Cambridge's Centre for Mathematical Sciences was completed from 1992-2003 and Oxford's Andrew Wiles Building opened in 2013. At Oxford, you'll benefit from views through the glass walls and a huge amount of working space. At Cambridge you might appreciate the geometrical features of the architecture and the ability to work on the grass roof (when it's sunny). Both are a decent walk from the city centre: around 15 minutes for Oxford and 20 for Cambridge.

## 1.3: Is maths at uni anything like maths at school?

At school, you first practise new methods by repetition and then by applying them to variations on familiar problems. For example, at school you may have a whole question on integrating a particular polynomial, which you will have practised many times in class. In contrast, at university you may be shown something in a lecture and immediately be expected to solve a rather different looking problem on the same topic. You have to work to understand the material independently and apply it to this new problem as you won't have done lots and lots of similar questions before.

You'll be expected to go back to square one and rebuild all of your mathematical knowledge. You'll spend time learning and exploring *how* and *why* methods work and under what circumstances. You can't take the core rules of algebra, differentiation and integration for granted—you'll prove them in depth. This process is the focal point of studying maths at university.

To give you an insight into what studying maths at university is like, and how it differs from maths at school, here's a list of the core modules covered in the first year at both the Oxford and Cambridge:[14]

## Analysis

*Analysis is very proof-heavy, and is central to the study of pure mathematics throughout your degree.*

Analysis in the first term has a focus on limits and convergence. When you think of a sequence converging to a limit, you might say 'it gets closer and closer to the final limit'. But that isn't rigorous enough for a pure mathematician. Suppose you have a sequence $u_n$ and the limit of this sequence as $n \to \infty$ is $3$. What we are really saying is that, eventually, the gap between each term $u_n$ and $3$ becomes very small. The two key words here are 'eventually' and 'very small'. We need to show that we can make this gap as small as we like, as long as we go far enough along the sequence, i.e. choose a large enough $n$.

At uni, you might express '$u_n \to 3$ as $n \to \infty$' more formally as:

> A sequence $u_n$ **converges** to 3 as $n \to \infty$ if and only if:
>
> For any real number $\varepsilon > 0$, there's an integer $N > 0$ such that: for all integers $n > N$, $|u_n - 3| < \varepsilon$

14 Check out oxbridgeformula.co.uk/bonus-chapter for more information about these topics.

Here, $\varepsilon$ is an arbitrary choice of what we mean by 'very small', i.e. how small we want the gap between the terms of $u_n$ and 3 to be. The $N$ represents what we mean by 'eventually', i.e. how far you need to go along the sequence until all subsequent terms are less than $\varepsilon$ away from 3.[15]

Starting by rigorously proving whether sequences converge or not, analysis builds up all of the results you've taken for granted at A Level, such as the definitions of continuous functions and derivatives, the chain and product rules, and the relationship between integrals and areas under curves.

Analysis is incredibly rewarding and interesting—and lays important foundations for other areas of mathematics. It's also challenging, because it will make you think in a new way.

An example of a question you would see on a problem sheet is:

*Prove that every **convergent sequence** is a **Cauchy sequence**.*

A **convergent sequence** is one that tends to a particular real number. A **Cauchy sequence** is one where the *difference between consecutive terms* of the sequence tends to $0$, as you look further down the sequence.

For example, the sequence $0.9, 0.99, 0.999, 0.9999, 0.99999\ldots$ is convergent—it converges to $1$. It's also a Cauchy sequence, as the difference between the $k^{th}$ and $(k+1)^{th}$ terms is $0.0\ldots09$, with $k$ zeroes between the decimal point and the $9$, so the difference tends to $0$ as $k \to \infty$.

## Linear Algebra/Abstract Algebra

*Cambridge calls it Abstract Algebra; Oxford calls it Linear Algebra. There is a large overlap in the content covered.*

Algebra in this format will focus upon the study of types of mathematical structure—in particular, the types called '***vector spaces***', '***groups***' and '***rings***'. These have many applications in different fields of maths.

15 Don't worry if this doesn't make sense yet—Analysis is one of the hardest things you'll learn in your first year!

## Vector spaces

A **vector space** is a set of vectors. At school, you might think of a vector as an arrow with a magnitude and direction or as something used to represent a translation in space, but in linear algebra they can be *any* objects that obey this set of axioms (rules) for adding and scaling them:[16]

(VS1) $\mathbf{u} + \mathbf{v} = \mathbf{v} + \mathbf{u}$, for any vectors $\mathbf{u}$ and $\mathbf{v}$

(VS2) $(\mathbf{u} + \mathbf{v}) + \mathbf{w} = \mathbf{u} + (\mathbf{v} + \mathbf{w})$, for any vectors $\mathbf{u}$, $\mathbf{v}$ and $\mathbf{w}$

(VS3) There is a vector $\mathbf{0}$ such that $\mathbf{v} + \mathbf{0} = \mathbf{v}$ for every vector $\mathbf{v}$

(VS4) For every vector $\mathbf{v}$, there's a vector $-\mathbf{v}$ such that $\mathbf{v} + -\mathbf{v} = \mathbf{0}$

(VS5) $a(\mathbf{u} + \mathbf{v}) = a\mathbf{u} + a\mathbf{v}$ for any scalar $a$ and any vectors $\mathbf{u}$ and $\mathbf{v}$

(VS6) $(a + b)\mathbf{v} = a\mathbf{v} + b\mathbf{v}$ for any scalars $a$ and $b$ and any vector $\mathbf{v}$

(VS7) $a(b\mathbf{v}) = (ab)\mathbf{v}$ for any scalars $a$ and $b$ and any vector $\mathbf{v}$

(VS8) $1\mathbf{v} = \mathbf{v}$ for any vector $\mathbf{v}$.

The types of vector you'll have seen at school obey all of these axioms. But there are many other *very different* examples as well.

**Did You Know?**

*The set of polynomials[17] is also a vector space.*

Let's check: let $f(x)$ and $g(x)$ be polynomials and let $a$ and $b$ be real numbers. Checking some of the axioms, we can see that the following hold true:

(VS1) $f(x) + g(x) = g(x) + f(x)$
(VS5) $a[f(x) + g(x)] = af(x) + ag(x)$
(VS8) $1(f(x)) = f(x)$

16 Note that '+' will mean different things for different vector spaces, in the same way that matrix multiplication is different from multiplication of real numbers even though they have the same name. Scaling simply means multiplying by a scalar, which could be a real number, or a complex number, or even something more exotic.
17 Polynomials with real coefficients.

You can check the other axioms and see that the set of polynomials, where the scalars are the real numbers, do in fact form a vector space.

A large part of the first-year course is spent studying **linear transformations**. These are functions of vectors that obey the rule $f(a\mathbf{u} + b\mathbf{v}) = af(\mathbf{u}) + bf(\mathbf{v})$ for any scalars $a$ and $b$ and any vectors $\mathbf{u}$ and $\mathbf{v}$.

## Groups

A **group** is a set of elements and a **binary operation**, which means a function that takes two elements from the set as inputs. For example, addition is a binary operation because it adds *two* numbers together, but squaring isn't a binary operation because it's only applied to *one* number at a time. A group must also satisfy the following axioms, writing its binary operation as $x \star y$.

(G1) For any $x$ and $y$ in the group, $x \star y$ is also in the group

(G2) For any $x$, $y$ and $z$ in the group, $x \star (y \star z) = (x \star y) \star z$

(G3) There is an *identity element* $e$ in the group such that $e \star x = x \star e = x$ for any $x$ in the group[18]

(G4) For any $x$ in the group, there's an *inverse* $x^{-1}$ in the group such that $x \star x^{-1} = x^{-1} \star x = e$.

For example, the set of all *integers* is a *group* with respect to the operation of *addition*, if we take the identity element to be $0$ and the inverse of an integer $x$ to be $-x$. Why not check for yourself that it obeys all the axioms? In contrast, the set of all *positive* integers *isn't* a group with respect to addition, because it doesn't obey rules G3 and G4.

Another example of a group is the set of all *rotations* of a plane, where the binary operation is *combining two rotations* by first doing one rotation and then the other. The identity is a rotation by $0$ degrees, and the inverse of a rotation is simply the one that takes you in the opposite direction by the same number of degrees.

18 Don't confuse this with the number $e = 2.718...$

A **ring** is a particular type of group that also has a *second* binary operation that obeys slightly different rules. An example is the integers, with addition as one binary operation and multiplication as the other.

A typical question you might see on an early Groups problem sheet is:

> *Determine with proof whether the affine transformations of 2D real vectors form a group. An affine transformation is any transformation that can be expressed as multiplication by a $2 \times 2$ matrix followed by a translation.*

To solve this, you would test whether these transformations satisfy all the group axioms (G1 to G4) under the binary operation of function composition (i.e. applying one function and then the other).

## Numbers and Sets

*At Cambridge, you study Numbers and Sets as a separate module in your first year. At Oxford, you study this topic in the Introduction to University Mathematics course.*

The Cambridge course explores sets, relations and functions, the integers, the real numbers and elementary number theory[19].

The Oxford course is shorter and covers sets, relations and functions, integers and real numbers. It also deals with mathematical reasoning.

A typical question you might see on an early Numbers and Sets example sheet is:

> *Given a **relation** $R$ on the natural numbers, we say that a set $S$ is $R$-closed if and only if: for any $m$ and $n$ such that $mRn$, if $m \in S$, then $n \in S$.*

19 The part of maths which studies integers—particularly facts about divisibility.

*The ancestral of $R$, written $R^*$, is defined by the rule that $mR^*n$ if and only if: for any set $S$ that is $R$-closed and contains every $k$ such that $mRk$, $S$ also contains $n$.*

*Show that $R^*$ is the smallest* ***transitive relation*** *that is identical to or larger than $R$.*

A **relation** is something that holds between pairs of numbers. Examples of relations are: '$<$', '$=$' and '$\neq$'.

A **transitive relation** is one where, if $xRy$ and $yRz$, then $xRz$. For instance, '$<$' and '$=$' are transitive, but '$\neq$' isn't.

For the relation $R$ to be **smaller** than the relation $R'$ simply means that $R'$ relates *all* the pairs of numbers $R$ relates and *more* (i.e. if $xRy$, then $xR'y$ too). For example, '$<$' is smaller than '$\leq$'.[20] So this question is asking you to show that:

(a) $R^*$ is transitive
(b) $R$ is either smaller than or identical to $R^*$ and
(c) $R^*$ is smaller than any other relation with properties (a) and (b).

## Differential Equations, General Calculus

*At Oxford, you'll study some form of calculus in all terms of your first year, including multivariable calculus[21] and differential equations. At Cambridge, the course focuses primarily on differential equations and goes into greater depth.*

These are the courses where the skills you developed at school come in the handiest. You'll explore more complex differential equations than at school, as well as new ways to solve them—but your A-Level knowledge will be the foundation.

Although you'll prove some theorems, these courses focus more on your ability to *apply* those theorems to different situations. You'll study the situations in which different types of differential equation can be used (such

20 This is because when one number is strictly less than another it is also 'less than *or* equal to' it.

21 Doing calculus with functions of more than one variable—for example $f(x, y, z)$.

as how the 'heat equation' describes a solid object that is cooling down). This will be one of the most 'applied' courses in your first year.[22]

A typical question you might see on an early Calculus problem sheet is:

*Find all the second-order* ***partial derivatives*** *of* $\cos(xy)$.

The **partial derivative** of a function $f(x,y)$ with respect to $x$, written $\frac{\partial f}{\partial x}$, is the result of differentiating it as if $y$ were a constant rather than itself depending on $x$.

For instance, calculating the standard derivative of $xy$ gives us: $\frac{d}{dx}(xy) = y + x\frac{dy}{dx}$, but differentiating partially gives us: $\frac{\partial}{\partial x}(xy) = y$ instead. The second-order partial derivatives are $\frac{\partial}{\partial x}\left(\frac{\partial f}{\partial x}\right)$, $\frac{\partial}{\partial x}\left(\frac{\partial f}{\partial y}\right)$, $\frac{\partial}{\partial y}\left(\frac{\partial f}{\partial x}\right)$ and $\frac{\partial}{\partial y}\left(\frac{\partial f}{\partial y}\right)$. Why not try working them out?

## Geometry

*Geometry is a first-year course at Oxford, but not at Cambridge. It builds and expands upon the geometrical techniques you'll have learnt in school.*

The course covers coordinate systems and how to represent and analyse curves and surfaces using vectors. You'll also study different vector products, including ***triple products***, and the use of matrices to represent transformations.

A **triple product** combines three vectors instead of two. For instance, the scalar triple product of vectors $\mathbf{a}$, $\mathbf{b}$ and $\mathbf{c}$ is defined as $\mathbf{a} \bullet (\mathbf{b} \times \mathbf{c})$.

22 Believe it or not, pretty much all the maths you study at school falls under the 'applied maths' umbrella at university.

**Did You Know?**

*If* $\mathbf{r}$ *is the position vector of a point in 3D space, then:*

a) *the set of points which satisfy the equation* $|\mathbf{r} - \mathbf{u}| = R$ *for some* $R > 0$ *form the surface of a sphere*

b) *the set of points which satisfy the equation* $\mathbf{r} \cdot \mathbf{u} = \alpha|\mathbf{r}||\mathbf{u}|$[23], *where* $\mathbf{u}$ *is a vector and* $\alpha$ *is a real number such that* $|\alpha| < 1$, *form the surface of an infinite cone with its point at the origin.*

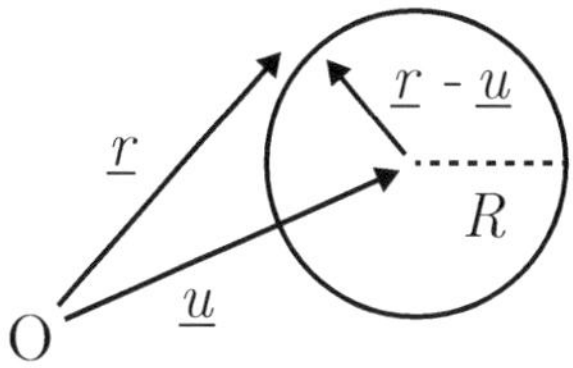


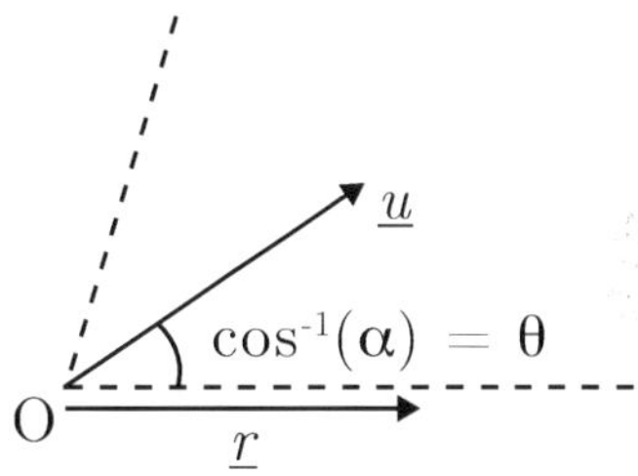


Centre given by $\underline{u}$
Radius is $R$
$\underline{r} - \underline{u}$ is a radius
So $|\underline{r} - \underline{u}| = R$

$\underline{u}$ is the direction the cone 'points' in. $\underline{r}$ is a constant angle $\theta$ from $\underline{u}$

$$\underline{r} \cdot \underline{u} = |\underline{r}||\underline{u}| \cos\theta$$
$$= \alpha|\underline{r}||\underline{u}|$$

## Dynamics and Special Relativity

*At Cambridge you'll study both dynamics and special relativity in the first year, whereas at Oxford you'll only study dynamics.*

Dynamics is essentially the study of how objects move in response to forces. Whereas at school you can usually assume that everything can be modelled as a particle in a vacuum, university-level courses allow you to model systems that are closer to real life. You'll study motion on curved paths such as planetary orbits, as well as oscillations and rotations of solid bodies. For more information on dynamics see page 150.

23 We could also write this as $(\mathbf{r} \cdot \mathbf{u})^2 = \alpha^2(\mathbf{r} \cdot \mathbf{r})(\mathbf{u} \cdot \mathbf{u})$.

At Cambridge, the study of special relativity allows you to see how the laws of Newtonian dynamics (what you learn in school) break down and must be corrected when you're dealing with objects moving close to the speed of light. For more information on special relativity, see page 153.

## Probability

*In Probability, you'll study various discrete and continuous distributions and find out what happens when you add a large number of random variables together. You'll also study random processes, which are sequences of random events.*

> *"Examples of new distributions I studied are the gamma and geometric distributions. The biggest difference between probability at school and uni is that we now prove everything we learn."*

Probability builds upon the material you'll have studied in statistics at A Level. However, you'll learn more complex theorems and techniques. It's an applied maths course, so although you have to be able to prove the theorems involved, you crucially need to be able to apply them. Once such theorem is the Central Limit Theorem, which says that random things tend to be normally distributed if there are enough of them. You'll also study how to solve questions about ***random walks*** and ***birth and death chains***, with a particular focus on interesting conditional probability questions.

> **A random walk** is a system that changes in fixed steps, where the change that occurs at each step is randomly selected from a limited set of options. For instance, if you play multiple rounds of a game where you can either win £2 or lose £1 each round, then each round is one step and the options are gaining £2 and losing £1 each time.
>
> **Birth and death chains** are a generalisation in which the random changes can occur at random times instead of in fixed steps.[24]

24 If you'd like to find out more, look up the Gambler's Ruin.

## Pure vs. applied maths at Oxbridge

Generally, the '*purer*' courses (such as Analysis, Abstract Algebra and Group Theory) differ most from school-level maths—whereas applied courses (such as Geometry, Probability and Dynamics) tend to build on what you already know. The Maths degrees at both Oxford and Cambridge feature compulsory pure modules at the beginning to give you the foundations you'll need later, but once you do start choosing options in your second and third years, you can focus more on applied maths if you want. At Cambridge in particular, there is plenty of overlap with the Physics department in terms of options you can take.

# 1.4: Doing a Maths degree (a typical work week)

A Maths degree is huge amount of work. Every week, you have lots of contact hours and problem/example sheets. In your first year at Oxbridge you'll typically have:

## Lectures: 12 per week

Lectures last 1 hour, and typically you'll have 2 per week for each module you study. The lectures will speed through lots of material—so don't expect to understand every minute of every one. To be able to complete your problem sheets, you'll need to review your written notes from your lectures and study the typed lecture notes you'll be given online. The lectures for first-year mathematicians are usually held in the morning, so get ready for daily 9 a.m. starts!

### Oxford

**Problem Sheets:** 4 or 5 problem sheets due weekly
Each problem sheet covers a few topics from one course. The questions vary in difficulty but generally get more involved and taxing towards the end, and there might also be some optional or extension questions to attempt. You're expected to spend 6–8 hours on each problem sheet in your first year—though don't be surprised if they take slightly longer as you'll need to set aside some time to understand and absorb the lecture content *beforehand.*

**Tutorials:** 3 or 4 tutorials per week
A tutorial will last between 1 and 2 hours, with 2–3 students per tutorial. Having such personalised tuition with an expert is an amazing opportunity to hone your understanding. Generally, in a maths tutorial, you'll

review the questions from the corresponding problem sheet with your tutor, with whom you can discuss different approaches to the problems and identify and eliminate any misconceptions you might have had. Sometimes you'll work through your solutions on a big whiteboard at the front of the room.[25]

After the tutorial, it's a good idea to revisit the questions you couldn't do the first time around. Try working without your tutorial notes to see if you can reach the correct solution on your own!

## Cambridge

**Example sheets:** At Cambridge, you'll be set 4 example sheets per course. You'll cover 4 courses per term, so that's 16 worksheets per term, or 2 per week. You're expected to spend 1 hour per question and each worksheet typically has around 14-15 questions on it, with the questions increasing in difficulty as you go on. It's actually pretty normal to find that the later questions on an example sheet take longer than an hour. Be prepared to spend a few hours on some of them because struggling with and solving them is one of the most rewarding parts of studying maths. It's also one of the best ways to improve your mathematical ability and understanding. Plus, if you've made an attempt and show your work in writing, your supervisor will at least have something to work on with you!

**Supervisions:** You'll have two 1-hour supervisions per week. As at Oxford, supervisions are held in groups of 2– 3, and you go through the example sheet assigned for it. This is your opportunity to really cement your understanding of the lecture content—so be engaged and ask questions!

> *"Especially in the first term, I found studying maths at university level quite a shock. The content and pace is very different from school. The lectures go fast! You'll be expected to do a lot of independent study afterwards, to get to grips with everything they cover. The content is also immediately a lot more advanced than at A Level, and you'll be expected to use a level of mathematical rigour that you've never needed before."* –Student, Maths, Cambridge

25 Or a rickety little blackboard in the corner of the room, depending on your college.

### Work/life balance

Although studying for a Maths degree presents a large workload, you'll definitely have time to socialise via outings, sports teams and other societies if you're organised and efficient. The problem sheets/example sheets (and related reading) take approximately 40 hours of focused study per week. If you study, say, for 6 hours 6 days per week and 4 hours on a Sunday, you'll comfortably stay on top of your workload with lots of time to get involved with other things.

It's also likely that not all 40 hours will be spent reading and scribbling your ideas on paper. Solving a maths problem is partly about letting the ideas fizz around your mind, which can happen during other activities like eating, walking or daydreaming. It's more about trying ideas to see if they'll help with a problem than it is about doing written calculations.

### Long holidays

At Oxbridge, holidays are called 'vacations'—times when you *vacate* Oxford or Cambridge to continue your studies at home!

You get very long vacations, which an ideal time to solidify everything you've learnt that term, including the proofs of key theorems, which you'll literally have to be able to regurgitate in the first parts of exam questions.[26]

> *"Cambridge is more fun and more work than I was expecting. It's just a lot more intense than other places, because the terms are unusually short—only 8 or 9 weeks. You should be up for the intense workload if you're considering applying!"* –Nick, Maths, Cambridge

## 1.5: Character profiles (spot the successful applicant)

In this section, we will look at the application journeys and outcomes for three students. This will give you an overview of the application process, but you can find more information in Part 1B: The Application Process, which starts on page 52.

26 You apply these to harder problems in later parts of the question.

## Applicant 1: Lina, 18 (Oxford)

**Before interview:**

- Lina is in her second year of A Levels and is studying Maths, Further Maths and Physics. She is predicted A*A*A. She has 10 GCSEs at level 8/9.
- Lina spends a lot of time preparing for the MAT. She looks over all of the required content to make sure she knows all the details. She practises a lot of A-Level questions and completes a couple of MAT papers, but focuses more on learning the content than doing past papers.
- She is interested in the entire syllabus and often reads ahead in her A-Level textbooks, something she puts in her personal statement.
- To prepare for interviews, Lina reads lots of popular maths books.
- In her personal statement, she describes much of the A-Level content she has covered, detailing the material she has studied and the parts she enjoys most.

**In her interviews:**

- Lina performs well in the early parts of the questions that the tutors have planned, since she has a good foundation of A-Level knowledge.
- She goes slowly and methodically thinking about the problem in her head, as she would do for a MAT question. She gets to some of the harder parts at the end of the interview, but runs out of time to give a complete answer.
- She finds her interviews easier than she was expecting, with much of the content focused on more preliminary, introductory questions.

## Applicant 2: Zayn, 17 (Oxford)

**Before interview:**

- Zayn is predicted A*A*AA in his A Levels: Maths, Further Maths, Computer Science and Physics. He has 5 GCSEs at level 8/9, which is much higher than anyone else at his school.
- Zayn prepares thoroughly for the MAT. He consolidates all of the A-Level material through practice, but spends more time looking through past MAT papers, attempting some in timed conditions.

- He works through a few of the extra MAT-style questions available in the Oxbridge Formula online academy after attending a 1-day course over the summer.
- His personal statement includes examples of lectures he has attended, extra reading he has done, and online courses he has completed. He describes an interest in mechanics he discovered during his A Levels.
- To prepare for interviews, Zayn practises a wide range of interview-style questions, including talking through the answers out loud and working through them on a whiteboard.

**In his interviews:**

- The college Zayn is invited to gives him a preparatory problem sheet that he completes upon arrival. He spends a good amount of time on this, working through each of the questions. He cannot complete all of the harder parts of the questions but writes down things he thought about doing for each one and how he could potentially solve it.
- In the interview, a tutor guides Zayn through some of the harder questions on the problem sheet that he couldn't answer on his own. He realises his mistakes and actively pushes the discussion forward throughout, taking on board the hints the interviewer gives him.
- Zayn really enjoys his interviews, even though he doesn't always reach a conclusive solution to the problems he attempts.

## Applicant 3: Michael, 17 (Cambridge)

**Before interview:**

- Michael loves maths and pondering over problems. He is predicted strong A Levels, including an A* in both Maths and Further Maths. He is also doing Physics and Chemistry. He has 11 GCSEs at level 8/9.
- Michael leaves starting his UCAS form till the last minute, so he doesn't have much time to think about his personal statement. He isn't much of a reader, so he writes about a few books he has skim-read and about a lecture he 'attended and enjoyed' (although it won't actually occur for another month).
- To prepare for his interviews, he practises vocalising his thoughts to his family and friends, chatting about A-Level concepts and anything else that comes to mind.

**In his interviews:**

- Michael is asked to sit a test when he arrives at Cambridge, which he thinks goes reasonably well. He leaves a few of the questions blank, but all the other applicants do too (this is normal).
- Michael's interviews go well, although he hasn't read some of the books he claimed to on his personal statement. He worries that this is apparent, as he couldn't effectively comment on one when asked.

After his interviews, Michael is made an offer, as his overall application is strong. However, he doesn't prepare fully for STEP. He finds A Levels easy and assumes STEP will be more the same. Michael scores 2 in both STEP II and STEP III, so he isn't accepted by Cambridge.

**Who is the best candidate?**

Zayn is the best candidate here.

**What did Lina do wrong?**

✘ Potential Lina tried hard to prepare for the MAT, but she didn't prepare in the right way. Knowing the A-Level syllabus is important, but it's far more important to practise questions in the style of the MAT as it is incredibly different from A Level. Her MAT score will have reflected this lack of preparation.

✘ Passion In her personal statement, Lina didn't talk about any extracurricular maths giving the impression of a passive interest in the subject, rather than an active one. She failed to further her interest from A Level through independent study.

✘ Ability Potential She didn't prepare properly for her interviews. She only read books that (although interesting) didn't directly help her improve her problem-solving abilities. As a result, Lina couldn't solve the harder types of questions, which is what the interviewers were interested in.

**What did Michael do wrong?**

✘ Michael put himself at risk with a weak personal statement, although this part of the application isn't as important for Maths as some other subjects and can be more than made up for by strong interview and test performance.

✘ Ability Potential His obvious downfall was not meeting his STEP offer. A Cambridge offer always includes STEP. If you don't make your STEP grades (many students don't), it's very likely that you won't get in, since STEP is designed to filter out candidates who wouldn't thrive at Cambridge.

✗ Ability Passion Potential Michael rested on his laurels, assuming that STEP would be just like A Level Further Maths. However, STEP is aimed at the top 2% of A Level maths students and requires a greater degree of unguided problem-solving. Given that Michael loves maths, he probably would have loved preparing for STEP, if he'd dedicated some time to it.

**What did Zayn do right?**

✓ Zayn did a lot of preparation for the MAT, certainly a lot more than just reviewing the A-Level content. Practising MAT-style questions is invaluable.

✓ Passion His personal statement describes things he has done to further explore his mathematical interest. This is exactly what admissions tutors want to see.

✓ Ability He prepared well for his interviews by practising the style of question out loud and working through them on a whiteboard.

✓ Potential Zayn allowed himself to be guided in the interview, which is important. The interviewers are trying to help you! Importantly, he was engaged rather than complacent—he took the advice and applied it rather than expecting the tutor to do all the work for him.

For more on the application process for Maths, see page 52. Check out page 143 for an interview with real Oxbridge interviewers.

# Chapter 2:
# Computer Science

## 2.1: Why Computer Science?

Computer science at university is very different to any subject you will have studied at school. Whilst computer science at school does cover a variety of ideas about computer programs and systems at an introductory level, an Oxbridge Computer Science degree will develop your understanding of *how programs really work*. It's significantly more grounded in maths, so a desire to explore mathematics further (and how maths applies to real-world computing scenarios) is essential.

> *"Essentially, Computer Science at university isn't a course about technology. It's a course about the principles of computing that underlie technology."* –Director of Studies, Computer Science, Cambridge

Computer Science might be for you if:

- ❑ **You're enthusiastic about solving maths and logic problems:** Maths is an essential skill in computer science. It's especially valuable if you're good at discrete maths and integer problems. The kind of eye for details and special cases that comes with maths problem solving is also really key. You'll spend a lot of time proving mathematical propositions and theorems, so it's important that these interest you. The Oxbridge Computer Science courses combine programming, practical applications and mathematical foundations.
- ❑ **You like to experiment with new tools:** Do you learn best by doing and making? For instance, maybe you enjoy making simple programs, like games or random generators, to practise a new programming language or technique? That's also exactly how you'll solidify new knowledge at uni. Although the theory you'll get in lectures is vital, you're unlikely to really grasp it unless you experiment with it in your own time.
- ❑ **You want to build working applications:** Does creating a program that solves a real-world problem give you satisfaction? Although the

Oxbridge Computer Science degrees do have a significant theoretical component, if you're excited by the prospect of creating fully-functioning software, they absolutely will give you that opportunity. For example, in the second year at Cambridge, you'll be assigned an industrial sponsor, who will give you a project specification, and you'll be tasked with creating a finished product that fits their brief.

- ❑ **You're interested in how technology really works:** Perhaps your interest in computers is about the technological side too, such as circuits and the physics of circuit components? An interest in electronics and the physics theory that underpins it is really useful in computer science—it's not all about software! Studying computer science is a great way of becoming able to understand the technology around you from top to bottom, inside out.
- ❑ **You care about both theory and practice:** If you just want to program, you don't need a Computer Science degree for it. And if you're just interested in maths problems, maybe a Maths degree would suit you better? In computer science, the theory you learn – about algorithms, complexity, and proofs – makes you a better programmer. And even if you love the theory for its own sake (which is natural—it's fascinating!), it helps to keep in mind its potential uses.
- ❑ **You're a team player:** If you're already interested in computer science, perhaps you've discovered for yourself that, contrary to some stereotypes, computer scientists tend to work in groups rather than alone. In a field that's about creatively solving practical problems, sharing ideas really speeds things up. Maybe you've already enjoyed working on an open source project, or designing an app in a team? If not, it might be worth trying it before you go to uni, because teamwork and communication are vital skills for both students and working computer scientists.

It's important to remember that enjoying ICT at school isn't a good enough reason to study Computer Science at university. Maths is the only compulsory prerequisite cited for Computer Science, and Cambridge admissions tutors value Physics far more than Level 3 ICT (in fact, having Physics at A Level is valued as highly as having Computer Science).

## 2.2: Computer Science: Oxford vs. Cambridge

The Computer Science degrees offered at both Oxford and Cambridge are some of their most employable degrees. Oxford offers Computer Science as part of two joint courses: with Maths and with Philosophy. If you're interested in a joint course, the information in the table below will still be useful to you, but see Sections 3.1 and 3.4 on pages 40 and 47 respectively for more details.

| OXFORD | CAMBRIDGE |
|---|---|
| **Entry requirements:** Generally, the offer is A*AA (with the A* in Maths, Further Maths or Computing/ Computer Science). Alternatively, the IB offer is 39, with 766 at Higher Level, including a 7 in Maths. | **Entry requirements:** Generally, the offer is A*A*A (with no restriction on where the A*s must be, although Maths A Level is essential). Alternatively, the IB offer is 42, with 777 at Higher Level. |
| **Admissions tests:** Oxford applicants must sit the MAT before their interviews. They sit slightly different questions to those applying to Maths/Maths & Philosophy/Maths & Statistics. There are a couple of computer-science-style questions. | **Admissions tests:** In 2019, Cambridge applicants had to sit the CTMUA, a pre-interview test.[27] Until 2019, Cambridge applicants had to sit the CSAT at interview, which is still used by several colleges. |
| **Applicants per place:** At Oxford, the 3-year average (2016–2018) is that 23% of applicants were interviewed and 7% were successful—giving an average intake of 33 students per year (or around 14 applicants per place). | **Applicants per place:** The Cambridge Computer Science Course is significantly bigger than Oxford's, with an average intake of 133. However, it's also very competitive, with 9 applications per place at present, and the number of applicants per place has been increasing rapidly in recent years. |
| **Course length:** In your third year, you can choose to leave with a BA, or continue to the fourth year and leave with an MCompSci. | **Course length:** In your third year, you can choose to leave with a BA, or continue to the fourth year and leave with an MEng. |

27 For the rest of this book, we will be working on the assumption that Cambridge will continue to use the CTMUA for Computer Science admissions.

| OXFORD | CAMBRIDGE |
|---|---|
| **First-year studies:** In your first year at Oxford, you'll study continuous mathematics, design and analysis of algorithms, digital systems, discrete mathematics, functional programming, imperative programming, introduction to formal proof, linear algebra and probability. You'll sit 4 preliminary exams at the end of your first year. The next section contains details of these courses. | **First-year studies:** In your first year at Cambridge, as at Oxford, you'll work for 4 preliminary exams. There will be 1 mathematics paper and 3 computer science papers, covering object-oriented programming, operating systems, digital electronics, graphics and interaction design. The next section contains details of some of these courses. |
| **After the first year:** In your second year at Oxford you'll sit 4 exams and you get a choice of options—in addition to the compulsory core modules such as Algorithms. You also have a compulsory group design practical. In your third year, your project work (and project paper) accounts for one-third of your grade, with the rest consisting of 10 exam papers. For the integrated master's programme, the structure of the fourth year echoes the third year, plus a compulsory project. | **After the first year:** Practical work is compulsory. In your second year, you'll undertake a group project that reflects current industrial practice. In your third year, you'll work on a substantial project culminating 12,000-word dissertation. You also have 4 compulsory papers in your second year spanning theory, systems, programming and applications. In your third year you'll have a wide range of cutting-edge computer science options—you can even specialise in robots! If you do the fourth year, it will include a substantial research project. |

**Did You Know?**

*In 2019, due to the highly competitive nature of the course, one large Cambridge college found that all of its Computer Science offers went to applicants with 4 predicted A* grades—and there were more such applications in the pool of rejected applicants, including some not invited to interview. If you're interested in applying to Computer Science at Cambridge, having stellar A-levels is a must, but your application needs to shine in other areas too.*[28]

28 You could say that great A Levels are a necessary condition, but not a sufficient one.

### Choosing between Oxford and Cambridge

The Oxford and Cambridge Computer Science courses have a lot in common, so how can you choose between them? Here are some more differences you might take into consideration:

- **Joint courses**: At Cambridge, Computer Science is studied on its own, but at Oxford you can also study it with Maths or with Philosophy. See Chapter 3 on page 40 for more details of these joint courses.
- **Careers**: Almost all Oxford Computer Science graduates (>95%) go straight into IT and telecoms jobs. 76% of Cambridge graduates do the same, but they are more likely than their Oxford counterparts to go into further study (O: approx. 0%, C: 10%) or other jobs (O: approx. 0%, C: 9%).
- **Size**: Cambridge's Computer Science intake is larger, at around 100–130, compared to Oxford's 30–40 (although Oxford's is also near 100 if you add the students studying joint courses). You might base your choice on whether you prefer to be part of a smaller or larger group.
- **Saturday lectures**: At Cambridge, you study the same maths as Natural Sciences students, which means you'll also have to attend their Saturday morning lectures. Oxford caters more to students who like to keep their weekends free, holding no lectures on Saturdays.
- **City and college**: As when applying for any course, you might find it really comes down to where you'd prefer to live. Try visiting both cities and some of the colleges to find out where you can best see yourself living for three to four years.

## 2.3: Is computer science at uni anything like at school?

Computer science is constantly evolving, with new programs and systems developed every year—so it's difficult to know every detail of what this subject will encompass. To give you a feel for the subject and to highlight links to the subjects offered at A-Level, we have put together a breakdown of the modules you can currently expect to cover in your first year.

> *"A degree in computer science is far more heavy on logic-based theory, programming and, importantly, maths, than A-Level Computer Science."* –Student, Computer Science, Oxford

## Maths

*First-year Computer Science builds on maths you may have met at school, including a closer look at vectors and calculus.*

In the first year of your Computer Science degree, you'll study maths as a standalone module. Through this, you'll gain the skills required for more advanced computer science modules in later years.

At Oxford, you'll cover linear algebra and probability, and you're taught alongside the students studying straight Maths (see page 9 to read more about these courses). You'll also study discrete and continuous mathematics, in which you'll see other topics from the Mathematics course in a condensed format that is more relevant to the Computer Science course. These topics include ***multivariable calculus***, Taylor's theorem and ***Lagrange multipliers***.

**Multivariable calculus** extends the rules of calculus you learned at A Level to functions of more than one variable. For example, $f(x,y) = x^2 + y^2$.

**Lagrange multipliers** are part of a technique for maximising or minimising functions of multiple variables when you're given extra conditions. For example, the minimum of $f(x,y) = x^2 + y^2$ occurs where $x = y = f(x,y) = 0$. But if you add the condition that $x = y + 2$, the minimum is at $x = 1$, $y = -1$, $f(x,y) = 2$ instead. An advanced way to approach this type of problem in multivariable calculus is to analyse the function $g(x, y, \lambda) = f(x, y) - \lambda(x - (y + 2))$ where $\lambda$ is a new variable: the Lagrange multiplier.

At Cambridge, the maths paper makes up 25% of your first-year exams, and the maths you're taught is identical to that taught to the Natural Sciences students (see page 210 for the Natural Sciences maths courses). This course builds upon the topics from Maths A Level—and although Further Maths A Level isn't a compulsory prerequisite, it does help. The content of this course includes multivariable calculus, vector algebra, differential equations, elementary probability theory and complex numbers.

In your first year studying maths for Computer Science, you're likely to learn formal proof methods—though the focus for Computer Science is on *understanding* the theorems and proofs, rather than on being able to *recreate* proofs and construct your own, as it is for Maths. Since so much of the maths you do in your first year builds upon the maths you did at A Level, a good understanding of this content is crucial.

> *"Computer Science isn't about sitting around programming all day. It's very mathematical and logical, and you have to be interested in the **theory** behind the programs and technology—not just how to use them."* –David, Computer Science, Cambridge

## Algorithms

*In your first year, you'll study algorithm design and analysis. You may have already started to explore a few well-known algorithms as part of A-Level Computer Science or the A-Level Further Maths Decision Maths modules, but here you'll see a greater variety and practise formulating them yourself.*

Here, you'll study the theory behind different algorithms—and how to write them. This is generally done on paper (not a computer), so you may use pseudocode[29] instead of a real programming language. The point is to communicate an understanding of how the algorithm works rather than develop your programming skills. Analysis involves developing and understanding techniques to show how fast and effective the algorithms you've constructed and studied are.

## Digital Systems/Electronics

*This is one of the more 'applied' courses. If you enjoy the electrical circuits element of your Physics A Level, this course will allow you to dive deeper into how they function.*

In your first year at Cambridge, you'll study Digital Electronics, and at Oxford you'll study a very similar course called Digital Systems. Each course allows you to explore the simple design of ***combinational*** and ***sequential circuits*** and get to grips with standard design elements such as ***logic gates***. You'll explore ***Boolean algebra***, a technique used to analyse and simplify digital circuits. With this course, you should reach a point

29 Pseudocode refers to writing out all the steps in an algorithm, but using English rather than any programming language.

where you are able to follow a specification to design and implement a simple ***finite state machine*** from scratch.

**Combinational circuits:** A combinational circuit is one in which the output only depends on the current input. Importantly, combinational circuits are memoryless: previous inputs do not affect the present state of the circuit.

**Sequential circuits:** A sequential circuit has memory (unlike a combinational circuit), so the output depends both on the current input and the sequence of inputs before that.

**Boolean algebra:** Boolean algebra is the branch of algebra in which the variables take the values true or false. These are usually denoted 1 and 0 respectively.

**Logic gates:** A logic gate is a circuit (or part of a circuit) that implements a function in Boolean algebra—it takes one or more inputs and produces an output. For instance, an 'AND' gate takes two inputs. It outputs a '1' if the first AND second inputs are '1's and outputs a '0' otherwise. '1' and '0' might correspond to high or low currents or voltages.

**Finite state machine:** A finite state machine is a model computer that performs tasks by switching between a finite number of states in response to different inputs. For example, you can make a finite state machine to decide whether an input number is odd or even.

For the Cambridge course, you have something called 'ticks', which are weekly assignments that you can complete in a lab or independently at home. Every week, you complete a project and take it to a marker to 'tick' it off. You design and construct functioning circuits, including gaining an understanding of MOSFETs (a type of transistor) to build digital logic circuits.

## Functional Programming

*Functional programming is touched upon in A-Level Computer Science, but not covered in depth.*

Functional programming involves programming in a language where the process the computer follows is described by defining the inputs and outputs of *mathematical functions* (and the rules for applying them), rather than by giving the computer step-by-step instructions.

> *"To put it simply, in functional programming you define a load of functions and compose them into one big function in complicated ways. You run this single function and it does everything you want the program to do."*

> A typical task you would see in an exam on functional programming in your first year is:
>
> *Write a function for differentiating polynomials.*

In addition to an exam, you may also have monitored labs. A typical first-year practical is defining a function to make a 2D maze and programming controls to allow the user to navigate their way out of the maze. In the lab, you would be expected to both make and annotate the code that would enable the user to move around.

> *"If there's one thing you do over the summer before arriving, I would recommend downloading and learning some Haskell"* –Student, Computer Science, Oxford

Here, we explain a snippet of code from a Functional Programming first-year task:

```
power f y x n -- implements y*x^n using a function f for
multiplication  (line 1)
  | n == 0 = y -- (line 2)
  | even n = power f y (f x x) (n 'div' 2) -- for even n,
    x^n == (x^2) ^ (n/2)  (line 3)
  | odd n = power f (f x y) x (n-1) -- y*x^n == (x*y)*x^(n-1)  (line 4)
```

This piece of code defines a function $power$ that can be used to perform exponentiation (i.e. perform calculations of the form $a^b$, like $137^{99}$). It has two important attributes:

1. It can be used to calculate integer powers of any kind of object that we have rules for multiplying—that might mean real numbers, complex numbers, or even matrices!

2. It's efficient, in the sense that it will complete its calculations quite fast compared to more straightforward ways of implementing exponentiation.

Let's see how it accomplishes these two things.

The **first line** says that $power$ is a function of four variables: $f$, $y$, $x$, and $n$. We could write it as $power(f, y, x, n)$.

A previous line in the code would define $f$ to be a function that multiplies two variables and $n$ to be an integer. $x$ and $y$ can be any two values that $f$ can multiply. So, we can say that $f(x, y) = x \times y$, but we have to remember that the meaning of '×' depends on whether we are talking about real numbers, complex numbers, matrices, or something else. Introducing this function $f$ is essentially a way of turning '×' into a variable to account for its different possible meanings and it's what allows the code to define exponentiation for any kind of object we know how to multiply.

The **comments** (in grey, after each --) say that $power(f, y, x, n)$ is intended to equal $y \times x^n$. We'll see in a second why this is better than just defining a function $x^n$.

The **second line** says that $power(f, y, x, 0) = y$. This makes sense because $y \times x^0 = y$. This line is the **base case** of the recursive definition.

The **third line** says that, when $n$ is even,

$$power(f,\ y,\ x,\ n) = power\left(f,\ y,\ f(x,\ x),\ \frac{n}{2}\right)\ (*)$$

This makes sense because $f(x, x)$ can be thought of as $x^2$, and $y \times x^n = y \times (x^2)^{\frac{n}{2}}$ when $n$ is even.

The **fourth line** says that, when $n$ is odd,

$$power(f,\ y,\ x,\ n) = power(f,\ f(x,y),\ x,\ n-1)\ (**)$$

This makes sense because $f(x, y)$ is $x \times y$, and $y \times x^n = (x \times y) \times (x)^{n-1}$.

Now we see why we defined $y \times x^n$ instead of just $x^n$. It allows us to move a factor of $x$ 'into' $y$ in line four, to reduce the power by 1. But we can just set $y = 1$ to get $x^n$, so this still helps us calculate simple powers.

What makes this code so efficient? Well, it's worth noting that we didn't *need* the third line to define the function. We could have just let the fourth line apply for both odd and even $n$. That would work because we could write:

$$y \times x^n = (x \times y) \times (x)^{n-1} = (x \times x \times y) \times (x)^{n-2} = (x \times x \times x \times y) \times (x)^{n-3} = \cdots$$

... and if we set $y = 1$, that will eventually evaluate to $x \times \ldots \times x$ with $n$ '$x$'s, which is what we expect. But we had to perform $n$ steps to get there, and $n$ could be quite a large number. $(*)$ lets us *halve* $n$ when it's even, which cuts out a lot of steps. For instance, if $n = 9$, we can reduce that to the case $n = 8$ with $(**)$, and then to $n = 4$, $n = 2$, and $n = 1$ with $(*)$, and finally, to $n = 0$ with $(**)$ again. That's only five steps, instead of nine. So it's line three that makes the code so efficient.

## Imperative Programming

*The basics of imperative programming are covered in A-Level Computer Science. Even if you haven't taken A-Level Computer Science, you're likely to know the basics if you've learnt any of the more common programming languages, such as C++, Java or Python.*

Imperative programming focuses upon more standard programming (in which the computer is given a step-by-step list of commands).

> *"The difference between imperative and functional programming is that imperative programming is about describing a list of steps to take to make a calculation—whereas functional is about describing a calculation in terms of combinations of simpler calculations."* –Student, Computer Science, Cambridge

In this course, you learn standard computer science essentials (such as writing algorithms) and write programs to perform basic operations (such as multiplying or inverting arbitrarily large matrices). This module is likely to involve more of the real-world applications of computer science, including an object-orientated programming project.[30] In this, you'll be expected to work in a group to break down programs into lots of little parts, so that different people can work on different parts and

30 In object-oriented programming, every object is part of a class, which determines what attributes it can have and what methods you can apply to it.

you combine your work to make a complete program. A typical practical might be creating a simple word processor in which different people implement different simple operations (e.g. one person implements Ctrl+C for copying text and another implements Ctrl+Z for undoing the last action).

*"In our first-year imperative programming course at Oxford we learned Scala, which is an Object-Oriented language. To use it, you have to think carefully about what your data is and how to structure it, for example with classes and subclasses. An example from my notes is:*

```
class Reptile {
    def legs = "Four"
    def skin = "Scaly"
}
class Snake extends Reptile {
    override def legs = "None"
}
val s = new Snake; println(s.legs); println(s.skin)
```

*It shows how we define snakes to be a particular subclass of reptiles. We need to add that they have no legs, instead of the usual four, but if we don't say anything about what their skin is like, our program already knows it's the same as for other reptiles (i.e. scaly). The last line is a test—if we ran the code, it would tell us what the legs and skin of an arbitrary snake are like."* –Student, Computer Science, Oxford

## Other Courses

You may also explore the real-world applications of computer science. For instance, at Cambridge, you can study operating systems, computer graphics and secure software. Often, these courses are more content-based, requiring you to learn and revise ideas you'll repeat back in an exam, rather than developing skills to tackle unfamiliar problems.

## After your first year

At both Oxford and Cambridge, the Computer Science course is extremely diverse—as you progress through your degree you have a broad choice of modules. Some examples are:

- ❑ **Artificial Intelligence:** The study of the simulation of aspects of human-like intelligence using machines. You might teach a computer how to recognise faces, or how to learn strategies in card games.
- ❑ **Databases:** The study of database design and the different models of databases in use. You learn what makes a database efficient, stable and user-friendly.
- ❑ **Logic and Proof:** Logic is central to computer science. This course provides an in-depth exploration of logical languages and systems for formalising and analysing proofs.
- ❑ **Bioinformatics:** Combines computer science and biology to construct accurate models for predicting and explaining biological phenomena (such as spikes in animal populations or genetic sequences).
- ❑ **Natural Language Processing:** Explores the application of computer science techniques to natural languages such as English. In particular, through natural language processing technology, computers can understand human speech.

You start to make choices in the second year at Oxford, and the third year at Cambridge. In the second year at Cambridge, you're not only graded on examinations—you also have a group project in which you're assigned an industrial client with a specification and you create and present a finished product to them.

Additionally, in the third year at both Oxford and Cambridge, you get assessed on a personal project, which allows you to put into practice all the skills you've gained over your degree.

## 2.4: Doing a Computer Science degree (a typical work week)

A Computer Science degree comes with an intense workload and, as with many STEM courses, a lot of contact hours.

In your first year at both Oxford and Cambridge, you'll likely have around 10 lectures per week. Some of these will involve a lecturer teaching you mathematical concepts and skills. You'll also have *guided lectures* on programming languages. These teach you the basics required for university programming, through screenshots of computer screens and step-by-step instructions.

> *"In the guided lectures, the lecturer might project a snippet of code on the screen with parts of it blanked out and they'll ask the students to suggest what might be missing. Or they might show some completed incorrect code and ask which line would produce an error. They'll do this for all the basic features of the language: how to use it and how not to use it."* –Student, Computer Science, Cambridge

Although the lectures aren't as interactive as tutorials or supervisions, it's vital that you attend. They provide you with a step-by-step walk-through of the programming skills you'll require and teach you how to construct and analyse algorithms. The majority of your learning will be through reading, completing exercises and problems, and independent practice. You'll have around two tutorials/supervisions a week to go through your problem/example sheets. It can take a while to get your head around any programming language, in the same way as if you were learning Japanese or Russian from scratch.

Your first year of Computer Science will include compulsory computer lab hours in which you'll complete assignments in programming and designing algorithms. After these labs, you'll be expected to write short reports on your work and the skills involved. Your practicals won't count directly towards your final degree classification, but they might lower it if you don't complete the work, or earn you an additional mark of distinction if you do very well.

> *"I love Computer Science because it's all about problem-solving. I think in that sense it's similar to Physics, which I also considered applying for. Both are about using your maths skills to tackle some kind of problem, just in different contexts."* –Student, Computer Science, Oxford

# Chapter 3:
# Maths/Computer Science joint honours

## 3.1: Maths & Computer Science

### Why Maths & Computer Science?

Computer Science is itself a mathematical degree, and an interest in maths is crucial to your success. However, if you really love maths and don't want to abandon it as a discipline in its own right, Maths & Computer Science might be a better course option for you.

Although there's a lot of interplay between the maths and computer science you study, this degree will allow you to explore other parts of maths (such as some applied modules and analysis) that you might not study if you choose straight Computer Science.

Some fields that might require deeper mathematical knowledge than the standard Computer Science degree can provide include:

- ❑ Applying computer science in highly mathematical scientific fields such as physics or economics
- ❑ Applying computer science in engineering—for instance, via robotics
- ❑ Working in artificial intelligence, which in particular often involves the study of statistics
- ❑ Studying the foundations of computer science—for instance, analysing the computational complexity of algorithms, or finding the most minimal assumptions needed for a particular type of computation.

The skills necessary for success in maths and computer science overlap, so the success you experience in one will likely reinforce the other.

### How do you apply for Maths & Computer Science?

Maths & Computer Science is offered as a separate degree at Oxford, but not at Cambridge. In your third year, you can choose to leave with a BA, or stay for a fourth year and leave with an MMathCompSci.

The typical offer is A*AA, with an A* in A-Level Maths or Further Maths. Alternatively, it's 39 in the IB, with 766 at Higher Level, including a 7 in Maths. You'll need to take the MAT, including one of the Computer Science questions (see Section 5.1 on page 70). On average, 1 in every 9 applicants is successful.

## What's it like to study Maths & Computer Science?

In your first year studying Maths & Computer Science at Oxford, you cover a broad range of courses from both Maths and Computer Science.

**Maths courses:** (Please see page 9 for more information)

- Introduction to university mathematics (learning about methods of proofs, terminology and using sets and correct mathematical notation)
- Introduction to complex numbers (a short course exploring complex numbers and ensuring everyone has the same level of basic skills)
- Linear Algebra
- Analysis (covers sequences and series, continuity and differentiation and integration)
- Probability
- Groups and group actions.

**Computer Science courses:** (Please see page 30 for more information)

- Functional programming
- Imperative programming
- Design and analysis of algorithms.

At the end of your first year, you have 5 written examinations covering this content. You also have about 5 projects over the year (you must pass these to continue your degree). Projects take one 2-hour session per week for 3 weeks (i.e. 6 hours per project). Although you get the option to do these in computer labs, you can do them independently if you prefer.

The labs diversify the degree, giving you a range of learning and assessment opportunities. Although the first year focuses heavily on maths, you can give more weight to the computer science modules as the degree progresses. You also get a wider selection of maths modules in later years, including some applied ones.

To read more about Maths at Oxford, check out Chapter 1, page 4.

To read more about Computer Science at Oxford, check out Chapter 2, page 26.

# 3.2: Maths & Statistics

## Why Maths & Statistics?

If you loved maths at school and particularly enjoyed the statistics modules, then Maths & Statistics is the course for you! You might find it particularly attractive if you're interested in applications of maths such as:

- **Collecting and analysing scientific data**—for instance, to judge how effective a new drug is or to combine inputs from two space telescopes to get a clearer image
- **Studying trends in society, or some part of it**—for instance, to improve political opinion polls, or to track the spread of a disease
- **Creating automated systems to respond to large quantities of information**—for instance, to keep an aircraft stable or to determine what news people receive via social media
- **Working with artificial intelligence**—for instance, to allow computers to recognise sounds and images, or to invent and prove mathematical conjectures without human input.

Many businesses and researchers use statistics and rely heavily on people with the expertise to design reliable techniques for making predictions and spotting errors. If you're the type of person who picks out statistical fallacies in the newspaper, or worries about how scientific results are reported, you might be right for this course. Studying statistics as part of a highly-rigorous maths degree will allow you to develop the expertise needed to devise procedures for avoiding and detecting statistical errors.

## How do you apply for Maths & Statistics?

Maths & Statistics is offered as a joint honours degree at Oxford.[31] In your third year at Oxford, you can choose to leave with a BA, or stay for a fourth year and leave with an MMath.

The typical offer is A*A*A, with an A* in both Maths and Further Maths. Alternatively, you need 39 in the IB, with 766 at Higher Level, including a 7 in Maths. You'll need to take the MAT. On average, 1 applicant in 17 is successful, making this a very competitive course!

31 If you want to study statistics with maths at Cambridge, you can just apply for Maths and pick more statistics options after your first year.

## What's it like to study Maths & Statistics?

The first year of Maths & Statistics at Oxford is the same as for students taking straight maths and it's only in the second year that the course starts to include more statistics.

In the second year at Oxford, you follow a similar course structure to students studying straight Maths, but with additional statistics elements. As a Maths & Statistics student, it will be compulsory for you to take both a probability and a statistics course (which are optional for other mathematicians). These build upon the probability and statistics covered in your first year. You'll also have the option to study statistical programming and simulation, as well as further options from the Maths course.

In the third year, you'll have even more statistical options, including:

- Applied and computational statistics
- Statistical inference
- Statistical machine learning
- Applied probability
- Statistical lifetime models
- Actuarial science.

To read more about Maths at Oxford, check out Chapter 1, page 4.

# 3.3: Maths & Philosophy

## Why Maths & Philosophy?

The relationship between maths and philosophy may not be obvious at first, but closer inspection reveals a rich intersection: the language of logic, set theory and the concept of number are central to both disciplines.

Maths & Philosophy is, unsurprisingly, the ideal course to study the **philosophy *of* maths**, so it's for you if you love doing mathematics and are also interested in analysing the 'how' *and* the 'why' of maths.

**Philosophy of maths** takes philosophical concepts from epistemology (the study of knowledge) and metaphysics (the study of what is real and how those things that are real are connected) and applies them in mathematics. This requires a good mathematical background, particularly in the abstract elements of mathematics, such as set theory and logic. The questions you might face include:

- Are sets real or a mathematical fiction?
- How is knowledge of mathematics possible and how does it differ from knowledge about everyday things?
- What foundational ideas are sufficient to derive each subfield of maths, and can studying those ideas help us answer the previous two questions?

However, this degree is also for you even if the philosophy of maths isn't your particular interest (though you'll have to be able to tolerate it for at least one term, as it's a required course in your second or third year). You might value continuing to study both quantitative and qualitative subjects—for instance, to continue to develop your analytical and communication skills. Or, you might have a primary interest in philosophy but want to use your mathematical skills to sharpen your philosophical ones. Many subfields of philosophy require the technical skills provided by the maths side of the degree, such as logic, philosophy of mind, and philosophy of science.

## How do you apply for Maths & Philosophy?

Maths & Philosophy is offered at Oxford but not Cambridge. In your third year at Oxford, you can choose to leave with a BA, or stay for a fourth year and leave with an MMathPhil.

The typical offer is A*A*A, with an A* in both Maths and Further Maths. Alternatively, 39 in the IB, with 766 at Higher Level, including a 7 in Maths. You'll need to take the MAT. On average, 1 applicant in 8 is successful. This is a demanding course because it requires you to have both numerical and analytical skills, as well as the ability to write essays. An A Level in Philosophy isn't a prerequisite, as no prior knowledge is required. However, having an essay-based A Level under your belt will make a difference.

*"I did English A Level, and the skills I obtained writing essays throughout sixth form have proved invaluable in my first two years at Oxford. For the Oxford course, Maths and Further Maths (both with an*

*A*!) are compulsory, and I also sat Physics, although this has not directly related to my course because the maths you study in the Oxford Maths & Philosophy course is very 'pure'. Some of my friends studying Maths & Philosophy also sat History, Religious Studies, Philosophy and Ethics, Chemistry and Economics as their other A Levels."* –Student, Maths & Philosophy, Oxford

## What is it like to study Maths & Philosophy?

Maths & Philosophy at Oxford allows you to explore university mathematics in depth: in your first year, you'll cover the core modules of Analysis, Linear Algebra, Introductory Calculus, Group Theory and Group Actions, and Introduction to Probability. Details of all of these courses can be found in Section 1.3 on page 9. In your first year, you'll also study logic: both an Introductory Logic course and a more advanced Elements of Deductive Logic course. This will be the biggest crossover between the two disciplines.

**Introductory Logic:** You'll learn about the language of ***predicate logic***, translate English sentences into this formal language, and consider possible ambiguities that could arise. You'll also learn about proof systems, including ***truth tables*** and a more complicated (but elegant) system called 'natural deduction'.

**Predicate logic** is a formal language used to translate statements of English or mathematical expressions. For instance, 'if John buys crisps, he will also buy dip' might be formalised as $B(j, c) \rightarrow B(j, d)$ where $B(x, y)$ is defined to mean '$x$ buys $y$', '$j$' means John, '$c$' means crisps, '$d$' means dip and '$\rightarrow$' is the logical symbol meaning 'if... then...' With a few more symbols, you can start capturing very complicated ideas and study how to prove or disprove them.

**Truth tables** are an important tool in logic. For example, if you had the statement 'John is tired and Mary is tired', you could formulate this as $P \wedge Q$, where the '$\wedge$' symbol is used to mean '...and...'

This would be formalised in a truth table as:

| $P$ | $Q$ | $P \land Q$ |
|---|---|---|
| $T$ | $T$ | $T$ |
| $T$ | $F$ | $F$ |
| $F$ | $T$ | $F$ |
| $F$ | $F$ | $F$ |

To formulate the truth table, you consider every combination of $P$ and $Q$ being true ($T$) and false ($F$) and consider the outcome this would have for the statement. It's clear that 'John is tired and Mary is tired' is true only if 'John is tired' ($P$) is true *and* 'Mary is tired' ($Q$) is also true.

**Elements of Deductive Logic:** This course will extend many of the basic concepts established in Introductory Logic. It will prove the correctness of the proof systems you used (and explore what 'correctness' is), cover proofs about natural numbers and explore the strengths and limitations of predicate logic.

In your first year, you'll also sit a philosophy paper that will be essay-based, unlike logic. You'll have a section on each of:

**General Philosophy:** In this course, you study notable philosophers (such as Descartes, Hume and Locke) and key philosophical issues (such as mind and body, God and evil, and scepticism). This course is a great chance to figure out which areas of philosophy you want to focus on after your first year.

The types of questions you might get asked in a General Philosophy paper include:

- *Does free will exist?*
- *How do we know we have any knowledge?*
- *The sun rose today—does that mean it will rise tomorrow?*

**Frege**: You'll also have an essay-based course focusing on the German mathematician and philosopher Gottlob Frege and his *Foundations of Arithmetic.* Here you'll explore Frege's ideas about the relationship between mathematics and formal logic, including how numbers are constructed through a small number of logical principles. This provides a foundation for the more in-depth Philosophy of Mathematics paper which you'll study for in later years.

To read more about Maths at Oxford, check out Chapter 1, on page 4.

To read more about Philosophy at Oxford, head to Part IV: Philosophy, on page 439.

# 3.4: Computer Science & Philosophy

## Why Computer Science & Philosophy?

This course combines two fields that initially may seem unrelated but in fact have a large overlap. For instance, artificial intelligence raises several ethical questions that are not necessarily studied within the domain of computer science.

> Questions that artificial intelligence raises include: *Could a machine ever be a person? Should we thank a robot? Could we ever have an artificially-constructed world leader?*

This degree is also a fantastic stepping stone towards working in ***cognitive science*** later in your academic or professional career. Cognitive science studies the human mind and brain from a computational angle. It's a rapidly growing field and will most likely increase in importance as both neuroscience and computing technology advance, since it provides a useful bridge between these areas.

You might instead choose this course because you're interested in logic. Logic is essential to both computer science and philosophy (as is set theory) and is fascinating in its own right. For instance, ***intuitionistic logic*** was invented as an approach to the philosophy of maths, but later developed further uses in philosophy, abstract models of computation, and automated proof checking—and is studied by both computer scientists and philosophers.

**Intuitionistic logic** is defined by a set of formal rules, but it can informally be thought of as a logic that replaces the concepts 'true' and 'false' with 'can be shown to be true' and 'can be shown to be false'. This results in rejecting some traditional rules of logic. A notorious example is that statements such as 'Every real number $x$ is either rational or not rational', which would be true using conventional logic, aren't necessarily true in intuitionistic logic. This is because, in intuitionistic logic, until each $x$ is *proven* to be rational *or proven* not to be rational, it doesn't count as either.

## How do you apply for Computer Science & Philosophy?

Computer Science & Philosophy is a joint honours degree offered at Oxford but not Cambridge. In your third year at Oxford, you can choose to leave with a BA, or stay for a fourth year and leave with an MCompPhil.

The typical offer is A*AA, with an A* in Maths, Further Maths, or Computer Science. Alternatively, 39 in the IB, with 766 at Higher Level, including a 7 in Maths (not Computer Science). You'll need to take the MAT, including both Computer Science questions. On average, around 1 applicant in 9 is successful.

The only compulsory prerequisite for this course is Maths A Level, with Further Maths recommended. Although an essay-based A Level isn't compulsory, it's definitely useful. You'll be expected to write sound and cohesive essays every week—and this may be difficult at first if it's not a skill you've already developed.

## What's it like to study Computer Science & Philosophy?

In your first year studying Computer Science & Philosophy at Oxford you'll take courses in:

- Functional programming
- Design and analysis of algorithms
- Imperative programming
- Discrete mathematics
- Probability.

These are the same courses that students taking straight Computer Science study—more details can be found on page 30.

You'll also take:

- **General Philosophy** and **Elements of Deductive Logic**: See page 45 for descriptions of these courses.
- **Turing on Computability and Intelligence**: This course touches upon some of the key philosophical issues in computer science. You'll learn about the ideas of the famous computer scientist Alan Turing, focusing on his 1936 paper *On Computable Numbers* and his 1950 paper *Computing Machinery and Intelligence,* the latter of which introduced the infamous Turing Test.

From your second year onwards, you'll take compulsory Computer Science modules alongside the students studying straight Computer Science, and have the opportunity to study some of the diverse optional Computer Science modules. You can also study philosophical papers on subjects that have numerous repercussions within computer science, such as the theory of knowledge and the philosophy of mind.

To read more about Maths at Oxford, check out Chapter 1, page 4.
To read more about Philosophy at Oxford, head to Part IV, page 439.

# 3.5: Maths with Physics

## Why Maths with Physics?

Maths with Physics is more *a route through* the Cambridge Maths degree than a degree in its own right. Roughly 25% of your first-year maths will be replaced with the physics content of the Natural Sciences degree. At the end of the first year, you can choose to continue with either the Maths degree or the Natural Sciences degree. In either case, you'll have the prerequisites to take options in both maths and physics.

This course is ideal for you if you're specifically interested in the mathematics behind physics—how the techniques used in physics are justified, what assumptions are made in using them, and what conditions there are on being able to use them. The application process is almost identical to that for Maths, as is a large part of the first-year course, so you'll need to be as enthusiastic and capable a mathematician as any other Maths applicant.

It's also the only way to study physics at Cambridge without also taking other sciences, since the only alternative is the Natural Sciences degree (in which it's impossible to specialise entirely in physics until second year).

To a certain extent, it's a course to take if you aren't sure whether you favour maths or physics, though you must be passionate about both to be successful in applying. You can change your mind about whether to pursue Maths with Physics or straight Maths at any point before you start your first year at Cambridge.

### How do you apply for Maths with Physics?

You apply for the Maths degree (G100) at Cambridge and simply state in your Supplementary Application Questionnaire[32] (SAQ) that you intend to follow the Maths with Physics route. Every other detail is the same as for a Cambridge Maths application (see Section 1.2) except that you're required to either take A-Level/Higher Level IB Physics or mechanics options in A-Level Further Maths, in addition to the other requirements.

### What is it like to study Maths with Physics?

Maths with Physics students study about 75% of the maths material learned by straight Maths students, as described in Section 1.3—your supervisors will focus on the parts of the maths syllabus they think are most relevant to you. A major topic that *is* mostly absent for Maths with Physics students is number theory.

See page 209 for details of the physics (Natural Sciences) modules you'll study. This part of the course will involve practical work.

After your first year, you'll have an enormous number of options from both Maths and Natural Sciences.

## 3.6: Is studying maths or computer science jointly with another subject more work?

Studying a joint honours degree isn't the same as doing two degrees at once—you won't take every module that would be compulsory for someone taking either of the standalone degrees. It's a large workload, but then all the degrees at Oxbridge are—especially STEM degrees, which include

32 The SAQ is an extra form you have to fill out online if you've applied to Cambridge.

more contact hours than humanities subjects. The amount you'll have to hand in to tutors, week-on-week, will be roughly the same as someone doing another deadline-heavy degree, such as Maths or Physics—but your course will probably be more time-consuming overall because you're refining two different skillsets independently.

It's also worth bearing in mind that, as you progress through the course, you'll have more choice in terms of how you divide your focus between the two disciplines. You can usually take up to 80% of your papers in either subject, so you'll have a lot of flexibility.

## Case Study: Maths & Philosophy

> *"In my first year, the mathematicians would generally have 5 problem sheets a week. I would have 3 problem sheets and an essay—or 4 problem sheets and 1 logic sheet. At Oxford, you're expected to spend 6–8 hours per problem sheet and up to 20 hours per essay (or that's what I was told anyway!). All in all, you'll be expected to do 35–40 hours of work per week, and the time spent on both essays and problem sheets for a Maths & Philosophy degree equates to the same number of hours as studying straight Maths."* –Student, Maths & Philosophy, Oxford

However, doing a joint honours degree is incredibly rewarding and enjoyable. It's nice having the variety of the two subjects, and you'll never be bored!

> *"I wish I'd thought about doing a joint honours at Oxford—studying just Maths for six hours every day can sometimes leave me craving a bit of variety."* –Peter, Maths, Oxford

If you absolutely love maths or computer science and never want a break from it, then a single honours degree is definitely for you! If, however, you're looking for a course with a broader scope, then a joint honours degree could be perfect.

# Part I B: The Application Process

Among the many courses that fall under the label of Mathematical and Computational Sciences, the admissions process varies a great deal. We'll discuss in detail how to get through each step of the admissions process – the personal statement, the admissions test and the interview[33] – for each of these courses.

33 If you're applying for Maths at Cambridge, you'll take your admissions test – STEP – at the very end of the process, but you should start preparing well before that! See page 80 for more info on STEP.

# Chapter 4: Personal statements

## 4.1: What to include in your personal statement

The point of your personal statement is to help admissions tutors answer this question:

> **"WHY should I accept *this* student to study *this* subject at *this* university?"**

If you can make sure that every sentence answers this question, then you'll undoubtedly have a very strong personal statement. Remember the intangibles: **Ability**, **Passion** and **Potential**? If you can demonstrate these, you're answering the question already. So keep them in mind at every stage of the writing process.

For maths and science subjects, you'll find that more weight is given to your admissions test score and interview performance than your personal statement. Nonetheless, you'll want to make your personal statement as representative of you as possible, because you could be asked about it at interview, and because information about your priorities and background can sometimes reassure tutors that you're a good fit for the course, especially if they are trying to decide between two candidates who are otherwise very similar.

You have a mere 4,000 characters (approximately 650 words) to make an impression. How can you show the admissions tutors, in so few words, that you're the perfect candidate for a place at their prestigious university? How can you demonstrate that you understand the degree you're applying for and have the ability, passion and potential to succeed in it? Here are some tips on making your personal statement show you off in your best light.

# General advice for Maths/Computer Science personal statements

## 1) Problem-solving Ability Potential

Problem-solving is such an important skill for maths/computer science, so you definitely want to show the admissions tutors how you've developed these skills. One of the best pieces of evidence you can give is extra problem solving you've done outside of your Maths A Level, such as in individual or team competitions.

## 2) Appreciation of undergraduate maths Potential

You'll want to show the admissions tutors that you know the difference between school and university maths. For instance, you might highlight the greater emphasis on rigour and proof rather than calculation.

## 3) Independent study Potential

Independent study is a large part of university, and anything you've done that shows off this skill should 100% be included. For instance, if you've completed a project over the summer, or as part of some work experience, that's perfect material to write about.

## 4) Extra reading Passion Ability

Reading widely on your subject is vital, and shows a willingness to expand your knowledge. But don't read a book just so you can write about it. Find books that you really enjoy reading and genuinely find interesting. Any of the books mentioned in the next section would be great to include—so long as you've actually read them! It's also good to write a couple of sentences about what you particularly enjoyed in the book, and what you did as a follow-up. For example:

> *"Reading the book Fermat's Last Theorem, I became fascinated by the history of maths and how different mathematicians approach the same problem in so many different ways. As a result, I completed a summer project focusing on the mathematicians of Ancient Greece."*

## 5) Extracurricular achievements in context Potential

Extracurricular achievements are fine to include in your personal statement, but it is vital that you link them back to the subject. Think about the perseverance you learnt when working towards your Gold Duke of Edinburgh award, or the self-discipline you achieved practising for your Grade 8 oboe—but discuss *how* these skills relate to your academics.

### 6) Concrete examples

Avoid flimsy sentences. Use concrete examples of how you've demonstrated passion for the subject. For example, instead of:

> *"I really love the concept of infinity."*

Use:

> *"The infinite has always intrigued me, and I became even more fascinated after reading Stewart's From Here to Infinity. As a result, I watched online lectures on Cantor's diagonal proof, and have been working on a project exploring different proofs of the uncountability of the real numbers."*

Your personal statement must be full of solid examples of your work ethic, as opposed to generalised, sweeping statements that don't convey anything more than you'd learn from a quick internet search.

### 7) 'I enjoyed x in school, so I did y...' Passion Potential

Admissions tutors want to know *more* than that you're good at the subjects you've covered in school. They also want to see what you do to deepen your understanding. In addition to further reading, you can expand your knowledge by doing online courses, attending public lectures, listening to interesting podcasts, or enrolling in a maths/computer science summer school.[34]

## Further advice for Maths applicants

There are plenty of extra mathematical problems out there to attempt in order to impress the admissions tutor reading your personal statement. Having said that, if you're only doing them for the sake of your personal

34 See oxbridgeformula.co.uk to learn more about our summer schools.

statement and not because you actually enjoy solving them, studying maths/computer science at Oxbridge probably isn't for you! Here are some good ways to find extra problems to improve your mathematical abilities before your interviews and admissions tests (and to discuss in your personal statement):

- Solve problems on the UKMT website. The Senior Kangaroo, in particular, is very useful
- Prepare with Oxbridge Formula resources and past papers
- Read maths books designed to bridge the gap between school and university—and solve the end-of-chapter questions (See Chapter 8 on page 140)
- Solve the weekly Nrich maths problems
- Solve problems in the Plus Maths magazine online.

## Further advice for Maths & Statistics applicants

For the most part, a Maths & Statistics personal statement will be the same as a Maths personal statement. You won't be expected to include lots of subject-specific examples for statistics, as the two are so closely linked. However, do show (even in one sentence) that statistics is a particular interest for you. This could mean drawing on a chapter in a maths book you read that focused on statistics or a particular problem in probability that intrigues you. Here's an example of a good sentence to include in a Maths & Statistics personal statement:

> *"I recently completed a five-week online course called 'Explore Statistics' in which I learnt a lot about handling and visualising data and different types of parametric and non-parametric hypothesis tests. Statistics is a fascinating and increasingly important subject that I would love to explore in more depth at university."*

## Further advice for Computer Science applicants

### 1) Try some programming Passion Potential

Although Computer Science is more than just programming, trying to get to grips with a programming language (such as Java, Ruby, Pascal, Haskell or Python) will give you a good indication as to whether the course is for you or not. Furthermore, it shows the admissions tutors that you have an active interest and have been exploring the various elements of course as much as possible. For practical experience using a language, you could try to contribute to an open source project or write a simple phone app. It's also useful to play around with hardware – anything from a Raspberry Pi, to a radio, to a robot – since circuit design will form a part of your first-year course at either Oxford or Cambridge.

### 2) Do extra Further Maths modules Ability Passion

Whether or not you take Further Maths, try to teach yourself a few (new) modules. Although the Further Pure A-Level content is taught in the first few weeks of your degree, it's covered very quickly—so already having a knowledge base will be invaluable. It also shows your drive and capacity for independent study, something that is very attractive to admissions tutors.

If you don't have a teacher at school to help with tricky areas in any extra topics you study, there are plenty of worked solutions and support pages available online—there's nothing stopping you. Although some of the maths you'll study at university is in the style of decision maths, the A-Level Further Pure modules cover the most useful topics to get to grips with ahead of time.

## Further advice for Maths & Computer Science applicants

In your Maths & Computer Science personal statement, aim for a roughly equal split of maths and computer science material. Demonstrate an awareness of the overlap between the two disciplines and how they influence one another. For example, discrete mathematics, linear algebra, vectors and transformation matrices, recursion, and approximations to functions (e.g. Taylor series) are all topics that play a significant role in both disciplines and could be good areas to research as you prepare your personal statement.

## Further advice for Maths & Philosophy and Computer Science & Philosophy applicants Passion

In your personal statement, you must touch upon both disciplines. As prior philosophical knowledge isn't a prerequisite for this course, your personal statement will probably be weighted towards the maths/computer science side—but make sure at least one third is philosophy-based.

The admissions tutors won't expect you to have a comprehensive understanding of philosophy by the time you write your personal statement—but they will look for your willingness to learn.

Reading a few philosophy books (see page 441 for a reading list), attending lectures, listening to podcasts, and thinking about key philosophical issues are the best ways to prepare. Here are some useful YouTube channels and podcasts you could investigate:

- Crash Course Philosophy YouTube channel
- The School of Life YouTube channel
- Philosophy Bites
- In Our Time
- The Philosopher's Zone.[35]

If you can start with a topic of interest and include a few sentences to demonstrate you're thinking about the questions it poses or analysing a response, that's great—it means you're starting to 'do philosophy'!

You'll also want to find a good way to connect the disciplines in the middle of your personal statement, as the intersection between maths/computer science and philosophy is central to each course.

For **Maths & Philosophy**, you could research:

- The concept of infinity
- Set theory
- Famous philosophers who were also mathematicians, such as Descartes, Leibniz, Russell and Frege
- Logic and some of its fundamental concepts, such as proof systems and formal languages
- Questions such as 'What is a number?' or 'What is probability?'

For **Computer Science & Philosophy** you could research:

- **Logic:** Boolean logic and logic gates are integral to computer science. Logic is also useful in many fields of philosophy.
- **Ethical questions about technology:** AI and other areas of modern technology have thrown up significant ethical questions. Ethics is central to philosophy, and an interesting way to connect the two disciplines in your personal statement. For example, you could think about how artificial intelligence might shift our concept of what it is to be a person.
- **The mind and brain:** Much as researchers study the mind and brain to improve AI, they also study AI to learn about the mind and brain. Evaluating the extent to which we can think of mental processes as compu-

35 You can find more links at oxbridgeformula.co.uk/bonus-chapter.

tational ones is a very vibrant field of study, and one where computer science and the philosophy of mind overlap.

- **Alan Turing and the Turing test**: This is an idea that's more significant than ever given ongoing advances in AI, and which you'll study in your first year.

## 4.2: Books to read if you're interested in Maths/Computer Science

Passion Potential

Reading around the subject you're applying for is a great way to show engagement and independent research in your personal statement. More than anything, reading outside of the syllabus is a way for you to develop a genuine interest and passion for your subject. Here are some maths/computer science books to give you a taste for university study:[36]

### Maths books

**Singh: *Fermat's Last Theorem***

An introduction to one of the biggest questions of mathematical history: Fermat's Last Theorem. It's also a fascinating exposition of mathematical methods, and how many mathematicians have attempted proofs of this intriguing theorem. If you study Maths at Oxford, your classes will be in the Andrew Wiles Building—named after the man who proved ***Fermat's Last Theorem*** in 1993.

**Fermat's Last Theorem** is the proposition that if $n > 2$ the equation $x^n + y^n = z^n$ has no positive integer solutions. Fermat claimed in his papers that he himself had a proof but that it was too big to fit in the margin where he was writing! It remained a famous unproven conjecture until Andrew Wiles proved it 358 years later, taking 129 pages to do so!

36 See oxbridgeformula.co.uk/bonus-chapter for links to these books and more.

### Stewart: *Seventeen Equations that Changed the World*

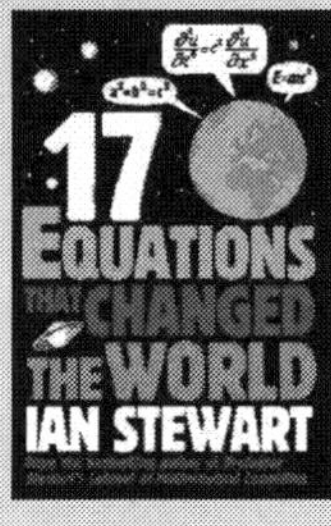


Considers some of the most crucial equations for the study of maths. It will be particularly useful when you're writing your personal statement because it's a good starting point for discovering and researching further things that interest you. For example, you could write something like:

> *"When reading* ***Stewart's Seventeen Equations that Changed the World****, I found the section on the Black-Scholes model extremely interesting. As a result, I did further research into how bankers use this model to predict the behaviour of markets, and I went to a lecture on the mathematics behind investment banking in London. I also did work experience with a bank, where I had the opportunity to ask more questions about market prediction—so I am particularly interested in the financial derivatives module in the course."*

### Singh: *The Simpsons and Their Mathematical Secrets*

This is a funny, entertaining read, showing some interesting mathematical secrets lying behind the cartoon *The Simpsons* (did you know, its main scriptwriters were a team of mathematicians?). It's amusing and engaging, and contains some really interesting mathematical theory presented in a digestible way.

### Allenby: *Numbers and Proofs*

A solid introduction to the notion of proof, which is crucial to the study of maths at university. If you're unsure if maths is for you, this book is a great way to start understanding the concepts and see if you'd enjoy the style of university maths.

**Hurst: *Bridging the Gap to University Mathematics***

This book is more systematic than others listed here and covers the most crucial core topics from undergraduate maths. Each chapter has an explanation, worked examples and exercises—and the chapters get harder (and closer to the style of university-level problems) as they progress. This is a book that is also worth coming back to the summer before you start your degree.

## Computer science books

**Hills: *The Pattern on the Stone***

An engaging exploration of the field of computer science, and a great starting point if you're relatively new to the subject. It offers a readable overview into a few highlights of the discipline such as parallel computing, quantum computers and genetic algorithms. It also begins with a clear account of Boolean logic—a popular interview topic.

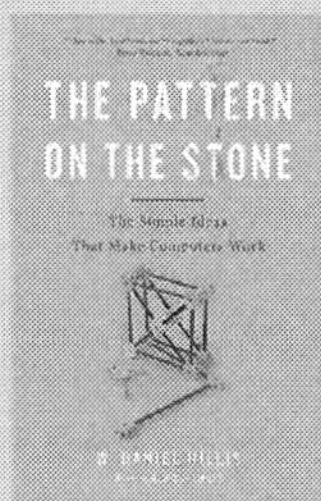


**Brylow and Brookshear: *Computer Science***

Another useful and accessible overview. It appears on a lot of pre-university recommended reading lists, as it touches on many of the key subjects explored at degree level, such as digital systems, algorithms and programming languages. Some of the topics covered are more advanced and begin to fall into undergraduate territory, but it's a good overall look at the subject.

**Kubica: *Computational Fairy Tales***

This is another overview of computer science, written in an accessible and engaging way. It consists of small bites of information that combine metaphor and allegory to set out a fairy tale world that helps the reader understand key concepts. As it's colloquial in style, some of the more technical mathematical elements of computer science are missed out for maximum accessibility.

## 4.3: Example Maths personal statement

Over the next few sections, we'll look at the personal statements of several students who are currently studying at Oxford or Cambridge. We've highlighted the points where each student has demonstrated their ability, passion, or potential in a way you could try to emulate, and we've also noted areas where the personal statements could be even more effective. Try to keep these notes in mind when drafting your own.

Here is the personal statement of a student who is currently reading Maths at Cambridge.

I am applying to study mathematics not only because it's an area of study that deeply fascinates me and is very applicable in the real world, but because it's something I have grown to love. Maths provides a deep and intricate world in which I lose myself for hours at a time, trying to find a solution to a challenging UKMT question I am set by the senior 'Elite maths' club.

**Passion** The student gives a concrete example of how their love for their subject is expressed, rather than simply stating that they do love it, which anyone can do.

Solving a hard problem and having to go out of my comfort zone to use a different method or approach to what might be considered 'conventional' at A Level is something I relish, and I believe it's one of the most rewarding things one can do. For example, proving that 'given any set of 100 integers, one can always find a subset of 15 integers such that any two of them have a difference which is a multiple of 7' is very different to the typical A-Level problem, but considering the integers modulo 7, and by use of the pigeonhole principle, the problem becomes beautifully simple.

**Ability** **Potential** Being ready to go out of your comfort zone is something that admissions tutors explicitly look for because someone who can't do that and learn from the experience will struggle with the challenges of an Oxbridge degree. The student again gives a concrete example—one that also serves to highlight their number theory skills.

For me, one of the most fascinating areas of mathematics is the notion of proof; it's simply amazing and often ingenious how one can show something to always be true in a particular set of circumstances using watertight and flawless logic. Being able to demonstrate a fundamental

**Potential** This student explicitly knows what they are getting into at university, and that maths is a rigorous discipline and not simply about calculation.

truth, applicable to infinitely many circumstances, be it by methods of contradiction, induction or construction is elegant and beautiful—except for the 4-colour theorem, perhaps one of the 'ugliest' proofs ever! I particularly enjoy number theory; recently I learnt how to use the various mean inequalities for problem-solving, something I found rewarding because the problems can seem unapproachable and daunting at first, but by application of one of these inequalities a quick solution can often be found.

While reading Ian Stewart's revised edition of Courant and Robbins's 'What is Mathematics?', I discovered how the two ancient problems of doubling the volume of a given cube and trisecting an angle (using ruler and compass alone) were proved impossible in the 19th century by constructing a series of fields of algebraic numbers, with each field and its possible constructions creating the next. I also have a great interest in some of the most simple yet complicated problems known—I can explain the Goldbach and twin prime conjectures to my younger brother, yet the proof/disproof of them has eluded the greatest minds for over 150 years.

**Passion** **Potential** The student spells out something they learned from the book, showing they engaged with it and were able to follow mathematical ideas beyond A Level.

Reading Mathematics at university would enable me to broaden my mathematical knowledge, gain a deeper understanding and grow my passion for the subject. I have a hunger for learning new things and ideas that has always been with me; I want to learn about Galois theory, Riemann sums, Ramsey numbers and everything else that the broad diversity of the subject offers. I thoroughly enjoyed attending two STEP maths courses this year because I learnt how to logically structure my solutions and clearly present them to others. My gold and silver awards in the chemistry and physics AS challenges (respectively) gave me further opportunities to solve problems at a high level; the questions are stimulating and fuel my interest in science as well.

**Passion** It's great to be explicit about what it is about this particular degree that you think will help you pursue your passion

**Ability** **Passion** You're allowed to have interests outside of mathematics—in this case, the student is careful to tie them back to their problem-solving ability and motivation too.

As a vice-captain, I am involved with running and organising many of the school's larger events, such as the Founder's Day Fête. I play rugby for the school's first team and have represented my county in triple jump and captained the athletics team. Mentoring physics, chemistry and also intermediate elite maths has been interesting and rewarding; I believe being able to explain things to others can be as important as understanding; which is why I mentor and also have a part-time job working as a maths, English and 11+ tutor at 'Explore Learning'.

In summary, I am applying to study mathematics because I enjoy it and want to take it further and to a higher level; I believe I have the ability, curiosity and perseverance to thoroughly enjoy university maths.

**Ability** **Passion** **Potential** Teaching and other extracurricular academic work with groups demonstrates commitment and work ethic, but it also tends to go hand-in-hand with understanding the subject matter better than students who haven't done that, because in explaining an idea you come to understand it better.

**Potential** Identifying qualities that admissions tutors value highly.

# 4.4: Example Computer Science personal statement

My interest in computing really took off when I realised I could tell the computer exactly what to do and hence, in turn, tell others what to do. This was something with an obvious appeal to a teenage boy with a strict mother. This drew me to a game design club at age eleven where, instead of passively accepting other people's ideas, I could create a game based on my own.

Although I sometimes became frustrated with my limited mathematical understanding, I quickly learned I could use algorithms to bridge the gap between my abilities and my imagination. For example, on a course at the University of Aberdeen I performed a dry-run of a typical classifier algorithm using Bayes' theorem, which taught me how easily formulae can be adapted to seemingly bespoke situations to produce exciting outcomes. This not only developed my Java programming ability, but also gave me an insight into mobile-telephone development, and the care that needs to be given to issues such as memory allocation and battery usage. I realised I could apply similar

**Ability** **Potential** A design activity that shows the student has the mix of creativity and accuracy needed for computer science. Other good examples would be amateur publishing and engineering contests—not all your experiences need to be directly related to computers.

**Passion** **Potential** This sentence shows a desire to further their knowledge beyond what is learnt at school, and it concludes with an example of how they've done this.

techniques to conserve resources in a desktop application and create a high-performance app using less processing power.

**Ability** **Passion** **Potential** This paragraph shows an active interest in computer science as well as independent research: the sort of things that stand out in a personal statement.

It's hard to predict the future, but it seems that computing will be increasingly dominated by artificial intelligence, specifically machine-learning algorithms. I am excited to see, and hopefully be part of, the shift from specialist AIs – which can only be considered 'intelligent' in one context – to a general AI which can potentially do most, if not all, of the computational tasks a human could. While attending the recent Computational Intelligence Unconference, I was struck by the suggestion that 95% of AI projects are unknown to the public; carried out by secret company labs and, perhaps more worryingly, by governments. Although there are possible negative consequences of such research, it's exhilarating as we are possibly on the verge of a key paradigm shift: the dawn of the age of artificial intelligence.

**Passion** **Potential** There is a successful balance of love for the subject on the one hand, and knowledge and concrete examples of exploring that interest on the other. Passion is important in a personal statement, but it's important to ground this in things you've done.

Teaching and mentoring students have required me to communicate my ideas effectively. As a Maths Prefect, it's encouraging to see students (who have previously only achieved limited results) flourish in the right environment. As such, I designed a tool to help sixth-form students learn about vectors. This required me to learn some of the FP3 content in advance, which improved not only my problem solving but also my ability to self-teach, a challenge I relished. I learnt how to expand my thinking when searching for a solution—a change from the majority of the maths course in which we tend to only be shown the relevant method.

**Ability** **Potential** Self-teaching is essential to success at university, so if you've done any independent learning, whether that be an online course, an EPQ, a school extended essay project, or teaching yourself a Maths module, include it.

I was appointed a House Leader in Year 12, which allowed me to voice the concerns of the student body to staff and make positive changes. Also, as a member of my school's Digital Council, I helped introduce new technologies and present them to the governing body.

**Potential** Extracurricular activities can be included if they link to the course you want to study, as this is ultimately what the admissions tutors are interested in. Group work is important in the Computer Science course, as in both academia and industry, so teamwork and communication are highly relevant skills for computer scientists.

At first, I was too directive, but over time I learnt to use open questions to allow the governors to express their understanding, which led to them being more receptive to my proposals. Furthermore, I delivered training to staff on several occasions, which was quite daunting at first but ultimately very rewarding. Unlike students, teachers are more resistant to change, which forced me to adapt my approach and build on the familiar, presenting it as an upgrade rather than a complete change.

Technology is evolving and reshaping old industries (for better or worse) because computer scientists are always trying to answer the question: 'How do we do it better?' After university, I plan to pursue a career in the computing industry; a degree will help provide me with the necessary skills and knowledge for my selected career.

**Passion** If you do have an idea of a career you intend to pursue and it plausibly adds to your suitability to study your chosen degree, include it. This isn't recommended for all subjects—for example, in maths they prefer you not to apply because of the amazing job prospects, but because of your love of maths instead.

# 4.5: Example Maths & Philosophy personal statement

During a Kent County Youth Orchestra rehearsal, playing Pärt's 'Cantus in Memoriam Benjamin Britten', I was struck by the vast influence and significance of mathematics. This beautifully poignant piece, solely reliant on mathematical ratios and patterns, widened my view of mathematics and its effect on numerous disciplines. Based on very simple patterns, Pärt's composition showed me that sometimes the beauty of mathematics lies in simplicity.

If you want to include extracurricular interests in your personal statement, that's great, so long as you link them back to the subject you're applying for, as that is what admissions tutors are interested in.

This was reinforced for me when I began investigating proof by contradiction more deeply, such as how to prove that $e$ is irrational. I was truly amazed to see that such a simple and succinct proof was possible. Bearing in mind the cross-fertilisation of mathematics with so many disciplines and having been inspired by a RIM

**Passion** **Potential** Instead of simply saying that they are interested in something, the student shows what they did to explore it, showing an active interest in the subject.

masterclass on music and juggling, I completed my EPQ entitled 'Whether music based on a mathematical structure is more satisfying.' Looking at more Pärt's music, observing the clean and simple use of symmetry, as well as observing Mozart's subtle use of the Fibonacci sequence, I wrote my own piece (and varied it by imitating their techniques)—which I tested on a sample group.

However, for me, the most beautiful part of mathematics is the study of infinity, which has sparked a particular interest in me. Having been introduced to some basic ideas of the concept of infinity at a lecture, I explored these further through reading Stewart's *From Here to Infinity*, which details the laws governing infinity. I watched an enthralling lecture showing some powerful Cantorian proofs about infinite sets. I continued my investigations through the harmonic series, gaining huge satisfaction from the integral test, which inspired me to further my knowledge by completing an online course on calculus. This allowed me to begin to use implicit differentiation, and the product and chain rules before we covered them at school, and gave me tools to start manipulating more complex functions and solve differential equations.

**Passion** Demonstrating an understanding of maths beyond school helps admissions tutors to see that you've researched what a Maths degree is really like

**Ability** **Passion** Including concrete examples of mathematical techniques you've learnt and developed is important, instead of using vague statements such as 'I really like calculus, so I learnt more about it.'

Beginning to connect the two disciplines together. The only discipline that seems comparable to mathematics in terms of the enormity of scale and its abstract nature is philosophy. Studying English, I have always had a passion for literature and words and this has fuelled my interest in philosophy. I began to see how philosophy could unlock meanings in various texts, including ontological issues in *Frankenstein* and existential questions in *Hamlet*—as well as how Hamlet's soliloquies interrogate the idea of the 'inner self', a concept I saw mirrored in Hume's writing. Reading *Sophie's World*, I took pleasure in the overt connection between the philosopher's tea party and Nagel's theory of the absurd in human life, which I found one of the most memorable extracts from Hanfling's compilation *Life and Meaning*. I earned a 97% mark in an online epistemology course, which led me to read Smith's *Philosophy of Mind*. I am constantly trying to widen my philosophical

**Potential** Linking philosophy to your other current studies is good because it shows that you have some of the skills needed for the course.

It would be even better if the student briefly explained what they think the connection between Hamlet and Hume is.

knowledge; I have been captivated by Plato's *Republic* and Descartes' *Meditations*, as well as listening to podcasts on relativism, beauty and scepticism.

This student is successful in showing they've read a wide range of philosophy, which demonstrates their enthusiasm, but don't worry if you don't have the same amount of reading under your belt yet—an insightful and enthusiastic description of one thing you've read is equally impressive, if not more so.

The self-discipline I have learnt through the meticulous nature of solving a mathematical problem I have channelled into being an officer in the Combined Cadet Force and my Gold Duke of Edinburgh Award expeditions. I recently spent a month in Borneo completing my jungle warfare training and volunteering as a school maths teacher. The latter experience showed me that, even when there's no common language, communication is still possible through the medium of numbers. I feel I have only scraped the surface of these two hugely influential disciplines, and I am keen to pursue mathematics and philosophy further, as I strive for a deeper understanding of the incomprehensible elements of the world.

**Potential** Good mention of other areas of interest, but constantly linking it back to skills required for the degree—this is really important!

# Chapter 5:
# Admissions tests

Different Oxbridge courses in the mathematical and computational sciences require different admissions tests. Even the specific questions you'll need to answer within the test can depend on your chosen course too.

Below is a table summarising the paper and questions you'll have to complete for each course. (Unlike other non-Oxbridge unis,[37] Imperial College makes MAT and STEP compulsory for some degrees, so we've added it to the table where relevant.)

| Course | University | Test (and Questions) | Page Number |
|---|---|---|---|
| Maths | Oxford | MAT (qs 1, 2, 3, 4, 5) | Page 70 |
| | Cambridge | STEP | Page 80 |
| | Imperial | MAT (qs 1, 2, 3, 4, 5) | Page 70 |
| Maths & Statistics | Oxford | MAT (qs 1, 2, 3, 4, 5) | Page 70 |
| Maths & Philosophy | Oxford | MAT (qs 1, 2, 3, 4, 5) | Page 70 |
| Computer Science | Oxford | MAT (qs 1, 2, 5, 6, 7) | Page 70 |
| | Cambridge | CTMUA[38] (as of 2019) CSAT (before 2019; still used at some colleges) | CTMUA page 74 CSAT page 102 |
| | Imperial | STEP | Page 80 |
| Maths & Computer Science | Oxford | MAT (qs 1, 2, 3, 5, 6) | Page 70 |
| Computer Science and Philosophy | Oxford | MAT (qs 1, 2, 5, 6, 7) | Page 70 |

37 Other unis that use STEP include Warwick, Bath, and UCL.

38 Colleges for mature students use an at-interview test instead of the CTMUA

## 5.1: MAT: The Facts

**Q Who wants the MAT?**

**A** MAT stands for Mathematics Admissions Test, and it's the admissions test set by Oxford for candidates applying to study:

- Maths
- Maths joint degrees
- Computer Science
- Computer Science joint degrees.

Imperial also requires you sit the MAT and other universities (such as Warwick and Bath) might make you a reduced offer if you get a good grade.

**Q When is the MAT sat?**

**A** It is sat in late October, or early November: before the interview stage of the Oxford application process.

**Q What is the purpose of the MAT?**

**A** Oxford only interviews 35% of its applicants for Maths and the MAT (alongside your UCAS application), helps to decide who gets an interview and who doesn't. After your interview, your MAT score is still taken into account in deciding whether you'll get an offer.

At Imperial, there's no interview for Maths applicants, so the MAT is arguably even more significant in deciding whether you get an offer.

**Q How long is the MAT?**

**A** The MAT lasts 2½ hours.

**Q How is the MAT structured?**

**A** The MAT is marked out of 100 and is made up of two sections.

***Multiple-choice (40 marks)***
Question 1 is multiple-choice and made up of 10 individual sub-questions. Each sub-question is worth 4 marks. The MAT is positively marked—you won't lose any marks for incorrect answers.

The multiple-choice test questions exist to challenge you on the full breadth of the A Level syllabus – everything from differentiation to circle theorems (or even both – e.g. to maximise the area of an inscribed triangle with some restraints). However, to test that you genuinely understand the underlying concepts, they force you to apply these skills in unfamiliar ways.

Question 1 also often tests your attention to detail. For instance, do you notice that one of the solutions you've found to a given equation is ruled out by an extra condition in the question?

***Long-answer questions (60 marks)***

You're expected to answer 4 long-answer questions. The questions you answer depend on the course you're applying for.

- For Maths, Maths & Statistics, and Maths & Philosophy, you answer questions 2, 3, 4 and 5.
- For Maths & Computer Science, you answer questions 2, 3, 5 and 6.
- For Computer Science, and Computer Science & Philosophy, you answer questions 2, 5, 6 and 7.

Each long-answer question is worth 15 marks.

These questions test your ability to solve more extended problems that the multiple-choice part does. They often ask you to explain results rather than just prove them, which is to test your depth of understanding, They frequently present you with definitions that will be new to you, and lean more on techniques like induction and recursion, proof by contradiction, and reasoning about limits than A-Level Maths does, since these are all skills that are more important at uni than at school. In other words, the MAT is testing your **Potential** as well as your **Ability**.

**Q What is the content of the MAT?**

**A** The content of the MAT is based upon the pure maths studied in the A-Level syllabus (as of 2018 guidelines), as well as some additional knowledge about sequences and series that appears in the second year of A Level.[39]

---

39 For a more detailed breakdown of the syllabus, see our free guidebook at oxbridge-formula.co.uk/mat.

**Q What do I get as well as the paper?**

**A** Nothing: the MAT is a non-calculator paper, and you don't receive a formula booklet.

**Q Where can I find MAT past papers?**

**A** Scan the QR code here to find MAT past papers:

**Q What does a MAT-style multiple-choice question look like?**

**A** D. The number of solutions of the equation $(5+\cos(x))^2 = 16 - 7\sin^4(x)$ in the range $0 \le x < 2\pi$ is:

(a) 0, (b) 1, (c) 2, (d) 3, (e) 4

**Q What does a MAT-style long-answer question look like?**

**A** 5. For **ALL APPLICANTS**

In this question, we consider repeating decimal expansions, such as $\frac{1}{9} = 0.111\ldots$ and $\frac{1}{11} = 0.090909\ldots$

We only consider decimal expansions that start to repeat immediately after the decimal place (e.g. $\frac{1}{6} = 0.1666\ldots$ is not counted).

A decimal expansion repeats with period $n$ if the shortest repeating block is of length $n$. For instance, $\frac{1}{11} = 0.090909\ldots$, which is of period 2 as the repeating block is '09'.

(i) Show that there are 90 numbers between 0 and 1 whose decimal expansion is repeating with period 2 and starts to repeat immediately after the decimal point.

(ii) Show that there are 9900 numbers between 0 and 1 whose decimal expansion is repeating with period 4 and starts to repeat immediately after the decimal point.

(iii) How many numbers are there between 0 and 1 whose decimal expansion is repeating with period 6 and starts to repeat immediately after the decimal point?

Let $N(n)$ be the number of numbers between 0 and 1 whose decimal expansion is repeating with period $n$ and starts to repeat immediately after the decimal point.

(iv) Show that: if $n$ is a product of two distinct prime numbers, then $\frac{N(n)}{10}$ ends in a '1'.

(v) Show that $\frac{N(n)}{10}$ ends in a '9' whenever $n$ is a product of three distinct prime numbers.

(vi) Explain why $\frac{N(n)}{10}$ ends in a '1' or '9' whenever $n$ has no repeated prime factors.

## Q Where can I find more details about the MAT?

For more details about the MAT, download our free guidebook at oxbridgeformula.co.uk/mat.

**Did You Know?**

*Some MAT statistics from the last 10 years:*
*Average score: 49.2*
*Average score to be invited to interview: 62.5*
*Average score to get an offer: 69.4*

*In 2018:*
*Average score: 50.8*
*Average score to be invited to interview: 67.1*
*Average score to get an offer: 72.9*

**Did You Know?**

*In 2017, 13 Computer Science applicants (representing a mere 2% of all applicants) scored 80 or more out of 100 in the MAT. That's an exceptionally strong score, but still, only 8 of them received offers. Don't be fooled into thinking that acing the MAT will guarantee you an offer. Although it plays a major part in the application process, your performance at the interview really matters too.*

## 5.2: CTMUA: The Facts

**Q Who wants the (C)TMUA?**

**A** The TMUA, Test of Mathematics for University Admissions, is a fairly new admissions test, introduced in 2016. In 2019, it was adopted by Cambridge under the name CTMUA.[40]

- You're required to sit the CTMUA if you're applying to study Computer Science at Cambridge.

40 'CTMUA' stands for Cambridge Test of Mathematics for University Admission, but in reality the CTMUA is exactly the same as the TMUA—it simply has a different name for Cambridge applicants. We will use the terms 'CTMUA' and 'TMUA' interchangeably from now on.

- You're encouraged to sit the TMUA if you're applying to study Maths or Maths joint honours courses at universities including Bath, Durham, Lancaster, LSE, Sheffield, Southampton and Warwick.

The test is only compulsory for Computer Science at Cambridge, but performing well in the TMUA can lead to a reduced offer at these other universities, giving you extra security when you take your A Levels.

**Q When is the CTMUA sat?**

**A** It is sat at the end of October, on the same day as the MAT.

**Q What is the purpose of the CTMUA?**

**A** The CTMUA functions similarly to the MAT in first helping to determine whether you get an interview, and then also whether you get an offer.

For universities other than Cambridge, a poor TMUA score won't hinder your offer, but a good TMUA score will give you a reduced offer.

**Q How long is the CTMUA?**

**A** It comprises two papers, each lasting 1 hour and 15 minutes.

**Q How is the CTMUA structured?**

**A** Each paper is made up of 20 multiple-choice questions:

- Paper 1: Mathematical Thinking
- Paper 2: Mathematical Reasoning

Although the CTMUA is multiple choice, the questions are designed to be answered by reasoning directly to the correct answer rather than by guessing, eliminating incorrect options, or using other tricks that rely on the choices you're given for the answer. The multiple-choice format seems to be used for ease of marking rather than ease of answering, because questions can have up to nine multiple choice options to choose from!

Both papers are positively marked, so you won't lose any marks for incorrect answers.

**Q What is the content of the CTMUA?**

**A** The CTMUA covers the same A-Level Maths content as the MAT. You're expected to have a good grasp of first-year A-Level pure maths, as well as second-year material on sequences and series. However, Section 2 has a very distinctive focus on logic and proof, which might need extra preparation.[41]

**Q What do I get as well as the paper?**

**A** Nothing, the CTMUA is a non-calculator paper and you don't get a formula booklet.

**Q How is the CTMUA marked?**

**A** You're assigned a score for each paper of the (C)TMUA, plus an overall score. It's scored between 1.0 and 9.0 (with 9.0 being the highest). A 'good' score is considered to be 6.5 or above, and in 2018 this was obtained by around 25% of candidates.

Here is the 2018 TMUA score conversion:[42]

| No. Marks | 40 | 39 | 38 | 37 | 36 | 35 | 34 | 33 |
|---|---|---|---|---|---|---|---|---|
| Score | 9 | 9 | 9 | 9 | 9 | 9 | 9 | 9 |

| No. Marks | 32 | 31 | 30 | 29 | 28 | 27 | 26 | 25 |
|---|---|---|---|---|---|---|---|---|
| Score | 9 | 8.8 | 8.4 | 8 | 7.7 | 7.4 | 7.1 | 6.8 |

| No. Marks | 24 | 23 | 22 | 21 | 20 | 19 | 18 | 17 |
|---|---|---|---|---|---|---|---|---|
| Score | 6.5 | 6.2 | 5.9 | 5.6 | 5.4 | 5.1 | 4.8 | 4.5 |

41 See oxbridgeformula.co.uk/bonus-chapter for a detailed look at exactly the extra skills you might need.
42 See oxbridgeformula.co.uk/bonus-chapter for score conversions for each paper.

| No. Marks | 16 | 15 | 14 | 13 | 12 | 11 | 10 |
|---|---|---|---|---|---|---|---|
| Score | 4.2 | 3.9 | 3.6 | 3.3 | 3 | 2.6 | 2.3 |

| No. Marks | 9 | 8 | 7 | 6 | 5 | 4 | 3 |
|---|---|---|---|---|---|---|---|
| Score | 1.9 | 1.5 | 1 | 1 | 1 | 1 | 1 |

| No. Marks | 2 | 1 | 0 |
|---|---|---|---|
| Score | 1 | 1 | 1 |

**Q What is CTMUA Paper 1 all about?**

**A** Paper 1 focuses on your **Ability** to apply your Maths A-Level knowledge in unfamiliar situations. The examiners want to see whether you can *apply* it, not just *memorise* it.

**For example, you may get questions about:**

- Differentiating functions and rearranging formulae
- Finding regions where certain inequalities of trigonometric functions are satisfied
- Finding the area of overlap of two shapes in the Cartesian plane
- Finding terms of a sequence using a recurrence relationship
- Working out when the trapezium rule gives an overestimate or an underestimate
- Solving non-linear simultaneous equations.

Paper 1 questions will be at least as difficult as the hardest questions that appear in your Maths A Level.

**Q What is CTMUA Paper 2 all about?**

**A** The purpose of Paper 2 is to test you on mathematical logic, something central to maths and computer science at university. I.e. it's testing your **Potential**, not just your **Ability**.
It assesses your skill at justifying and interpreting mathematical arguments and conjectures, as well as your ability to deal with basic concepts from logic. This is a greater departure from the style of A-Level questions than in Paper 1, so it's worth doing more preparation and practice for this paper. You'll still face some

questions about functions, calculus, geometry and sequences that are similar to those that you answer at the harder end of A Level. However, you will also find some questions that are very different in style. For instance, you might find that:

- You're presented with a step-by-step attempt at a proof of a mathematical statement and have to work out where the proof went wrong.
- You must select which statement in a list is a counterexample to a given proposition.
- You're given statements about prime numbers, square numbers or cube numbers—and must work out which statement universally holds.
- You're given a statement and have to deduce which of a list of options is a ***sufficient condition*** or a ***necessary condition*** for that statement to hold.

A **sufficient condition** is something that is *enough* for something else to be true.

For example. 'I am drinking a cappuccino' is enough, or a *sufficient condition*, to conclude that 'I am drinking a coffee'.

A **necessary condition** is something that *has* to be true when something else is true.

In the above, 'I am drinking a coffee' is a necessary condition, because drinking a cappuccino means I'm necessarily drinking a coffee.

In other words:

'A implies B'

means the same as:

'A is a sufficient condition for B'

which means the same as:

'B is a necessary condition for A'.

**Q Where can I find (C)TMUA past papers?**

**A** Scan the QR code here to find (C)TMUA past papers:

**Q What does a question in the style of CTMUA Paper 1 look like?**

**A** **Question 14, Paper 1**

The ratio of the $11^{\text{th}}$ term of an arithmetic progression to the $21^{\text{st}}$ term is 9:8.

What is the ratio of the $51^{\text{st}}$ term to the $91^{\text{st}}$ term?

A 1:2 B 2:1 C 1:5 D 5:1

E 1:10 F 10:1 G 1:1

**Q What does a question in the style of CTMUA Paper 2 look like?**

**A** **Question 8, Paper 2**

Consider the following problem:

Solve the inequality $\sqrt{(y-1)^2+6} > 3$.

A student submits the following answer:

$$\sqrt{(y-1)^2+6} > 3 \qquad \text{(Step 1)}$$

$$(y-1)^2+6 > 9 \qquad \text{(Step 2)}$$

$$(y-1)^2 > 3 \qquad \text{(Step 3)}$$

$$(y-1) > \sqrt{3} \qquad \text{(Step 4)}$$

$$y > 1+\sqrt{3} \qquad \text{(Step 5)}$$

Which steps of the argument are invalid?

A There are no invalid steps; the argument is correct.
B Only step 1 is invalid; the rest are correct.
C Only step 2 is invalid; the rest are correct.
D Only step 3 is invalid; the rest are correct.
E Only step 4 is invalid; the rest are correct.

**Q Where can I find more details about the CTMUA?**

**A** For more details about the CTMUA check out our free guidebook at oxbridgeformula.co.uk/ctmua

**Did You Know?**

*In 2019, the CTMUA Paper 1 scores of successful applicants to Queen's College Cambridge ranged from 4.8 to 9, whereas for Paper 2 they ranged from 6.5 to 8.1. It seems, therefore, that a high score in Paper 2 was a greater predictor of being made an offer in this instance than Paper 1.*

## 5.3: STEP: The Facts

**Q Who wants STEP?**

**A** STEP (Sixth Term Examination Paper) is used predominantly by the University of Cambridge. It forms part of every Cambridge

Maths offer. Some colleges may choose to use it for subjects like Economics and Engineering too.

Other universities such as Warwick, Imperial, UCL and Bath also make Maths offers involving STEP, especially if you did not have the chance to take the MAT or TMUA in the autumn. Imperial also regularly make offers involving STEP for Computer Science.

**Q When is STEP sat?**

**A** STEP is sat at the same time as your A Levels—in your *sixth term* of sixth form. It forms part of your conditional offer, rather than deciding whether you get an offer in the first place.

**Q What is the purpose of STEP?**

**A** STEP is an incredibly challenging paper, aimed at the top 2% of A-Level mathematicians. It's modelled on the style of university mathematics and designed to indicate whether you would flourish in an undergraduate Maths degree. For instance, there is a much greater focus on proof, and you'll need to see how results can be generalised, apply them to additional cases, and check whether they must be subject to conditions.

> *"STEP is an excellent predictor of success in the Mathematical Tripos, partly because the questions are less standard and less structured than, for example, A-level questions, which helps to distinguish between ability (or potential) and good teaching."* –Maths Faculty, Cambridge

**Q How is STEP graded?**

**A** STEP is graded on a scale of S to U:

- S (Outstanding)
- 1 (Very good)
- 2 (Good)
- 3 (Satisfactory)
- U (Unclassified).

**Q What will an offer with STEP look like?**

**A**
- The standard Cambridge offer is A*A*A (A* Maths and Further Maths), plus a grade 1 in both STEP 2 and STEP 3. Individual colleges may choose to make a slightly different offer if they think it's appropriate.
- Other universities will typically reduce one of the A*s in your offer to an A on the condition you get at least a grade 1 or 2 (depending on the university) in any STEP paper. For instance, a common Warwick offer is: 'Either A*A*A, or A*AA and a grade 1 in any STEP paper'. If you take the STEP paper and do not achieve a grade 1, but still get A*A*A, you'll meet the offer and not be any worse off for attempting STEP.

**Q How long is STEP?**

**A** Each STEP paper is 3 hours long.

**Q How is STEP structured?**

**A** **STEP 1**

The paper consists of 11 questions in 2 sections:

- Section A: Pure mathematics, 8 questions
- Section B: Mechanics and probability/statistics, 3 questions— with at least 1 on probability/statistics and at least 1 on mechanics.

**STEP 2 and STEP 3**

These papers are divided into 3 sections. Each paper will consist of 12 questions.

- Section A: Pure mathematics, 8 questions
- Section B: Mechanics, 2 questions
- Section C: Probability/statistics, 2 questions.

Every question is worth 20 marks. You'll be assessed on the 6 best answers given for every paper, but there's no restriction on the number you can try. There is also no restriction on which sections the questions come from. For example, you could answer 6 questions from the pure mathematics section without answering any applied mathematics questions.

**Q What is the content of STEP?**

**A** STEP is based on the A-Level syllabus, though the questions are longer and more difficult. STEP 1 covers Maths A-Level; STEP 2 additionally covers Further Maths AS level; STEP 3 covers the breadth of both A-Level Maths and Further Maths. For a full breakdown of the syllabus, download our free guidebook.[43]

**Q What do I get as well as the paper?**

**A** Neither formula books nor calculators are allowed in STEP exams. On its website, Cambridge specifies the exact formulae you should know, as some are beyond the A-Level syllabus.[44]

**Q Where can I find STEP past papers?**

**A** Scan the QR code here to find STEP past papers:

**Q What does a pure maths question in the style of STEP 1 look like?**

**A** **Question 2, STEP 1**

Given a positive real number $m$, find in terms of $m$ a real number $c$ such that the curve with equation $y = e^x$ touches the line with equation $y = mx + c$.

43 Find it here: oxbridgeformula.co.uk/step.

44 Find this and other great resources at oxbridgeformula.co.uk/bonus-chapter.

(i) Hence or otherwise, find the greatest $m$ such that $e^x \geq mx$ for all $x$. Find also the least $n$ such that $nx \geq \ln(x)$ for all $x$.

(ii) Find the real number $k$ such that the curve $y = e^{x^k}$ touches the line $y = x$ and deduce that $\sqrt{x} > \ln(x)$ for all $x > 1$.

## Q What does a mechanics question in the style of STEP 1 look like?

**A Question 9, STEP 1**

A particle $P$ of mass $m$ kg falls from rest through a fluid. It experiences a constant gravitational force and a drag force that opposes its motion through the fluid, but no other forces. It is found that the downwards acceleration $a$ of $P$ at time $t$ after it begins to fall is given by $a = ge^{-kt}$, where $g$ is the constant gravitational acceleration in $ms^{-2}$ and $k$ is a constant.

(i) Find the velocity $v$ of $P$ as a function of $t$ and hence find the drag force as a function of $v$. Find also the eventual speed of $P$ as $t$ grows very large.

(ii) A second particle $Q$ of mass $m$ kg falls from rest through a different fluid. This particle also experiences only a constant gravitational force and a drag force that opposes its motion. It's found that the downwards acceleration $a$ of $Q$ at time $t$ after it begins to fall is given by

$$a = 4g\frac{e^{-rt}}{(1+e^{-rt})^2}$$

where $g$ is the constant gravitational acceleration in $ms^{-2}$ and $r$ is a constant.

Find the velocity $v$ of $Q$ as a function of $t$ and hence find the drag force as a function of $v$. Find also the eventual speed of $Q$ as $t$ grows very large.

(iii) Given that $g$ is the same for both particles and they both approach the same eventual speed as $t$ grows very large, which of them reaches 99% of this eventual speed in the shortest time?

## Q What does a probability question in the style of STEP 1 look like?

**A Question 11, STEP 1**

By considering the binomial expansion of the expression $(a+b)^n - (a-b)^n$ or otherwise, find in terms of $n$ the probability that, when $n$ fair, 6-sided dice are rolled, there is an odd number of dice showing '1'.

(i) Show that the probability that there are an odd number of dice showing '1' and an odd number of dice showing '2' can be written as

$$\frac{3^n - 2^{n+1} + 1}{4 \times 3^n} \qquad (*)$$

and find an expression for the probability that, for at least one of the results '1' and '2', there is an odd number of dice showing that result.

What happens to $(*)$ as $n$ grows large? Explain briefly why your answer is sensible.

(ii) Find the probability that the sum of the numbers rolled on the $n$ dice is odd.

## Q What does a pure maths question in the style of STEP 3 look like?

**A Question 7, STEP 3**

An operator $A$ corresponds to an operation or series of operations that can be applied to functions. '$Af(x) = g(x)$' means that applying $A$'s corresponding operation(s) to $f(x)$ produces $g(x)$.

If $A$ is an operator such that $Af(x) = kf(x)$ for some complex number $k$, we say that $f(x)$ is an *eigenfunction* of $A$ and that $k$ is the corresponding *eigenvalue*.

(i) Show briefly that $f(x) = e^{\alpha x}$ is an eigenfunction of the operator $\frac{d^n}{dx^n}$ for all $n$ and for any complex number $\alpha$. Find the corresponding eigenvalue in terms of $n$ and $\alpha$.

Hence show that $y = e^{\alpha x}$ is a solution to the differential equation

$$\frac{d^3y}{dx^3} + \frac{d^2y}{dx^2} + \frac{dy}{dx} + y = 0 \qquad (*)$$

if $\alpha$ is a solution to the cubic equation

$$\alpha^3 + \alpha^3 + \alpha^3 + 1 = 0$$

and solve equation $(*)$ for $y(0) = 0$ and $y'(0) = y''(0) = 2$.

(ii) Let $B$ be the operator such that $Bf(x) = f(x+1)$ for all $f(x)$. Show that, for any complex number $\beta$, $u(x) = \beta^x$ is an eigenfunction of $B$.

Suppose that $(u_n)$ is a sequence for which $u_0 = 0$ and $u_1 = 1$ and which satisifies the recurrence relation $u_{n+2} = u_{n+1} + u_n$. Show that:

$$u_n = \frac{1}{\sqrt{5}}\left[\left(\frac{1+\sqrt{5}}{2}\right)^n - \left(\frac{1-\sqrt{5}}{2}\right)^n\right]$$

(NB: These are the *Fibonacci Numbers*)

(iii) Let $C$ be the operator such that $Cf(x) = (f(x+1))^2$ for all $f(x)$. Find a function $g(x)$ such that $v(x) = e^{i\gamma g(x)}$ is an eigenfunction of $C$ for any complex number $\gamma$.

By considering $v(n) + v(n)^{-1}$, determine the value of the following expression when it contains $n$ '2's:

$$\sqrt{2+\sqrt{2+\sqrt{2\ldots+\sqrt{2}}}}$$

**Q Where can I find more details about STEP?**

**A** For more details about STEP, check out our free guidebook at oxbridgeformula.co.uk/step.

**Did You Know?**

*The most common reason by far for missing your Cambridge Maths offer is a disappointing STEP score. Only around 50% of offer holders make the cut.*

# 5.4: Preparing for MAT/CTMUA/STEP

## When should you start preparing?

For all of these tests, the summer between Year 12 and 13 is an incredibly useful block of time, and you should take advantage of it for preparation! We don't recommend starting your preparation as late as September—that's when you'll be focused on writing your personal statement and getting your UCAS form done by mid-October! Cramming isn't the way to go if you're serious about Oxbridge. In our experience, the best and most dedicated candidates will start preparing around May or June, after their internal exams or AS levels.

For MAT and CTMUA: if you're studying all of A-Level Maths first, followed by Further Maths, you're likely to have covered almost all the Year 12 Maths syllabus by April. This means you might even start your preparation in the spring. Remember the adage: 'Slow and steady wins the race'. If you're doing the Maths and Further Maths A Levels alongside each other instead, you should nevertheless be in a good position to attempt full papers by the beginning of the summer holidays.

For STEP, you almost certainly won't have covered all of Further Maths before the summer, so you probably won't be able to attempt many STEP 3 past paper questions. That means it's better to start with STEP 1 and STEP 2 (STEP 1 first, because the questions are not quite as difficult as in STEP 2) and start to work on the STEP 3 questions as you cover the material at school. Some Cambridge colleges ask you to sit a test at the interview. This is similar in difficulty to STEP 1, so any exposure you have to STEP 1 early on will hold you in good stead.

You may also not have covered all the Maths A Level material by the end of Year 12, in which case you'll have to pick questions from the past papers more carefully. However, it's best to start in summer, as STEP is so demanding that having nearly a full year of experience is really valuable.

## What should you do to prepare?

There are numerous ways you can prepare for your admissions tests. In spite of the differences in format, the tests are all designed to identify similar qualities in candidates – in particular, your Ability and Potential in your subject – so many tips will apply to more than one test. See which columns are ticked to see which admissions test the tip applies to.

| MAT | CTMUA | STEP | Preparation tip |
|---|---|---|---|
| ✓ | ✓ | ✓ | **Getting the basics down: formulae and arithmetic**<br>It's hugely important to have a solid grasp of all the content that the tests are based upon. It's also crucial to remember the formulae from this content, as they won't be given to you in a formula booklet.<br><br>*"My Maths teacher told me to learn all of the A-Level formulae before the MAT and I'm so glad I did—it allowed me to work really quickly because I wasn't desperately struggling to remember different formulae!"* –Jess, Maths, Oxford<br><br>You also won't have a calculator, so make sure your arithmetic is up to scratch. You don't want to find yourself in a situation where you're applying for Maths at a top university but can't perform simple long division! |
| ✓ | ✓ | ✓ | **Preparing for the style of question**<br>To prepare yourself for the style of these tests, look for some harder, more abstract questions for the topics you're studying at school. This will help you apply the concepts you're learning in an unfamiliar and more complex context. Sources for such questions include AEA papers, BMO Papers, Nrich and Underground Maths.[45] |

45 See oxbridgeformula.co.uk/bonus-chapter for more on these.

| MAT | CTMUA | STEP | Preparation tip |
|---|---|---|---|
| ✓ | ✓ | ✓ | **Do past papers!**<br>This is the best way to prepare and to get a grip on the style of the questions. There are three useful ways you can do past papers:<br><br>**1.** First, do some papers with the aim of getting the hang of their format and style. Familiarise yourself with how the questions are structured and phrased.<br><br>MAT past papers:<br><br>(C)TMUA past papers:<br><br>STEP past papers: |

| MAT | CTMUA | STEP | Preparation tip |
|---|---|---|---|
| | | | **2.** Answer some papers as perfectly as you can. Take your time to do these—go way beyond the time allotted. Try to make your answers neat and perfect. Write full solutions to all the multiple-choice sections in the MAT and CTMUA. You can use worked solutions to give you a hint if you're stuck with the beginning of the question, but try to compile two or three perfect solutions, so that you know what you're aiming for.<br><br>Also, check your long-answer solutions (in STEP and the later parts of the MAT) against the mark scheme to ensure you're picking up all the marks you possibly can.<br><br>This will ensure that you're completely comfortable with the papers and, if any of the questions are similar to the exam you sit (which is highly likely), it will give you a real advantage.<br><br>**3.** Do some papers in timed conditions to test how much you can do in the time given. Mark the paper afterwards using the mark scheme and use detailed solutions to make sure you approached the question in the best possible way.<br><br>*"Past paper questions are key. The style of MAT questions is very different to GCSE and A Level, and something you have to get used to. The examiners are not looking to see you use content in a context you've already been taught, but in new ways—you have to use your initiative. This is especially true for the longer questions, which you have to learn to persevere at."*<br>–Anya, Maths, Oxford |

| MAT | CTMUA | STEP | Preparation tip |
|---|---|---|---|
| ✓ | | ✓ | **Brainstorm approaches to long questions**<br>A good way of developing the type of thinking required for the long-answer sections of MAT and STEP is through mind maps. Find a question from a past paper and draw a mind map about that question. Write all the possible methods you could use in this question, brainstorming concepts and potential routes through it. Then try and answer it and, if one route through it failed, try another route outlined on your mind map. From doing a few of these, you begin to identify which methods are useful in each sort of question.<br><br>Over time, you should start to see why some methods worked and others didn't. You want to get to a place where, on first reading a question, you can already see a route through it and have a vague understanding of how each part links to the next. |
| ✓ | | ✓ | **Learn to justify your reasoning**<br>Very often in long-answer questions, you need to include succinct written explanations to justify parts of your solutions. Practise writing explanations and ensure they have all the points required to gain all the marks available. You can practise this by studying the mark schemes and watching video solutions.[46] |
| ✓ | ✓ | | **Learn what to look for in graphs**<br>Complicated graphs often appear in multiple-choice questions. You may either be given a tricky function and be asked which graph it corresponds to, or be given a graph and be asked which function would produce it. To help you prepare, look at some unfamiliar |

46 You can find solution videos at oxbridgeformula.co.uk/mat.

| MAT | CTMUA | STEP | Preparation tip |
|---|---|---|---|
| | | | functions[47] and see what you can identify about their graphs. Can you work out:<br>■ Their x- and y-intercepts?<br>■ Their turning points?<br>■ Their behaviour at infinity?<br>■ Any other asymptotes—horizontal, vertical or oblique?[48]<br>■ Whether they are a transformation of a more common graph? |
| ✓ | ✓ | ✓ | **Get experience with integer problems and number theory**<br>In your multiple-choice questions, expect some basic number theory, particularly having to think about factors. It may be worth reading through an elementary number theory book, such as Ogilvy and Anderson's *Excursions in Number Theory.* STEP papers *tend to include number theory questions too.* |

# MAT-specific preparation advice

## 1) Other admissions tests

To prepare for the MAT, you can practise other exams. For example, the CTMUA Paper 1 has questions that are similar to the multiple-choice section of MAT. These can be useful to 'warm-up' to the style of MAT questions. Attempting selected questions from STEP papers (especially STEP 1, which shares a lot of content with the MAT) are a great way to practise, and are of similar difficulty to (or a bit harder than) some of the MAT long-answer questions.[49] (See page 74 for CTMUA and page 80 for STEP.)

47 A great way to create these is to combine more familiar functions. You could replace one or more '$x$'s in one function with another function, e.g. by starting with $y = e^x$ to get $y = e^{\sin(x)}$. Or look at products of familiar functions, as in e.g. $y = xe^x$.

48 An oblique asymptote is a diagonal line that the graph approaches as $x \to \pm\infty$.

49 At oxbridgeformula.co.uk/mat, you can find a range of in-person and online courses to help you develop your problem solving skills for the MAT.

## 2) UKMT questions

The style of MAT questions is similar to some UKMT maths challenge questions, so this can be a useful source of practice. In particular, the MAT Computer Science questions rely on logic and unpicking puzzles in a similar way to some of the UKMT questions.

## 3) ProjectEuler

Another great online resource is the ProjectEuler website. It offers a rich archive of mathematical problems similar to those in questions 2, 5, 6 and 7 of the MAT, the questions aimed at Computer Science applicants. The problems involve integers, iteration, and absorbing new definitions—skills that are central to these MAT questions.

## 4) Time-management preparation for the MAT

The **multiple-choice section** of the MAT allows you to pick up 40 marks (10 x 4-mark multiple-choice questions), but no marks are given for working. While you don't want to waste time, what working you do does need to be clear enough for *you* to follow to avoid silly mistakes. To prepare, make a habit of writing concise but clear working whenever you're doing any calculation, e.g. in A Level Maths or Physics, so you don't have to worry about it in the MAT.

Another way to prepare is to practise some multiple-choice MAT questions under extreme time pressure, allowing (for instance) 4 minutes per question. Based on the number of marks these questions are worth, you could spend up to an hour on this section (i.e. 6 minutes per question)—but it might be worth allocating more time to the long-answer section if you find that more difficult, so being prepared to go a bit faster is very handy.

Many students do find the long-answer section quite a lot more difficult than the multiple-choice 'section, in which case it requires more preparation too. If you do spend a full hour on the multiple-choice section, you only have around 20 minutes per long question, plus 10 minutes to check your work.

**Top Tip**

*If you struggle with the* ***long-answer section****, we recommend spending at most 45 minutes on the multiple-choice questions, leaving 1 hour and 45 minutes for the long-answer sections. This can give you more time to properly digest the long questions and consider possible routes for answering them.*

Work out how much time you need for each part by doing timed mocks. Experiment with different ways of dividing your time between the multiple-choice and long questions until you find the way that scores you the most marks.

### 5) Making full use of past papers

If you have to do questions 6 and 7, it's important to remember that any preparation you do for MAT questions you may not be examined on (such as question 3, which is often graph-based, or question 4, which is often geometry-based) will improve your general problem-solving skills, which will translate to improved performance in questions 6 and 7 too. You'll also find practising these questions will improve your general maths skills—very helpful for your interview.[50]

Likewise, if you aren't applying for Computer Science and won't have to do questions 6 and 7 on the day, try a few of them from past papers anyway to work on your logic, problem-solving, and proof skills.

**Top Tip**

***Maths is maths; problem-solving is problem-solving.*** *Don't fall into the trap of only practising one style of question that you may have seen in past papers. If the examiners decide to change things up this year and test you from a different angle (as they frequently do), you'll be stuck! MAT 2019 is a prime example of examiners introducing a different style of question and many students being tripped up.*

## CTMUA-specific preparation advice

In Paper 2 of the CTMUA, you'll get logic- and proof-based questions that focus more on your mathematical *thinking* than the A-Level content. Here's some advice to help you prepare for this paper:[51]

- ❑ **Look over some instructive proofs:** You'll need to gain a solid understanding of proofs before sitting this exam, beyond what is taught in A Level. Research some basic proofs to familiarise yourself with how

50 We run specialised sessions for those applying for Computer Science on our MAT long-answer question courses, including plenty of material online.

51 Check out oxbridgeformula.co.uk/ctmua for online video resources and in-person courses for the CTMUA.

they work. For example, look at some of the many different proofs of the irrationality of the square root of 2.

- ❑ **Practise breaking proofs down into steps:** The questions in the CTMUA often rely on locating flawed steps in proofs. To practise viewing proofs in this way, break down standard proofs into sections and make sure you're completely confident with how every line follows from the previous one.
- ❑ **Use other maths papers:** A lot of the logical techniques you'll need for CTMUA Paper 2 can be found in STEP questions. Although STEP questions have a different format, tackling them will allow you to develop skills that can be directly applied to CTMUA questions—the underlying maths is the same. To prepare for CTMUA Paper 1, the multiple choice questions from the MAT are a useful source of extra practice.

## STEP-specific preparation advice

- ❑ **Familiarise yourself with classic proof techniques:** Make sure you know how the main proof techniques function. These are proof by contradiction, direct proof, proof by exhaustion and proof by induction.

**Types of proof**

- **Proof by contradiction** is when you assume the opposite of the statement you're trying to prove and show it results in a contradiction, meaning the statement you're trying to prove must be true instead. Proving the square root of 2 is irrational is an example.
- The simplest form of proof, **direct proof,** is when you repeatedly manipulate your starting information until you reach the result you're trying to prove, as seen when you solve equations or inequalities by performing one rearrangement in each line.
- **Proof by exhaustion** is when you set out all the possible cases and check what happens in each one. For instance, try proving by exhaustion that, if the last digit of $n^2$ is 1, then the last digit of $n$ is 1 or 9. (Hint: the possible cases are all the possible last digits, from 0 to 9.)
- **Proof by induction** is in the form of:
  ***Base case*:** Consider the result when your variable $n$ is at its minimum value, typically 0 or 1

  ***Inductive hypothesis*:** Assume the result holds for $n = k$

> ***Inductive step:*** Show the result holds for $n = k + 1$
>
> You can conclude from here that the result always holds for all natural numbers. For instance, try proving by induction that $1 + 4 + 9 + \ldots + n^2 = \dfrac{n(n+1)(2n+1)}{6}$ for all $n$.

- ❑ **Practise with others:** Since STEP questions are extended problem-solving exercises and having a big toolbox of techniques and approaches for unpicking them is vital, it's great practice to share your ideas on questions with friends who will also be taking STEP.
- ❑ **Practise all three papers:** Even if you're not taking all three STEP papers, the others are an invaluable source of practice questions.
- ❑ **Use the Siklos booklets:** Stephen Siklos, the former chief examiner for STEP, created these booklets to help students prepare for the test. Each booklet introduces STEP questions that deal with key topics or techniques, bookending each one with warmup questions and a discussion of what can be learned from the example. Using these booklets is a very good way to start your STEP preparation. You can download them for free at oxbridgeformula.co.uk/siklos-download
- ❑ **Identify tricks you can reuse:** After you practise a question, make a note of any techniques it taught you. Try to think of other questions you've seen where it would be applicable, or even create a question inspired by one you've seen before and practise applying the technique, since that will ingrain it in your intuition.[52]
- ❑ **Play around with results from past papers:** You'll often find that past paper questions involve proving or using a particular result, such as the fact that a differential equation has solutions of a certain form, or that they teach you to use a method, such as a way of evaluating an infinite sum, and ask you to apply it in a few cases. It's great practice to try to generalise any results you prove, or apply them in new cases. This will improve your proof skills and mathematical intuition. Likewise, if the question teaches you a new method, see if you can think of any more applications for it. This will expand your toolbox of techniques—you never know what will prove useful in your own exam!

> *"When looking at mathematical statements and problems, practise asking yourself questions such as: "What if ...?" (for example*

52 Check out oxbridgeformula.co.uk/step to find out about our series of in-person STEP courses and 300+ STEP video solutions.

> *what if, instead of all natural numbers in this problem we look at only even numbers?), or "Can this be extended ...?" (for example, something valid for a particular function, which happens to be an even function, can it be extended to all even functions? Yes/no - why?)."*
> –Maths Faculty, Cambridge

## 5.5: Exam techniques to ace MAT/CTMUA/STEP

Exhaustive preparation is important, but it's only half the battle. Solid exam technique is invaluable on the day. Picture this: you walk into the exam room (generally a chilly sports hall) and an incredibly intimidating paper stares back at you. It's nerve-wracking—this paper could secure you a place at one of the top universities in the world.

So what do you need to do when you're in the exam room? Here are some top tips for getting through the admissions test with your sanity intact:

| MAT | CTMUA | STEP | Examination technique |
|---|---|---|---|
| ✓ | ✓ | | **Eliminate incorrect options**<br>The multiple-choice section is less of a struggle if you can easily eliminate incorrect options. For example, there's usually a graphical question where you have to guess which graph fits a complicated equation. In this case, you should be looking for things such as:<br>■ **Roots:** Where does the graph cross the x-axis?<br>■ **Y-intercept:** Where does the graph cross the y-axis?<br>■ **Behaviour as the graph goes to infinity:** Look at how the equation would behave as you increase x to positive infinity or decrease it to negative infinity.<br>■ **Is the graph even?**[53] Is the behaviour in the quadrants where $x$ is negative a reflection of the behaviour in the quadrants where $x$ is positive? (Think of the function $f(x) = \cos(x)$ here, or $f(x) = x^2$. For even functions, $f(x) = f(-x)$.) |

53 Or odd for that matter! An odd function has order 2 rotational symmetry about the origin: $f(x) = -f(-x)$.

| MAT | CTMUA | STEP | Examination technique |
|---|---|---|---|
| | | | ■ **Turning points:** Although this takes a little longer, see if you can tell where the stationary points will be and what kind they are, with or without differentiation.<br>■ **Transformation:** Look at the equation. Is it in the form of a transformation of a function whose graph you know? |
| ✓ | | ✓ | **Skip *parts* of a question—don't sacrifice the whole question**<br>Remember, even if you start on a long-answer question, you can leave later parts. Have a go, but it's not the end of the world if you can't get an answer. Unlike for multiple-choice questions, there are marks available for working here. In fact, this is what the examiner is interested in: seeing your mathematical reasoning.<br><br>A good example of this is a question in which you're first asked to 'show that' statement P is true and then to deduce statement Q from it. If you don't know how to do the first 'show that' part, you can still show how to deduce Q from P and get the marks for that step. |
| ✓ | ✓ | | **Guess**<br>If you simply can't answer a multiple-choice question, just guess. There's no harm in it: you won't lose a mark! |
| ✓ | | ✓ | **Use strategies for long questions**<br>If you can't answer a long question, there are various strategies to try:<br><br>■ Even if you're unsure about them, at least attempt the harder parts. Write what you're doing as clearly as you can, and even include comments about what you're trying to do, if you don't think your working is strong enough to stand by itself. |

| MAT | CTMUA | STEP | Examination technique |
|---|---|---|---|
| | | | ■ Try different methods, but don't cross anything out, in case your later attempts lead you further away from the correct solution.<br>■ If you can't find a full solution and there's a clear equation to start from (such as a function or a recurrence relationship for a sequence), try to consider particular cases (e.g. the behaviour of the function or sequence at $x = 0$).<br>■ Use these things to pick up marks along the way, and they might give you ideas for finding the full solution.<br><br>*"Even if writing out what you **would** do only nets you an extra mark, that mark could be the difference between grades. I'm pretty sure it was for me."* –Nick, Maths, Cambridge |
| ✓ | | ✓ | **Include diagrams**<br>Include diagrams in your long answers, especially when you have to explain or justify something—this can really help clarify to the examiners what you're thinking! Here are some tips for graph drawing:<br><br>■ **Do:** Draw them big<br>■ **Do:** Leave space for labels, extra lines and working<br>■ **Do:** Use rulers, and colours, if they make your diagrams clearer<br>■ **Don't:** Draw tiny circles that become cluttered with lines and angles<br>■ **Don't:** Draw graphs with short axes that end up useless and illegible. |
| ✓ | | ✓ | **Know when to move on**<br>The best way to answer long questions is to keep going until you reach some kind of wall. It's time to move on when you realise you've spent five minutes gnawing your pencil without writing anything down. |

| MAT | CTMUA | STEP | Examination technique |
|---|---|---|---|
| | | | Before you move on, however, re-read the later parts of the question. They can fizzle in the back of your mind while you move on to other questions. Then, when you have time to come back to them at the end, you may find additional ways to try to tackle them. |

**Did You Know?**

*The college you apply to gets your STEP script, not just your mark. The Cambridge Maths Faculty says this is so "it is possible to make allowances for a near miss and to make judgments on the actual work rather than on just the marks or grades."*

## MAT-specific exam techniques

### 1) Multiple-choice questions

If you allocated your time in line with the marks available for each question, you would do the multiple-choice questions in an hour and the long-answer questions in 1.5 hours. This can work for some students. But if you find the longer questions harder, you might want to get the multiple-choice questions finished more quickly to have more time for the long-answer section.

### 2) Long-answer questions

- Spend a few minutes at the start to read and digest the question and perhaps jot your initial ideas down.
- Remember that all the long questions are worth an equal number of marks, but some may be easier for you than others. You don't have to attempt the questions in order, so grab what you think will be the easier marks first.
- Don't dedicate too much time to any one question. If you're stuck (which is very normal, especially as you progress through a question), move on. You can come back if you have time at the end, but don't spend ages attempting to answer just one question when you could be picking up easy marks from the earlier parts of other questions.

## CTMUA-specific exam techniques

### Don't spend too long on each question

Remember: you only have 1 hour and 15 minutes to answer 20 multiple-choice questions. You could try to answer all 20 questions within an hour and spend the last 15 minutes checking these answers and filling in the correct boxes.

**Top Tip**

*If you've solved an equation and are now **checking your answer**, instead of simply re-solving the equation as you did the first time, check whether your solution matches up with the original information given—by inputting your solution(s) into the original equation, for instance. Alternatively, use a different method and see if you still get the same answer.*

## STEP-specific exam techniques

In STEP, you have to spend time at the beginning of the paper choosing which questions to answer. You'll be marked on your six best answers, but it's worth knowing how many questions you need to answer to achieve the grade you're aiming for. By looking at recent grade boundaries, you can approximate how many questions you'll need to answer fully (or strongly) to meet your target.

It's generally accepted that if you're aiming for a:

- ***Grade S***: You should try to fully answer 5 questions
- ***Grade 1***: You should try to fully answer 4 questions plus some partial answers
- ***Grade 2***: You should try to fully answer 3 questions plus some partial answers.

However, the grade boundaries do vary each year and between different papers, with STEP 3 generally having the lowest boundaries and STEP 1 the highest. We suggest choosing six questions at the outset, because you may start a question and quickly realise it was more difficult than expected and need to abandon it.

Here are three questions to ask yourself when choosing which STEP questions you want to answer:

### 1) 'What are my strengths and weaknesses?'

Most STEP questions can be categorised by the topics they test you on, varying from geometry to logic to simple harmonic motion. Undoubtedly, you'll be better at some of these topics than others. Also, in your preparation, you may have chosen to focus on certain question areas.

It's important to understand this and to know your strengths and weaknesses. During your preparation, it may be worth keeping track of the questions (and the topics) with which you had the most success. Doing so might turn up surprises: for instance, you may feel you're good at integration questions, whereas in fact you rarely complete them. In the exam, this understanding will guide you to select the best questions for you. The exam is *not* the time to give a vectors question a go for the first time!

### 2) 'What happens later in the question?'

There is more to choosing questions than just looking at the overall topic. Looking for elements of questions you've seen before or mathematical techniques you prefer (for instance proofs or graph sketches) can be very helpful when making your choices. It's especially important to look beyond the first part of the question, as later parts can be harder. It's a good idea to try to spot the links between each part of the question when you are initially looking through the paper, as this will give you a good idea of whether you actually have a decent shot at being able to do most of the question.

### 3) 'Are any of the applied questions worth looking at?'

Both the mechanics and statistics sections often have nice, accessible questions. However, the mechanics questions can be time-consuming, with lots of algebra. Try plenty of each type of question before the exam and see if they suit you, and be aware of the areas you want to focus on before you go into the exam. Remember: even if you haven't studied much statistics at A Level, there's often a probability question that doesn't require much A-Level knowledge.

## 5.6: The CSAT

### What is the CSAT?

The CSAT is the Computer Science Admissions Test: the Cambridge admissions test for the Computer Science course (used up until 2019 at all colleges)[54] that is sat on the day of the interview.

54 Some colleges still use it as a basis for the interview, in addition to the CTMUA.

The questions are completely mathematical—you are unlikely to be asked *'How does a computer work?'* or *'How do you program this particular function?'* However, there is more of a focus on discrete maths and algorithms/procedures than other maths admissions tests. The CSAT will also test your problem-solving and proof skills.

The CSAT is a 2-hour paper made up of two sections, where the second section is the more challenging one. In each section, your best five answers count towards your mark. You can attempt as many questions as you like. There are eight to choose from in the first section and twelve in the second section—but to avoid rushing we recommend that you aim to answer only five questions from each section. The paper comprises a wide range of questions, so if you don't like geometry or integration or integer problems you can avoid them (to an extent).

For sample CSAT papers, please scan this QR Code:

## Section A

The questions in Section A are based on the first year of the pure maths A-Level content—but they are more difficult, abstract and unstructured than A-Level questions. For example, you may be expected to sketch the graph of a function – a standard technique – but the function may include unknown parameters, so you can't simply calculate roots or turning points numerically as you would at A Level. The questions are not multiple-choice, and you may be asked to give a proof rather than simply do a calculation.

An example question is:

*For every $a \geq 1$, a function $f_a(x)$ is defined as follows: $f_a(x) = \int_0^x t^a \sin(t)dt$.*

*Show by means of a sketch that, for every $a \geq 1$, $f_a(x) = 0$ for infinitely many positive values of $x$.*

## Section B

In Section B, the questions are more difficult. For instance, they might require you to write a proof that requires a few tricky steps or work with an unfamiliar concept. They sometimes have multiple parts, but typically give you little guidance as to how to answer. Each question is similar to the final part of a MAT question 5, 6 or 7 (but without all the examples and guidance). They are also comparable to BMO[55] questions in that they often test number theory, combinatorics, algorithms and functions.

An example question you could expect is:

*Let $k$ and $n$ be positive integers such that $k$ is a prime factor of $n$. Determine the set of possible values of $k$ in the case that $2^n + 1$ is prime and prove mathematically that these are the only possibilities.*

Although the CSAT isn't currently in use at all colleges, doing past CSAT papers is great preparation for your Computer Science interviews at both Cambridge and Oxford and any at-interview tests you may have to complete at either Oxford or Cambridge. For more details and video solutions to the CSAT sample papers, check out oxbridgeformula.co.uk/csat

55 The British Mathematical Olympiad. See oxbridgeformula.co.uk/bonus-chapter for more info.

# Chapter 6: Interviews

## 6.1: What will your interviews be like?

As you travel to Oxford or Cambridge for your Maths or Computer Science interviews[56], it's difficult to know what to expect. To make the experience a little less intimidating, we'll cover some logistics of the interview process, as well as the form your interviews will likely take.

### How many interviews will you have?

#### Oxford

At Oxford, you're expected to go up and stay in a college, usually for two to three nights. Your interviews will be scheduled while you're there, and you may be called for further interviews at any point. You should remain in college until you're told you're free to go, and look out for information on where and when your interviews will be. Typically, you'll have two or three interviews at the college you're staying at and one at a different college. You're interviewed at a second college so that Oxford can standardise the calibre of applicant they accept across the university. If you're applying to a joint honours course, you're likely to have more interviews, as the tutors will want to fully test your abilities in both subjects.

> *"I really enjoyed my Oxford interview experience. Staying in college for a few days meant I made lots of friends. We played games and chatted in the common room—it was great fun!"* –Student, Computer Science & Philosophy, Oxford

56 Some overseas candidates won't have to travel to the UK. You'll receive specific information when you apply, but it can be worth contacting the university earlier to be able to make plans either way.

### Cambridge

At Cambridge, you typically don't need to stay overnight unless you live more than a few hours away. In that case, you'll be offered college accommodation. You'll probably only have one or two interviews, usually back to back. You'll know the times of your interviews before you arrive and won't be called for an interview at other colleges. At Cambridge, you may spend the morning doing an at-interview test and have an interview in the afternoon. The at-interview test is typically one hour, although it varies between colleges, and some don't use them at all.

## How much are your interviews worth?

Remember: interviews form a piece of a larger jigsaw puzzle. Your personal statement, grades and predicted grades all enter into the equation, along with your score on the admissions test. However, this is the only opportunity the admissions tutors have to meet you, so it's your biggest chance to demonstrate your mathematical abilities and make them want to teach you for three or four years.

**Did You Know?**

***Oxford vs Cambridge:*** *As there's no pre-interview test at Cambridge for Maths, more candidates are invited to interview (and more offers are made) than at Oxford. This is due to the STEP requirement in the offer: roughly 500 offers are made for 250 places. The biggest 'culling' of candidates at Cambridge occurs on results day in the summer, following the STEP results. For Computer Science, the CTMUA is used to select who to invite to interview, just as the MAT is at Oxford.*

## How long will your interviews be?

Interviews are generally 30 minutes, give or take. The tutor wants to give you sufficient time to work through the problems they present to you and explore them in detail.

## Where will you have your interviews?

If you submit an open application, you'll be assigned a college and interviewed there. This is also where you'll stay if you're required to stay overnight. If you apply directly to a college, you'll likely be interviewed there, but if they have an excess of applications you may be sent to another college. At Oxford, you'll also be interviewed at a second college either way.

## Who will be interviewing you?

The subject tutors from your respective college will be the ones interviewing you. In a typical interview, there are two tutors in the room. Often one engages in conversation while the other takes notes. Less typically, you might have up to four or five tutors if the Maths department at your college is particularly large, or if they are training up someone to do interviews in future.

## What can you expect from your interview?

### Maths interviews

Maths interviews are very technical, in the sense that you'll spend almost all of the time attempting hard maths problems with the tutor. They form a conversation between yourself and the interviewer, who may respond to your answers by (gently) pointing out mistakes, offering hints and leading questions, or extending the problem. Usually, they'll start with a fairly easy preliminary question such as curve sketching. From here, the questions will become trickier, and the tutor will pay attention to how you attempt the harder parts. There won't be a huge focus on your personal statement in your interviews—many Maths applicants aren't even asked about it.

To answer the question, you'll either be given paper and a pen, or a big whiteboard. You'll be expected to show all of your working, and it's *always* a good idea to verbalise your thinking along the way rather than working things out in your head.

Often in an interview, you'll only be presented with one question, which will be broken down into parts and taken in different directions by the tutors. Sometimes, you may have a couple of unrelated questions to test multiple skill sets.

### Computer Science interviews

As with Maths, your Computer Science interviews will be very technical: the tutor will set a problem to see how you fare in solving it. Maths is essential to computer science, and your interviews will include maths questions. You may also be given problem-solving questions that do not relate to any specific A-Level Maths topic. In particular, questions on devising, following and analysing procedures are popular, because they test skills that are needed for computer science. Questions 5, 6 and 7 of the MAT, and Section B of the CSAT, are good sources of practice for these.

If you're applying to Cambridge and have to sit an at-interview test, there's a chance that the interviewers may go through some of these questions with you as the basis for the interview. Alternatively, at some colleges across both universities, you may receive a problem sheet to work on immediately before your interview, which will be discussed and dissected in your interview. Furthermore, at Oxford, the tutors may pick up on some of the questions you struggled with in the MAT and see if you can find a solution with hints and guidance from them.

## Joint honours interviews: What form will they take?

### Maths & Statistics interviews

When it comes to Maths & Statistics, you're unlikely to have any 'statistics only' interviews, as the two subjects are so closely linked. However, do go into your interviews expecting a probability-style question, as this is how the admissions tutors will test that you're the right candidate to cope with the statistics course.

### Maths & Computer Science interviews

For Maths & Computer Science, you'll probably have (at least) one interview in each subject. Although the style of the questions will differ, both will be technical interviews in which you're expected to solve mathematical problems. However, you may get asked some questions such as *'Why Maths?'* or *'Why Computer Science?'* as preliminaries, so make sure you've prepared answers!

### Maths & Philosophy interviews

The interviews you can expect for Maths and Philosophy are very different to each other. Unlike the technical Maths interviews, Philosophy interviews will be more of a discussion led by the tutor. You'll be asked a philosophical question and the tutor will judge how you answer. They'll lead you in a debate, but, unlike in a maths question, there isn't always a final answer you're working towards—the questions are more open-ended. You're unlikely to be sat around a table—instead you'll be in a more lounge-like environment, and there won't typically be paper for you to do your working on (unless you feel the need to ask for it).

It's also unlikely that you'll have a 'crossover' interview: your Maths and Philosophy interviews will probably be kept completely separate. However, in your Philosophy interview, you can expect some questions that relate to maths, such as: *'Could we ever grasp the infinite?'* or *'What is a number?'* See page 446 for more on Philosophy interviews.

### Computer Science & Philosophy interviews

The interviews for Computer Science & Philosophy work in a similar way to Maths & Philosophy. They'll probably be distinct, but again, the topic of the philosophy questions may have origins in computer science. For example, you may be asked: *'If a robot says it feels unwell, should we comfort it?'* See page 446 for more on Philosophy interviews.

## Will they ask general questions about you?

In your subject-specific interviews, it is unlikely you will get too many questions about yourself, your interests and why you want to study there. At Cambridge, you may have a 'general interview', although these are not usually done at Oxford. In a general interview, you won't necessarily be asked straightforward questions about your interests. To avoid students just repeating prepared answers, and to get a better sense of your personality, the tutors could ask more job-interview-style questions such as:

- If you were in my position, would you let yourself into Cambridge?
- What achievement to date are you most proud of?
- What do you expect to get out of this degree?
- What is your favourite number?
- What is your biggest weakness?

They also may ask you subject-related questions in the general interviews once the general part is done. Cambridge states that the general interview is there to ensure you understand (and are suited to) the intensity and highly academic nature of Cambridge and what your chosen course entails.

## Will they try and catch you out?

### NO!

The most common misconception about interviews is that the tutors are trying to trip you up. This is simply not true. The tutors are there to guide you through the problems and to give you hints. They are looking to see how *teachable* you are and how you adapt to new information being thrown at you. If they give you a hint, they are generally trying to help you and steer you in the right direction, so don't ignore them!

## How can you know if the interview went well?

How you feel about an interview once you've left isn't always a good reflection of how it actually went. For instance, it might be the reason you feel it went well is that you didn't appreciate the importance of some of the details the interviewer was trying to point out, or that you you worked slowly and silently to avoid making errors, in which case the interviewer may have had less opportunity to challenge you. Likewise, if you feel an interview went badly, it might just be because you needed more guidance to get through the question than you're used to at school, or because your mistakes stand out to you in hindsight more than your impressive moments.

Remember: if you're being challenged and led down difficult paths in your interview, it's because your interviewer is enjoying challenging you. This is what Oxbridge teaching and learning is all about! Your interviews *should* be taxing and difficult—if you come out of them feeling as if you were completely lost by the end, that isn't necessarily a bad thing.

Check out page 143 for a real Oxbridge interviewer's explanation of what your interviewers will be looking for.

# 6.2: Preparing for your Maths/Computer Science interviews

Maths/Computer Science interviews are very different to the comfortable-sofa-chat interviews associated with the humanities, and you'll need to make sure you prepare yourself for the types of challenge they'll present.[57] Typically, you'll be sitting at a table with one or two tutors, and you'll be expected to work through some questions on paper or a whiteboard.

## When should you prepare?

If you're taking a pre-interview admissions test such as the MAT or CTMUA, it's best to focus on that before thinking too much about your interview, since:

**a)** You need to do well on the test to even be offered an interview
**b)** Preparing for the test also helps you prepare for the interview, since it improves your technical and problem-solving skills.

57 See oxbridgeformula.co.uk/maths-interview for information on our interview-preparation courses. Each course is an entire day focused on tackling tough mathematics questions with interview-style prompts and extensions from an expert maths interviewer.

If you're taking STEP, your admissions test is less imminent, so you can choose to start your interview prep earlier in the autumn or summer. But still, if you haven't been doing STEP test prep already, start that too, as it will also help get you ready for interview-style problems.

Whichever test you have to take, it's always worth spending some time over the summer to read widely on your subject and do more recreational maths or problem-solving.

## What should you do to prepare?

**Top Tip**

*Practise going through questions on a big **whiteboard** before your interview. Ask your teacher if you can solve some questions on their board. Working out a problem on a whiteboard is different than doing it on paper!*

### 1) Vocalise your thoughts

One of the hardest parts of a Maths/Computer Science interview is talking through your reasoning and thought processes out loud rather than simply working the problem out in your head. You need to let the interviewer see how you approach a problem and how your thoughts follow from each other to reach a conclusion.

Vocalising maths is very different to communicating in regular conversation, so you need to practise working through problems out loud. Some ways to practise are:

- ❑ **Talk out loud when working:** Talk to yourself while you do your maths homework, working through the harder problems slowly and vocalising your thoughts. You could record yourself and listen to it back to check your explanations are clear and useful.
- ❑ **Get help:** Ask your parents, siblings or friends to listen to you explain a mathematical concept (such as trigonometry or differentiation), or an area of computer science that particularly interests you. Have them ask you questions when they don't understand. You're aiming to clarify your thoughts and communicate them concisely and accurately, so addressing someone with little subject knowledge is useful, because they can't fill in the gaps from their knowledge and will get lost if you're not explaining clearly enough.

- ❑ **Work with a buddy:** If you have a friend applying for a similar course, have a conversation with them where you solve hard questions together. Help each other out with hints, as this is similar to the form your interview will take.

### 2) Review your A-Level content

You need to know your A-Level content inside and out, as any interview question will rely on this knowledge. Often, a Maths or Computer Science interview will start with a graph-sketching question or a function to integrate or differentiate. Here, the skills you've accumulated from your A Levels are really important.

**Top Tip**

*Your interview will test your mathematical reasoning skills, not just your A-Level knowledge. However, it's important to have a* ***solid foundation*** *of mathematical knowledge so you don't fall at the first hurdle.*

### 3) Review admissions tests

Even if you've already sat the MAT or CTMUA, all the preparation you've done will be useful for your interviews too. In particular, the style and standard of questions are likely to be similar to the MAT long-answer questions. If you didn't sit the MAT, doing a couple of MAT papers is good preparation. If you want further practice, working through some STEP questions is also useful.

## Maths-specific interview preparation advice

### 1) Graph drawing

Interviewers love to ask you to sketch graphs. This is often how they start a question, and they may ask you to do further work with the graphs: translating them, estimating their, or testing their behaviour as a parameter varies.

Make sure your graph-drawing abilities are top-notch and you're not a slave to your graphical calculator! Practise drawing neat axes and sketching functions concisely and accurately. Making sure you're able to sketch simple functions such as $f(x) = \tan(x)$ and $f(x) = x^3$ is a great place to start. Be sure you're confident with the subtler details, such as the fact that $f(x) = x^3$ should not be sketched as if it has a positive gradient at the origin, but $f(x) = \tan(x)$ should.

It's also worth trying to sketch less-familiar functions that combine the functions you've seen at A Level. Some we would recommend are:

- $f(x) = e^{\sin x}$ or $f(x) = e^{\cos x}$
- $f(x) = \sin(e^x)$ or $f(x) = \cos(e^x)$
- $f(x) = x^x$.

Practise performing transformations on these graphs, thinking about what they tell you about the derivative and integral of $f(x)$, and comparing them to one another. Also be on the look out for symmetries and periodicities. These are ways that the interviewer may develop a question in an interview.

### 2) Key maths terms

Familiarise yourself with key mathematical words. Your mathematical prowess may shine in an interview, but it will slow things down if you're confused about the meaning of a fundamental term. Do of course tell your interviewer if you don't understand something, but be sure you know all the mathematical terminology that appears in the A-Level syllabus so as not to be caught short. Some key examples are:

- Function[58]
- Real and irrational
- Reciprocal and inverse
- Converse and contrapositive
- Root and factor
- Stationary point and turning point.

## Computer Science-specific interview preparation advice

### 1) Unfamiliar problems

Your Computer Science interviews are likely to contain a high proportion of mathematics. As Computer Science A Level isn't a compulsory requisite, you probably won't be tested on this content if you haven't studied it—but you'll probably be asked about your interests in computer science or things you've written in your personal statement. You need to be very secure with the maths you've covered at school, but what matters is how

58 A good test of whether you genuinely understand the meaning of 'function' is: can you explain why there are $n^n$ functions from the set $\{1, 2, 3, ..., n\}$ to itself?

you can apply it to unfamiliar problems. Your mathematical intuition, skills and understanding are what the interviewer is looking to test.

Project Euler is a good source of unfamiliar problems that are similar in style to some you may receive in your interviews. These maths-based problems will require you to apply your A-Level skills in new scenarios and settings.

### 2) New computer science topics

Your interviewer may also explain an unknown computer science topic and ask you questions centred on it. A good way to prepare for this would be doing independent research on basic computer science concepts and briefly presenting what you've learned to someone (such as a family member or friend). Some concepts you could start with are:

- Sorting methods
- Big O notation
- Recursion
- Data structures
- Parallelism.

### 3) Admissions test questions

You might receive a diagram or game set up to analyse and manipulate. Many of these questions are real-life versions of the questions 6 and 7 from the MAT paper, so focusing on these in past papers is a good way to prepare. The CSAT is also an excellent source of tough maths questions aimed specifically at computer scientists. After all, this used to be the test that you'd sit before and discuss in a Cambridge Computer Science interview.

## 6.3: A script of an Oxbridge Maths interview

This section will present three different Maths interview questions with a scripted model interaction between the interviewer and the student working through the solution. Each question will touch on a different topic, giving you a feel for the broad variety of questions you may be asked. Have a go at each question first, and then read through, going back to add to your own answer if you get a hint from the script. Note how the student doesn't find the answer immediately but works it out in conversation. (Much of what is said will also be written down on paper or a whiteboard by the student or tutor.)

See also page 143 for an interview with real Oxbridge interviewers.

## Maths interview question 1 (Geometry/Spatial Reasoning)

**Question: Consider the unit cube. Can you find the shortest distance between the points (0.2, 0.3, 0) and (0.5, 0.5, 1), travelling along the surface of the cube?**

(If you aren't familiar with the term 'unit cube', the interviewer may clarify what they mean by this. For example: 'The cube with the vertices (0, 0, 0), (0, 0, 1), (0, 1, 0), (1, 0, 0), (0, 1, 1), (1, 1, 0), (1, 0, 1), (1, 1, 1).' Alternatively, the interviewer may have drawn up a unit cube for you on a piece of paper or a whiteboard before you enter the room.)

The interviewers aren't trying to trip you up with terminology—they want to see how you think in response to these questions.

### Model interview

**Student:** I see that the path must go along the face of one of the other sides of the cube, and the two faces that the points are on. I'll try drawing the cube first to visualise it.

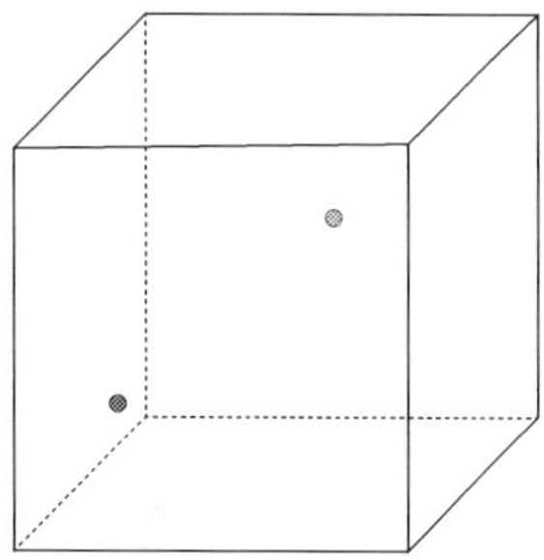

**Tutor:** Okay. What should the path look like on each of the faces it crosses?

**Student:** The path must be a straight line on each of the faces.

**Tutor:** Good. (*Pause.*) How will you go about calculating the distance?

The interviewer pauses to give the student time before offering a prompt. This is the typical dialectical style used in an interview.

**Student:** I suppose I should use Pythagoras' equation to calculate the distance between two points across a face, but I'm not sure which face it should go across.

(*Silence.*)

**Tutor:** Can you rule out any possibilities?

Student draws the following diagram, which is a cube net with front face in the centre and the opposite face (the destination) repeated 4 times so that the path can be drawn without breaks.

**Student:** If we go along the 'bottom' face, the distance will be $\sqrt{0.3^2+(1+0.5+0.3)^2}$, whereas if we go along the 'left' face, the distance will be $\sqrt{0.2^2+(1+0.5+0.2)^2}$, so the answer is $\sqrt{0.2^2+(1+0.5+0.2)^2}$, which is...

**Tutor:** That is a good-enough answer, you don't need to simplify it more than that. Why have you excluded going along the 'right' or 'top' faces?

**Student:** Clearly the point (0.2, 0.3) is in the bottom left-hand corner of the square, so for the shortest distance we should be travelling along the 'bottom' or 'left' faces.

**Tutor:** Thank you.

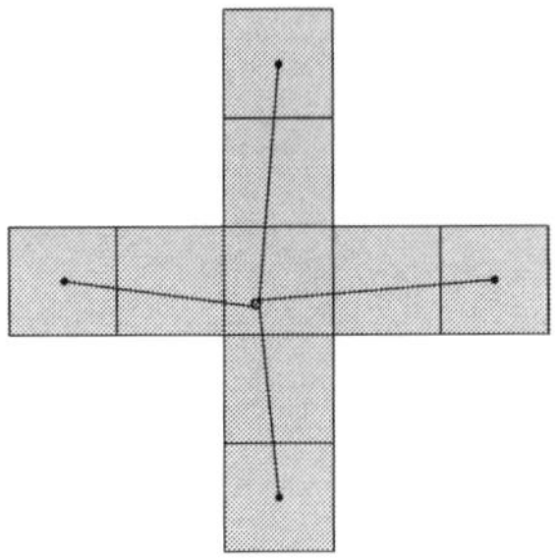

Unlike at A Level, interviewers are more interested in the process rather than the exact numerical answer.

## Further hints

- If you haven't drawn a diagram, or your diagram is unclear, you might be asked: 'Would a (new/larger) diagram be useful?'
  Don't be afraid to start drawing on the paper in front of you while you think about the question. It's better to think out loud if you have an instinct about the geometry of the problem.
- If you're stuck, you could get the prompt: 'What is special about the point (0.5, 0.5, 1)?'
  You might notice that the second listed point is in the centre of the opposite face, which should make the question a little easier.
- If you're struggling to get started, the interviewer may also offer a simpler version of the problem. For example: 'What is the distance between the points (0.5, 0.5, 1) and (0.5, 0.5, 0) travelling along the surface of the cube?'

## Extending the question

Depending on how quickly you arrive at the answer and how much prompting you need, the interviewer may extend it to a somewhat more general question, for example: 'How would you go about finding the shortest distance between the points $(x_1, y_1, 0)$, $(x_2, y_2, 1)$ travelling along the surface of the unit cube?'

Interviewers often generalise results as a way of extending questions—if you're given a sheet of questions beforehand by your college, it might be useful to think: 'How might I generalise this result?'

In this instance, the interviewer might be looking for you to say something such as: 'We know a lot less about the points in this case. We would have to find all four possibilities and take the minimum.'

### What is the question testing?

The tutors want to test your spatial reasoning, as well as how you respond to a question where you can't simply apply a formula. Most A-Level students should be familiar with finding the Euclidean distance between two points in space (i.e. $\sqrt{(1-0)^2+(0.5-0.3)^2+(0.5-0.2)^2}$) and this might be your initial response—however, this question should stretch you to thinking about the shortest paths that are restricted to particular surfaces.

### Related topics from university

The shortest paths around a solid (or in space) are called 'geodesics', a concept you may meet in your second or third year at Oxbridge, depending on the options you take.

## Maths interview question 2 (Definitions/Modulus)

**Question: How would you define the maximum of two real numbers, $x$ and $y$?**

### Model interview

**Student:** The maximum of $x$ and $y$ is the biggest of the two numbers.

**Tutor:** Ok, yes, but do you think you could formalise that more?

**Student:** (*Pauses to think.*) The maximum is $x$ if $x$ is bigger than $y$, and it is $y$ otherwise.

The interviewer will typically try and get you to formalise your thoughts and move away from vague language.

**Tutor:** Can you write that down for me?

**Student:** $maximum(x, y) = x$ when $x > y$ and $maximum(x, y) = y$ when $y > x$.

**Tutor:** Are you sure?

**Student:** (*Pauses to think.*)

Often the interviewer will ask you if you're certain, whether you have the answer right or wrong. They aren't trying to trip you up! Instead, they're usually prompting you to reconsider or to give a fuller explanation.

**Tutor:** Have you considered the case where $x = y$? What happens then?

**Student:** Well, in that case, they are the same number, so either of them could be the maximum.

**Tutor:** Can you write that down for me?

**Student:** $maximum(x, y) = x$ when $x > y$ and $maximum(x, y) = y$ when $y \geq x$.

**Tutor:** Good. How might you write this down in one formula?

**Student:** (*Pause.*) I'm not sure. I don't really know how we could do it without cases.

**Tutor:** Okay. Maybe think about the average of the two numbers and the difference of the two numbers? How do they relate to each other?

Don't worry about needing hints from interviewers. They are trying to push you to tackle new material!

(*Brief silence—this is natural during difficult steps.*)

**Student:** Ah. I see that one of the numbers is the average plus half of the difference and the other is the average minus half of the difference.

**Tutor:** Ok, so can you now have a go at writing the maximum function down?

**Student:** I think I should be writing something like: $max(x, y) = \frac{x+y}{2} + \frac{x-y}{2}$ but I know that's not quite right because the difference should always be positive.

Even if you know you've not quite got the answer, tell them what you're thinking!

**Tutor:** Do you know a way of making it always positive?

**Student:** Oh yes, I can take the modulus, so I think the formula is $max\ (x,\ y) = \frac{x+y+|x-y|}{2}$.

**Tutor:** Yes, that's it.

## Further hints

If you're truly struggling, the tutor may give more comprehensive hints. For example: 'Can you write down $x$ and $y$ in terms of $\frac{x+y}{2}$ and $\frac{x-y}{2}$?' This technique is often used in mathematical proofs. It's a nice way of regrouping $x$ and $y$ so that $x = \frac{x-y}{2} + \frac{x+y}{2}$ and $y = \frac{x+y}{2} - \frac{x-y}{2}$.

## Extending the question

- A next step could be: 'If that is your formula for maximum, can you write down your formula for the minimum?', prompting you to reflect on your responses from earlier and write $min(x,\ y) = \frac{x+y-|x-y|}{2}$.

- They might ask: 'Can you write a formula for the maximum and minimum of three numbers?', which might prompt you to note that the $max(x,\ y,\ z) = max(max(x,\ y),\ z)$, for which we can use the formula derived above.
- A more challenging extension to this might be: 'What is the middle number in $x$, $y$, $z$: can you write down a formula for it?' This could be approached a few ways and you might notice that: $mid(x,\ y,\ z) = x + y + z - min(x,\ y,\ z) - max(x,\ y,\ z)$.

### What is the question testing?

This question is testing how well you can formalise your own intuitive ideas of maximum and minimum and use what you already know about the modulus function.

Much of the focus of pure maths at university is on rigour and formality. You can only use terms that you've defined properly. This question aims to challenge you to do just that.

### Related topics from university

Ideas of maximum/minimum and inequalities form part of the Analysis course in your first term at both Oxford and Cambridge.

## Maths interview question 3 (Prime Numbers/Möbius Function)

**Question: The Möbius function, $\mu(n)$, is defined as follows for natural numbers: $\mu(1) = 1$ if $n$ is square-free and has an even number of prime factors. $\mu(n) = -1$ if $n$ is square-free and has an odd number of prime factors. $\mu(n) = 0$ if $n$ isn't square-free. Please could you calculate $\mu(35)$, $\mu(66)$ and $\mu(35 \times 66)$?**

### Model interview

**Student:** I'm not sure what it means for $n$ to be square-free, can you clarify what you mean by this?

Don't be afraid to ask for clarification on key terms and concepts. They don't expect you to know everything!

**Tutor:** Of course. A number is square-free if it doesn't have any squared prime numbers as factors. For example, 6 is square-free because its only factors are 2 and 3, and neither is repeated.

**Student:** Ok, I think I understand that. (*Pauses to think about the calculation.*) So, $35 = 5 \times 7$ and 5 and 7 are both prime so $\mu(35)$ must equal 1. And $66 = 6 \times 11 = 2 \times 3 \times 11$, and 2, 3 and 11 are all prime so $\mu(66)$ must equal -1.

**Tutor:** Before you work it out, do you have any instinct on what $\mu(35 \times 66)$ might be?

**Student:** Well 35 has an even number of prime factors, and 66 has an odd number of prime factors, so together there'll be an odd number of prime factors, so I think $\mu(35 \times 66) = -1$.

**Tutor:** That's correct. Can you state the connection between $\mu(35)$, $\mu(66)$ and $\mu(35 \times 66)$ more exactly?

**Student:** (*Pauses.*) It seems as though $\mu(35)\mu(66) = \mu(35 \times 66)$... Yes, I think that's the rule.

**Tutor:** Okay. Does this rule work for any two numbers $x$ and $y$?

**Student:** Yes, I don't see why it shouldn't. The total number of prime factors of $xy$ is equal to the sum of the numbers of prime factors of $x$ and $y$. So, if the number of prime factors of each of them is both odd or both even, the factors of $xy$ will be even and $\mu(xy) = 1$, whereas if one has an odd number of factors and one an even number, there will be an odd total and $\mu(xy) = -1$. Although, saying that out loud, I'm now thinking that it won't work if $x$ and $y$ share factors, because then $xy$ won't be square-free...

If you think you've taken a wrong turn don't be afraid to correct yourself—in fact the sooner you do the better! It shows you're able to question yourself and listen to the advice of the interviewer.

**Tutor:** Continue. Can you give me an example?

**Student:** Well $\mu(6) = 1$ but $\mu(6 \times 6) = 0 \neq \mu(6)\mu(6)$. I think that this relation will only hold when $x$ and $y$ don't share factors. That is, they have to be coprime.

**Tutor:** Can you explain why it will always hold in cases like this?

**Student:** Well, if $x$ has a squared prime factor so will $xy$, and therefore $\mu(xy) = 0 = 0 \times \mu(y) = \mu(x)\mu(y)$. If neither has a squared prime factor, and since they are coprime, their factors are different, so the total number of *unique* factors of $xy$ is equal to the sum of the numbers of unique factors of $x$ and $y$. So, by the reasoning I gave before, it must hold that $\mu(xy) = \mu(x)\mu(y)$.

**Tutor:** Good. This property is called *multiplicativity.* Can you think of any other examples of a multiplicative function?

**Student:** I guess a simple function such as $f(x) = x$ will be multiplicative, because $f(xy) = xy = f(x)f(y)$. Thinking about it, any function such as $f(x) = x^n$ will work.

**Tutor:** That's right.

## Further hints

- If you haven't noticed that the rule $\mu(xy) = \mu(x)\mu(y)$ has exceptions, the interviewer might prompt you by saying: 'What is $\mu(x)^2$ going to be for any $x$?' or 'Can you think of a simple counterexample to this?'
- When asked to think of an example of another multiplicative function, it needn't be complicated. The interviewer may prompt you in this way by asking something like, 'What are some easy functions you know—are they multiplicative?'

Thinking of counterexamples and proving things go hand in hand. Seeing where your attempt at a proof fails can help you construct a counterexample and vice versa.

## Extending the question

- A natural follow-up is to ask you to prove the statement: 'If $xy$ is square-free, then $x$ is square-free'. You could explain this by saying: *'$xy$ being square-free means that whatever $x$ and $y$ are, they must be coprime'* and '$\mu(xy) \neq 0$ implies that $\mu(x) \neq 0$ and $\mu(y) \neq 0$'.
- Alternatively, the interviewer could give you a function you probably won't have seen before and ask you to prove that it's multiplicative. For example, they might give you the unit function $u(n)$ for positive integers, defined as $1$ when $n = 1$ and $0$ otherwise, and ask you to show that it's multiplicative. This could be done by splitting it into the cases of $x = y = 1$, $x \neq 1 \neq y$ and $x = 1, y \neq 1$. Proving properties of functions/objects is commonplace in pure mathematics.
- If you've shown competency in the question, the interviewer could ask you about other functions in the realm of number theory, such as Euler's totient function, $\phi(n)$, which counts how many numbers less than $n$ are coprime to $n$—or the divisor function, $\sigma_k(y)$, which sums the $k^{\text{th}}$ powers of all the divisors of $n$.

## What is the question testing?

This question is testing your skills in number theory and numerical reasoning. You're purposefully exposed to a function that you're unlikely to have seen before so the interviewers can see how you respond to new material. The ideal student will, even in unfamiliar territory, be able to understand and apply the definition to calculate and prove results. Working from definitions is a vital skill to have, as the pace of learning maths at Oxford and Cambridge is fast.

### Related topics from university

Number theory is part of the Cambridge Numbers and Sets module in the first year. At Oxford, you'll study less number theory directly until you begin to take options in your second year, but the reasoning used in this question about factors, co-prime numbers, etc. is relevant to the Groups and Group Actions course in the second and third terms of the first year at Oxford.

## 6.4: A script of an Oxbridge Computer Science interview

Below are three example Computer Science interview questions worked through by a model student. If you want to practise answering interview-style questions, try to answer the question as best you can on your own before working through the script, and when you do read through, try to do each step *before* you read the student's response. Remember, with interview questions, you aren't expected to be able to do them all right away—the interviewer wants to be able to talk to you about the questions and work them through with you.

### Computer Science interview question 1 (Recursion/Iteration)

**Question: The 'iterated logarithm', $\log^*$, is defined as the number of times one needs to apply the base-2 logarithm to a number before it is less than, or equal to, 1. I'd like you to find a recursive formula for $\log^*$ and use this to find $\log^*(8)$.**

Many Computer Science interviews focus on mathematical questions, rather than anything explicitly linked to programming or technology.

### Model interview

**Tutor:** Are you familiar with the definition of recursion?

Don't panic if you're not! The interviewer will explain unfamiliar terms—they're testing what you can learn, not what you already know.

**Student:** Yes, it's when something is defined in terms of itself.

This might not be the most precise answer ever, but it sounds relevant enough that the interviewer can wait to see what the student comes up with to see if they really do understand.

**Tutor:** Okay, so let's find a recursive formula for $\log^*$.

**Student:** Recursive formulae have base cases. In this case, we stop applying $\log$ when the number is less than 1. So, we have $\log^*(n) = 1 \text{ } if \text{ } n < 1$.

**Tutor:** Is that correct?

**Student:** (*Pauses.*) Oh, should it be 0 instead of 1? (*Thinks.*) Yes, it should be, because you don't need to apply $\log$ any times once the number is less than 1... or equal to 1. So it should be $\log^*(n) = 0 \text{ } if \text{ } n \leq 1$.

**Tutor:** Okay, and otherwise?

**Student:** Well, that's the base case. If we have a number bigger than 1, then we apply the logarithm. And then we want to find the iterated logarithm of that number. So we have $\log^*(\log\ n)$... And then... (*Pauses.*) I'm not sure.

**Tutor:** If I gave you the value of $\log^*(\log\ n)$, call it $k$, what is the value of $\log^*(n)$?

**Student:** Well, $\log$ applied $k$ times to $\log(n)$ is less than or equal to 1... and then $\log$ applied $k + 1$ times to $n$ is less than or equal to 1. So it's $\log^*(n) = \log^*(\log\ n) + 1$. And that applies for $n > 1$.

**Tutor:** Okay, good. So then what is the iterated logarithm of 8, using this formula?

**Student:** So if we start with 8 and take the logarithm... and we're using base 2... then $2^3 = 8$ so we get 3. Applying the logarithm again... (*Pauses.*) We're looking for a number where $2^x = 3$. But this isn't going to be a whole number.

**Tutor:** Right. Can we work out an upper bound and a lower bound for $x$?

This is often a useful technique in integer questions.

**Student:** (*Pauses to think.*) $2^1 = 2$ and $2^2 = 4$ so it should be between 1 and 2.

**Tutor:** Yes. What's the next step?

**Student:** If we take the logarithm of 1 we get 0, which is less than 1.

**Tutor:** Does the number need to be less than 1?

**Student:** (*Looks at formula again.*) Oh no, actually it can be equal to 1, so we stop there.

**Tutor:** And that means the iterated logarithm of 1 is?

**Student:** 0?

**Tutor:** That's right. And the iterated logarithm of 2?
**Student:** It's $\log_2 2 = 1$, and we stop at 1, so it's 1?

**Tutor:** Yes. What about the iterated logarithm of 8?
**Student:** We do it once to get 3, and a second time to get a number between 1 and 2 and a third time to get a number between 0 and 1 so it's between 2 and 3.

**Tutor:** Can the iterated logarithm be a non-integer?
**Student:** Oh, it's the number of times you apply the logarithm so it has to be a whole number. So with 8 we either did it 2 or 3 times.

**Tutor:** Which one, 2 or 3?
**Student:** Well it depends if it's 1 or 2 after we've done it twice.

**Tutor:** Can it be exactly 1 or 2?
**Student:** (*Thinks for a second.*) No, because it's bigger than 2 and less than 4.

**Tutor:** Yes, so we know that our $x$ satisfying $2^x = 3$ is more than 1 and less than 2.
**Student:** And we do have to apply the iterated logarithm a third time, so it's 3.

**Tutor:** Yes. Now please find all numbers that have an iterated logarithm of 3.
**Student:** Okay. So those are the numbers that have $\log\log\log n \leq 1$. So if we raise each side to the power of 2, we get $\log\log n \leq 2$ and then $\log n \leq 4$ and then $n \leq 16$.

Interviewers will often ask questions that generalise the results you've worked out.

**Tutor:** Is every number less than or equal to 16 suitable?
**Student:** No, because some might have an iterated logarithm of 0, 1 or 2. So we also need $\log\log n > 1$. That's the same as $\log n > 2$ or $n > 4$. So $n$ has an iterated logarithm of exactly 3 if it's in the range $4 < n \leq 16$.

**Tutor:** Okay, thank you.

## Further hints

- The interviewer might prompt you to give an example of a recursive formula. If you're stuck at first, you can establish what properties recursive formulae have (they consist of base cases and recursive cases).

- If you're stuck on how to find all numbers with iterated logarithm 3, the interviewer might ask you something like: 'What is the smallest number with iterated logarithm 3?'

## Extending the question

When you take the equation $\text{logloglog } n \leq 1$ and raise each side to the power of 2 to get $\text{loglog } n \leq 2$, this only works because $2^x$ is an 'increasing function'. This means that if $x > y$, then $2^x > 2^y$. Not every function is increasing (e.g. $f(x) = -x$ and $f(x) = \cos(x)$ are not), so you can't just apply any function you want to both sides of an inequality. The interviewer could ask follow-up questions about this if it comes up in the discussion (for instance, if you ask if you're allowed to raise each side of an inequality to the power of 2).

In fact, $\log^*$ itself is an increasing function. This lends itself to another way of deriving the range in which numbers have an iterated logarithm of 3: find the smallest numbers with iterated logarithms 3 and 4, and any number with iterated logarithm 3 is between these values. Calculation shows that $2^2 = 4$ and $2^{2^2} = 16$ are these bounds, so we get the interval $4 < n \leq 16$ as before.

If there's time, the interviewer could ask a follow-up question: 'For a positive number $k$, find all numbers $n$ such that $\log^*\ n = k$.' The solution (which the interviewer will help the student construct) is to consider a 'power tower' of $k$ lots of 2s stacked on top of each other (e.g. for $k = 4$, we have $2^{2^{2^2}} = 2^{16}$ $[= 65{,}536]$ as the upper bound). Write this number as $\text{Tower }(2, k)$. The numbers $n$ that have iterated logarithm $k$ are the ones satisfying $\text{Tower }(2, k-1) < n \leq \text{Tower }(2, k)$.

## What is the question testing?

The question tests your ability to learn a new concept and apply it to your existing knowledge of logarithms. It also tests your understanding of recursion and your ability to derive formulae.

## Related topics from university

Recursion is one of the most common techniques for writing algorithms and occurs widely throughout computer science as well as mathematics.

The iterated logarithm is used in computer science as a measure of 'complexity' of some algorithms—that is, how quickly they run. If you've come across 'big O notation', the iterated logarithm (written $\log^*$) is interesting as it's a function that grows very, very slowly—much slower than any function in $\text{O}(\log\ n)$ or even $\text{O}(\text{loglogloglog } n)$.

The additional material relating to 'power towers' relates to a function in arithmetic known as 'tetration'.

## Computer Science interview question 2 (Graph Sketching/Inequalities)

**Question: Put the following functions in increasing order in terms of how fast they grow as $n$ tends to infinity: $100n^3$, $n^4$, $\log\ n$, $(\log\ n)^{\log\ n}$, $\text{loglog}\ n$, $n^{\log\ n}$.**

### Model interview

**Student:** When the question says 'log', does it mean 'base 10 log'?

**Tutor:** In fact, it doesn't matter—but let's say it's the common logarithm. That is, the base 10 logarithm.

**Student:** Okay. (*Pause.*) I'll start by sketching the graphs of some of these functions.

**Tutor:** Good.

**Student:** So here's $y = 100n^3$. And $y = n^4$.

Graphs can just be rough sketches, unless you're asked for more detail. Remember to always label axes though!

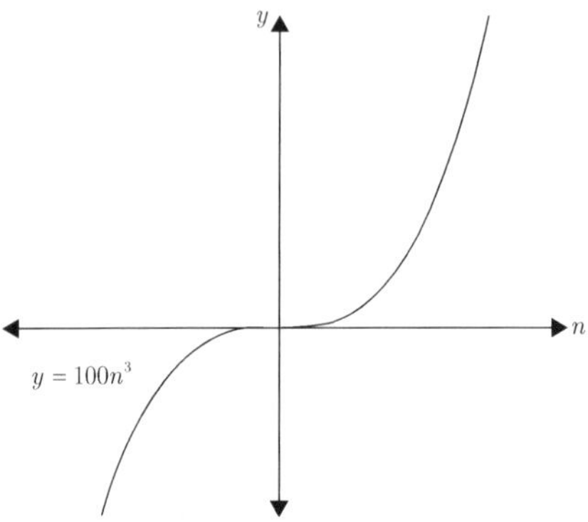


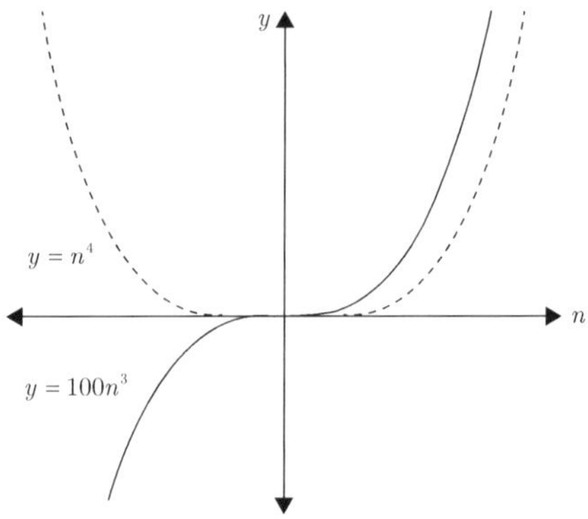


As for which one is bigger... we're looking at the right-hand side of the graph and it looks as though $100n^3$ is the one on the inside so it's the one that's growing fastest.

**Tutor:** Is that right?

**Student:** No, actually shouldn't $n^4$ grow faster?

It's okay to change your answer or to be unsure. It's best to say your vocalise thoughts rather than sitting in silence so the interviewer can see how you're thinking.

**Tutor:** Why would that be?

**Student:** Because 4 is a higher power than 3. (*Pause.*) Okay, so maybe $n^4$ overtakes $100n^3$ higher up.

**Tutor:** How can you tell if that happens?

**Student:** Well, if we solve $100n^3 = n^4$ we can see where they intersect. And we get $n^3(n-100)=0$, so they intersect at 0 and 100. (*Pause.*) So the graph of $n^4$ overtakes $100n^3$ past 100.

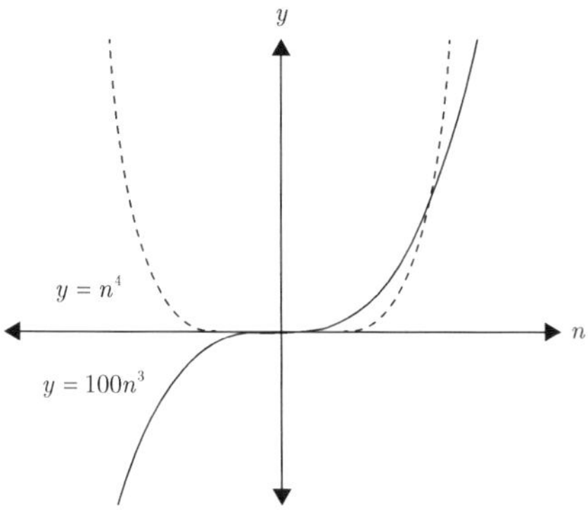


**Tutor:** Okay, so which is growing slower?

**Student:** $100n^3$.

**Tutor:** What about the other functions?

**Student:** Well, $\log\ n$ is going to grow very slowly and $\log\log\ n$ will grow even slower.

**Tutor:** Why is that?

**Student:** If I draw $\log\ n$...

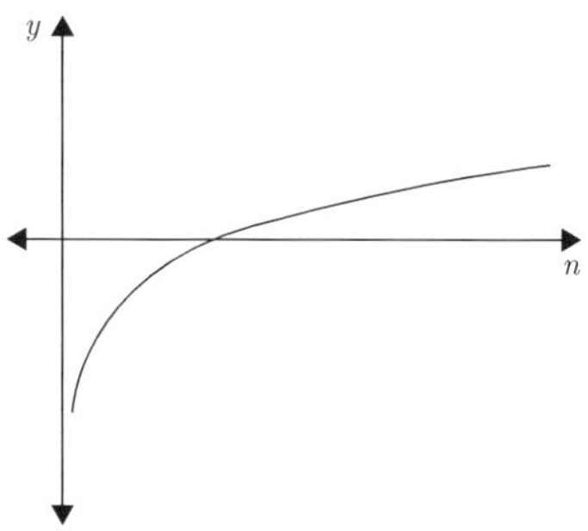


It's growing slower than $100n^3$ or $n^4$. And if we take the logarithm of that, it becomes even smaller... (*Pause.*) because $y = \log\ n$ grows slower than $y = n$, so if we replace $n$ with $\log\ n$ we get that $\log\log\ n$ grows slower than $\log\ n$.

**Tutor:** Okay. How about the remaining functions?

**Student:** By the same reasoning, $(\log\ n)^{\log\ n}$ must grow more slowly than $n^{\log\ n}$. And if we compare $(\log\ n)^{\log\ n}$ to $n^4$... firstly, we see that $n^4$ grows slower than $n^{\log\ n}$ because $\log\ n$ will be bigger than 4 as $n$

gets bigger. Finally, to solve $(\log n)^{\log n} = n^4$, I'll put 10 to the power of each side. That means the left-hand side is $10^{(\log n)^{\log n}} = 10^{(\log n)^2}$...

Is this right? Make sure you're very confident with the rules for logs and powers!

**Tutor:** What if, instead, we try to take the logarithm of the equation $(\log n)^{\log n} = n^4$?

The interviewer may give you advice if you go down the wrong track.

**Student:** I think that $\log((\log n)^{\log n}) = (\log n)(\log\log n)$ and $\log(n^4) = 4 \log (n)$.
That means $(\log n)^{\log n} > n^4$ if $(\log n)(\log\log n) > 4 \log (n)$, which is true if $\log\log n > 4$, which is true for $n > 10^{10^4}$. Therefore, $(\log n)^{\log n}$ grows faster.

**Tutor:** Okay, thank you.

*Note: Final order (slowest to fastest) is:* $\log\log n$, $\log n$, $100n^3$, $n^4$, $(\log n)^{\log n}$, $n^{\log n}$.

## Extending the question

The interviewer could introduce more functions such as: $(\log n)^n$, $2^n$, $\sqrt{n}$, or $(\log n)^{(\log n)^{\log n}}$.

They could also ask you to compare the derivatives of some of the functions (treating $n$ as a continuous variable) to test your calculus skills too.

## What is the question testing?

The question requires a thorough understanding of logarithms, exponentials, polynomials and graph sketching.

## Related topics from university

The question relates to 'big O notation', a way of classifying functions in terms of how fast they grow. This is important in computer science as a way of classifying how efficient an algorithm is. It's also used in analysis, an area of mathematics, as a way to find limits.

You may have already encountered Big O notation in your Computer Science A Level or elsewhere. If this is the case, the interviewer may add more functions or continue pushing to find an area you're unfamiliar with. The interviewer cares more about finding out how you think (and respond to new information) than how much information you already know.

## Computer Science interview question 3 (Algorithms/Automata)

*At the beginning of the interview, the interviewer hands the candidate the question on a piece of paper and asks them to read the material.*

A *deterministic finite automaton* (DFA) is a machine that can be in one of a finite number of states. It starts in an initial state and changes state according to the input it receives. Some states are *accepting*: if the machine is in an accepting state when the input terminates, then it 'accepts' the input. Otherwise it 'rejects' the input.

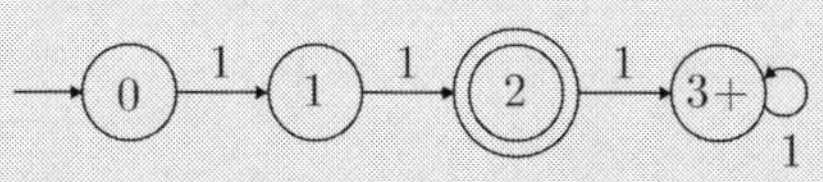


The automaton represented by this diagram can only recognise strings of 1s. The arrow going into the state $0$ indicates that $0$ is the start state. The double circle around the state $2$ indicates that it's an accepting state. An arrow from state X to state Y labelled with a $1$ indicates that when the machine is in state X and receives a $1$ as input, it moves to state Y.

For instance, with the input $111$, the machine moves from state $0$ to $1$ to $2$ to $3+$, and as $3+$ isn't an accepting state, the machine rejects $111$.

**Questions:**

**i) What strings does this machine accept?**

**ii) Let $1^n$ be the string consisting of $n$ repetitions of the character $1$, where $n$ is a fixed number. Explain how to construct a DFA that accepts only the string $1^n$.**

**iii) How can this be extended to make a DFA that accepts a finite set of strings: $1^a$, $1^b$, ..., $1^z$?**

### Model interview

**Student:** It seems the only thing this machine accepts is the input $11$.

**Tutor:** Correct, and how can we show that?

**Student:** If we put in $11$ then the machine goes from state 0 to 1 to 2, and 2 is an accepting state, so the machine accepts $11$.

In a case like this, it's important to explain each step of the algorithm or process, even if it seems easy at first, because the tutor needs to see that you're thinking clearly about how it works.

**Tutor:** Okay. And if we input something else?

**Student:** Well, if we put in three or more 1s then the machine goes to state $3+$ and stays there forever. And $3+$ isn't an accepting state so it will reject the input. And if we put in just the input $1$ then it goes to state $1$, which isn't accepting.

**Tutor:** Okay. We can also input the empty string.

**Student:** Meaning zero 1s? Then the machine stays where it started, in state $0$. And $0$ isn't an accepting state.

Always be on the lookout for special cases like this!

**Tutor:** Okay, good. Now I'd like you to read question ii.

**Student:** (*Reads the question.*) The original machine solves this problem when $n$ is $2$. And we can do the same method for any $n$.

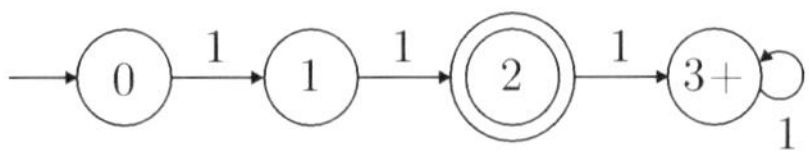


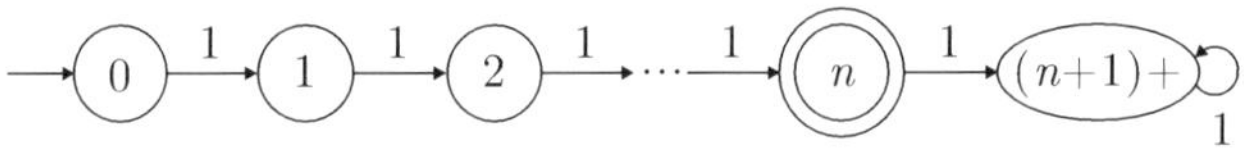


**Tutor:** Yes. And if we want to change this to accept the strings $1^a, 1^b, \ldots, 1^z$?

**Student:** We can change the accepting state from $n$ to the numbers $a, b, \ldots, z$.

**Tutor:** Okay. And what is $n$ in this case?

**Student:** We could just get rid of $n$ and have one state from each number $0, 1, 2, \ldots$

**Tutor:** In that case, the machine isn't finite.

**Student:** Oh, okay. Then we can just go up to the largest number out of $a, b, \ldots, z$.

**Tutor:** Yes, good. Next, I'd like you to make a DFA that accepts strings of the form $1^n$ where $n$ is a multiple of $2$.

The tutor is now extending the question beyond what was asked on the paper the student was given at the start. Your interviewers may well keep adding to a question in order to stretch you.

**Student:** Right. We can't have a separate accepting state for each of $1^0, 1^2, 1^4, \ldots$ because that wouldn't be finite.

**Tutor:** No.

**Student:** (*Thinks.*) We only need to know whether the number of 1s inputted is an even or odd number. We can have one state for $even$ and one for $odd$. It would look something like this:

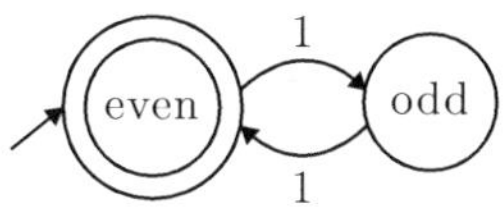


**Tutor:** Yes. And if instead of multiples of $2$, what if we looked at multiples of $n$?

**Student:** Then we need $n$ states. So, would this work?

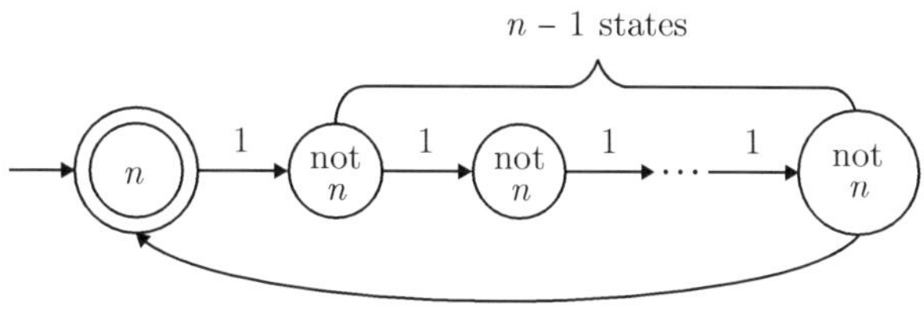


**Tutor:** Yes, although it might have been better to label the states $0, 1, ..., n - 1$. Right, now I'll ask you to think about DFAs that take as input not just a sequence of $1$s but a sequence of digits 0, ..., 9. In that case, the number $981$ would be represented by inputting a $9$, an $8$ and a $1$. Our diagram can have one arrow per input digit per state. I'll ask you to make a DFA that accepts decimal numbers[59] that are a multiple of 2.

If you've ever studied modular arithmetic, this might seem familiar.

**Student:** Okay. Again, we just need to know whether the input is even or odd. And we can keep track of that by seeing whether the last digit is $0, 2, 4, 6, 8$ or $1, 3, 5, 7, 9$. The DFA would be:

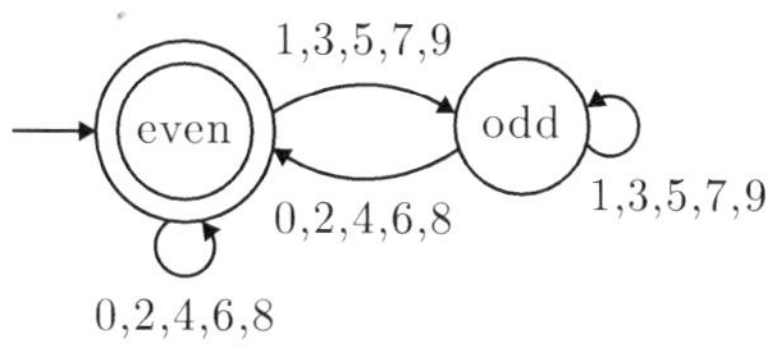


*[An arrow with '1, 3, 5, 7, 9' is shorthand for 5 arrows with 1, 3, 5, 7 and 9 as labels.]*

**Tutor:** Good. Now how could we write a DFA to determine if a number is a multiple of 3?

**Student:** We can't do this just by looking at the last digit, because multiples of 3 can end in any digit. There's a test to see if a number is divisible by 3 by adding all of its digits together.

59 Meaning our normal counting system with digits from 0 to 9.

**Tutor:** And how do you tell if the number is divisible by 3 with that test?

**Student:** A number is divisible by 3 if you add all its digits together and get a multiple of 3. Or, if that number is still too big to work out if it's divisible by 3, you can keep adding its digits together until you get down to a single-digit number.

**Tutor:** Okay. How can we use this idea to construct a DFA?

**Student:** Well, we can just keep a running count of the sum of the digits. But we can't store the number because we don't know how big it will be.

Identifying the obstacle you're facing is a good thing to do when you don't have a complete answer yet.

**Tutor:** Okay. Do we need the whole number? (*Waits.*) Or just a property of it?

**Student:** Oh, we only need to know whether or not the running total is a multiple of 3. Or, whether it's 1 or 2 more than a multiple of 3. If the next digit is 0 mod 3, the state doesn't change. If it's 1 mod 3, the value of the running total mod 3 increases by 1, and so on. So it would look like this.

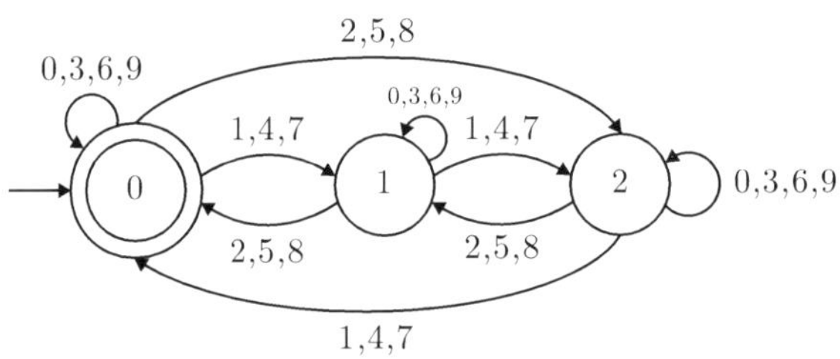


*[Note: The interviewer would not make the student add all of the labels, only those necessary to explain how the DFA works.]*

**Tutor:** Okay, thank you.

## Further hints

The interviewer will prompt you to correct any small mistakes you've made, such as forgetting to draw an arrow for the initial state, or a double circle for accepting states.

If you were stuck on the last part, the interviewer might prompt you to think of any divisibility tests for 3 that you might know—and if you don't know any, the interviewer will likely explain one.

## Extending the question

As well as multiples of 2 and 3, we can make a DFA to test divisibility by any number for which we have a divisibility rule involving the digits they end in, or some type of digit sum.

For instance, a number is divisible by 8 if its last three digits are divisible by 8. For example, 713,564,256 is a multiple of 8 because 256 is a multiple of 8. We can have one state for each of the last three digits, from 000 to 999, and make all the multiples of 8 (000, 008,..., 992) accepting states. However, this does require a DFA that has 1,000 states. Can you think of a DFA that does the same thing with fewer states?

A number is divisible by 11 if its alternating digit sum is a multiple of 11 (e.g. 83,929,032 is a multiple of 11 because $8-3+9-2+9-0+3-2=22$ is a multiple of 11). How can we make a DFA for multiples of 11 using this rule?

Additionally, given two DFAs, $M_1$ and $M_2$ that accept multiples of $m$ and $n$, we can make a DFA $M_3$ that accepts multiples of $mn$. Can you work out how? (Hint: if we enter a number and this causes $M_1$ to move to state $x$ and $M_2$ to move to state $y$, we want $M_3$ to be in a state $(x,\ y)$.)

## What is the question testing?

You may already be familiar with deterministic finite automata, perhaps under the name 'finite state machines', but the interviewer is testing how well you can learn new information. As a result, if you already know some of the background material, you'll be pushed further into the extension material to a point where you're asked a question you haven't come across before.

The question tests your ability to learn new information quickly and to design abstract procedures. Candidates with programming knowledge may have written algorithms to test divisibility of numbers, but with DFAs there's a constraint that only a finite number of states can be used, making things more difficult.

## Related topics from university

Deterministic finite automata are used in the theory of computation in computer science. We say a language (set of strings) is decided by a DFA if the DFA accepts every string in the language and rejects every string that isn't in the language. Not every possible language can be decided by a DFA—the languages that can be are called 'regular languages'.

At Cambridge, DFAs are covered in the Digital Electronics and Discrete Mathematics modules in the first year. At Oxford, the second year Models of Computation course covers DFAs and their properties, as well as *non*-deterministic finite automata and several other types of theoretical machine.

# 6.5: More examples of maths and computer science interview questions

Here are some more examples of types of question that are common in maths and computer science interviews. If you're applying for Computer Science, check out the maths questions too, and vice versa. You might also benefit from looking at some of the maths questions for physical science applicants on page 312.

## Examples of short maths interview questions

- Differentiate $\sin x$ with respect to $\cos x$.
- I colour the vertices of a cube either red or blue at random. What's the probability that no two adjacent vertices are the same colour? What's the probability that every face contains vertices of both colours?
- Evaluate the sum $\sum_0^n \frac{2^{-k} \cdot (k+3)}{(k+1)(k+2)}$.
- Sketch $y = \frac{2x^2 - 1}{x^2 - 1}$.
- If a piece of paper of length $x$ and width $y$ is folded so the top left corner meets the bottom right corner, what is the length of the fold?
- Show that the sum of two consecutive positive cubes is never a power of 2.

## Examples of longer maths interview questions

- What is $\int_{-1}^{1} x^{-2} dx$? Consider its geometrical meaning. Comment on $\int_{-1}^{1} x^{-1} dx$.
- Sketch $y = x^2 - x^3$, $y^2 = x^2 - x^3$ and $y = \ln(x^2 - x^3)$.
- If the two of us stand at random places in a queue of $n$ people, what is the expected number of people in between us?

- Can you find a non-constant polynomial $p(x)$ with leading coefficient 1 such that $p(n)$ is even for every whole number $n$, but $p(n)$ is never a multiple of 4?
- What is $\frac{d}{dx}(\cot x)$? Can you find the Maclaurin series for $e^{-\cot^2 x}$? Why is your answer interesting?

> *"In the Trinity at-interview test, I had very little clue what was going on. I had five jumbled attempted solutions without clear answers, and one answer with no working for a different question. In the interview, the tutors gave me small hints on the questions I'd attempted, which allowed me to solve them all correctly, and my answer with no working ended up being correct. So my advice for an at-interview exam would be to focus on working through a question as far as you can, and then move on. Getting no clear cut answer does not take away anything from your work, and if anything it gives your interviewer something to challenge you with during the interview."* –Student, Maths, Cambridge

## More examples of computer science interview questions

- There are two piles of cards in front of you. We take turns taking any number of cards from either pile. Whoever takes the last card loses. Should you go first or second?
- You are given 90 cards with numbers from 1 to 100 written on them. The cards are in order, the first numbered 1, and the last numbered 100. What's the most efficient way to find at least one number between 1 and 100 that isn't on any of the cards? To find all of them?
- Describe the best procedure you can think of for completing a jigsaw puzzle. Imagine each piece is a unique shape, but is blank, and that you know the completed puzzle is a 50cm by 1m rectangle.
- Given a screen with cartesian axes on, describe an algorithm for producing an image of a parabola with a given equation pixel-by-pixel. How about a circle?
- Prove that $\binom{n}{k}$ is the $(k+1)$th number in the $(n+1)$th row of Pascal's triangle.
- How can we use only NAND gates to create a logic gate that takes three inputs and returns 1 if an odd number of them are 1 and 0 otherwise?

> *"There were a couple of times when it helped me to be able to think about adding numbers modulo 2. For instance, one question started with determining which Fibonacci numbers are even. There were also a couple of logic puzzles. On the day, I'd advise not doing any extra preparation except trying to keep your head clear, as it's more about being able to tackle new material than about how much you have memorised."* –Student, Computer Science, Oxford

# Part I C: Before Your Degree

# Chapter 7:
# A packing list of skills to bring from school to your degree

Although the Maths/Computer Science courses at Oxbridge are a different kettle of fish to A-Level Maths, there's a set of transferable skills that will take you a long way if carried through from school to your degree. These include:

## Attention to detail

It's essential to pay attention to detail in university-level maths and computer science, especially when it comes to writing proofs. Solving a maths problem can be an intricate process, requiring precision and clarity in your working. The same goes for writing a program, and for learning the rules a programming language is built on in the first place. This is important both at A Level and throughout your degree.

## The content of your A Levels

The content of Maths A Level (and Further Maths A Level for many courses) will be assumed throughout your degree. Much of the undergraduate content does not directly build on your A-Level knowledge, but it's required for many topics (such as differential equations, number theory and geometry).

All of the equations on the A-Level formula sheets are useful at university, but they won't be written out for you anymore, so it's worth taking the time to memorise key formulae or (even better) learn how to re-derive them quickly.

## Visualisation skills

Being able to roughly sketch functions is important because using a diagram in formulating a question will give you a better grasp of the concepts you're dealing with. It's especially helpful if you can develop an intuitive understanding of how a function should behave based on its equation—when it should go to 0 or infinity, where it should have turning points, what range it should lie in, and so on. In contrast, calculating specific coordinates will be less important at uni than at school.

Additionally, picturing things in 3D (trajectories, surfaces, vectors, rotations and other transformations) will help with both pure modules relating to vectors, matrices, and geometry, and applied modules in mechanics.

## Skills in structuring mathematical proofs

Your teachers will often nag you to show all of your working, something that is of the utmost importance at university! During your degree, a large proportion of your marks are given for proving theorems and formulae—meaning there are plenty of 'show that' questions. You must be able to present and structure your proofs clearly, exactly as you're pushed to do at school.

Moreover, you'll need to be fluent with proofs by contradiction and by induction—not just presenting them, but also figuring out where the contradiction is likely to come from, or how the induction step is going to work.

## A word on gap years for Maths and Computer Science

There's no right or wrong when it comes to taking a gap year at Oxford or Cambridge, but if you do want to take a gap year, then bear the following in mind:

### 1) Spend your time in ways relevant to your subject

> *"Deferred entry applications in Mathematics, its Joint Schools, and Computer Science will be considered from applicants who have planned structured activities in their gap year; activities might include technical employment relevant to Mathematics, Statistics or Computer Science, teaching abroad or a gap year programme."* –Oxford

### 2) Make sure to keep up your skills

> *"It would be wise to take steps to ensure that your maths does not get rusty during your year out. Many students take a further qualification in maths (A-Level Further Maths, STEP, etc.)."* –King's College, Cambridge

# Chapter 8:
# What should you do over the summer before your degree?

Here's a list of things you can do to prepare yourself for studying Maths/ Computer Science at university:

## General advice

### 1) Do any summer work set by the university

It's likely that you'll receive problem sheets designed to help you bridge the gap between school and university. Don't let them get lost in your email inbox—it's vital to have a good attempt at them. These questions will cover the content your lecturers think it's important you know and they'll give you a good indication of the topics you'll be expected to be fluent in from the start.

### 2) Read widely around your subject

Your interest may have waned over the gruelling A-Level period, so take some time to dive into the subject and further explore the ideas that originally attracted you to it. If you're a computer scientist, why not read news articles on AI, investigate uses of technology that interest you, or watch YouTube videos on key computer science concepts?[60] Likewise, as a mathematician, you could read up on current developments in maths, research famous problems and their solutions, or listen to lectures on the role of maths in society.

### 3) Attempt some problems in a bridging book

There are lots of books out there to help students to bridge the gap between school and university maths. Why not get one of these and work through some of the problems over the summer?

60 We recommend the YouTube channel Computerphile.

Looking for a great bridging book?[61] Try these titles:

**Hurst: *Bridging the Gap to University Mathematics***

*Focuses on consolidating the knowledge accumulated at A Level that is required at university level study.*

**Alcock: *How to Study for a Mathematics Degree***

*Concentrates more on the adjustment to the new style of maths at university, which can be a shock at first.*

**Houston: *How to Think Like a Mathematician***

*Works through the key skills required for university maths, such as using axioms to construct a proof. Useful to have on hand at the beginning of your degree, as it will clarify ideas that are skimmed over in lectures.*

# Advice for Maths offer-holders

## 1) Look over your notes from A Level

It is important to be completely confident with all of the A-Level content in Maths and Further Maths. If you didn't take A Levels, or if you did but there were areas that let you down in your exams, look over the syllabi and revise them a bit before heading to university. Don't assume that the first few lectures will recap A-Level Maths and Further Maths. Some of your first-year courses will review sections of the relevant A Level material, but the core A Level topics will mostly just be assumed to be common knowledge. And the material that *is* recapped will fly by in just a couple of lectures.

You might also want to spend some time looking through modules you didn't cover at school. Some of the later Further Pure modules and Mechanics modules will hold you in good stead for what you're about to study at university.

## 2) Try some STEP questions

STEP questions emulate the unstructured style of undergraduate problem sheet and exam questions. The more you practise such questions, the

61 See oxbridgeformula.co.uk/bonus-chapter for links to these books and more.

easier it will be to hit the ground running in your first year. Even though you might be too late to sit the exam, the extra practice won't be in vain.[62]

> *"I decided to take the STEP papers because I really loved maths. Little did I know how much they were helping me bridge the gap between school and university. I think I started the year off struggling a lot less than my friends."* –Student, Maths & Computer Science, Oxford

# Advice for Computer Science offer-holders

## 1) Revisit Project Euler

The problems on Project Euler will get you in the right frame of mind for solving university-style problems. The website is refreshed constantly with new problems and is a great way to get your brain back in gear!

## 2) Practise programming and learn a language

Programming is an essential part of any university Computer Science course, so it's a good idea to get some more practice before arriving. It's not essential to learn the programming language associated with your course before you arrive, as it will be covered from the foundations when you start. However, the technique of learning and applying a language is a vital skill. A highly accessible language such as Python is a good place to start.

## 3) Revisit your pure maths A-Level content

It's important to be confident with all your A-Level Maths content, as this will be assumed in many of your courses at uni. Further Maths, although not compulsory for Computer Science at either Oxford or Cambridge, is highly recommended. If you didn't study Further Maths (or did Scottish Highers or the IB instead), it's worth getting hold of some Further Pure textbooks and trying to understand some of the essential content they contain.

62 You know where we are if you're looking for further help!

# Q&A with real Oxbridge interviewers

To help you get inside the minds of your Oxbridge interviewers, we've put together a case study based on our conversations with two admissions tutors from Oxford: one in Maths, and the other in Physics. We hope it will give you a glimpse into the inner workings of the applications process!

## Are applications done internally by colleges, or across the whole university?

**Maths interviewer:** In Maths, the MAT isn't marked by the colleges, but by the Maths faculty. After that, your application is primarily dealt with at your college. Everyone gets two interviews in their first-choice college, and one in another college.

**Physics interviewer:** In Physics, the students are ranked as a cohort across the department, not across colleges. This is to ensure that no one misses out on a place because they applied to the wrong college. You'll have three interviews: two in your first-choice college (or the one assigned to you), and a third at another college.

## How is the MAT/PAT score used?

**Maths interviewer:** We use the MAT as the primary filter to determine who is invited to interview and who isn't. For Maths applications, it's a lot more important than the personal statement. However, we do look at other contextual information, such as the quality of the teaching a student has had, and take that into account in evaluating the MAT mark.

**Physics interviewer:** The PAT score is used to shortlist the best candidates. We select the majority of candidates to invite to interview from the top of the list, but also consider candidates who didn't get as high a score based on contextual factors such as postcode, school GCSE average, whether they've been in care, and whether they have a disability. This can pull people up to be interviewed if, for example, the teaching they received isn't good enough.

## How are the interviews marked?

**Maths interviewer:** At my college, we mark each interview on a form that contains fields such as how good the candidate is in making analytical judgments, how far they got with the question, their clarity, how many hints they needed and how they responded to those hints. Each question is given a mark from 0 to 8, and the average of your scores across all the questions is your overall mark. The students who score the top few marks definitely get an offer, and we debate who to take out of the students who didn't score as highly. Every college does it differently. I like having a detailed breakdown of the whole candidate, so I can remember them later.

**Physics interviewer:** A candidate is given a score out of 10 in the interview. This is an overall mark for performance. A 10 means 'we have to take this person'; a 5 means 'this person might struggle'; a 3 means 'we shouldn't take this person'.

## Can you name some candidate 'dos and don'ts' in an interview?

**Maths interviewer:** The interview isn't necessarily about solving the question—I'm looking for people to show how they think about the question and the methods they use. I try and base my questions on *understanding* more than knowledge, so it isn't so dependent on how good your previous education has been. I usually choose a question that doesn't need that much A-Level knowledge – basic number theory, for example – so everyone is familiar with the ideas, but to solve it you need analytical skills, good logic and deduction.

**Physics interviewer:** The absolute worst thing you can do is to not speak because that gives us nothing to go on.

## How do you structure an interview?

**Maths interviewer:** I don't ask anything about the personal statement or reading—just a few maths problems. Sometimes it will be one or two problems broken down into lots of parts. The interview will start with something easy and get harder as it goes on.

**Physics interviewer:** We just ask physics and maths questions, often ones involving mechanics. The interviews are short, only 20–25 minutes, so we usually only have time for two to three questions. Essentially, we ask questions that you won't know how to answer straight away. We're looking to see how you think.

# Part II:

# Physical Sciences

# Part II A: The Courses

In this part, we will discuss the various physical science courses offered at Oxford and Cambridge, including:

- Physics (and joint courses)
- Engineering
- Materials Science
- Chemistry
- Physical Natural Sciences (including Physics, Chemistry, Materials Science and Earth Sciences)
- Chemical Engineering.

Each chapter will dive into the details of one of the above degree subjects, its pre-requisites, and what's involved in studying the subject at university level.

# Chapter 9: Physics

## 9.1: Why Physics?

Physics is a rich, multi-layered subject that fundamentally shapes the way we view the world. Operating at the frontier of human knowledge, physics is both an exciting and relevant field of study. Physics at Oxbridge is intense but extremely rewarding. It may be the course for you if:

- ❑ **You enjoy problem-solving:** You enjoy the types of question that appear on the Physics Olympiad or UKMT papers[63] (if you have never seen these before, look at the standard of the Senior Kangaroo rounds). Much of physics is about solving a mathematical problem in an applied context—which is why a love of problem-solving is crucial.
- ❑ **You aren't afraid of maths:** At every stage of your Physics degree, the subject matter will be very maths-heavy. In your first year, you'll study maths far beyond the Further Maths A-Level syllabus, and you'll face at least some abstract maths questions with no immediate application to physics. Although you'll later learn to apply the maths you learn to physics problems, you'll definitely enjoy the course more if you can appreciate the maths as a discipline in its own right.

> *"I was surprised at the amount of 'mathsy-maths' I was expected to do in the first year of my Physics degree. It's not like school, where the maths in physics is never particularly complicated; at uni, maths dominates lots of the physics topics you'll do."* –Jake, Physics, Oxford

Note that both A-Level Maths and Physics are required subjects for Physics at Oxford. If you apply to Natural Sciences at Cambridge with an application that focuses on physics, you'll be expected to take Maths A Level.

63 Find the link at oxbridgeformula.co.uk/bonus-chapter.

- ❑ **You're hard-working and committed:** Physics is a tough, time-consuming degree, especially in the early stages when you're working to grasp all the concepts involved. Not only are the contact hours high (with lots of lectures and labs), but the course requires a large amount of independent study—so you must really love the subject and be prepared for the journey ahead!
- ❑ **You enjoy practical work:** Your Physics degree will include compulsory practical assignments. These will be in small groups (often pairs) in a lab and can often fill an entire day, after which you'll need to complete a post-lab report. These are compulsory and contribute to your final degree classification.
- ❑ **You don't hate statistics:** In your post-lab reports, you'll be expected to analyse your results in depth. This includes a variety of statistical analyses and detailed evaluation of the content. You'll be taught to use all the necessary techniques and software, and the required statistical methods will be included in the lab instructions. Crunching through all that data can be time-consuming, so it's important you don't absolutely hate it!
- ❑ **You love physics, and you want to understand it in great depth:** Clearly, it's important to love your degree subject. If you love Physics and Maths at A Level, Physics may be the course for you! Physics at university-level opens your eyes to a previously inaccessible realm of natural phenomena, such as in special relativity and quantum mechanics—if you want to speak the language of the universe, you're looking in the right place!

## Choosing between Oxford and Cambridge

When deciding between Oxford and Cambridge, it's important to note the differences in course structure. At Oxford, you apply to study Physics as a course, and all 3–4 years are entirely focused on the subject. At Cambridge, you have to apply for Natural Sciences (see Chapter 14) if you want to study Physics. This means studying other subjects such as chemistry alongside physics. If you have a strong interest in pure maths as well as physics, you can instead apply for Maths with Physics at Cambridge (see page 49). You can also study Maths at Oxford (see Chapter 2) and switch to Maths and Theoretical Physics in your fourth year.

This chapter will be focused entirely on physics, and is therefore centred on the Oxford course. However, it contains a lot of useful information for Cambridge Natural Sciences applicants who are interested in specialising in physics. Chapter 14 on page 205 if you want to read about Natural Sciences before coming back here.

## 9.2: How do you apply for Physics at Oxford?

The typical offer is A*AA at A Level. Maths and Physics are compulsory A Levels, and Further Maths is also recommended. In particular, all the Mechanics options offered within the A-Level Maths syllabus are highly recommended. You must get an A* in at least one of Maths, Further Maths and Physics. If you take the IB, the typical offer is 39, with 766 at Higher Level, and a 7 in Maths or Physics. Every applicant will also need to take the PAT (Physics Aptitude Test).

Overall, about 1 in every 7 applicants is successful.

In your third year, you can choose to leave with a BA, continue to a fourth year and leave with an MPhys, or switch to a one-year master's in Maths and Theoretical Physics in your fourth year and leave with an MMathPhys instead.

## 9.3: What is it like to study Physics?

Much of the physics you study at university develops key concepts you're exposed to at A Level. For example, you'll study circuits, electromagnetism and optics.

However, the crucial difference is that at university you're expected to understand these topics in much greater depth and rebuild your knowledge of the science from its *mathematical foundations*. You'll not only learn what laws and equations to apply to each type of physical system you study, but also how they are derived from first principles. In school, you *learn* definitions and formulae—whereas at university you'll work to *understand* them using mathematical skills you may not have needed before.

To give you a taste of Physics at university and how it compares to A Level, here's a breakdown of the first-year Oxford Physics syllabus. See page 208 for a similar breakdown of the Cambridge Natural Sciences course.

### Classical Mechanics

*Classical Mechanics builds upon the Newtonian mechanics you study at school (force diagrams, F=ma and SUVAT), but generalises to more difficult situations (e.g. rotational mechanics) and goes into greater depth concerning the derivations of the equations and their wider repercussions.*

In this course, you'll focus on the study of Newton's laws of motion and the content that follows from these—including collisions, orbits and the difference between ***rotational*** and ***translational mechanics***. You'll study further conservation laws, including conservation of angular momentum.[64]

> **Translational mechanics** studies the motion of bodies that aren't spinning, whereas **rotational mechanics** studies ones that are, such as the Earth rotating on its axis. Rotational mechanics can also be used to analyse rotation around a point in space, such as the Earth's orbit around the Sun.

If you haven't studied Further Maths A Level, it's definitely worth looking over it before you start studying physics at university. Although your introductory courses will cover this content, these go very quickly, and you'll need a significant amount of independent study to fully understand it. For example, an understanding of polar coordinates and hyperbolic curves will make sure you aren't left behind when you start the Classical Mechanics course.

> An example of a question on this topic would be:
>
> *Derive the radial and tangential accelerations[65] of a particle moving with coordinates $(x(t), y(t))$ in terms of $x'$, $x''$, $y'$ and $y''$.*

## Electromagnetism

*The study of electric and magnetic forces, touched upon in most A-Level syllabi, but taught and explored from first principles at university.*

In this course, you'll explore how electromagnetism works and learn and understand a variety of new laws, such as ***Gauss's law***, ***Ampère's law*** and the ***Biot-Savart law***. You'll be expected to apply vector operator

64 Analogous to linear momentum, but for rotating bodies.

65 In 2D, the tangential acceleration of an object is the component of its acceleration in the direction it's currently moving, and the radial acceleration is the component perpendicular to this.

identities and vector analysis to electromagnetic questions and manipulate equations involving charged particles.

**Did You Know?**

*A simple example of a vector operator is the derivative, and an example identity for it is:* $\mathbf{v}\cdot\frac{d\mathbf{v}}{dt} \equiv \frac{1}{2}\frac{d}{dt}(|\mathbf{v}|^2)$. *Can you see why that's true?*

*You'll also study electromagnetic induction and the way charges move in electromagnetic fields.*

**Gauss's law:** *The total of the electric flux out of a closed surface is equal to the charge enclosed divided by the permittivity of free space.*

Some concepts here may seem familiar, but this law also introduces new concepts, such as electric flux (a measure of electric field strength and direction across a surface in 3D space). This law can also be employed and manipulated in an integral form, so integration becomes a key technique in this field.

As an illustration: if we rub a balloon to make it statically charged and put it in a sealed box, we can measure the total charge on the balloon just by measuring the electric field across each side of the box, even if we don't know how close the balloon is to the edge (which we might have thought, based on Coulomb's Law,[66] would affect the measurement).

**Ampère's law:** An equation that allows you to relate the ***permeability*** and current in a loop to the magnetic field.

**Permeability** is a measure of the ability of a material to support the formation of a magnetic field within itself, and is another new concept introduced in university-level physics.

66 That the repulsive or attractive force from a charge is inversely proportional to the square of its distance from you.

**Biot-Savart law:** An equation that describes the magnetic field created by a current-carrying wire; it allows you to calculate the field's strength at any given point around the wire.

## Special Relativity

*A new topic explored at university that is crucial to the subsequent (optional) study of general relativity and quantum mechanics.*

Special relativity considers the physical effects that occur when particles move at speeds approaching the speed of light. You learn to draw space-time diagrams (see our sample drawing) that show how the distance an object travels (or the time it takes to travel) will appear to be different depending on the motion of the observer. This leads to some astounding results; for example, to some observers, a pole of a greater length than the longest dimension of a barn can fit entirely within the barn. You'll study how to calculate the discrepancies between results observed by different observers using a family of ***co-ordinate transformations*** called ***Lorentz transformations***.

A **co-ordinate transformation** is a change of co-ordinates that models the point of view of a moving observer. For instance, suppose a particle $P$ is at $(0, 0)$ in the $x$-$y$ plane, and an observer is moving along the $x$-axis at speed $v$, starting at $(0, 0)$. When we think about what the observer sees, we take them to be using a different set of co-ordinates in which they are always at the origin. From their point of view, $P$ will be moving to the left at speed $v$, so if we don't take relativity into account they would measure its position at time $t$ as $(-vt, 0)$. So, we've performed a transformation in changing $P$'s position from $(0, 0)$ to $(-vt, 0)$. This is not a Lorentz transformation yet because we've ignored relativity – the answer should really be $\left(-\frac{vt}{\sqrt{1-\frac{v^2}{c^2}}}, 0\right)$ – but you'll see all the details at uni!

If you're interested in exploring special relativity, investigate the *twin paradox* or *the barn paradox*.[67]

67 See oxbridgeformula.co.uk/bonus-chapter for more information.

*"This is an example of a space-time diagram from my notes"*
–Student, Physics, Oxford

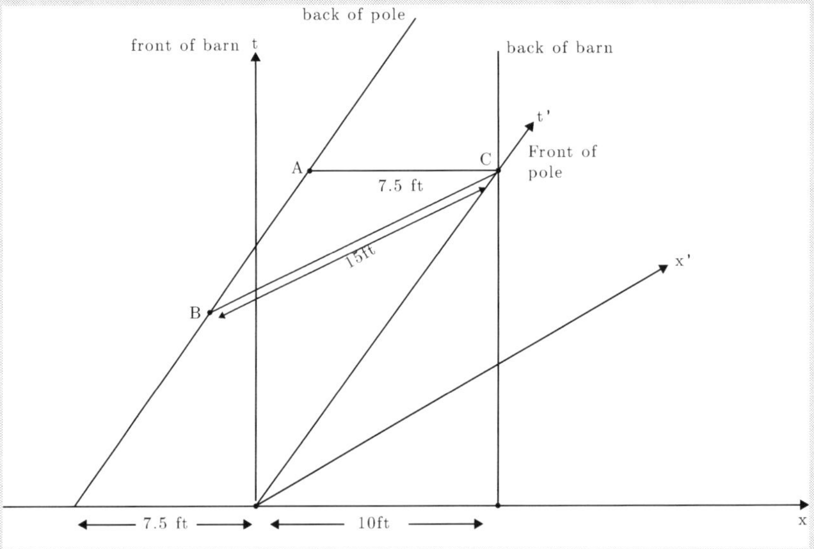


This diagram shows a 15ft pole fitting into a 10ft barn! Don't worry if it makes no sense yet, as you'll learn all about it at uni. However, if you're interested, here's a brief explanation:

Each point in the diagram represents a point in space at a particular time. The point C is the point where the pole meets the back of the barn at the time when it reaches it. In the barn's frame of reference (defined by the vertical t-axis and horizontal x-axis) the pole's other end is at A at that time, which is 7.5ft from C, so it fits in the barn. Whereas, in the pole's frame of reference (defined by the skewed t'-and x'-axes), its other end is at B at that time, which is 15ft from C, so it's still 15ft long.

You could say the reason it works is that the barn and pole disagree about which of points A and B is at the same time as C. This is called 'relativity of simultaneity'.

## Circuit Theory

*At university level, you build upon the concepts you learnt at A Level such as resistance and capacitance, but apply more sophisticated and more general mathematical techniques to them.*

You'll study the use of summation, integration and differentiation in investigating circuits, as well as the growth and decay of currents in circuits—for instance, how to derive the time constant for capacitor-resistor circuits. The circuit symbols you learnt at A Level will be used in circuit theory at university, so make sure you're familiar with them! The course also introduces you to key concepts such as ***inductance*** and ***impedance***.

**Inductance** is an electrical component's capacity to create an emf in response to changing current. This could either be an emf across itself ('self inductance') or in another part of the circuit ('mutual inductance').

**Impedance** is a generalisation of resistance for circuits with changing current. Notably, its value can be a complex number.

*"Imaginary numbers are introduced obscurely and abstractly in Maths A Level. Circuit theory is one of the first times you see imaginary numbers applied directly to physics."* –Jake, Physics, Oxford

## Waves and Optics

*Optics is featured in some A-level syllabi whilst absent in others. It describes the fundamental properties of how light behaves, and will build up from a few foundational principles due to the disparity in students' prior knowledge.*

In your first-year Optics course, you'll look at familiar properties such as reflection, refraction and diffraction. You'll also study the effects of light having wave-like properties. Although it may not introduce any more theory than is included at A Level (for instance, you'll still use the lens equation and ray diagrams), it does involve applying it in a wider variety of cases. For example, you'll study combinations of converging and diverging lenses, variously shaped mirrors, and how lenses are used in telescopes and medical devices.

First year optics has a greater focus on geometric optics—that is, treating light rays as straight lines, using mirrors and lenses, etc. From your second year, you'll primarily study wave optics—treating light as a propagating electromagnetic wave that can diffract and interfere.

An example of a question from this course would be:

*Describe the conditions necessary to observe optical interference fringes in Young's double-slit experiment.*

# Maths

*As you've probably realised by now, maths is a hugely important part of a Physics degree. In order to build up your mathematical toolbox for the later years of your degree, you'll have two compulsory maths papers in your first year. They will both build on your A-Level knowledge and also introduce you to entirely new fields of mathematics, together with their applications in physics.*

**Maths exam 1**

Exam 1 includes[68]:

- Differential equations (first- and second-order) and their application to forced vibrations of mechanical or electrical resonant systems
- Complex numbers (including Argand diagrams and de Moivre's theorem)
- Vector algebra and its applications in classical mechanics
- Eigenvalues, eigenvectors and matrix diagonalisation.

*"The notion of vector spaces and linear algebra[69] can seem abstract at first, but is incredibly useful for quantum mechanics, which is a big part of the second year."* –Jake, Physics, Oxford

**Maths exam 2**

Exam 2 includes content such as:

- Fundamental ideas about series expansions, evaluating limits and convergence of series

68 These all build upon Further Pure A-Level knowledge. If you haven't studied Further Maths, these are all topics you might want to read up on before your degree starts.

69 See page 11 to read more about vector spaces and linear algebra.

- Differentiation techniques, including ***partial differentiation*** and Taylor series expansions to explore maxima, minima and saddle points[70]
- Integration (including double integrals) in Cartesian, polar and other specified coordinate systems
- Performing coordinate transformations using ***Jacobians***
- Basic probability theory
- Derivation of the 1-dimensional ***wave equation***, its solutions and applications.

A **partial derivative** of a function $f(x, y)$ with respect to $x$ is the result of differentiating it as if $y$ were a constant rather than potentially depending on $x$. For instance, at A-level you would differentiate $f(x, y) = xy^2$ implicity to get $y^2 + 2xy\frac{dx}{du}$ , whereas the partial derivative with respect to $x$ is just $y^2$.

A **Jacobian** represents the scaling that takes place when you change from one coordinate system to another. You may have come across a 1D version of this when doing integration by substitution. If you use the substitution $u = x^2$, you would usually 'replace' the $dx$ with $\frac{dx}{du}du$. Here, the $\frac{dx}{du}$ is the Jacobian. In 2D and higher dimensions, the Jacobian is the determinant of a matrix, where each entry of the matrix is a partial derivative of the change of coordinates or 'substitution'. For instance, converting from two Cartesian coordinates ($x$ and $y$) to two polar coordinates ($r$ and $\theta$) requires a $2 \times 2$ Jacobian matrix, and its determinant is used to prove that the expression for an area in polar coordinates is $\int \frac{1}{2} r^2 d\theta$ instead of $\int y dx$ in Cartesian coordinates. You may recognise this from A-Level Further Maths.

The **wave equation** is a partial differential equation that is used to describe waves. For a simple example, suppose $P(x, t)$ is the pressure at a distance $x$ along a tube, such as a musical instrument, at time $t$. The wave equation for a sound wave in this tube would be $\frac{\partial^2 P}{\partial t^2} = k\frac{\partial^2 P}{\partial x^2}$,

70 A saddle point on a surface looks like a lowest point if you're going in one direction, but looks like a highest point if you go in another. For instance, a horse-rider's saddle bends upwards in front and behind them, but downwards to the left and right where their legs are, so the centre is a saddle point.

where k is a constant, $\frac{\partial^2 P}{\partial t^2}$ is the result of taking the partial derivative twice with respect to $t$, and $\frac{\partial^2 P}{\partial t^2}$ is the same but with respect to $x$.

## Practical assessment

Each week, you'll be expected to complete practical projects that contribute to your mark at the end of your first year. You'll need to evaluate and understand your results and use statistical analysis to present them.

You take part in labs based on topics from of the main courses covered in the first year. Here are examples of the labs for each course:

- **Electronics**
  *Example lab: Excitation of circuits by step emfs*
  You study 'equivalent' circuits, which are simplified models of real circuits that replicate an aspect of their behaviour, such as what happens when you apply a particular emf. In this lab, your model circuits are excited by emfs that 'step' (jump abruptly) from one steady value to another.
- **General physics**
  *Example lab: Radioactivity and statistics*
  The first part of the experiment uses random radioactive decay to create models of different probability distributions. The second is on the properties of alpha, beta and gamma radioactivity, and how they can be measured in the lab.
- **Optics**
  *Example lab: Grating monochromator*
  The monochromator is an instrument used to detect ***spectral lines***. In this lab, you calibrate it via an observation of mercury vapour and then use it to investigate the ***Balmer lines*** of atomic hydrogen and calculate the ***Rydberg constant***.

**Spectral Lines:** Each type of atom emits or absorbs light at specific wavelengths. A spectrum is a graph of light intensity against wavelength, and a line appears where a specific wavelength is emitted or absorbed more than others. Locating different spectral lines allows you to tell what elements are present in the material you are looking at. **Balmer lines** and the **Rydberg constant** are specific features of the spectrum of atomic hydrogen.

- **Electrostatics and magnetism**
  *Example lab: Self and mutual inductance and Faraday's law of induction*
  You'll explore the self-inductor as a circuit element, using air-filled coils and ferrite core inductors. You'll explore the relationship between self and mutual inductance. (See page 154 for a definition of inductance.)

**Computing labs** also form a major part of the practical course in the first year. No previous computing experience is required. You'll learn to use the MATLAB language[71], and you'll be tested via two-day computing projects. Computing labs are massively important because you'll use the skills you learn in MATLAB for data analysis in the main practical labs.

Each day in a physics lab or computer lab counts for an equal amount of **'lab credit'**. There are 17 days of labs available and you need a total of 12 days of lab credit to pass the year.

We've described the core of first-year Physics at Oxford, but you'll also have the opportunity to study short options including complex numbers, astrophysics and quantum mechanics. In later years, the options become more advanced and more diverse. Some examples of courses from later years are thermodynamics, fluid dynamics, climatology, biophysics, nuclear physics, and general relativity.

As you can see, the Physics course builds upon pre-existing knowledge but reworks the way in which you study physics, focusing on derivations and maths—not just the accumulation of facts. However, if you love both physics and maths at school, it's a good indication you'll enjoy the content of the degree.

## 9.4: Doing a Physics degree (a typical work week)

This isn't meant to scare you... but, due to the large amount of content as well as the practical lab hours, your Physics degree definitely won't be a walk in the park! In your first year you'll likely have:

71 A programming language that is designed to enable you to perform complex mathematical calculations, such as evaluating integrals and multiplying matrices, with relatively short commands.

- 8–10 one-hour lectures per week, covering either mathematical methods or physics content.
- Two small-group sessions (tutorials or classes) per week.
- Eight hours of independent study per hour of tutorial or class. This is normally centred around completing a problem sheet. You'll also need to spend time looking over lecture notes and doing extra reading in order to give the problems your best shot.

## Problem sheets

Problem sheets consolidate the material covered in lectures by seeing how effectively you can apply the material to problems yourself. They may start with basic questions you can answer quickly, but will ramp up in difficulty, ending in more involved questions that require more time and often multiple attempts. They're meant to be challenging, as that's how you'll improve your problem-solving abilities and learn what makes for a good solution. You won't be expected to get full marks on all problem sheets—but your tutors will want to see that you've made a good attempt at every problem.

## Tutorials vs. classes

A tutorial (two or three students) is more intense than a class (more than three students). At the start, your tutor will hand you back your marked problem sheet, and you'll spend most of the time going through the questions that you or your tutorial partners struggled with. A tutorial will typically be more interactive and personalised than a class. As a part of a tutorial or class, you may be asked to explain concepts or present solutions on a whiteboard.

Classes are generally more relaxed, because there are more students present (less attention on you![72]) and your tutor is more likely to go through the problem sheet on the board. They might include all the Physics students from your year in your college, or a group of students from various colleges.

## Labs

Labs form the backbone of the Physics course because they provide an opportunity to develop a concrete understanding of the theoretical content covered in lectures. You'll have 6–8 hours of labs every week, and will be assessed on how successfully you follow the plan for the experiment that is given to you, as well as your post-lab write up.

72 Not that tutorials are scary—they're actually quite fun if you've done the work!

### Independent study

As with all Oxbridge degrees, Physics requires a great deal of independent study. Lectures will introduce you to the content, but you'll be expected to develop a comprehensive understanding of this content through reading textbooks and lecture notes, solving exercises and doing problem sheets.

> *"I didn't quite appreciate the amount of self-study that goes into an Oxford Physics degree. Most of the deep dive into a topic takes place outside of lectures and tutorials."* –Jack, Physics, Oxford

## 9.5: Character profiles (spot the successful applicant)

So, what does the ideal Physics candidate look like? Here are some profiles of different applicants to illustrate the key traits sought by admissions tutors. In this section, we present three applicants; one of them is successful. We will discuss what makes that candidate successful and identify the hurdles where the others stumble.

While discussing the candidates, we'll talk about the different steps of the application process. You can read more about these starting on page 216.

### Applicant 1: John 19 (re-applying to Oxford)

**Before interview:**

- John is currently on a gap year. He achieved A*A*A in his Maths, Physics and Further Maths A Levels, respectively.
- John is travelling and playing gigs in his gap year and taking some time off from studying.
- He does some preparation for the PAT, but mostly thinks he will be okay considering he got an A* in his Physics A Level.
- He did a lot of preparation and extra study when he first wrote his personal statement back in Year 13, and re-submits that original personal statement (which he and his teachers thought was strong).

**In his interviews:**

- In his interviews, John manages to complete the basic parts of all the problems, recalling some of the information from his A Levels.
- However, as he has not recently done any interview practice, he struggles as he gets deeper into questions that begin to veer further from familiar territory.
- He tries to bring in some facts and knowledge he accumulated from his A Levels that he thinks may be relevant, but doesn't manage to directly apply it to the problems at hand.
- When asked about a book he listed on his personal statement, it has been a long time since he's read it and he can't discuss its subject matter coherently.

## Applicant 2: Zara, 17 (Oxford)

**Before interview:**

- Zara is predicted 2 A*s and 2 As in her A Levels: Maths, Physics, Biology and Further Maths.
- She particularly loves physics and regularly competes in the Physics Olympiad, in which she scores well.
- She has recently completed work experience in a lab investigating the stresses on ball bearings in a rotor, using her knowledge of circular motion and elastic forces.
- To prepare for the PAT, she does all the past papers and hones her skills by solving other problems she finds in the ENGAA and NSAA[73] as well as extra questions from the Oxbridge Formula website.
- She verbally explains some of her solutions from these papers to her parents, preparing herself for having to explain her reasoning when it comes to interviews.

**In her interviews:**

- Zara faces a difficult question about planetary motion, something she is yet to do in-depth at A Level. However, she tries to apply principles she has learnt at school such as conservation of energy, and listens to the interviewer's guidance. Although she doesn't complete all the parts, she makes a lot of progress in solving the problem.

73 See page 240 for more information on the ENGAA and NSAA.

- Her mathematics is sound, and she enjoys working through the differentiation problem thrown at her.
- She engages with her interviewers, listening to their advice and taking it on board as best she can.

## Applicant 3: Tomo, 18 (Oxford)

**Before interview:**

- Tomo is predicted all A*s in Maths, Physics and Further Maths, and does little extra work to prepare for the PAT, as he is confident in his maths and physics abilities.
- He decides to apply to Oxford because all his teachers tell him to but has little desire to put in work beyond what he already does for school.
- He reads a couple of books his teachers direct him towards, and writes about them on his personal statement.
- He doesn't start to prepare for his interviews until after he knows he's been invited. He does manage to look over all his A-Level content, especially maths and physics, and revises late into the night before his first interview.

**In his interviews:**

- In his interviews, Tomo is shocked by how different the problems are compared to A-Level questions.
- Having not done much extra preparation, he stumbles with problems quite early on and seems to quickly give up hope of solving them.
- When asked why he applied for Physics, he simply answers that he thought he was good enough and it would have been a shame not to.

**Who is the best candidate?**

Zara is the best candidate here. She is well-prepared and passionate about the subject: a potent mix. She is receptive to feedback throughout the interview and engages with the interviewers, meaning she becomes an attractive student to teach.

**What did John do wrong?**

- ✘ Although John's grades and credentials may be strong, he showed a lack of motivation to continue exploring physics in his gap year or to do something physics-related. This contributes to his physics and maths skills declining.
- ✘ As his personal statement was recycled material that was not fully relevant to his current situation, the admissions officers could see that he wasn't driven to continue exploring the subject. Try and discuss your gap year if you're taking one, and relate the experiences you've had to the course you're applying for.
- ✘ He didn't realise that the PAT requires preparation regardless of whether or not you've completed your A Levels.
- ✘ The moral of this story is: if you're going to take a gap year and reapply for a technical subject like Physics, it's crucial to spend at least some of your time continuing to explore your subject[74]. You want your gap year to be an opportunity to strengthen your application—not weaken it.

**What did Tomo do wrong?**

- ✘ It was clear to the interviewers that Tomo's motivation was more about being able to tell his friends that he was accepted by Oxford, and less about actually studying Physics.
- ✘ An Oxford Physics degree is a lot of work, and you should be deeply engaged with (and enthralled by) the subject if you're thinking of applying. Tomo's bare minimum preparation did not convey this.
- ✘ The fact that Tomo waited until he knew he'd be interviewed contributed to his lack of time for preparation. He was competing with far more motivated students who didn't need the excuse of an interview to seek out and tackle challenging physics problems.
- ✘ Good A-Level grades and teacher references aren't enough. You need to show the interviewers that you have embarked on independent study and are keen to further your understanding of the subject. Almost every applicant will have similarly good grades and references, so you really have to make yourself stand out.

For more on the application process for physical sciences, see page 216.

74 We're not saying everything you do has to be related to your subject—it's about striking a balance.

# Chapter 10: Physics & Philosophy

## 10.1: Why Physics & Philosophy?

Physics and philosophy appear, at first glance, to be two very different subjects. However, there's a rich overlap between them. If you're interested in the 'big questions', in examining not only the foundations of our universe but also the very methods we use to investigate them—this may be the course for you.

Some of the questions this course seeks to answer include:

- What methods are acceptable in science?
- What are the differences between mathematical knowledge and knowledge based on experience?
- What does it mean for one event to cause another?
- Is a physical object simply a collection of particles?
- Could space exist if there were no objects to occupy it?
- What does it mean for an event to have a probability $p$ of occurring?
- How can we learn the laws of physics that resulted in the Big Bang when there are no other examples of Big Bangs to study?

This course may appeal to you if you study Physics A Level alongside an essay-based subject such as English, History or even Philosophy itself[75]. Physics & Philosophy might be for you if you're strongly interested in the history of science and/or the philosophy of science.

It's also the course for you if you want to leave with a very wide range of skills and be able to move into one of a very large number of fields after you graduate. You'll leave with experience of mathematics, coding, lab work, problem-solving, analysis of texts, essay writing and verbal debate/discussion—all in the context of some of the hardest questions known to humanity.

75 Be aware, however, that the philosophical content does not follow directly on from the A-Level Philosophy syllabus.

## 10.2: How do you apply for Physics & Philosophy?

Physics & Philosophy is offered at Oxford, but not Cambridge. The typical A-Level offer is A*AA, with an A* in at least one of Maths, Further Maths, or Physics. Physics and Maths are compulsory subjects, and it's recommended to take mechanics modules in Maths and Further Maths if possible. The typical IB offer is 39, with 766 at Higher Level, including a 7 in Maths or Physics. On average, around 1 in 11 applicants will be successful.

Although it's not essential to have an A Level in a humanities subject, essay-writing is a large part of this degree—so honing these skills to A-Level standard will prove invaluable.

The application process for Physics & Philosophy is very similar to the one for Physics. You'll sit the PAT and have physics interviews. The differences are that:

- Your personal statement needs to show an understanding of the philosophy side of the degree
- You'll have at least one interview in philosophy. See page 446 for more information.

In your third year, you can choose to leave with a BA or continue to a fourth year (the integrated master's) and leave with an MPhysPhil. You can also switch directly to a 1-year master's in Maths and Theoretical Physics for your fourth year and leave with an MMathPhys.

## 10.3: What's it like to study Physics & Philosophy?

Although you may appreciate the intersection (and harmony) between the two subjects, it may be difficult to picture what it's really like to study them both alongside each other. We've included a breakdown of the first-year Oxford course to give you a feeling for how the course operates and how the two disciplines interact. If you'd like more information about any of these, we've included references to other parts of the book that discuss them in more detail.

In your first year, your physics courses are split into three exam papers:

- Mechanics and Special Relativity
- Differential Equations and Matrix Algebra
- Calculus and Waves.

These are taken directly from the Physics syllabus—you study the content and sit the exams alongside students studying straight Physics. For more details about the physics included in these courses see page 150.

At the same time, you study philosophy to prepare for two exam papers. One of these exams comprises two topics:

- Elements of Deductive Logic
- General Philosophy.

These courses are also studied by those taking Maths & Philosophy, and details can be found on page 45. You'll also study:

## Introductory Philosophy of Physics

In this course, you'll read and analyse the ***Leibniz-Clarke correspondence***. This means studying a historical text, but with the help of a modern translation and commentaries, and in a way that relates the topics to modern debates.

The **Leibniz-Clarke correspondence** was a famous scientific and philosophical debate held in a series of letters between Leibniz and Clarke in the early 18th century. The exchange began as a result of Leibniz's criticisms of Isaac Newton, who was defended by his follower Clarke. Their discussion ranged across topics including the nature of space, the nature of causation, the role of God in physics and whether all motion is relative.

After your first year, the course becomes more flexible. The advantage of doing a joint honours course is that you get to choose your favourite bits from both courses! Throughout your studies (up until your fourth year) you'll have a roughly 50/50 split between physics and philosophy, with flexibility as to which modules you choose within each. There will, of course, be some compulsory courses. For example, everyone has to study the following physics courses:

- Thermal Physics
- Electromagnetism
- Quantum Physics.

Your physics options will include:

- Subatomic Physics
- General Relativity and Cosmology
- Classical Mechanics.

Similarly, the compulsory philosophy courses include:

- Philosophy of Science
- Philosophy of Special Relativity
- Philosophy of Quantum Mechanics.

Your philosophy options include:

- Feminism and Philosophy
- Philosophy of Mathematics
- Early Modern Philosophy
- Knowledge and Reality.

If you're continuing into the fourth year to get an MPhysPhil, it will involve completing three research projects on particular areas in either discipline that interest you. You'll be able to split the balance in any way you like—you can do 100% physics or 100% philosophy if you choose.

# Chapter 11: Engineering

## 11.1: Why Engineering?

Engineering involves applying science, maths and practical reasoning to real-world problems. It's a lively discipline, evolving every time a new microchip is developed or a new design for an oil tanker is suggested. Engineering never rests and will always be essential to science, industry, and society more broadly. It is, therefore, a highly employable subject to study at university.

> *"A high level view of Engineering is that it's about learning the skillset where you can look at a problem and find a pathway to a solution. Engineering is very iterative. Something I've learnt is that you never ever ever get to the optimal solution the first time you try to solve something—you'll most likely start with a brute-force basic solution and then iterate it. Everyone will tackle problems in different ways and still get to the answer. You might draw a series of diagrams to find out how a mechanism works, or write down a bunch of equations and solve them algebraically, or use software to simulate a mechanism and iterate through to the solution."* –Pranay, Engineering, Cambridge

This may be the course for you if:

- ❑ **You enjoy maths and physics:** While Engineering is a practical discipline, there's no getting away from the fact that it requires a very broad theoretical skillset, drawing on the maths and physics (and chemistry and biology!) you learn at school. A significant proportion of the written work you'll do will involve solving problems using maths and physics techniques learnt in lectures. Unlike a 'pure' science or maths degree, however, you won't be expected to be able to *prove* theorems, but rather to *use* them. If you love mechanics in A-Level Maths or the mathematical parts of A Level Physics, it's a good sign you could enjoy studying Engineering too.

- ❑ **You want to put the theory into practice:** The learning process for an engineer is very hands on. If you think too much theory will bore you and you want to be able to apply what you've learnt in a practical way, an Engineering degree definitely offers this. At Oxbridge, you'll typically have around 4 hours per week of practicals (known as labs) and be exposed to plenty of software packages for design, manufacturing, analysis of materials, and more. You'll have access to tools like 3D printers, which you can use for projects as part of your course, or even any other personal projects you might have in mind.
- ❑ **You like the idea of designing something others will find useful:** If you feel a sense of satisfaction from creating a 'final product' which can be used to solve real world problems, Engineering certainly fits the bill. Over the course of your degree, some of your practical projects will have briefs relating to problems that the university's industrial partners are facing right at that moment. Problem-solving in a practical context requires a high degree of creativity, which the Oxbridge engineering courses explicitly aim to instil in you.
- ❑ **You enjoy working with others:** If you don't want your degree to just mean sitting in your room, alone, thinking, and you enjoy collaborating with others instead, it's a good sign you might be well suited to Engineering. Teamwork is a huge part of being an engineer, and during your degree you'll need to work with other students, both in your regular practicals, but also over the course of extended one-off projects which include collaborative design as well as a practical element. These will give you vital communication and presentation skills.
- ❑ **You want a career as an engineer:** If you specifically want to be an engineer, then doing an Engineering degree will put you at a particular advantage. That said, with the vast array of skills you'll develop, you can do almost anything with an Engineering degree—from software development to finance to academic study to entrepreneurship. Both Oxford and Cambridge offer courses on business and management (within an engineering context) as part of the degree, giving you the skills to lead a team of engineers.
- ❑ **You want to keep your options open:** The advantage of studying Engineering at Cambridge or Oxford is that both courses start with an incredibly broad overview of the entire discipline. At many other universities, you have to choose which branch of engineering to specialise in when you apply. In contrast, at Oxbridge, you begin your degree by learning the fundamental aspects of ***mechanical*** and ***electrical***

***engineering***, allowing you to specialise in one of a highly varied selection of engineering fields later in the course.

**Mechanical engineering:** The discipline within engineering that studies mechanical systems. This includes crucial fields such as construction, transportation and manufacturing. Examples of mechanical engineering in practice include designing a wind turbine, testing the response of a racing car's suspension to different stresses, and choosing the right material and manufacturing process for the bell of a rocket.

**Electrical engineering:** Focuses upon the design of electrical systems. You learn how electricity can be used for energy transmission, telecommunications and automation, as well as other topics within electromagnetism. Examples of electrical engineering in practice include designing transformers for the national grid, constructing a mobile phone network, and creating sensors for a plane's autopilot.

Engineering at both Oxford and Cambridge is a four-year master's course and you leave with the accreditation required to become a chartered engineer. In the first two years, you study many different fields of engineering, with few options. In your last two years, you can start to specialise. You leave with an MEng.

## 11.2: Engineering: Oxford vs. Cambridge

Engineering is offered at both Oxford and Cambridge[76], so to help you choose which university is best for you, we've put together a table outlining the similarities and differences between the two courses.

At Cambridge, you can also apply for Engineering and move into Chemical Engineering later. See Chapter 15 on page 213 for more details.

76 At Oxford, the degree is technically called Engineering Science, but don't be put off by the difference in names—the Oxford course isn't any less practical, and the Cambridge course isn't any less scientific.

| OXFORD | CAMBRIDGE |
|---|---|
| **Prerequisites:** Maths, with Further Maths highly recommended. You must also sit the PAT (the Physics Aptitude Test). | **Prerequisites:** Maths, with Further Maths recommended. Cambridge has its own admissions test for Engineering: the ENGAA. There is, however, some discrepancy between colleges; some require Further Maths, or even STEP.[77] Some colleges also have at-interview tests. |
| **Offer:** The typical A-Level offer is A*A*A, with an A* in Maths and a second A* in either Further Maths or Physics. The typical IB offer is 40, with 776 at Higher Level, including 7s in Maths and Physics. You can also apply with a Level-3 Diploma in Engineering, if you take A-Level Physics too. | **Offer:** The typical A-Level offer at Cambridge is similar to that at Oxford: A*A*A, with an A* in Maths. The typical IB offer is 40-42, with 776 at Higher Level, including Maths and Physics. You can also apply with vocational qualifications in Engineering if you take A-Level Maths too. |
| **Statistics:** Of those who apply, 48% are interviewed and 18% are successful. This means fewer than 1 in 5 applicants is offered a place and achieve the required grades. | **Statistics:** Of those who apply, 1 in 7 is successful, meaning they are both offered a place and achieve the required grades. |
| **First-year studies:** You'll study:<br>■ Structures and Mechanics<br>■ Electrical and Information Engineering<br>■ Energy and the Environment<br>■ Mathematics<br>■ Practical work | **First-year studies:** The content is divided into 5 sections:<br>■ Mechanical Engineering<br>■ Structures and Materials<br>■ Electrical Engineering<br>■ Mathematical Methods<br>■ Coursework and labs |
| **Later years:** In your second year at Oxford you'll have compulsory courses in the same five subject areas as in first year. In your third year, you'll have lots of options (of which you specialise in five) and | **Later years:** At Cambridge, your second year is completely mapped out for you just like the first, and covers the same subject areas, plus Information Engineering and Business Economics. In your third |

77 See page 80 for more information about STEP.

| OXFORD | CAMBRIDGE |
|---|---|
| some compulsory modules such as Engineering in Society and a group design project. In your fourth year, you complete a major research project and six options chosen from within any of these eight specialisms:<br><br>■ Biomedical Engineering<br>■ Chemical and Process Engineering<br>■ Civil and Offshore Engineering<br>■ Control Engineering<br>■ Electrical and Opto-electronic Engineering<br>■ Information Engineering<br>■ Solid Materials and Mechanical Engineering<br>■ Thermofluids and Turbomachinery | and fourth years, you're able to specialise within a variety of engineering disciplines:<br><br>■ Aerospace and Aerothermal Engineering<br>■ Bioengineering<br>■ Civil, Structural and Environmental Engineering<br>■ Electrical and Electronic Engineering<br>■ Electrical and Information Sciences<br>■ Energy, Sustainability and the Environment<br>■ Information and Computer Engineering<br>■ Instrumentation and Control<br>■ Mechanical Engineering<br>■ General Engineering<br><br>You'll also have several industrial placements. In your fourth year, as at Oxford, you complete a major research project. |
| **Style of teaching:**<br>Lectures: 10 per week<br>Tutorials: 2 per week<br>Lab hours: Up to 5 hours per week. | **Style of teaching:**<br>Lectures: 12 per week<br>Supervisions: 2–5 per week<br>Lab hours: 4 per week in weeks with lectures, 21 per week in weeks without lectures. |

**Top Tip**

*Some colleges encourage **gap years** for Engineering applicants, some discourage them and some are neutral—so it's best to check with the college(s) you're thinking of applying to find out their stance.*

## Choosing between Oxford and Cambridge

As you can see from the above, there are few obvious practical differences between the Engineering courses at Oxford and Cambridge. They both start general and only allow you to specialise after two years. They are both highly technical and intellectually demanding. They both put less emphasis on industrial placements and more on academic prowess than engineering at other universities.

So how can you choose which is for you?

- ❑ **Course size:** Cambridge admits more than twice as many Engineering students each year as Oxford. It's the second largest Cambridge course. If you value meeting and exchanging ideas with many other students, Cambridge might be for you; if you value being part of a tight-knit group, Oxford might suit you better.
- ❑ **Different specialisms:** Cambridge offers one specialisation that Oxford doesn't—Aerospace Engineering. Oxford offers an 'entrepreneurship pathway', whereas Cambridge allows you to move into Manufacturing Engineering after two years. Both will teach you about management in an engineering context, but the Oxford course is more about entrepreneurship, and the Cambridge course is more about working in or leading a team of engineers. See page 180 for more information on the different specialisms.
- ❑ **Future plans:** Cambridge Engineering graduates are more likely than their Oxford counterparts to go into engineering (O: 14%, C: 45%) or IT and telecoms (O: 7%, C: 15%). On the other hand, Oxford graduates are more likely to go into further study (O: 21%, C: 12%) or business and administration (O: 20%, C: 5%).
- ❑ **Different cities:** If you can't decide on the basis of the courses themselves, why not visit both to get a feel of the different atmospheres and decide which suits you best? You might also want to visit individual colleges at both to see if you fall in love with one.

> *"When I visited the Oxford Engineering department on the open day, I was really impressed with the facilities they had, as well as how lovely the staff were there. I also visited Cambridge at their open day, and as impressive as their department was, I personally felt Oxford was more welcoming. I also preferred Oxford as a city over Cambridge, as everything is closer together. The collegiate system also really appealed to me as you live in these close-knit communities, giving you more of a sense of belonging."* –Sophie, Engineering, Oxford

*"I didn't really even consider Oxford because a lot more students from my school had gone to Cambridge in the past, so I was able to learn more about the application processes from them. The main thing that confirmed the decision for me was visiting my college at an open day. It just felt right."* –Student, Engineering, Cambridge

# 11.3: What's it like to study Engineering at Oxbridge?

Both Oxbridge Engineering degrees are intense and the work is challenging. Here's a breakdown of the first year of the course at both unis to give you a taste of the content you could be studying as an engineer.

## First-year courses at Oxford and Cambridge

The first years of both courses are designed to give you an insight into the discipline of Engineering as a whole.

*"I almost didn't bother to apply to Cambridge because I thought any other top uni would be as good for Engineering and easier to get into. But I learned that Oxford and Cambridge are the places to go if you want to start with general study before specialising. I'm so glad we started general as I initially wanted to specialise in electronic engineering, but I discovered a passion for aerodynamics during my degree."* –Student, Engineering, Cambridge

### Mechanical and Structural Engineering

*Falls under 'Structures and Mechanics' at Oxford; split between 'Mechanical Engineering' and 'Structures and Materials' at Cambridge*

What will you study within these courses?

- **Newtonian mechanics**: extends the mechanics you're learning at school to handle rotating bodies, variable forces, and variable mass. Similar to the Classical Mechanics course for Oxford physicists—see page 150 for more information.

- **Thermodynamics**: introduces you to the laws relating heat, mechanical work, and entropy[78], and their applications in studying heat flows and the operation of simple machines like turbines.
- **Fluid mechanics**: studies flows in liquids and gases, and the behaviour of objects moving through them, introducing you to the physics behind lift, drag, and pressure.
- **Vibrations and damping**: extends A-Level ideas about springs, elasticity, and simple harmonic motion to investigate systems that are damped or driven, and oscillations in two or more dimensions.
- **Design of structures**: looks at the way in which different kinds of structure (including beams and jointed frameworks of multiple beams, columns, cables, pressure vessels, etc.) support the loads applied to them and bend and twist under forces.
- **Materials**: analyses the different classes of engineering materials, like metals, ceramics, glasses, polymers, and composites. You'll learn to understand and measure properties like compressive vs. tensile strength, and mechanisms of failure such as fracture, wear, and deformation.

## Electrical Engineering

*Split between the 'Electrical and **Information Engineering**' and 'Energy' courses at Oxford; simply 'Electrical Engineering' at Cambridge*

> **Information engineering** is the study of systems that must receive and organise large amounts of information, such as a digital model of a large business and its inputs and outputs.

What will you study within these courses?

- **The physics of electromagnetism**: you'll study both electromagnetic fields in general, and they ways in which they produce the phenomena of current, voltage, capacitance, inductance and impedance in circuits. See page 151 and page 154 for a discussion of some important concepts in electromagnetism.
- **Circuits**: how to analyse and design both AC and DC circuits containing components such as inductors, capacitors, amplifiers, and transistors.

78 Entropy is notoriously difficult to understand, but it can be thought of as measuring a) given a system's temperature, how much of its energy is unavailable to do work, b) how uniformly the system's energy is spread across its parts, and c) how 'disordered' the system's internal state is.

- **Digital circuits**: an introduction to the theory of formal logic, binary arithmetic, Boolean algebra, and logic gates, together with their application in designing and analysing digital circuits (i.e. circuits that perform calculations on inputs that are '1's and '0's). See page 32 for information on digital circuits and their theory.

## Energy and the Environment

*Studied at Oxford only*

Examines how different systems affect the environment in different ways, and how we can ensure future sustainability. Sustainability is an important theme of the Oxford course.

## Maths

*Called 'Mathematical Methods' at Cambridge and 'Mathematics' at Oxford. Both have similar content.*

At first, you'll study complex numbers, vectors, matrices, and eigenvectors and eigenvalues. You'll also study probability, including discrete and continuous probability distributions, conditional probability, and hypothesis testing. These are similar to pure topics in A-Level Further Maths, plus statistics topics from Maths and Further Maths, but here you'll complete them in one eight-week term rather than a whole year, which you would get for Further Maths.

Later, you'll study more advanced maths, particularly calculus and its applications. You'll be introduced to multivariable calculus and partial differential equations. See page 15 and page 156 for more information about these. There will be a particular focus on techniques for analysing signals (e.g. radio waves). These include ***step functions***, ***impulse functions***, ***convolution***, and ***Fourier series***.

A **step function** changes discontinuously between two constant values. For instance, the function $f(x)$ such that $f(x) = -1$ for $x < 0$ and $f(x) = 1$ for $x \geq 0$. An **impulse function** describes a sudden change to a system. You'll see a relationship between idealised instantaneous impulses and step functions.

A **convolution** is an operation that is most often applied to waves and can be thought of as combining or averaging two waves.

**Fourier series** are infinite sums of sine and cosine functions that are used to approximate other functions.

> *"Further Maths A Level will help you hit the ground running with this course because many of the techniques follow on from that content."*

**Coursework/labs**

> *"Our coursework counts towards our final grade for the year, but via standard credit, which means that as long as you turn up to every practical and meet an adequate standard, you get full marks for the coursework for that year. It's a good way to be able to experiment to learn the basic skills without fearing you'll harm your final mark if whatever you try doesn't quite work out."* –Latoya, Engineering, Cambridge

Coursework and labs come in five main varieties:

- **Short 'turn up and do' experiments:** You'll perform an experiment with your lab partner and analyse the results in the form of a lab report using some of the physics and maths techniques you've learned recently. Some examples include:
  - **Fluid dynamics lab**: Investigating the relationships between pressure, temperature, and fluid flow in a complicated system of tubes with adjustable parameters
  - **Electrical engineering lab**: Measuring the oscillations in current in different parts of a circuit using an oscilloscope
  - **Structural engineering lab:** Testing different steels to destruction after e.g. heating, or cooling by liquid nitrogen
  - **Vibrations and damping lab:** Observing the ways a model skyscraper can vibrate.
- **Projects lasting a week or longer:** These include both design and construction. Some examples include making an AM radio and creating a structure to support a given object.
- **Programming coursework:** In each computing practical/lab, you'll be asked to write a program to complete a different task, which might mean performing basic arithmetic at the start of the year and implementing efficient sorting algorithms at the end.
- **Design:** Computer-assisted design as well as manual drawing coursework.
- **Exposition classes**: Includes written reports and spoken presentations.

When you begin an Engineering degree at Cambridge, the entire first week is dedicated to a lab in which you learn some fundamental engineering principles through Lego Mindstorms![79] This gives you the opportunity to explore and understand many of the key parts of doing an engineering lab.

There are also optional projects throughout the year, which will allow you to combine and consolidate what you've learned so far.

> *"At the end of my first year, we were given a summer project where we had to write some code in C++ to safely land a Mars probe using the drag equation and Newton's equations. What was cool about this project was that it extended to the second year. Each problem sheet we got in second year had an optional extension on it, which related to this project. For example, we applied what we learnt in Information Engineering or Chemical Engineering to iterate and improve our Mars lander project, which was really effective in reinforcing the new concepts we were learning."* –Student, Engineering, Cambridge

> **Case study:** *"One of the most difficult and rewarding things I did in first year was a term-long project where we had to build a bridge. It was everything we'd normally do on a problem sheet, but in real life.*
>
> *For example, during lectures for the Structures course, we'd be learning how to analyse forces around a point or in, say, a T-shaped bar, which would be tessellated to create a bridge. Then we'd have problem sheets giving us model systems and asking 'what is the force in this bar?', or 'is this beam under tension or compression?', or 'what would change if we removed this bar?', or 'what would happen if we changed this tension to a compression?'*
>
> *At the same time, in our practicals, we were designing and testing our model bridge using exactly what we were learning. We found ourselves asking very similar questions to what we had be asked in the problem sheets. For example: 'how many supporting tessellations do we need?', 'is it supposed to be under tension or compression?' or 'how many T-bars do we need to add here?'*

79 A system for making robots with Lego.

*We had some initial ideas and intuition from the example structures we'd seen in lectures and the problem sheets. When we analysed our ideas on paper the first time (for example, by resolving forces) we realised that the designs would have failed in practice. We therefore had to do a few iterations of the design on paper until we found something that should theoretically work. We also discovered some practical considerations that made us change our plans, such as that some types of joint are more fragile under compression than others."*

## Work experience

Work experience is imperative for an engineer. To qualify for accreditation, you'll need to complete a specific minimum number of weeks of work experience over the first two years of your degree. You can find this on your own, through the university's careers service, or through the Engineering department. Most students try to get some work experience every year.

## In later years

In your second year, you'll continue with a similar broad syllabus to your first year, building on the core themes of mechanical engineering, electrical engineering, maths, practical and computing skills, and work experience. In your third and fourth years, you'll be able to specialise. The specialisms offered at both Oxford and Cambridge all fall under one of the following (all the example projects have really been done by Oxbridge students):

- **Bioengineering/biomedical engineering**: engineering in a medical or biological context, such as creating medical instruments, prosthetics, and artificial tissues and organs. *Example projects: a probe to measure currents around swimming microorganisms; a device for destroying tumours with ultrasound.*
- **Chemical engineering**[80]: the study and design of chemical processes and plants, for instance, to produce a new drug or a new plastic efficiently and in high quantities. *Example projects: hydrophobic coatings that can be applied to arbitrary metal surfaces; a cement that stays liquid until exposed to air.*
- **Civil engineering**: designing and constructing infrastructure, such as bridges, dams, and buildings. *Example projects: optimising concrete structures for increased lifespan underwater; measuring and minimising the $CO_2$ emitted in constructing a brick-and-mortar house.*

80 At Cambridge, you would need to switch to the Chemical Engineering degree course after your first year to study this.

- **Control/instrumentation**: designing sensors and systems for using them in automation, such as in launching an unmanned rocket or allowing a manufacturing robot to handle parts gently. *Example projects: coordinating electricity supply based on second-by-second demand; increasing the precision of a 3D printer.*
- **Electrical engineering**: covers everything electrical, from microprocessors to power stations and transmission, though you'll likely specialise in one subfield. *Example projects: a light-sensitive switch; a plan for a modular nuclear power station.*
- **Information engineering**: the design of systems for collecting and organising large amounts of data and making it usable to human beings, such as in digital libraries, business modelling, and software for planning large projects. *Example projects: AI for improved climate change predictions; software for coordinating infrastructure projects across a city.*
- **Mechanical engineering**: the design and construction of mechanical systems, from nanobots to trains to turbines. *Example projects: a robot than runs like a dog; cooling an engine using sound waves.*

Cambridge also allows you to specialise in **Aerospace/Aerothermal Engineering**, i.e. the study of aerodynamics and its application to aircraft, land vehicles, or even buildings. *Example projects: a wing that reduces ice build-up; reducing the effect of the wake of one wind turbine on another.*

At Oxford, an alternative specialism is the '**entrepreneurship pathway**'[81], in which you also take economics and management courses (see Chapter 23) in order to prepare you to run a business in an engineering context.

At Cambridge, you can move into **Manufacturing Engineering** after your second year, in which you'll learn about the practical aspects of applying engineering in manufacturing industries, such as the typical challenges, manufacturing tools and processes, and decision-making processes. You'll spend time in a variety of industries as part of your practical work for the course.

> *"In my third year in Manufacturing Engineering, I got to visit the plants of eight different manufacturing companies. At the end of each industrial visit, we had to do a presentation about each company we visited to the rest of the cohort, as not all students visited the same*

81 Its full title is 'Engineering Science, Entrepreneurship and Management'

*companies. In fourth year we had to carry out projects with three different firms. We were involved in solving real problems for these companies. One of our assignments was at a car manufacturer. Our team was asked to automate the logging of repairs that were needed, to eliminate human error. We started the project and then handed it off to another team, who carried on working on it while we finished a project another team had started."* –Student, Manufacturing Engineering, Cambridge

## A typical week in contact hours

In the first year at both Oxford and Cambridge, you'll typically have 10–12 lectures per week and 2–5 tutorials or supervisions in college in which you review problem sheets you have completed. In each tutorial or supervision, you'll be going through a problem sheet with your tutor; the sheet will include questions that test and extend what you've learned in lectures that week. Every week you'll also have practical work, usually lasting 4–5 hours.

**Did You Know?**

*At Oxford, your practical work for the year will consist of:*

- *10 hours of drawing and design*
- *2 hours of workshop practice*
- *25 hours of computing labs*
- *25 hours of mechanical engineering labs*
- *25 hours of electrical engineering labs*
- *5 hours of thermodynamics labs*

*"I rarely needed to read a book because the lecture notes were so complete. You'll need to revisit them multiple times to be able to do your example sheets, but the lecture notes are so well structured and summarised that they'll give you a really solid understanding of everything you need as long as you put in the work to read and understand them."* –Student, Engineering, Cambridge

# 11.4: Character profiles (spot the successful applicant)

Now that you know what you'll be studying and what the workload will be like, you're probably wondering: 'What are the admissions tutors looking for in an ideal Engineering candidate?'

In this section, you'll meet three different applicants, one of whom is successful. We'll explore what makes that candidate so successful and identify the hurdles at which the others stumble. See page 216 for more information about each stage of the application process.

## Applicant 1: Charlie, 18 (Cambridge)

**Before interview:**

- Charlie is in their second year of A Levels, studying Maths, Further Maths, Physics and Biology. They are predicted A*A*AA.
- They particularly love the mechanics modules of Maths, which is why they have decided to apply to Engineering. They do lots of extra mechanics questions from STEP papers in their free time.
- They've read a bit around Engineering and enjoyed the books they've read. They've also done some work experience in a consultancy firm. It wasn't directly linked to engineering, but they included it in their personal statement as they thought it showed dedication, explaining *what* they did rather than the skills learned from it.
- They do a couple of ENGAA papers as preparation but don't practise them in timed conditions.
- They struggle for time with the ENGAA, but they're happy with the questions they do arrive at an answer to.

**In their interview:**

- Charlie is given an at-interview test upon arrival at Cambridge. They are shocked by this, as they are only expecting to have an interview.
- They run out of time and haven't prepared much maths, as they aren't expecting questions on pure maths in their interviews, so they flounder on a few of the questions.

- With a little guidance, Charlie manages to find the answers to some of the maths questions, although it's clear that they haven't prepared maths as comprehensively as they should have.
- Charlie does better on the physics questions as they have done lots of revision and are able to show off their understanding.

## Applicant 2: Alicja, 19 (Oxford)

**Before interview:**

- Alicja is currently on a gap year completing an industrial placement at a large electrical engineering firm.
- She has A*A*A in her Maths, Physics and Chemistry A Levels.
- She does lots of practice for the PAT during her gap year, to make sure she has not forgotten any of the skills she accumulated during her A Levels. She checks her solutions using the Oxbridge Formula website and seeks out extra questions from UKMT papers.
- She reads a lot around the subject and has attended a series of evening lectures about sustainable development and how engineering can help preserve dwindling natural resources.

**In her interview:**

- Alicja performs well in her interviews. She's done a lot of preparation, talking to her friends about engineering and the work she's been doing during her placement.
- Her graph-sketching question goes well, and she isn't flustered by the more complicated maths content.
- She struggles more with the physics questions but listens to the guidance of the interviewer and manages to reach a solution.

## Applicant 3: Bea, 17 (Cambridge)

**Before her interview:**

- Bea is in her second year doing A-Level Maths, Physics and Biology. She is predicted 3 A*s.
- She is also doing an EPQ on how electrical engineering is used in iPhones. She has not done any work experience but has enjoyed exploring the theoretical side of the subject through her EPQ.
- To prepare for the ENGAA, she thoroughly revises all of her A-Level content.

- She hasn't done any past papers and is shocked by how time-pressured the ENGAA is.
- To prepare for her interviews, she reads a lot about engineering and memorises lots of information about different mechanical and digital systems.
- She does a bit of problem-solving, but not much, as she thinks her A Level practice will be sufficient.

**In her interview:**

- Bea is very nervous in her interview. As a result, she doesn't speak very much, and just writes her working on the whiteboard.
- She is silent as she attempts the problems, so the interviewer doesn't gain much insight into Bea's reasoning and how she is thinking about the problems.
- She is stronger in the earlier parts, but gets flustered when she gets to the harder parts of the questions and struggles to take on board the interviewer's advice.

**Who is the best candidate?**

Alicja is clearly the best candidate here. Although they all have sufficiently strong predicted grades, Alicja prepared thoroughly and ticked many of the boxes that admissions tutors are looking for.

**What did Charlie do wrong?**

✘ Charlie's work experience was not relevant to engineering. Work experience is only worth including in your personal statement if it's directly relevant to the course or if you can show you developed skills that will help you succeed in your degree.

✘ Ability Potential Charlie did not do sufficient preparation for the ENGAA. In particular, they didn't attempt papers in timed conditions.

✘ Ability Charlie was not fully prepared for their interviews and was caught out by the maths aspects of the at-interview test and interview questions.

**What did Bea do wrong?**

✘ Although Bea's EPQ was relevant, she hadn't done any practical preparation for her application. Practical preparation, such as work experience, is highly valued by admissions tutors, as it shows an active desire to engage in engineering as a career and field.

✘ Potential Furthermore, she was completely underprepared for the ENGAA, not even knowing how the sections were divided.

✘ Potential She was also too closed off in her interviews, not giving the interviewers a chance to fully see and understand how she reasons. Although her answers were clear and she grasped most of the content, she didn't come across as a 'teachable' student (i.e. someone the tutors would be able to have productive discussions with during tutorials).

**What did Alicja do right?**

✓ Potential Passion Alicja maintained her interest in engineering during her gap year, attending relevant lectures and engaging in useful work experience.

✓ Ability Potential Passion Despite having achieved A*s in her Physics and Maths A Levels, she didn't rest on her laurels and active prepared for the PAT (which she found challenging but enjoyed), so she performed very well.

✓ Potential She communicated well in her interviews, and acted on the advice of her interviewers, which is really important.

For more on the application process for physical sciences, see page 216. See page 143 for an interview with real Oxbridge interviewers.

# Chapter 12:
# Materials Science

## 12.1: What is Materials Science?

Materials science spans physics, chemistry and maths. It's the study of materials, their chemical composition, their physical properties, their applications in science and engineering and how they are manufactured. It focuses on the materials we need in modern society and how they can be optimally produced to cause the least possible harm to the environment. As a discipline, it's in a constant state of flux, as society's material needs change over time.

> *"Materials Science is the study of materials, their properties, and why they have them. In other words, looking at the microstructure of a material to see why it has particular properties and using this knowledge to design new materials."* –Student, Materials Science, Oxford[82]

This may be the course for you if:

- ❑ **You're an all-rounder:** Materials science can't be categorised under any one of physics, chemistry, design, and engineering—it lies on the boundary between all four. That means if you have an aptitude in several of these (and maths), you might find that materials science is a way to engage in all your interests at once.
- ❑ **You like applying your knowledge in creative ways:** Do you love open ended problems and combining ideas in new ways? Are you creative in the way you approach problems, and happy to face and overcome many obstacles before finding a solution? These skills are central to the design element of materials science, i.e. in applying what you've learned about existing materials to create entirely new ones, and applications for them.

82 From the Oxford website.

- **You're driven to understand the world around you:** An engineer might look up the tensile strengths of two alloys to *decide* which to use, whereas a materials scientist will *explain* what determines the tensile strength and then develop new alloys in which it's even higher. If you want to learn *why* things work, starting from a molecular level, and then apply those lessons, materials science might be what you're looking for.
- **You're fascinated by modern technology:** Do you like to read articles and watch videos about invisibility cloaks, aerogels, self-healing concrete, nanotechnology, superconductors, nuclear fusion, quantum computers, and more? All these cutting-edge technologies rely on advances in materials science. If working at the frontier of human technological research matters to you, you might find materials science is the place to be.
- **You love to be part of a small, tight-knit group:** Materials Science at Oxford has a small intake – around 30 to 40 per year – which means you get to know all your course-mates quite well. Some people enjoy being part of a smaller, cosier, slightly niche community—you might think about whether it would suit you.

At Cambridge, Materials Science is offered as part of the Natural Sciences course. At Oxford, you can take it as a standalone course (the focus of this chapter). See Chapter 14 on page 205 for information on Natural Sciences at Cambridge. Materials Science is the course to study at Oxford if you want to continue with both chemistry and physics (much like the role Natural Sciences plays at Cambridge).

**Did You Know?**

*Materials Science is used in all of the following areas:*

- ***Aeronautics:*** *Designing materials for parts of aeroplanes*
- ***Biomedical science:*** *Is there a material analogous to bone that we can use to coat metal implants? Can we find a material from which we can create human organs?*
- ***Ceramics:*** *Can we find a ceramic material or alloy that is both hard enough and light enough for use as body armour?*
- ***Entrepreneurship:*** *Learning how to develop and market idea, and create a business around it*
- ***Nanotechnology:*** *Precision engineering at the atomic level, with many applications in medicine and manufacturing*
- ***Polymers:*** *E.g. using the electrical properties of certain polymers to create cheap solar panels.*

The Oxford Materials Science degree lasts 4 years and you leave with an MEng, which gives you the accreditation needed to become a chartered engineer (if you wish to pursue that path). You can also leave after 3 years with a BA that isn't accredited. You'll engage with many different sciences and develop a variety of skills, including computing and laboratory work.

> *"Materials is a lot more applied than Physics. It's much closer to Engineering in that sense."* –Student, Materials Science, Oxford

You'll have the opportunity to study a foreign language, which can be useful for securing internships and lab work abroad later on in your degree, and there's even a course on entrepreneurship[83] and the practical aspects of setting up a business. The degree also includes group projects and courses in research skills, culminating in an 8-month full-time research project in the fourth year, in which you'll join a research team and make a genuine contribution to the field of materials science.

This should make it clear that you'll leave Oxford with a very broad range of skills and ready for a career in engineering, research, or the business side of manufacturing, among others. If this flexibility is important to you, perhaps Materials Science is the degree for you.

## 12.2: How do you apply for Materials Science at Oxford?

The compulsory A-Level/Higher Level subjects for Oxford Materials Science are Maths and Physics; Chemistry is also highly recommended. Further Maths is seen as useful, as is Design and Technology. The usual offer is A*AA, with an A* in Maths, Physics or Chemistry. For the IB, it's 40, with 766 at Higher Level, including a 7 in Maths, Physics or Chemistry. You'll also need to take the PAT. Materials Science is only available at a handful of colleges.

On average, around 1 in 4 applicants is successful, and approximately 30 students are accepted each year.

83 Taught partly by the Saïd Business School.

# 12.3: What's it like to study Materials Science?

In your first year studying Materials Science, you'll build upon skills taught in your Maths, Physics and Chemistry A Levels, and learn new ways to develop and apply these skills. Here's a breakdown of the first year of studying Materials Science at Oxford, to give you a sense of how it builds on your A-Level studies.

In your first year at Oxford, you'll study for four Materials Science exams:

- Structure of Materials
- Properties of Materials
- Transforming Materials
- Mathematics for Materials Science.

There will also be three practical components that are assessed across the year, equivalent to a fifth exam paper:

- Crystallography[84]
- Computing
- Other practical work.

You typically have two to three days to carry out practicals, which take place approximately once a fortnight, and you'll have a week to hand in your written work.

**Structure of Materials**

This course covers:

- Crystallography and diffraction
- Metals and alloys
- Ceramics and semiconductors
- Defects in crystals
- Polymers
- Composites
- Elementary quantum theory
- Bonding.

84 Crystallography studies crystals, often through the way electromagnetic radiation passes through them. Since 'crystals' refers to all materials whose molecules form into lattices (including metals and semiconductors), crystallography is a vital discipline with a wide range of applications.

Some of the content covered in early lectures from these subjects will overlap with that of your A Levels. For example, optics (including diffraction) is covered in A-Level Physics. Furthermore, if you've studied A-Level Chemistry, the knowledge you've gained about bonding will come in useful here. However, this course requires you to analyse in depth how bonding actually functions.

> *"I enjoyed Structure of Materials because we learned how individual electrons are actually distributed within molecules."* –Angus, Materials Science, Oxford

**Properties of Materials**

This course covers:

- Elasticity and structures
- Electrical and magnetic properties
- Mechanical properties
- The kinetic theory of gases.

Much of the content in this course follows directly from A-Level Physics, such as the study of ideal gases and elasticity. The course will explore the laws and properties you already know in greater depth, and fill in the missing gaps as to why things work as they do! This course will also involve laboratory work, some of which is assessed across the year.

**Transforming Materials**

This course covers:

- Thermodynamics
- Kinetics
- Electrochemistry
- Polymer synthesis
- Microstructure of materials.

Again, lots of the foundational content can be spotted in the A-Level Physics syllabus and also the Chemistry A-Level course. However, as Chemistry A Level is not a compulsory prerequisite, none of the knowledge will be presupposed. This module will also draw on your mathematical skills to monitor the behaviour of materials before and after some transformation.

## Maths for Materials Science

Maths is a big part of the Materials Science course, and the first year allows you to study the maths required for more advanced materials science. In this course, you'll be exposed to a variety of university maths concepts, including:

- Vectors, matrices and determinants
- Ordinary and partial differentiation[85]
- Indefinite and definite integrals
- Taylor and Maclaurin series
- Complex numbers
- Ordinary differential equations.

Having a Further Maths A Level is really valuable here, as many of the skills studied in this course follow directly from or overlap with the Further Maths syllabus. If you have an opportunity to look over the Further Maths content before starting this degree, it will be extremely helpful!

> *"In my interview, I was asked to sketch a graph of the relationship between two variables and explain why this would be the shape of the graph if the* two *variables were, say, the density and temperature of a material. Next, I was asked how I could turn the graph into a straight line, i.e. by using logs."* –Student, Materials Science, Oxford

## A typical week in contact hours

In the first year, you'll have 2-3 hours of lectures every weekday, and every second week you'll have two afternoons (around 3 hours per day) of labs.

> Some first-year Materials Science labs include: using lasers to examine materials, casting metals and finding the glass transition temperature of a rubber ball (i.e. when it goes from rubbery to hard and brittle).

There are typically 3 problem sheets per week and a 1-hour tutorial on each. You're expected to spend roughly 30 hours working on the problem sheets compared to around 15 contact hours (lectures and tutorials, excluding labs), so it's important to be able to motivate yourself to work independently.

85 For more on partial differentiation, see page 156

# Chapter 13: Chemistry

## 13.1: Why Chemistry?

The focus of this chapter is Chemistry at Oxford, where it's offered as a standalone course. At Cambridge, you can study chemistry as part of either Natural Sciences (see Chapter 14 on page 205) or Chemical Engineering (see Chapter 15, page 213).

Chemistry is a wide-ranging science that draws on many disciplines such as maths, physics and biology. It's a diverse and innovative subject. If you love chemistry at school, that's a good place to start, as university chemistry develops and *explains* many of the secrets behind the A-Level Chemistry course, as well as adding a whole host of new topics.

This may be the course for you if:

- ❑ **You love chemistry:** If you're genuinely inspired by chemistry at school and *need* to know more, the picture only gets more intricate and interesting at university—you're only going to enjoy it more. If you want to ascend to the next plane of understanding, a Chemistry degree might be for you.
- ❑ **You have interests in maths and physics too:** If you're not afraid of an integral and you always wondered what quantum mechanics is really all about, you're well set to deal with the more theoretical side of chemistry, which is a core part of the Oxford course.
- ❑ **You crave variety:** Chemistry isn't just sitting in front of a laptop, or scribbling answers to a problem sheet. You'll have to solve equations and memorise facts, but also spend whole days in labs getting to grips with processes and equipment, and on top of that spend a lot of time discussing all the concepts you're picking up with peers and tutors.
- ❑ **You're not afraid of hard work:** The Chemistry course has a reputation at Oxford as being one of the degrees with the heaviest workloads, but that suits students who prefer having lots of contact hours. If you love the idea of literally working 9 to 5 on chemistry, and if you have the determination to master all the different aspects of the course, you might find that the intensity is a blessing rather than a curse.

- ❑ **You want to be at the forefront of research:** If you're looking to contribute to the long-term future of science, Chemistry might suit your ambitions. Unlike in Engineering or Materials Science, you might be instrumental in discovering entirely new scientific techniques at a fundamental level—things that might not find their way into everyday applications for decades. The Oxford course is particularly research-focused, and your tutors will literally be world experts—the people who write the textbooks. If you love the idea of being able to discuss cutting-edge ideas with leading researchers, that's an extra bonus of the Oxford system.

> *"I noticed a trend we're discussing more and more is eco-chemistry: minimising waste in terms of energy efficiency and 'atom economy'—i.e. trying to have every atom that goes into a process either end up in a useful product or be available to be reused next time. Batteries, hydrogen storage and solar panels are also big topics because there's so much research into them right now."* –Michał, Chemistry, Oxford

The Oxford degree is a four-year course and you leave with an MChem. It has a focus on preparing you for the option of going into research, to the extent that the fourth year is entirely research-based: you join the research group of an Oxford academic and write a dissertation on your results.

**What Oxford students wish they'd known before applying for Chemistry:**

> *"The course is a lot of work, but on the other hand, because you spend a lot of time in labs, you become really close friends with your classmates, so there are a lot of people to talk to about chemistry problems with. There's a real teamwork element to the degree."* –Daniel, Chemistry, Oxford

> *"Many people say it's the hardest degree, and the labs are full-on, but if you work hard at the right time you'll always see rewards, and you'll still find the time to be involved in extracurricular clubs and societies."* –Michał, Chemistry, Oxford

## 13.2: How do you apply for Chemistry at Oxford?

The typical Oxford A-Level offer is A*A*A, with the two A*s in maths or science subjects. For IB, it's 40 points, with 766 at Higher Level. Chemistry and Maths are both compulsory A Levels for studying Chemistry at Oxford. Maths is not a compulsory Higher Level subject for the IB, but if you don't have it, you'll need 7s at Higher Level in both Chemistry and another science. Physics, Biology and Further Maths aren't compulsory, but are highly recommended.

You'll also need to take the TSA (Thinking Skills Assessment). See page 373 for more details.

Of those who apply to study Chemistry, around 1 in every 4 applicants is successful.

## 13.3: Is the chemistry at uni anything like chemistry at school?

Important aspects of university chemistry are:

- ☐ **Synthesis:** Combining two simpler chemicals to form a more complex product
- ☐ **Structure:** The arrangement of the chemical bonds between atoms in molecules
- ☐ **Reaction mechanisms:** The sequences of elementary reactions by which chemical change occurs
- ☐ **Properties:** Investigating the nature of different chemicals and how they behave under particular conditions.

Chemistry at university does build on your A-Level Chemistry. However, at university you'll be required to explain in depth many of the things you just accept as fact at A Level. In particular, *molecular orbital theory* will be introduced to fully *explain* much of what you see at A Level—it describes how electrons are distributed across whole molecules, and does so in quantum mechanical terms.

Organic Chemistry in particular is more closely related to the Chemistry A-Level syllabus than other areas of the course, but you go into much more depth than you did at school. The boundaries between organic and inorganic chemistry have become thinner as we investigate further intermediate compounds, but they are still taught as two distinct disciplines.

First-year Chemistry at Oxford can be divided into four areas; at the end of your first year, you'll sit an exam in each area.

## Organic Chemistry

- Organic Chemistry expands on your A-Level knowledge, and you'll be introduced to further mechanisms and reactions. An example is the Diels-Alder reaction, which you'll learn as part of your study of carbonyl compounds.
- Organic Chemistry is made up almost entirely of mechanisms at university. Everything you're learning at A Level, plus reactions you'll see for the first time, will be explained using mechanisms.
- At the end of your first year, you'll study some biological chemistry. This involves learning more about amino acids and proteins, and even the workings of animal cells. You'll also study DNA and its construction. If you're taking A-Level Biology, you'll see some connections to that material, but with a much greater focus on the chemistry of the processes involved.

> *"My first term did start with a recap of the A-Level organic chemistry material to get everyone up to speed... but the lecturer covered the whole A Level in an hour! You've barely touched the tip of the iceberg of organic chemistry at school."* –Kay, Chemistry, Oxford

## Inorganic Chemistry

- The inorganic course offers great variety. You'll perform a survey of all the properties and compounds of main group elements and transition metals. Many of these properties may be familiar from A-Level Chemistry, but the way they'll be explained is far more involved.
- You'll study the bonding patterns of different compounds, as well as the symmetry and structure of compounds, via molecular orbital theory (just as in organic chemistry).
- There will be an element of applied physics, in that you'll take a quantum mechanical view of electrons in atoms and molecules, thinking of electrons as wave functions rather than tiny point charges.

## Physical Chemistry

- Physical Chemistry examines motion, forces and energy within substances or molecules.

- This course will contain topics such as electromagnetism, thermodynamics and quantum mechanics—so it's very useful to have A-Level Physics when studying this course. However, it's not a prerequisite, and any of the A-Level topics used will be explained as they arise.
- Instead of examining the physics of large systems (such as cars driving down a road), the Physical Chemistry course focuses on physics at the atomic or molecular level. For instance, you might consider the ***particle in a box***.

The **particle in a box** is an idealised physical scenario in which a particle is trapped between impassable walls and bounces back and forth between them. Under the quantum mechanical way of viewing the particle, it turns out that its kinetic energy can only take discrete values[86]. I.e. there is a lowest possible energy, and a second lowest, etc., and nothing in between those energies is physically possible. When we generalise the particle in a box to a particle in a ring, and then to a particle in a sphere, we get a model of an electron in an atom.

*"In organic and inorganic chemistry, we were shown the wave functions of electrons within molecules – whether they were spread out over the whole thing, or localised around one constituent atom or bond – but it was in physical chemistry that we actually solved the Schrödinger equation, which is what tells you what the wave functions have to be."*
–Student, Chemistry, Oxford

## Maths

- Maths is central to university chemistry and, in your first year, you'll study it as a standalone discipline.
- You'll study Taylor series and techniques for integration and differentiation. Unlike if you were studying for a Maths degree, you won't be expected to *prove* the theorems you learn in an exam, although sometimes the lecturers will show the proofs to aid understanding.

86 This is analogous to the way in which a standing wave in a tube of fixed length can only have wavelengths from a discrete set of values, since the energy of a particle is inversely proportional to its wavelength.

- You'll build upon the calculus you're learning at school by being introduced to new concepts such as ***partial derivatives*** (see page 15 and page 156) and path-dependent integrals.[87]
- You'll cover matrix algebra such as finding eigenvalues and using matrices to solve sets of simultaneous linear equations. Matrices will also be useful for studying quantum mechanics and group theory later. See page 13 for more information about group theory. In chemistry, groups are used to study symmetries of molecules and of electron orbitals *within* molecules.
- You'll study probability and statistics, partly for the sake of applying these skills to your lab reports, but also so you can study ***statistical mechanics***. For instance, you might have seen a graph of the Maxwell-Boltzmann distribution at A Level, but in statistical mechanics you'll derive the function which describes this distribution.

> **Statistical mechanics** is essentially an approach to thermodynamics that studies the distribution of speeds and energies of molecules within a substance.

## Labs

As well as the four written examinations, you'll have practical lab work that counts as coursework. At the beginning of the year, your computer labs will cover the Python programming language. This language is used throughout the year in your experimental labs to help you analyse and understand the data.

Labs are central to the Chemistry degree; they're where you apply the theoretical work covered in lectures.

> **An example lab from first-year Chemistry at Oxford**
>
> ***Interhalogen compounds:*** In this lab, you react gaseous chlorine with fluorine, bromine, and iodine to synthesise a set list of compounds. Then you analyse the output compounds, checking that they behave how you would expect them to. For example, you consider how they absorb UV radiation and analyse this graphically.

87 Like the definite integrals from A Levels, except that they don't only depend on the limits of the integral, but also the way the system changes in going from one limit to the other.

*"All labs are really hands-on. We're given a really quite detailed procedure to follow at the start, but there's also guidance from an instructor throughout. Afterwards, we submit an online report with a full write-up: introduction, method, data and analysis. We also complete an online risk assessment before we start each lab."* –Student, Chemistry, Oxford

## After first year

In your second year, you'll continue with the same core topics as in your first year. In your third year, there are still compulsory courses in organic, inorganic, and physical chemistry, but you can choose to specialise in one of those fields by taking more options in it. You can also specialise in techniques like spectroscopy, or applications like semiconductors and superconductors.

Unlike in a Natural Sciences degree, the only physics and biology topics you learn in the Oxford Chemistry degree are the ones directly related to chemistry. However, there is some overlap with the other sciences. You'll have core courses on thermodynamics, quantum mechanics, and biochemistry, and some of your third-year options include the chemistry of lasers (physics) and the chemistry of proteins and DNA (biology).

You'll usually spend your fourth year in a research lab in Oxford, working under academics as they perform cutting-edge, publishable research. This is excellent preparation for going into research yourself, either in academia or in industry. Although the particular subject matter you study depends on the lab, they will seek to give you opportunities to pick up new skills.

*"The fourth-year research project is a fantastic opportunity – in one year researching superconductors I learned glass blowing, arc welding, and how to operate a particle accelerator – but it's not completely obligatory to be in a lab. One of my friends chose to do a project on the history of the science of photography instead, which meant more historical research in conjunction with the History department than actual lab work!"* –Graduate, Chemistry, Oxford

## 13.4: What's the workload like for Chemistry?

This section is designed to give you a taster of what studying Chemistry at Oxford is really like. It will describe the workload and contact hours in each week and what's expected of you in terms of practical work.

### Lectures and labs

A Chemistry degree is full on and includes a high number of contact hours. Almost every day you'll have at least two lectures (for example at 9 and 10 a.m.). In your first year at Oxford, you'll have labs in half of the weeks. In weeks with labs, there will be two days per week in which you have contact hours (both labs and lectures) from 9 a.m. to 5 p.m.! On these days, you head to labs straight after lectures. Days without labs are more relaxed, allowing you independent study time to complete problem sheets.

> *"Chemistry is a busy degree! There's a lot of contact hours and they're all vital: you can't miss any lectures because that's where you get the depth, but your tutorials and labs are just as important, and then you have to do the same amount of independent work as any other degree too..."* –Student, Chemistry, Oxford

### Tutorials

On two or three days, you'll have tutorials or classes, held in your college in small groups (typically 2–3 students plus a tutor for tutorials, and a larger group for classes). You'll discuss a problem sheet[88] that you completed beforehand, review and correct your answers, and expand on the questions. In your first year, you'll typically have 1–2 tutorials per week on chemistry and a class on maths.

> *"I used to keep a diary of elements. I had one page per element, and I would keep adding information to it and randomly test myself on elements throughout the year! In our exams, we had to be able to write*

88 Or in some cases an essay question. For instance, you might be asked to 'compare the transition metals', in which case you'd need to respond by describing and explaining differences in properties like crystal structure, conductivity, reactivity, and so on.

*about any given element, or to compare and contrast elements, so this came in really handy."* –Student, Chemistry, Oxford

# 13.5: Character profiles (spot the successful applicant)

What does a successful Chemistry candidate look like? We've put together some character profiles of different applicants to illustrate the traits admissions tutors are keen to see. Here, you'll meet three applicants, one of whom is successful. Afterwards, we'll discuss what the best candidate did right—and the hurdles where the other ones stumbled. You'll find more information about the application process from page 216 and more information about the TSA on page 373.

## Applicant 1: Nikhil, 18

**Before his interview:**

- Nikhil is on a gap year, and has already secured A*A*AA in his A Levels: Maths, Further Maths, Chemistry and Biology.
- During his gap year, he is doing an internship in a lab, researching energy alternatives to fossil fuels and determining their sustainability.
- He is reading around the subject and regularly answering chemistry problems from Chemistry Olympiads[89] so as not to let his A-Level skills decline. He also does some maths problems from the Nrich website.[90]
- To prepare for the TSA, he completes eight timed papers. He checks his answers against the mark scheme and generally scores fairly well (after looking at the score conversion).
- His problem-solving skills are quite strong so he spends more time practising his critical-thinking skills by analysing the arguments in newspaper editorials, and learning techniques from the Oxbridge Formula website.
- He doesn't quite finish the TSA when he sits it, but gets most of it done.
- To prepare for his interviews, he talks through lots of key chemistry concepts with his mum, which proves very useful as it makes all the content fresh in his memory and he has to learn to make his explanations clearer so they are understandable to a non-expert.

89 See oxbridgeformula.co.uk/bonus-chapter.
90 See the bonus chapter for a link to some relevant problems.

**In his interview:**

- Nikhil finds the preliminary questions (in which he is asked to draw and interpret some graphs), fairly straightforward.
- As the interview progresses, the questions get harder, but he draws diagrams, which gives him the time and tools to understand the questions better.
- He doesn't reach a solution for one of the questions, but with the tutor's guidance gets very close. He probably would have got there with a bit more time.

## Applicant 2: Stefan, 17

**Before his interview:**

- Stefan is in his second year of A Levels, studying Maths, Chemistry and History.
- He is enthusiastic about chemistry, and has read ahead a lot in the syllabus.
- As a history student, he finds the history of chemistry very interesting and has read a lot around this—he focuses upon this reading in his personal statement.
- He does a fair amount of preparation for the TSA, but it always seems to take him longer than the time allocation.
- To prepare for his interviews, he revisits all the books he has read and written about in his personal statement.

**In his interview:**

- Stefan doesn't get any questions directly about his personal statement in his interview, so he tries to shoehorn in the names of some of the historical chemists he has learnt about. The tutor seems a little confused by this.
- He struggles with the more-complicated parts of the chemistry questions and is shocked by how they differ from what he's seen at school; he thought he would only be answering advanced A-Level questions.

## Applicant 3: Josie, 18

**Before her interview:**

- Josie is finishing off her A Levels in Maths, Chemistry, Physics and Biology, and is predicted A*AAA.
- She has also recently completed a project on air pollution in rapidly industrialising countries.
- She competes in the Chemistry Olympiad, which she really enjoys.
- She does a lot of preparation for the TSA and thinks it goes quite well.
- To prepare for her interview, she solves chemistry problems online.

**In her interview:**

- She performs well on the basic parts of the chemistry questions, and with some guidance from the tutors, can attempt the more-involved parts, as long as they don't get too mathematical.
- However, she isn't expecting any maths questions, so she struggles a lot more with those. She can't remember anything about binomial probabilities and when she's asked to sketch a complicated-looking function that arises in a physical chemistry question, she doesn't know how to start.

### Who is the best candidate?

Nikhil is the best candidate. While the other two both get caught out in different ways, Nikhil keeps up his Chemistry skills during his gap year and prepares well for both the TSA and the interviews.

### What did Nikhil do right?

✓ Nikhil's gap year reflected his interest in chemistry and gave him experience with lab work, which is always attractive to Chemistry admissions tutors because labs are a vital part of the degree.

✓ He also used his gap year to keep his chemistry and maths in top form.

✓ He prepared well for the TSA, being aware of the time constraints and practising in timed conditions.

✓ He also practised communicating verbally in preparation for his interview, which allowed him to make the most of the tutor's guidance and advice on the day. This showed him to be an engaged and teachable student—exactly what they are looking for.

**What did Stefan do wrong?**

- ✗ Although reading widely around your subject is good, Stefan focused too much on increasing his knowledge of the history of chemistry and not enough on his technical chemistry skillset.
- ✗ If you're applying to a STEM rather than a humanities subject, being well-read is not the priority. Instead, focus on ensuring your skills and understanding are as good as they can be.
- ✗ Stefan also tried to shoehorn content from his personal statement into the interviews instead of focusing on understanding the problem and exploring different methods of solving it.

**What did Josie do wrong?**

- ✓ Josie prepared well and was a strong candidate.
- ✗ However, she was ill-prepared for the mathematical side of the interview. Maths is such an important part of the Chemistry degree, and it is vital that you are well prepared for it.

For more on the application process for physical sciences, see page 216.

# Chapter 14: Physical Natural Sciences

## 14.1: Why Natural Sciences?

Natural Sciences is a broad degree offered at Cambridge but not Oxford. It's an umbrella course under which the majority of science-based subjects are taught. For example, in the first year of studying Natural Sciences at Cambridge, you choose three of the following science subjects:

- Biology of Cells
- Chemistry
- Earth Sciences
- Evolution and Behaviour
- Materials Science
- Physics
- Physiology of Organisms.

Plus, you have to take one maths option (either Mathematics or Mathematical Biology.)

At Cambridge, the flexibility of the course makes it possible to:

**a)** focus solely on the biological sciences
**b)** focus solely on the physical sciences
**c)** combine the two!

In this book, we focus on the physical natural sciences route (options b and c above), which are more quantitative in nature.

The physical natural sciences are:

- Chemistry
- Earth Sciences
- Materials Science
- Physics
- Maths.

The Earth Sciences and Materials Science courses begin from scratch, whereas the Maths, Physics and Chemistry courses build quickly from their respective A Levels.

Natural Sciences is a popular course because it offers such a broad scope for study and you don't have to specialise right away. Even further into the degree, you can study up to three sciences; at Cambridge you can keep your degree broad throughout or specialise in a wide variety of subjects in your third year, including astrophysics, biochemistry and history and philosophy of science.

Physical Natural Sciences may be the course for you if:

- ❑ **You have broad interests:** Do you love learning about all aspects of the physical world, enjoying physics and chemistry at school, but find yourself fascinated by the idea of branching out into earth sciences or materials science if you choose? The Natural Sciences degree is a home for students who have a broad set of scientific skills and would love to develop them all instead of specialising right away.
- ❑ **You love applied maths:** Studying physical sciences is inherently mathematical. But if it's specifically seeing the power of maths in constructing scientific theories and deriving results from them that interests you, then you might particularly enjoy Natural Sciences. The degree isn't about proving theorems for their own sake, but instead about exploring all the ways maths can be applied, from fundamental physics to gas laws to seismic waves.
- ❑ **You want to *understand* everything:** Although Natural Sciences students do practicals, the degree is really about developing a broad and deep understanding rather than immediate practical applications. Natural Sciences might be for you if you're fascinated by examining and explaining scientific curiosities. For instance, an engineer might learn about a few common substances, especially their structural properties, but a natural scientist would be able to *explain* the physical and electromagnetic properties of many common and exotic substances starting from a molecular level.
- ❑ **You're good at making connections:** If you love science, perhaps one thing that really to you is the connections between different fields. Natural Sciences isn't just about studying two or more subjects at the same time, but instead it's about understanding each subject better by means of the other. For instance, much of what you learn in chemistry and materials science might be explained based on fundamental physics, but at the same time it's examples from chemistry and materials science that allow those physical laws to be investigated and understood in the first place.

- ☐ **You like to be spoilt for choice:** Cambridge states that there are over 100 different combinations of courses taken by Natural Sciences students each year. If you want to keep your options open and enjoy daydreaming about all the possible directions you could take, a Natural Sciences degree might be for you.

You can leave after three years with a BA, or continue to a fourth year for an MSci.

> *"I applied to Natural Sciences because of its interdisciplinary nature. At A Level, I was unsure what type of science I wanted to specialise in, so this course seemed the natural choice (if you'll pardon the pun). Cambridge seemed the best place to do this degree because of its immense research output and its unique supervision system, allowing for the learning to be tailored."* –Jake, Natural Sciences, Cambridge

> *"When applying to university, I was torn between physics, chemistry and maths. I didn't want to commit to a single subject in case I changed my mind once I started. Natural Sciences was very appealing because I could start broad and specialise later. Studying a wide range of subjects also helped me see problems from several perspectives."* – Harry, Natural Sciences, Cambridge

## 14.2: How do you apply for Natural Sciences at Cambridge?

The A-Level offer is typically A*A*A, with A*s in science or Maths A Levels. Some colleges require three science or Maths A Levels—and although some may accept you with two, this will limit the options you can take throughout your degree. Cambridge asks for 40–42 IB points with 7, 7, 6 in Higher Level, with two 7s in Maths or science subjects.

Although Further Maths is not required, it's a great advantage throughout the course and can potentially lead to a lower offer overall. It will *definitely* help with the maths, physics and chemistry elements of the course when you start your degree!

> *"For Natural Sciences at Cambridge, it might be beneficial to sit four A Levels instead of three, to allow you to include Further Maths."* –Admissions Tutor, Cambridge

You'll also need to take the NSAA—see page 250 for more information.

Cambridge offers approximately 580 Natural Sciences places per year and has around 2700 applicants, giving a success rate of around 1 in 5.

## 14.3: Is Natural Sciences at Cambridge anything like the sciences at school?

You'll take three separate subjects in your first year, to give you a taste of some of the options you might specialise in later. Some will be more closely related to what you have studied at A Level than others. Of the Physical Natural Sciences options, Earth Sciences and Materials Science will likely be completely new to you.

### Earth Sciences in Natural Sciences

The first year of Earth Sciences is a general introduction to the planet—what we know and don't know about it. It doesn't rely on any specific A-Level knowledge and relates to all of the sciences and maths. To take this course, you must have studied at least two sciences at A Level.

In your first year, you'll study key topics like the origins of the Earth and major events in its history (such as the ice ages) and examine the currently pressing issue of climate change. The course also involves practical work, in which you'll study different types of rocks and minerals.

> *"Earth Sciences is a fully interdisciplinary field with ample room for geologists, biologists, climatologists, chemists, mathematicians and many others."* –University of Cambridge

### Materials Science in Natural Sciences

Materials science is a physical natural science you can pick up in your first year. You must have studied Maths and at least one of Physics and Chemistry at A Level to take this option.

Materials science is a cutting-edge science studying the diversity that arises among materials due to their atomic and molecular structures. It looks at the physical properties and behaviours that follow as a result. For more information on materials science as a discipline, see Chapter 12 on page 187.

In the first year of the Natural Sciences, you'll be given a broad overview of materials science, covering:

- Atomic structure of materials
- Materials for devices
- Diffraction[91]
- Microstructure
- Mechanical behaviour of materials
- Biomaterials
- Materials under extreme conditions.

## A-Level subjects in Natural Sciences

Other sciences falling under the remit of physical natural sciences include maths, physics and chemistry—and these follow on from their respective A Levels. Here's an outline of what you'll study in the first-year course of each of these sciences, and how the content relates to your A Level.

## Physics in Natural Sciences

To study physics in your first year at Cambridge, you must have Maths and Physics A Level, or Maths and Further Maths A Level (with a high proportion of mechanics). The first year is assessed through one written examination and regularly assessed practical work.

The first-year course aims to prepare you for further undergraduate study of physics by introducing you to the foundations of the subject. The aim is to convey the scope and breadth of physics and give you a basis to work from before you specialise later on. In your first year, you'll study:

- Mechanics
- Relativity
- Oscillations and waves
- Quantum waves
- Fields.

91 The diffraction of light and other EM radiation is used to examine crystals.

See the Physics Chapter starting on page 148 for more information about these topics.

## Chemistry in Natural Sciences

The first year of chemistry will give you a broad overview and strong foundation before you decide where (and whether) to specialise. The prerequisite for studying this course is A-Level Chemistry, but you'll be severely restricted in how many later chemistry modules you can study if you don't also have A-Level Maths. In your first year, you'll study the following topics:

- **Shapes and Structures of Molecules:** introduces modern theories of bonding to explain why molecules have the shapes they do, and how those shapes affect their other properties. It's useful for both the organic and inorganic parts of the course.
- **Reactions and Mechanisms in Organic Chemistry:** falls under organic chemistry
- **Kinetics of Chemical Reactions:** falls under physical chemistry
- **Chemistry of the Elements:** reviews the elements of the periodic table and their different properties—falls under inorganic chemistry.

For more information on organic, inorganic, and physical chemistry see the Chapter on Chemistry starting on page 195.

## Mathematics in Natural Sciences

A-Level Maths is a prerequisite for this course, and Further Maths is highly recommended.

When doing this course, you'll choose either Maths Course A or Maths Course B. Both cover mathematical methods for the sciences, but Course B also treats maths as a discipline in its own right. As a result, Course B has more complicated pure maths, but less applied probability and statistics.

Students are encouraged to take Course A unless they did Further Maths A Level and have a strong understanding and a desire to take it further. Course B moves at a significantly faster pace and covers a wider range of content.

The content covered by both courses includes:

- Vector calculus (including multivariable calculus)
- Vector algebra

- Matrices
- Complex numbers
- Ordinary and partial differential equations
- Elementary probability theory
- Computing techniques.

See page 156 to find out more about partial derivatives and multivariable calculus.

## 14.4: What's the workload like?

Natural Sciences entails an intense workload and a contact-heavy week. All-in-all, you'll be expected to spend around 40 hours a week on academic study, the equivalent of a full work week. You'll have 12 lectures per week and practical labs for all subjects (except maths). Your computer labs for maths and the other sciences will help you learn your way around the programming you need for data analysis in practical labs.

Natural Sciences is one of those subjects for which you'll have to attend the infamous 'Cambridge Saturday lectures' (infamous because most other unis are kind enough to give students the entire weekend off!).

You'll also have one supervision per week for each subject in which you'll go through a problem sheet you handed in. Supervisions are held with a supervisor (a subject expert) and a small group of 2–5 students. The supervisor is there to support you—and to stretch you in preparation for your exams.

To give you an idea of what it's like to be a Natural Sciences student in your first year at Cambridge, here's what a typical day might look like:

| | |
|---|---|
| 8 a.m. | Wake up, eat breakfast, cycle to lectures |
| 9–10 a.m. | Lecture |
| 10–11 a.m. | Lecture |
| 11–12 p.m. | Independent study |
| 12 p.m. | Lunch |
| 1–3 p.m. | Labs |
| 3–4 p.m. | Supervision |
| 4–6 p.m. | Independent study |
| 6 p.m. | Dinner |
| 7 p.m. | Study, sports or a society. |

If this schedule seems daunting, you'll be relieved to hear that some days are a lot easier. Labs only happen twice a week, so other days you'll typically have more time for independent study and extracurricular activities. And although the contact hours are intense in the first year, they drop from 30 hours to 10–15 hours per week as the course progresses, allowing more time for private study.

# Chapter 15: Chemical Engineering

## 15.1: What is Chemical Engineering?

Chemical engineering studies the processes by which chemicals are manufactured. That might mean pharmaceuticals, plastics, electrical components, jet fuel, beer, perfume, powerful acids and any number of other substances ranging from the essential to the esoteric. You will, naturally, have to learn a great deal about chemistry, but you'll also study the engineering behind the processes and reactors used to manufacture different substances, drawing on fields of physics such as thermodynamics and fluid dynamics.

This may be the course for you if:

- ❑ **You love the idea of being an engineer but don't want to give up chemistry:** At both Oxford and Cambridge, you can study Chemical Engineering via the Engineering degrees[92]. Have a look at the Engineering chapter on page 169. If this appeals to you but you want to keep up some chemistry, you can specialise in chemical engineering later down the line.
- ❑ **You're happy to continue studying maths and physics.** Chemical Engineering is, at its heart, an engineering degree, so if the thought of continuing with advanced maths and physics fills you with dread, then this probably isn't the degree for you. Bear in mind, however, that even if you do a pure Chemistry degree (see page 193), you won't completely be able to escape maths and physics—they underpin all of the physical sciences.
- ❑ **You like the sound of producing useful products**: For instance, chemical engineers are heavily involved in producing medical drugs and fuels[93]. Chemical engineers develop practical processes and design manufacturing plants—if that sounds like something you'd find reward-

92 At Cambridge, you can also study Chemical Engineering via the Natural Sciences route.

93 The pharmaceutical and energy industries are among the most popular destinations for chemical engineers.

ing, chemical engineering might be for you. If you prefer the idea of researching new materials or reactions, without having to worry about the practicalities of producing them, maybe Materials Science and Chemistry are degrees to consider instead? See page 187 and page 193 respectively for more details[94].

- ❑ **You like the idea of creating efficiencies:** A major consideration in actually producing chemicals is efficiency. If you have a strong interest in science and technology, but it matters a lot to you that their environmental impacts are positive rather than negative, pursuing chemical engineering is a great way to help work towards reducing waste, pollution, and energy consumption.
- ❑ **You are interested bringing products to market:** Part of being a chemical engineer is taking new chemical discoveries and figuring out how to make them affordable and profitable. So if you have an interest in both business and science, this degree might be the one for you.

Chemical Engineering is offered at Cambridge as a standalone degree. However, you start the degree as either an Engineering or Natural Sciences student, and take up Chemical Engineering from your second year onwards. See Chapters 11 and 14 (on pages 169 and 205 respectively) for information about these first-year courses. Cambridge states that the Engineering and Natural Sciences routes are equally good preparation for Chemical Engineering.

You can leave after 3 years with a BA, or after 4 years with an MEng that gives you the accreditation needed to become a chartered engineer[95]. To some extent, this degree could be thought of as the engineering-oriented complement to Oxford's research-oriented Chemistry degree. If you love chemistry as a subject, you might base your choice between the Chemistry and Chemical Engineering degrees on the types of work you can most see yourself doing after you graduate.

At Oxford, Chemical Engineering isn't offered as a standalone subject, but is something you can specialise in as part of the Engineering Science degree (see Chapter 11).

94 If you apply for Chemical Engineering via Natural Sciences at Cambridge, you'll have the chance to check out both these fields in your first year to decide what you want to focus on.

95 You can also move into Manufacturing Engineering after your second year. See page 180 for more details.

# 15.2: How do you apply for Chemical Engineering?

The application process will be the same as applying for Engineering or Natural Sciences, depending on which route you choose, except that Chemistry is a required A Level. See page 171 for the Engineering route and page 207 for the Natural Sciences route.

The typical offer is A*A*A, or 40–42 in the IB with 776 at Higher Level. Chemistry and Maths are required A-Level/Higher-Level subjects for all applicants; Physics is required for applicants taking the Engineering route, but also for Natural Sciences applicants at some colleges. You'll need to take the ENGAA (page 246) or NSAA (page 250), depending on the route you choose.

On average, around 1 in 8 applicants is successful via the Engineering route, and 1 in 9 via the Natural Sciences route.

# Part II B: The Application Process

Hopefully you've managed to have a look at Part IIA and figured out which physical science course is for you—now let's make sure you get in! In this part, we'll discuss the demands of each step of the application process for each course – from personal statement, to admissions test, to interview – and give you a step-by-step guide to getting your offer.

# Chapter 16: Personal statements

In this chapter, we'll give you some tips on preparing for and writing your physical science personal statement. It could be argued that the personal statement is given less weight for physical sciences than other parts of the application process such as admissions tests and interviews. Nonetheless, your personal statement should show you in your best light by highlighting your Ability, Passion and Potential and by using concrete examples.

You need to remember that every sentence of your personal statement needs to answer this specific question for the admissions tutor:

**"Why would *this* student succeed in studying *this* subject at *this* university?"**

And remember, it's a *personal* statement. Make sure you talk about yourself, your achievements, and *why* you think *you* would be suitable for the course that you are applying for.

In the next few sections, we will touch upon the types of things you might want to include in your personal statement and present books that you can read in advance of writing it. Finally, we'll show you some examples of real personal statements from current Oxbridge students.

## 16.1: What to include in your personal statement

The most important rule to follow is that everything your personal statement should provide evidence for at least one of:

- Your current **ability** in your subject and all the different associated skills
- Your **passion** for your subject and an understanding of what it really entails
- Your **potential** as a student and your capacity for study and mastering new skills.

In our example personal statements in the next few sections, you'll see how to demonstrate each of these points.

## General physical science personal statement advice

### 1) Extra problem solving Ability Passion

A good thing to include in your personal statement is any further exploration of the subject you've done. This could be through school competitions relevant to your subject, or extra problems found in books or online.

### 2) Lectures and online videos Passion

Another way to showcase your passion for your subject is by referencing lectures and videos you have enjoyed, and further study you have done as a consequence of these videos. For example, a good sentence to include would be:

> *"After attending a lecture at Imperial College about optical computing, I decided to use some of the ideas in my team's entry for the Schools Aerospace Challenge. Using a series of online videos to learn more about fibre optics, I managed to create a workable design for a fly-by-light system."*

### 3) Independent study Ability Passion Potential

Independent study is a crucial skill at university, and admissions tutors are looking for examples of this. Here are ways you can engage in independent study and show it off on your personal statement:

- If your school offers the EPQ (Extended Project Qualification) or indeed any type of extended essay project in sixth form, this is a great way to explore a topic in depth.[96] Include information in your personal statement about your independent research and how you wrote the essay out of your passion to increase your knowledge. Here are some example EPQ topics relating to the physical sciences:
  - The history of quantum mechanics
  - The first trip to the moon and the engineering behind the rocket
  - The chemistry behind chocolate and what makes it so addictive.

---

96 Note: although an EPQ is a great way of demonstrating independent study, if you have an opportunity to study Further Maths A Level instead, this is generally preferred for physical sciences at Oxbridge.

- You can also develop your independent study skills by completing an online course. There are many online short courses listed on websites such as Coursera or FutureLearn.[97] You can find a variety great courses here, from Forensic Science to Atmospheric Chemistry. Courses typically include a certificate of completion, which is a brilliant thing to include in your personal statement.
- If there's a topic that really interests you, why not consider doing a project on it? Not only will this give you the opportunity to investigate something you find fascinating, but you'll also end up with a tangible outcome which will demonstrate that interest to others.

### 4) Internships or further lab study Passion Potential

If you've completed relevant work experience or extra lab work, it will make a brilliant addition to your personal statement! You could include a sentence such as:

> *"This summer, I arranged a placement with an engineering firm at Southend airport. I was fascinated to learn how passing a current through a wing could be used to detect metal fractures. I'm really looking forward to learning more about the crystal structure of metals in the Materials Science degree."*

However, if your work experience is not relevant to your subject, don't force it to appear so. Instead, use it to demonstrate different skills relevant to university study, for example:

> *"I'm particularly fascinated by the entrepreneurial and management aspects of engineering. In my roles as Head Girl and leader of my school's team for the Magistrates Mock Trial Competition, I have developed leadership, communication and teamwork skills which I believe will prepare me for the group project work that an Engineering degree will demand of me."*

Oxford and Cambridge both value industrial experience particularly highly for Engineering, as well as for related courses such as Materials Science and Chemical Engineering. If you have an opportunity for work experience in any field of engineering or science, this will strengthen your personal

97 Find links to some good courses at oxbridgeformula.co.uk/bonus-chapter

statement! Even if it's only for a few days, engaging practically with the profession will make your application stand out.

**Top Tip**

*Finding* ***relevant work experience*** *isn't always easy, but you could try some of the following:*

- ***Contacts:*** *Take advantage of the support of your school or the university where you're applying; your teachers or advisors will often know where previous students have found work experience, and might even be able to make a warm introduction. Likewise, ask your family, and family friends, if they know anyone in a relevant field.*
- ***Initiative:*** *Feel free to reach out to labs and businesses within engineering industries who might be willing to look kindly on a polite and eager student.*
- ***Social media:*** *Use social media sites such as LinkedIn to help you connect with people in your field.*

*Remember: cold contacting people can be hit-or-miss, but admissions tutors know that not everyone can find work experience. If you only manage to find a couple of days of work experience make sure you can comment intelligently on what you learnt.*

*"You could contact local companies such as car manufacturers for engineering work experience. There are also organisations such as The STEM Exchange and In2Science,[98] which might be able to help you get relevant experience."* –Kim, Engineering Science, Oxford

## Further personal statement ideas by subject

### Physics

**Lectures and videos:**
Some good online resources are for further research are:

- Feynman's online lectures
- The Minute Physics YouTube channel

98 See oxbridgeformula.co.uk/bonus-chapter for more information on these schemes.

- The Physics Girl YouTube channel
- The Physics Crash Course YouTube channel.[99]

## Physics & Philosophy

**History of science:** Finding reading relating to both philosophy and physics can be hard, whereas books and videos on the history of science are relatively plentiful—but they often touch on the philosophy of science anyway. Any time you read about scientists using thought experiments, thinking about the scientific method, or engaging in debates with each other, there's often a philosophical idea you can extract to talk about in your personal statement or interview.

## Engineering

**Practical hobbies:** Rather than just talking about sport or music, it could benefit you to be able to talk about something you enjoy designing or making, especially if it requires problem-solving ability, use of technology, iterated design or teamwork, since these all require skills that are relevant to an Engineering degree.

## Materials Science

**Further research:** Reading around materials science through any of the books mentioned in the next section is a good way to explore the discipline. Here are a few resources offering interesting insights on materials science you can mention in your personal statement.

- **The BBC** covers stories such as 'Could plant-based plastics help tackle waste pollution?' or 'How plastic became a victim of its own success'. These will offer insights into the current issues faced by materials scientists. Programmes to watch or listen include:
  - 'Horizon'
  - 'How to Build...'
  - 'Inside the Factory'.
- **New Scientist** magazine gives a great overview of science in the news.
- **Materials Today** contains articles that are more technical than the others, but they give you a strong idea of highly relevant research areas.

99 See oxbridgeformula.co.uk/bonus-chapter for links to these and plenty of other useful resources.

## Chemistry

**Chemistry problems:** It's useful to compete in the UK Chemistry Olympiad—or to simply do the papers, all of which can all be found online. Also, the Cambridge Chemistry Challenge has lots of problems to solve, all of which will be good fodder for your personal statement and useful interview preparation.

## Physical Natural Sciences

**Connections between the sciences:** An important technique to master when writing your personal statement for Physical Natural Sciences is linking the different sciences together. To make your personal statement flow, avoid just writing about each as a standalone subject, and find a way to connect them.

**Top Tip**

***Laboratory experience*** *can be linked to more than one science by talking about how the skills you developed are transferable. For example, you could have a sentence linking chemistry to physics such as:*

> *"While investigating halogens in a lab over the summer, I developed a collection of practical skills, including writing risk assessments and data analysis. These skills will be directly transferable to my degree in terms of the chemistry practical work and the physics lab work. The practical side of a Natural Sciences degree really interests me because..."*

**Top Tip**

*Find topics that straddle two or more subjects and use these to link two together on your personal statement.*

- **Maths and physics:** *Think about mechanics modules, or how integral maths is in deriving equations that are central to physics. Physics requires a strong mathematical skillset, so you can easily link the two subjects.*
- **Physics and chemistry:** *Many subjects sit on the boundary between physics and chemistry, such as materials science. If materials science interests you, this may be a nice way to weave together physics and chemistry.*

- **Chemistry and maths:** *Describe the mathematical skills required in analysing data from a chemistry lab (for example, calculating yield), or the maths required for physical chemistry.*

*You can also discuss the general scientific skills you've learnt (through lectures, extra problems or work experience) and use these as a way of connecting two disciplines.*

## 16.2: Books to read if you're interested in the physical sciences

Reading is a fantastic way to investigate your subject outside of the school curriculum and gauge your interest in it. Including a sentence or two in your personal statement about a book you particularly loved (with a brief analysis of your favourite section) is also a great way to show the admissions tutors your passion to explore the discipline. Be sure to clearly link the books to your passion for the subject and *explain why each book made you want to study the course.*

Here are some of our favourite books on the physical sciences:[100]

### Physics books

**Feynman: *Six Easy Pieces***

This book covers the most accessible material from Feynman's university lecture series on the major concepts of contemporary physics. This book is a useful 'taster' of the style of physics you'll be exposed to at university. As it covers a broad range of topics, it can help ignite an interest in a specific area and lead you to further investigation—something that will impress admissions tutors when it comes to your personal statement! If you enjoy Feynman's lectures, you can watch and read a wide variety of them online, and read his follow-up book *Six Not So Easy Pieces*, which is focused on relativity.

100 See oxbridgeformula.co.uk/bonus-chapter for links to all of these books, and more!

### Hawking: *A Brief History of Time*

This classic physics book asks many of the questions central to the subject:

- Was there a beginning of time?
- Will there be an end of time?
- Is the universe infinite?
- Is anything infinite?

This book is a great overview of the major thinkers in the field (including Newton and Einstein), and covers key physics topics such as spiral galaxies and black holes. If you enjoy this book, you can also read his follow up: *The Universe in a Nutshell.*

### Bryson: *A Short History of Nearly Everything*

This is a popular science book, covering the basics of key physics concepts such as:

- The solar system
- Quantum developments
- The history of physics
- Einstein's theory of relativity.

Although the physics included is not particularly technical, it's an enjoyable read and gives an accessible and informative overview of the subject.

### Povey: *Professor Povey's Perplexing Problems*

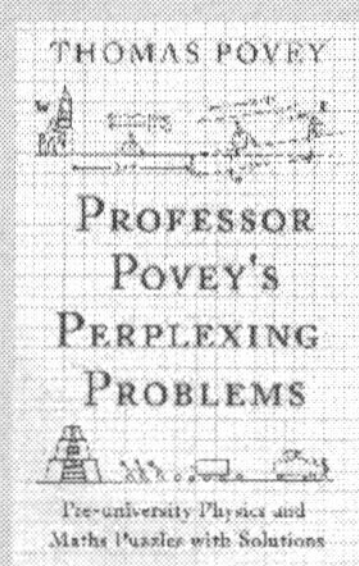


This is less of a 'sit down and read' book than the others, but still a hugely useful introduction to university physics. It includes over 100 physics and maths problems that traverse the boundary between school and university study. It will massively hone your problem-solving skills and give you a good indication of whether or not physics is indeed the course for you! This book is also useful preparation for admissions tests and (especially) interviews.

## Physics & Philosophy books

### Kuhn: *The Structure of Scientific Revolutions*

This is a landmark text about the history of science, written by the philosopher Thomas Kuhn. It revolutionised the way that both physicists and philosophers view and approach science and introduced the term 'paradigm shift', which is now fully integrated into everyday speech. It explores how science has developed over time and explores many of the central discoveries through a philosophical lens. If you don't have the time to read the whole text, it's worth reading a summary, because it contains ideas that are still important in both physics and philosophy today.

### Becker: *What is Real?*

This is a historical and philosophical discussion of a number of influential approaches to understanding quantum mechanics. This book is highly opinionated in the sense that it criticises commonly-held ideas about quantum mechanics, but it attempts to provide reasons for its criticisms and gives an even-handed overview of other positions without favouring one. A great way to get an insight into the types of debate that quantum mechanics has inspired since its creation.

### Albert: *Time and Chance*

An introduction to the problem of the arrow of time. The 'arrow of time' refers to the fact that some physical processes can be reversed and others can't. For instance, a cake can be put down and picked up again, but it can't be burned and then unburned—burning is irreversible. The problem is that the interactions between particles that make up the cake and the air around it aren't irreversible, at least not in the same way, and burning is merely a particular rearrangement of those particles, so how do we explain the fact we can't unburn the cake? Albert discusses the relationship of this problem to thermodynamics and probability and attempts to describe a solution.

For further recommendations of philosophy books, head to page 441.

## Engineering books

**Blockley: *Engineering: A very short introduction***

Engineering has a rich and varied history, and this book is a great introduction to the broad scope of the discipline. It outlines many of the key fields in engineering and how the systems we employ today came to be. It traces engineering all the way from its Archimedean roots to the modern world, exploring the role of engineering in the techno-era that is the21st century.

**Norman: *The Design of Everyday Things***

A famous text in the fields of engineering and psychology, this book considers why some products appeal to human nature and others don't. It explores what makes a system appeal to the human psyche—and why some designs are less attractive and usable than others. Although you won't find many equations or heavy scientific theory in it, it's an important investigation into why we need well-designed systems and an interesting take on engineering as a discipline.

**Lawlor: *Engineering in Society***

This book outlines the role that engineering plays in a wide variety of careers. It includes a diverse spectrum of fields in which engineering is essential, and aims to show the prospective engineering student where their degree might take them.

**Gordon: *Structures: Or Why Things Don't Fall Down***

This book provides an insight into some of the core concepts of engineering in a way that is stripped of jargon and complicated equations. In an accessible, engaging style, it offers intuitive answers to everyday questions such as: 'Why don't suspension bridges collapse?' and 'How do dams hold back water?' If you want an overview of the type of problems you'll solve in an engineering degree, this is a good place to start.

**Petroski: *Pushing the Limits: New Adventures into Engineering***

This text is an overview of the feats of modern engineering. It examines many of the failures and success stories of modern engineering, focusing on the author's personal experience with large engineering projects such as the Three Gorges Dam in China. If you're interested in learning about how engineering has shaped history, this is a brilliant book!

## Materials Science books

**Miodownik: *Stuff Matters: The Strange Stories of the Marvellous Materials that Shape Our Man-Made World***

Mark Miodownik's book is the most accessible of the works listed here, and it's a great entry point into materials science. We love how Miodownik describes his view of the world. He unpicks everything from the viewpoint of a materials scientist, breaking down why specific materials lead to successful products. Before your interview, it might be useful for you to mentally dissect objects around you in the same manner.

**Ball: *Made to Measure: New Materials for the 21st Century***

> *"I read this book in the summer holiday before interviews and found it fascinating. It's very readable and covers some of the more technological advances in materials."* –Inigo, Materials Science, Oxford

*Made to Measure* explores a wide range of technological advances, including a light-activated walking table! Bear in mind that this book was written in 1997—so imagine how advanced research must be over 20 years later!

**Cotterill: *The Material World***

This is an extremely detailed book covering many of the essential concepts in materials science, from supernovae to consciousness and everything in between. It's a great way to start looking at the world as a materials scientist would. The fact that it doesn't go into much *mathematical* detail makes it all the more accessible and enjoyable.

**Gordon: *The New Science of Strong Materials: Or Why You Don't Fall Through the Floor***

Gordon is definitely more interested in the engineering side of materials science, and this comes through in his book. He answers questions that are vital for engineers, such as: 'Why is wood a suitable material for certain objects and not others?' The book is similar to *Made to Measure* in that the world is presented from a materials perspective but in a very readable fashion.

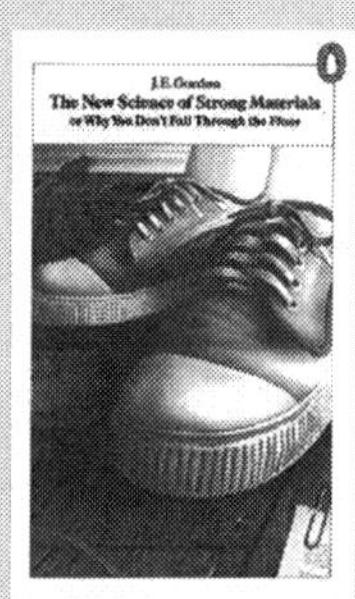

**Martin: *Materials for Engineering***

This book tackles the hard maths and engineering aspects of materials, as well as materials properties. It's not as easy to read as other books listed here, but it's worth a skim if you can get a copy. Usefully, each section ends with a series of questions that make valuable pre-interview practice questions.

## Chemistry books

**Keeler and Wothers: *Why Chemical Reactions Happen***

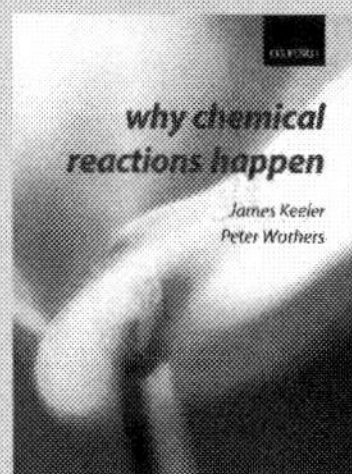


This book offers an overview of the subject, exploring what chemical processes are and why they happen. It does not make the traditional divide between physical, inorganic and organic chemistry. It explains (with diagrams) how bonding in molecules occurs, how molecules interact, how different reactions occur and what their outcome will be. This is a good book to give you a sense of the key topics in chemistry at university.

***Chemistry World Journal***

This is a monthly chemistry journal published by the RSC (Royal Society of Chemistry). It's great to read because it covers recent developments and current affairs in chemistry.

**Sykes: *Mechanisms in Organic Chemistry***

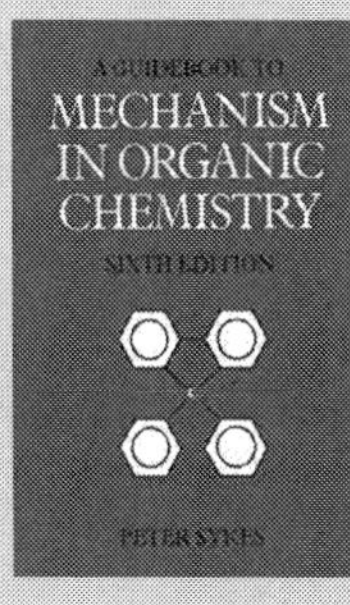


This is a textbook on organic chemistry, so parts will be inaccessible to an A-Level student. However, much of it is comprehensible due to its clarity and multitude of examples. It's aimed at university students, but if you want a taster of the type of study you'll do at university and to push your understanding a bit further—this is a great book to dip in and out of.

**Atkins: *What is Chemistry?***

This is an accessible text designed to help you to see chemistry through a chemist's eyes. This book touches on the relationship of chemistry to the wider world, such as chemistry's role in power generation and transport. This is a comprehensive guide to chemistry's central role in society, and it will give you an insight into the breadth and depth of the discipline.

**Emsley: *Nature's Building Blocks***

This is an A–Z guide to the elements. Each element is discussed in terms of its history, structure, uses and means of identification. In the process, the book introduces a range of chemical techniques and key facets of chemistry. It's highly readable, and also great to dip in and out of if you want to pick one element to read about at a time.

## Earth Sciences books

This is a standalone degree offered at Oxford (and which is beyond the scope of this book), but it's also one of the subjects you can study as part of Cambridge's Natural Sciences programme. Although you most likely won't be interviewed on earth sciences for Natural Sciences (as it's taught from its foundations), reading around the subject will demonstrate your independent studying abilities and give you a feel for the subject.

**Hazen: *The Story of the Earth***

This book takes a historical approach to the formation of the Earth. Hazen also tackles issues the Earth is currently facing and introduces the key concepts and methods of Earth Sciences. It's an accessible read, covering the entire scope of the history of the Earth. Another highly accessible history of the Earth and its features, such as mountain ranges and ice caps, is Fortey's *The Earth: An Intimate History.*

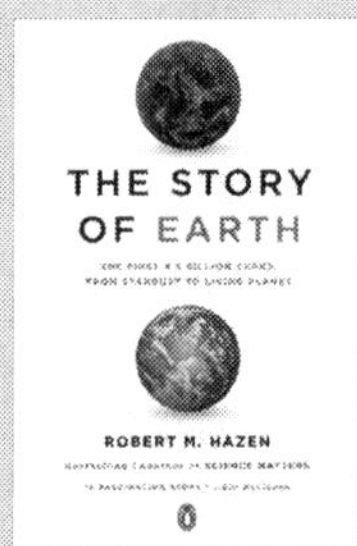

**Press: *Understanding Earth***

This is more of an academic textbook, and is a solid insight into university-level Earth Sciences. It provides introductory lessons into much of the theory of Earth Sciences, as well as the experimental fieldwork techniques required. Fieldwork is a big part of the Cambridge course and is assessed throughout the degree.

**Stow: *Vanished Ocean***

A history of the Tethys ocean; don't be embarrassed if you haven't heard of it, as it no longer exists. This book discusses how scientists can learn about the features of the Earth in the distant past. This means discussing the relationships between land, ocean, atmosphere and life—and the traces they leave on the present (for instance, the distribution of fossils and oil reserves).

# 16.3: Example Physics & Philosophy personal statement

The following four sections show you how to use the tips from the previous two sections to write a brilliant personal statement. The personal statements you see here are real personal statements of successful Oxbridge applicants.

You'll benefit from reading any of these personal statements, no matter what degree you end up applying for—as the techniques are applicable to any scientific subject.

I have always been passionate about hiking. I love climbing to new altitudes, and reached 4228m last year. Ironically, at these heights, the hackneyed phrase 'time flies when you're having fun' carries new meaning—as time passes slightly faster at high altitudes due to time dilation. I read about this in 'Quantum Theory Cannot Hurt You' by Marcus Chown, though I think this book confined itself to a list of pop physics facts rather than explaining the mechanism by which they work. In contrast, in

'The Order of Time', Carlo Rovelli uses general relativity to explain that due to space-time distortion caused by masses—our straight, inertial trajectory through a curved space-time causes us to accelerate towards large masses.

**Passion** **Potential** Critiquing and comparing the books you've read demonstrates genuine interest and a capacity for critical reflection that is vital for further study of science and philosophy.

I found another example of the flexibility of time in Curiosity, an app that collates science articles. There, I read about John Wheeler's *gedankenexperiment* in which the pre-conceptualised double-slit experiment is carried out, but the screen showing interference can be removed instantly to reveal a detector for each slit—demonstrating that the final conditions of the experiment retroactively determine the initial state of the photon. I look forward to studying physics because I want to delve deeper into the mechanisms of phenomena (such as the double-slit experiment or time dilation) to achieve a more precise model of the universe, and I look forward to learning the mathematical mechanisms behind well-known facts.

**Passion** Feel free to be this direct about why you want to study the subject. That is, after all, what the personal statement is for.

**Passion** Wanting to know 'why' things work is always a positive.

Rovelli's ideas on time intrigued me so I attended New Scientist Live, where he stole the show and I discovered a fascination for his theory of quantum loop gravity. I have subsequently read 'Reality Is Not What It Seems' and 'Anaximander'. I revelled in the philosophical discussion that ensued from Rovelli's talk (especially his confutation of block universe theory), and I look forward to returning next week! I find myself at home in the intellectual atmosphere of the lectures at the Royal Institution and Royal Society. Studying Theory of Knowledge helped me appreciate epistemology and the importance of analysing the scientific claims we make, which is touched on by both Rovelli and A.J. Ayer in 'Language, Truth and Logic'.

**Passion** **Potential**: Giving the admissions tutor some reassurance that the student is suited to a highly academic setting.

In an independent experiment for my coursework, I collected data to model the synchronisation of coupled metronomes, and demonstrated that the time taken for synchronisation varies sinusoidally with the initial phase difference of the pendula. I also wrote an essay on heat treatments of aluminium alloys, which required deep

**Ability** Describing a project you've done is worth much less without a precise, quantitative description of what you found—this is a great example of how to do it right.

independent research into their material properties and how these could be improved on a microscopic level. This taught me the importance of academic rigour and precise data analysis. I have been on a work placement in an R&D centre at Brunel University, where I became familiar with the life of a researcher and the applications and limitations of physics in industry by collecting data and optimising industrial processes.

**Ability** **Potential** Notice how the student summarises the key skills learned from every experience they mention that will come in handy at university.

I chose to apply post-qualification and take a year out, and I was successful in securing a position as software engineer on a full-year contract for a publicly listed software development company. I am adding to my existing coding and analysis skills, having now mastered C# and SQL. This experience is allowing me to apply my academic learnings in real-life business and social contexts. Alongside coding, I enjoy applying my problem-solving skills in the Maths and Physics Olympiads, scoring in the top third of the BPhO last year. My hobbies include playing the classical and electric guitar, and I have been in an eclectic mixture of bands, ranging from playing in a jazz band to starting my own rock band, and even playing as session guitarist for Jesus Christ Superstar. I led my school's chess team in the Briant Poulter league, and I intend to keep up my chess and music at university. I also founded our student-led Logic Puzzle Club, in which we met to solve and discuss puzzles and paradoxes.

**Ability** Taking a year out is not in itself a problem, but the admissions tutors will want to know you have kept intellectually active and on top of your subject. Ideally, you would have picked up useful skills (in this case, coding is widely applicable in modern physics and in your degree).

## 16.4: Example Chemistry personal statement

Nearly all children experience an astonishing urge to ask every question that comes to their heads. Despite having grown up, I find I still wonder: How have the things surrounding me been made? What materials have been used and why? That is why I love chemistry, a science that gives logical answers to questions resulting from basic curiosity. What's more, hard work in a laboratory, however painstaking, assures me we can find solutions that are more than theoretical, but connected with the practical world.

**Passion** Everyone says they love their subject, but adding a touch of explanation helps make it feel genuine.

**Potential** acknowledging the work is hard but worth it anyway already marks you as better prepared for the degree course than the average applicant.

'Organic Chemistry', written by John McMurry, highlights how basic information about molecules or reactions relates to biochemistry, life processes and the pharmaceutical and chemical industries—and thus I consider it one of the best books I have ever read. For certain, it has shaped the way I look at chemistry.

Good to include books you have read and particularly enjoyed, but make sure you know the topics inside out—you may be (gently) quizzed on them at interview.

I have been working in a school laboratory since 2012, learning the basics of analytical chemistry. I also attended chemistry workshops at Warsaw University of Technology in 2013, 2014 and 2016—and at the University of Warsaw in 2014 and 2016. The workshops covered a wide range of topics such as organic chemistry, classical analytical chemistry, NMR spectroscopy and crystallography. I took part in the Fifth National Meeting of Young Chemists organized by the University of Gdańsk and Gdańsk University of Technology. My level of knowledge and skills, in both theoretical and analytical chemistry, has been proven in the 61st and 62nd National Chemistry Olympiad (against about 1000 participants), in which I came 24th and 9th, respectively. I also won the 52nd Antoni Swinarski Chemistry Contest, organized by Nicolaus Copernicus University in Toruń, as well as some local competitions.

**Potential** Laboratory work is a huge part of studying chemistry at university, and therefore if you do have experience it's highly valuable.

**Ability** A great, concrete example of success in a relevant field.

I learn chemistry in individual lessons, which is a privilege for those most eager to learn and with outstanding potential and prospects. The organisation of these tutorials, similar to Oxford's style, has strengthened my ability to effectively organise my timetable and study independently, and also allowed me to study chemistry to an advanced level with added content from the university programme. I also have extended-level classes in English, Physics and Mathematics. I find the latter two subjects crucial for deepening my understanding of chemistry. Evidence of my high level of knowledge in those two fields can be seen in my outstanding results in the LXVIIth Mathematical Olympiad (places 28th–41st) and the 65th Physics Olympiad (a title in the national stage). I have been a Scholar of the Prime Minister of Poland for the academic year 2015/16. These results show my ability to think creatively, logically and learn exact sciences fast and easily.

**Potential** Examples of independent study, showing the admissions tutor that this candidate is well-suited to the style of teaching at Oxbridge.

**Ability** (if not yet potential): It's great to draw out the skills that these achievements demonstrate, and could be made even better by stating how they would make you successful at university.

I have been engaged in organising extra classes on advanced chemistry and research group meetings at school for the past three years. Helping teachers communicate complex problems and prepare lessons, materials, tests and samples for analytical chemistry has helped me consolidate my knowledge. Currently, I lead two 1-hour workshops per week with students four years my junior, and help prepare lessons for those who are a year or two older than that. I also create study materials to prepare other students from my high school for various contests and the Chemistry Olympiad. These experiences with teaching are a wonderful challenge, and are very rewarding because I enjoy helping other students very much. I look forward to widening my perspectives and to learning as much as possible from the best chemists.

**Ability** **Potential** Again, drawing out what was learned; perhaps being so keen to discuss the subject with others also demonstrates passion.

## 16.5: Example Engineering personal statement

Having been fascinated from an early age by the way things work, in school I enjoyed not only the challenges posed by science and technology, but also the many ways in which they provide the answers to questions. I currently hold an Arkwright Engineering Scholarship (sponsored by the RAF), which has given me invaluable opportunities and insight.

While studying for my GCSEs, I took part in engineering projects such as designing a hybrid rocket engine and building a voice-controlled robot. These projects involved a large amount of research (such as engine and nozzle design, propellants, use of 3D modelling software, Python, and printed circuit board design and manufacture). By the end, I had designed a de Laval nozzle and fabricated a PCB using school's facilities. These projects culminated in my selection for a residential trip to Keble College Oxford for an Ogden Trust Science Camp. We toured the Engineering and Materials Science departments, and throughout the trip we solved various problems with basic tools. This strengthened my ambition to study engineering at university.

**Potential** Knowledge of things such as Python and modelling software is impressive, but what's even more impressive here is that the student has demonstrated they can do independent research and apply it.

That summer I spent a week at the Italian Institute of Technology in Genoa shadowing working engineers; this gave me a solid insight into the workplace. I was based in their Robotics Engineering department and was able to witness how all the disciplines of engineering connected to produce a product. One of the robots was a quadruped designed to navigate uneven terrain, such as that found after an earthquake. From this I learned about the hydraulic systems powering the movement, and also the complex programming and electronics that allowed it to stabilise itself. I saw how the robot used a laser to scan the environment and build a point cloud map based on the time taken for the laser light to bounce off objects in its surroundings. Using funds from my Arkwright Scholarship, I attended a Smallpiece Engineering Course at the University of Leeds entitled 'Advanced Nuclear Engineering'. Here we learnt about the nuclear industry, which gave me a better understanding of what nuclear engineers do. We researched different types of reaction cycles and how reactors are designed to harvest the greatest yield of energy. Nuclear engineers also design systems to reduce nuclear waste; this includes the extraction of certain isotopes, such as strontium-89, that can be used in medicine. We attended several workshops and lectures, some of which included lab work, to help us understand how the UK uses an open fuel cycle and how spent fuel is reprocessed at sites such as Sellafield. I was also invited to RAF Cranwell and later RAF Odiham to learn about engineers in the RAF. We were also given leadership training, which has improved my team building and communication skills.

**Potential** Work experience in the engineering industry makes you a much more convincing candidate to admissions tutors, but don't panic if you can't organise a whole week in one place![101]

**Passion** **Potential** It's imperative to link something you were exposed to in a practical context to something interesting you learnt from it.

**Ability** **Passion** **Potential** Any extra courses you have done, whether in person or online, are great to include in your personal statement, as they show you can handle the material, are motivated to do extra work and are able to learn independently.

This sentence on its own doesn't tell us much about the person who wrote it, so it could have been left out. If kept, it would be even better to link it to the university course or degree applied for, or your own interests.

Would be great to link these transferable skills to how they will help make you successful in a degree course such as Engineering.

101 For ideas on how to find relevant work experience, please see oxbridgeformula.co.uk/bonus-chapter.

To complement my school work I read 'Space Race' by Deborah Cadbury, which chronicles the history of space missions from 1945 up to the historic Apollo 11 of 1969. This book detailed not only the numerous engineering challenges faced by both nations but also the human aspects of engineering such as being able to present ideas, raise funds and deliver on time. I will also be attending a Masterclass on Aerodynamics at the University of Bolton in October. In school, I have taken part in many competitions such as the Chemistry Olympiad, the Alan Turning MathsBombe challenge and the UKMT Senior Maths Challenge, in which I received a Bronze Certificate. I have volunteered as a mathematics tutor at a local primary school, and worked with the local Guide Dogs to raise awareness and funds. This has helped to improve my leadership and people skills.

I believe I will enjoy an Engineering degree, as it will challenge me to think about problems in a new way and help me apply my knowledge of mathematics and physics to benefit society. After university, I intend to join the RAF as an engineering officer.

**Passion** **Potential** You don't need to have settled on a specific career. In fact, the Oxford and Cambridge Engineering courses are unusually broad and theoretical, and being too specific might suggest you're not interested in that approach. But this student manages to emphasise their motivation without falling into that trap.

# 16.6: Example Physical Natural Sciences personal statement

As a student with a genuine scientific curiosity, I wish to gain a more rigorous understanding of the natural laws which govern the world around us. As such, I take as many opportunities as possible to challenge myself in my A-Level subjects. For the last 2 years, I have attained a merit in the first round of the British Mathematical Olympiad. Moreover, this year I won a gold award in the Cambridge C3L6 Chemistry Challenge and silver in the British Chemistry Olympiad.

**Ability** **Passion** **Potential** Solid examples of achievements in your discipline beyond the A-Level course really enhance your personal statement; here the student manages to do more than merely demonstrating their ability by explaining their motivation to take on new challenges—which is promising for their further development as a scientist.

The book Professor Povey's Perplexing Problems has provided me with regular and fun challenges; after attempting all of these, I have also deeply relished the opportunity to teach myself the new maths and physics required to solve the site's weekly challenge boards. Thus, I want to read this course at university because I want to dive even further into the mathematical and physical sciences.

This summer, I wrote an essay explaining the significance of each of Maxwell's laws; I found it astounding how his electromagnetic wave equation led him to predict that light was in fact an 'electromagnetic disturbance'. I also conducted an investigation into the mathematics behind radioactive decay that looked at the equations governing a chain of two radioactive decays and concluded with the general case involving n-nuclides. This project, more than any other, brought home to me the necessity of mathematical rigour and persistence in problem-solving. More recently, I completed a research project on 'Millikan's Oil Drop' experiment, the first to find the value of the electronic constant e. Learning about how Millikan minimised systematic error in his setup, including measuring the viscosity of air using 5 unique methods, helped me appreciate the incredible degree of precision needed in experimental science.

**Potential** Great! This student is showing they understand what the degree course would be like.

**Potential** Details of specific research projects completed are great, as long as they explain what you gain from them and why they made you want to study the course.

However, it's the interface between the sciences which fascinates me most of all. A first lesson in these connections came when I read *Why Chemical Reactions Happen* by Keeler and Wothers, a book that explains the mechanisms at the heart of chemistry using molecular orbital theory. I found it revelatory that the second law of thermodynamics and quantum mechanics drive all chemical interactions, a fact that forced me to recognise that a solid background in physics is critical to understanding chemistry at a basic level. A work placement at Oxford University on tissue engineering was an even more striking lesson on the importance of this interface; while reviewing literature on the latest methods of 3D bioprinting, I realised that a thorough understanding of chemistry, biology and material science was required to synthesise animal tissue using cell-laden hydrogels. I now know that pursuing a career in research science often requires an ability to work between the disciplines.

**Passion** **Potential** This paragraph gives a very good reason for wanting to pursue Natural Sciences (as opposed to a single science) and demonstrates an understanding of the demands of the course.

I am also passionate about spreading my love of maths and science to others. Last year I ran weekly Maths A Level mentoring sessions a local school; I found it challenging (but rewarding) to explain core mathematical concepts in a way that my mentees could fully understand. As an editor of my school's academic yearbook, as well as the maths and science magazine, I encourage my peers to write STEM articles. Through reviewing and editing intriguing pieces, I hope to not only introduce myself to areas of STEM I haven't met before but also to spark an interest in such subjects in my fellow students.

Outside of the classroom, my adventurous attitude has led me to engage with as many activities as possible. I love long-distance running, singing bass in choir, as well as rowing and playing the piano. Balancing these commitments with the responsibility of being an academic prefect has taught me how to manage my time wisely and prosper in a high-pressure environment. And so, combined with my enthusiasm for the subject, I believe that these qualities will enable me to thrive as I work towards my ambition of becoming a practising scientist.

**Passion** **Potential**
Linking extra-curricular interests back to the discipline and why you would thrive at university is a nice way to conclude.

# Chapter 17:
# Physical science admissions tests

Once you've written your personal statement and submitted your UCAS application, the next step is your admissions test. The following table shows you which test you'll need to take. In this chapter, we'll discuss what the different physical science admissions tests (PAT, ENGAA, NSAA) entail and how to prepare for them, and suggest exam techniques to help you ace them!

| Course | University | Test | Page Number |
|---|---|---|---|
| Physics | Oxford | PAT | Page 240 |
| Physics & Philosophy | Oxford | PAT | Page 240 |
| Engineering[102] | Oxford | PAT | Page 240 |
| | Cambridge | ENGAA[103] | Page 246 |
| Materials Science | Oxford | PAT | Page 240 |
| Chemistry | Oxford | TSA, Section 1 only | Page 373 |
| Natural Sciences[104] | Cambridge | NSAA[105] | Page 250 |

## 17.1: PAT: The Facts

**Q Who wants the PAT?**

**A** The PAT is the Physics Aptitude Test set by Oxford. It's a mixture of physics and maths questions based on the Physics and Maths

102 Applicants for Chemical Engineering via Engineering also take the ENGAA.
103 Colleges for mature students don't use the ENGAA and use an at-interview test instead.
104 Applicants for Chemical Engineering via Natural Sciences also take the NSAA.
105 Colleges for mature students don't use the NSAA and use an at-interview test instead.

A-Level syllabi. It must be sat as a pre-interview assessment by all Oxford applicants for:

- Physics
- Physics & Philosophy
- Engineering
- Materials Science.

**Q When is the PAT sat?**

**A** It's sat in late October or early November before the interview stage of the application process.

**Q What is the purpose of the PAT?**

**A** It's designed to determine your academic potential and assess your ability to use scientific and mathematical knowledge in unfamiliar contexts. As many candidates applying for Physics will be predicted the typical offer grades or above, the PAT acts as an important differentiator when selecting candidates for interview, indicating whether or not you would cope well with university physics.

**Q How long is the PAT?**

**A** The PAT lasts 2 hours.

**Q How is the PAT structured?**

**A** The PAT is made up of multiple-choice and long-answer questions. Each multiple-choice question is positively marked,[106] and in long-answer questions your working is marked. There are 100 marks available across the paper and there are no optional questions to choose from: you're expected to answer every question. There are 12 2-mark multiple-choice questions, and around 10–12 long-answer questions worth varying numbers of marks.

**Q What is the content of the PAT?**

**A** The PAT is designed to test both your maths and physics skills, so the content is broadly taken from the A-Level syllabus. As syllabi differ between exam boards, it's important to familiarise yourself with what is actually required for the PAT.

106 Positively marked meaning you don't lose marks if you get a question wrong.

**Maths:**

The maths tested won't go beyond the scope of A-Level Maths, but it may include topics from later on in the A-Level course that you haven't yet covered in school. You should get to know the full syllabus, which is available in our free guidebook.[107] The maths topics covered include:

- **Elementary maths:** Arithmetic, geometry, coordinate geometry, probability
- **Algebra:** Polynomials, graph sketching,* differentiation, transformations, inequalities, trigonometry
- **Logs and exponential functions:*** Graphs, properties and identities
- **Series:** Arithmetic and geometric
- **Binomial expansions:** For integer powers $\geq 2$
- **Calculus:** Advanced differentiation* and advanced integration.*

*(*) Topics you may not have covered at school by the time you sit the PAT.*

**Physics:**

The physics covered is based on the A-Level syllabus. Note that the A-Level syllabus differs between exam boards, and our free guidebook contains a comprehensive view of the PAT syllabus. When your paper is marked, you won't receive special compensation if you haven't studied the topic the question tests. The onus is on you to study the extra material; this is a great example of the type of independent study required at university.

Broadly, the physics topics covered are:

- **Mechanics:** Distance, velocity, speed and acceleration equations, graphical analysis, response of a system to multiple forces, circular motion, levers/pulleys, springs, kinetic energy, conservation of energy
- **Waves and optics:** Longitudinal and transverse waves, amplitude, frequency, period, wavelength and speed of a wave, electromagnetic spectrum, reflection at plane mirrors, refraction, interference, diffraction, standing waves

107 Find it at oxbridgeformula.co.uk/pat.

- **Electricity and magnetism:** Current, voltage, resistance, transformers, circuit diagrams, electrostatic forces, photoelectric effect
- **The natural world:** Atomic structure, the solar system, the Earth-Moon system, circular orbits, satellites.

Although the focus is on maths and physics, you may also be faced with general problem-solving questions that test skills developed over both your Maths and Physics A Levels and GCSEs.

**Q What do I get as well as the paper?**

**A** You can use a calculator for the PAT. However, you don't get a formula booklet.

**Q What score do I need?**

**A** The average score among all applicants is around 60, but to guarantee an interview and increase your likelihood of receiving an offer, you want to be scoring above 70 out of 100.

**Q Where can I find PAT past papers?**

**A** Scan the QR code here to find PAT past papers:

## Q What does a PAT multiple-choice physics question look like?

**A** A child stands on a roundabout facing the centre. They throw a ball to the centre of the roundabout twice—first when it is still, and then when it is rotating clockwise. How should they adjust their throw the second time compared to the first time? [2]

| A | B | C | D | E |
|---|---|---|---|---|
| Aim more to the left | Aim more to the right | Throw straight, but harder | Throw straight, but less hard | Throw the same as before |

## Q What does a PAT multiple-choice maths question look like?

**A** I roll a 6-sided die. If the result is a 1, I will re-roll, but I will not re-roll more than twice. What is the probability that the final result is less than 3? [2]

| A | B | C | D | E |
|---|---|---|---|---|
| $\frac{36}{216}$ | $\frac{43}{216}$ | $\frac{44}{216}$ | $\frac{86}{216}$ | $\frac{87}{216}$ |

## Q What does a PAT long-answer physics question look like?

**A**

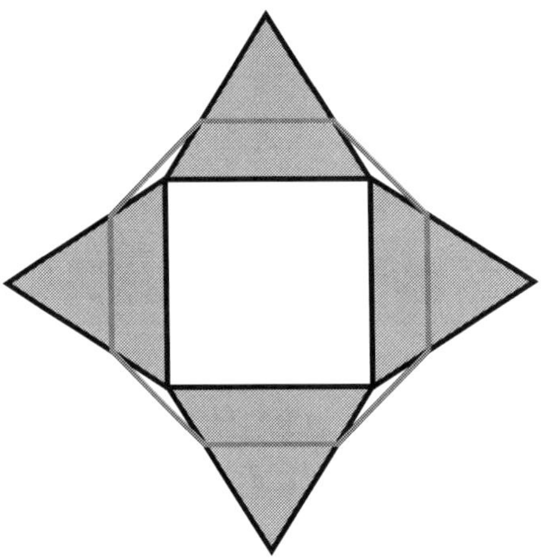

Four identical glass prisms are arranged as shown, with their bases meeting at right angles. The cross-section of each prism is an equilateral triangle with sides of length 1cm.

A ray of monochromatic light passes through each prism in turn, completing a loop. The path traced out by the ray is a regular octagon.

(a) Find the refractive index of the glass. [3]
(b) Describe the path of the ray if its wavelength is increased slightly. [2]

**Q What does a PAT long-answer maths question look like?**

**A** Sketch the graph given by the equation $\log_2(y) = \log_3(x+1)$. [5]

**Q Where can I find more details about the PAT?**

**A** For more details of the PAT find our free guidebook at oxbridgeformula.co.uk/pat or scan the QR code below.

**Did You Know?**

*In 2019, the average score in the maths section of the PAT was around 13 percentage points higher than the average physics score. Unlike in previous years, the two sections were mixed (instead of a separate maths section first), meaning the disparity can't have been due to students running out of time to do the physics. An explanation might be that the physics questions tend to be a bit more out of the ordinary—you often have to interpret an unfamiliar physical scenario quickly and intuitively to be able to find the answer.*

## 17.2: ENGAA: The Facts

**Q Who wants the ENGAA?**

**A** The ENGAA (Engineering Admissions Assessment) is a test taken by applicants for Engineering and Chemical Engineering at Cambridge.

**Q When is the ENGAA sat?**

**A** It's sat in late October or early November, before the interview stage of the application process.

**Q What is the purpose of the ENGAA?**

**A** The ENGAA is used to decide whether or not you'll be invited to interview. It's also used in deciding who gets offers.

**Q How long is the ENGAA?**

**A** The ENGAA is divided into two sections, and you have an hour for each.

**Q How is the ENGAA structured?**

**A** **Section 1**
This is a multiple-choice section including both maths and physics questions. It consists of 40 multiple-choice questions, and is divided into two parts:

- Part A: Maths and physics (20 questions)
- Part B: Advanced maths and advanced physics (20 questions)

**Top Tip**

*The ENGAA is* ***positively marked****, so there's no harm in guessing if you run out of time. You do not lose marks for incorrect answers. Each question in Section 1 is equally weighted; you get 1 mark if your answer is correct, and 0 marks if it's not.*

**Section 2**

Section 2 is multiple-choice, but it focuses on advanced physics only. You only have 20 questions to answer, but they are more difficult than Section 1 and more often than not require knowledge from several topics.

**Q What is the content of the ENGAA?**

**A** The ENGAA uses content from the A-Level Maths and Physics courses, but does not include any Further Maths content.

Topics covered in Section 1:

Part A:

**Maths:** Content from the first year of A-Level Maths: numbers, algebra, geometry, measures, statistics and probability.

**Physics:** Content from the first year of A-Level Physics: electricity, motion and energy, thermal physics, waves, the electromagnetic spectrum and radioactivity.

Part B:

**Advanced Maths:** Content comes from later on in the A-Level course:[108] algebra and functions, sequences and series, coordinate geometry, trigonometry, exponentials and logarithms, differentiation, integration and graphs of functions.

**Advanced Physics:** Extra topics include: forces and equilibrium, kinematics, Newton's laws, momentum and energy.

Topics covered in Section 2:

You can be tested on anything that appeared in Section 1, as well as some more involved concepts from the A-Level syllabus. These are: vectors and scalars, mechanics, mechanical properties of matter, electric circuits, waves and quantum and nuclear physics.

**Q What do I get as well as the paper?**

**A** Nothing; the ENGAA is a non-calculator paper and you also don't get a formula booklet.

108 Some of which you might not have studied yet.

**Q What score do I need?**

**A** The ENGAA is marked on a scale of 1.0–9.0, and although different colleges will use different criteria, you want to be scoring about 6.0 to be in with a decent chance of success. Aim to score 70% in each section.

Extrapolating from previous years, the number of correct answers needed for each score in Parts A and B of Section 1 are roughly:

Part A:

| Standardised score | Correct answers out of 20 |
|---|---|
| 1.0 | 0 |
| 2.0 | 8 |
| 3.0 | 10 |
| 4.0 | 12 |
| 5.0 | 13 |
| 6.0 | 15 |
| 7.0 | 16 |
| 8.0 | 17 |
| 9.0 | 18 |

Part B:

| Standardised score | Correct answers out of 20 |
|---|---|
| 1.0 | 0 |
| 2.0 | 4 |
| 3.0 | 5 |
| 4.0 | 6 |
| 5.0 | 8 |
| 6.0 | 10 |
| 7.0 | 12 |
| 8.0 | 14 |
| 9.0 | 16 |

In previous years, Section 2 has not been marked on the 1.0–9.0 scale and instead has been kept as a raw score.

**Q Where can I find ENGAA past papers?**

**A** Scan the QR code here to find ENGAA past papers:

oxbridgeformula.co.uk

**Q What does an ENGAA Section 1 maths question look like?**

**A** You are given that, for $x$ measured in radians,

$$\int_0^{\frac{\pi}{2}} \sin(x)dx = 1$$

Find the value of the integral

$$\int_0^{\frac{3\pi}{2}} (1 + |\sin(x)|)\mathrm{d}x$$

**A** $\frac{\pi}{2}+1$ **B** $\frac{\pi}{2}+3$ **C** $\frac{3\pi}{2}+1$ **D** $\frac{3\pi}{2}+3$ **E** $\frac{9\pi}{2}+3$

**Q What does an ENGAA Section 1 physics question look like?**

**A** A scientist calculates that: for some quantity $X$ associated with the electric field around a charged particle, $X > 0$ within a radius $R$ related to the charge $Q$ and mass $M$ of the particle.

If $c$ is the speed of light and $k$ is the constant in Coulomb's Law $F = \frac{kq_1q_2}{r^2}$ for the force between charges $q_1$ and $q_2$ separated by distance $r$, which of the following could conceivably be an expression for $R$?

**A** $\frac{2kMc^2}{Q}$ **B** $\frac{2kMc^2}{Q^2}$ **C** $\frac{2kQ}{Mc^2}$ **D** $\frac{2kQ^2}{Mc^2}$ **E** $\frac{2k}{c^2}$

**Q What does an ENGAA Section 2 question look like?**

**A**

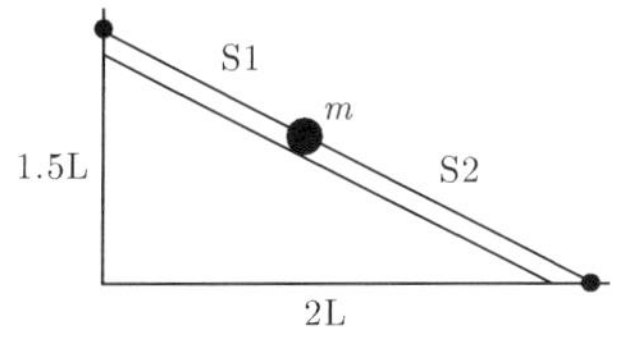


A point mass $m$ lies on a smooth wedge as shown, joined to the ends of the top face of the wedge by springs S1 and S2. Each spring has natural length $L$ and stiffness $k$. The vertical height of the wedge is $1.5L$ and its horizontal width is $2L$.

Find the height of the mass above the horizontal base of the wedge when the system is in equilibrium. (Gravitational field strength = $g$.)

**A** $\frac{3}{32}\left(10L - \frac{3mg}{k}\right)$ **B** $\frac{3}{100}\left(25L - \frac{6mg}{k}\right)$ **C** $\frac{3}{20}\left(5L - \frac{6mg}{k}\right)$

**D** $\frac{1}{25}\left(25L - \frac{8mg}{k}\right)$ **E** $\frac{1}{10}\left(12.5L - \frac{3mg}{k}\right)$

**Q Where can I find more details about the ENGAA?**

**A** For more details of the ENGAA, find our free guidebook at oxbridgeformula.co.uk/engaa.

**Did You Know?**

*A few Cambridge colleges have chosen to make STEP offers for Engineering in the past. In 2016 and 2017, Christ's College made STEP offers to 19 out of 22 of their Engineering intake. It's best to check the website of the college you're thinking of applying to, to check the latest guidance in your year of application. For more information about STEP, see page 80.*

## 17.3: NSAA: The Facts[109]

**Q Who wants the NSAA?**

**A** The NSAA (Natural Sciences Admissions Assessment) is Cambridge's pre-interview Natural Sciences aptitude test; it's designed to test how you think, using what you know.

**Q When is the NSAA sat?**

**A** It's sat in late October or early November, before the interview stage of the application process.

109 At the time of printing, Cambridge has announced that the NSAA will be changing, but has not released details. Please see oxbridgeformula.co.uk/bonus-chapter for updates.

**Q What is the purpose of the NSAA?**

**A** It's used as an indicator as to whether or not you should be invited to interview, and whether you would be able to cope with the taxing nature of a Natural Sciences degree.

**Q How long is the NSAA?**

**A** It's composed of two sections and lasts 2 hours overall.

**Q How is the NSAA structured?**

**A** **Section 1:**
A multiple-choice assessment consisting of five parts, of which you must answer three. You have 80 minutes for this section. The five parts are:

- Part A: Mathematics
- Part B: Physics
- Part C: Chemistry
- Part D: Biology
- Part E: Advanced Mathematics and Advanced Physics.

Each part contains 18 questions of equal weighting. You'll score 1 mark for each correct answer, and you won't lose marks for incorrect or unanswered questions.

**Section 2:**
Section 2 is not multiple-choice; you might be asked for numerical calculations, written explanations or diagrams. It consists of 6 questions, of which you must answer 2. You have 40 minutes for this section. There are 2 questions each on biology, chemistry and physics. In this section, you may be expected to draw diagrams and analyse data, including drawing graphs. If you can't answer one part of a question, later parts may still be solvable. You can answer any 2 of the 6 questions; they don't have to be from the same science.

**Q What is the content of the NSAA?**

**A** The content covered in the NSAA is largely based on the first-year courses of the respective A Levels. However, there may be some discrepancies due to differences between syllabi. You're not required to have done Further Maths A Level to answer the questions in Section 1 Part E, but there may be some topics beyond the first year of Maths A Level; it's good to review these before sitting the NSAA if you intend to answer this section.[110]

**Maths content required (Section 1):**
The content for the maths section is taken from the first year of the A-Level Pure Maths course. You'll potentially be asked questions on topics such as numbers, algebra, geometry, statistics and probability.

**Physics content required:**
Most content required for the physics section of the NSAA is taken from the first year A-Level Physics course.

***Section 1***
The topics include electricity, motion and energy, thermal physics, waves, electromagnetism and radioactivity.

***Section 2***
For the long-answer questions in this section, you're expected to understand: vectors and scalars, mechanics, mechanical properties of matter, electric circuits, waves and quantum and nuclear physics, as well as the content in Section 1.

**Chemistry content required:**
***Section 1***
The topics covered in the chemistry syllabus for Section 1 are atomic structure, the periodic table, chemical reactions and equations, quantitative chemistry, oxidation, reduction and redox reactions, chemical bonding, structure and properties, group chemistry, separation techniques, acids, bases and salts, rates of reaction, energetics and electrolysis.

***Section 2***
You can be tested on any of the content examined in Section 1, and you must be familiar with: formulae, equations and amounts of substances, atomic structure, bonding and structure, energetics, kinetics, equilibria, inorganic chemistry and organic chemistry.

110 Details of all these topics can be found in our free online NSAA guidebook here: oxbridgeformula.co.uk/nsaa.

**Advanced maths and physics content required:**

***Maths:***

The topics covered include algebra and functions, sequences and series, coordinate geometry, trigonometry, exponentials and logarithms, differentiation, integration and graphs of functions.

***Physics:***

The topics covered include forces and equilibrium, kinematics, Newton's laws, momentum and energy.

If you are applying for Biological Natural Sciences, it is likely that you will sit Section 1 Part D, Biology. As we are only discussing the Physical Natural Sciences in this book, we won't discuss the Biology syllabus here. Please see oxbridgeformula.co.uk/nsaa for resources and extra questions for Biological Natural Sciences.

**Q What do I get as well as the paper?**

**A** Calculators cannot be used in Section 1 of the NSAA, but they can be used in Section 2. You do not get a formula booklet.

**Q How well do I need to do on the NSAA?**

**A** The NSAA Section 1 is graded on a scale of 1.0–9.0, and a score of 6.0+ (about 60%) is generally seen as a good score: this is where you should be aiming. Very few applicants will achieve a perfect score of 9.0.

In 2016, the score conversion for Section 1 was:

| Raw mark in any part | Part A: Maths standard-ised score | Part B: Physics standard-ised score | Part C: Chemistry standard-ised score | Part D: Biology standard-ised score | Part E: Adv. Maths and Physics standard-ised score |
|---|---|---|---|---|---|
| 0 | 1.0 | 1.0 | 1.0 | 1.0 | 1.0 |
| 1 | 1.0 | 1.0 | 1.0 | 1.0 | 1.0 |
| 2 | 1.0 | 1.0 | 1.0 | 1.0 | 1.0 |
| 3 | 1.0 | 1.0 | 1.0 | 1.0 | 1.8 |
| 4 | 1.0 | 1.7 | 1.2 | 1.0 | 2.7 |

| Raw mark in any part | Part A: Maths standard-ised score | Part B: Physics standard-ised score | Part C: Chemistry standard-ised score | Part D: Biology standard-ised score | Part E: Adv. Maths and Physics standard-ised score |
|---|---|---|---|---|---|
| 5 | 1.3 | 2.5 | 2.0 | 1.0 | 3.4 |
| 6 | 1.8 | 3.2 | 2.7 | 1.0 | 4.0 |
| 7 | 2.3 | 3.8 | 3.4 | 1.5 | 4.6 |
| 8 | 2.7 | 4.5 | 4.0 | 2.1 | 5.1 |
| 9 | 3.1 | 5.1 | 4.6 | 2.7 | 5.7 |
| 10 | 3.6 | 5.7 | 5.2 | 3.3 | 6.2 |
| 11 | 4.0 | 6.3 | 5.8 | 3.9 | 6.7 |
| 12 | 4.5 | 7.0 | 6.5 | 4.6 | 7.3 |
| 13 | 5.0 | 7.7 | 7.1 | 5.3 | 7.9 |
| 14 | 5.5 | 8.5 | 7.9 | 6.0 | 8.6 |
| 15 | 6.2 | 9.0 | 8.7 | 6.9 | 9.0 |
| 16 | 7.0 | 9.0 | 9.0 | 8.1 | 9.0 |
| 17 | 8.3 | 9.0 | 9.0 | 9.0 | 9.0 |
| 18 | 9.0 | 9.0 | 9.0 | 9.0 | 9.0 |

Section 2 is left as a raw mark, but you should again aim for at least 60%.

**Q Where can I find NSAA past papers?**

**A** Scan the QR code here to find NSAA past papers:

## Q What does an NSAA multiple-choice biology question look like?

**A** A woman has a mutant allele in one of her X-chromosomes, which is associated with a recessive genetic condition. The only effect of this condition is that, if a fertilized egg has it, it will develop into identical twins.

The woman has children with a partner who does not have the mutant allele. All of her children also have children with partners who do not have the mutant allele. Which of the following could happen?

**1** All of her children and grandchildren are twins

**2** None of her children are twins, but all of her grandchildren are

**3** All of her children and grandchildren are male non-twins

(Assume the rate of bearing twins in mothers without the mutant allele is 0%.)

**A** none of them
**B** 1 only
**C** 2 only
**D** 3 only
**E** 1 and 2 only
**F** 1 and 3 only
**G** 2 and 3 only
**H** 1, 2 and 3

## Q What does an NSAA multiple-choice chemistry question look like?

**A** Monochloramine reacts with ammonia to give hydrazine and hydrogen chloride. The following equation describes the reaction, with some details obscured:

$$N_xH_2Cl + A \rightarrow N_2H_y + B$$

where A represents a single molecule of ammonia and B represents a single molecule of hydrogen chloride.

Which of the following are true of monochloramone and hydrazine?

**A** Neither contains any N-N bonds

**B** One contains no N-N bonds; the other contains an N-N single bond

**C** One contains no N-N bonds; the other contains an N-N double bond

**D** Both contain an N-N single bond
**E** One contains an N-N single bond; the other contains an N-N double bond
**F** Both contain an N-N double bond

**Q What does an NSAA multiple-choice physics or maths question look like?**

**A** The NSAA Part A (Maths) and Part B (Physics) questions are almost identical to the ENGAA Section 1 Part A questions.

The NSAA Part E (Advanced Maths and Advanced Physics) questions are almost identical to the ENGAA Section 1 Part B questions.

See the ENGAA table starting on page 246 for examples of these.

**Q What does an NSAA Section 2 question look like?**

**A** An NSAA Section 2 Physics question looks as follows[111]:

A car of mass $M$ accelerates along a flat road, starting from rest at time $t = 0$.

The effects of friction and air resistance are negligible. Its motor provides constant power $P$, independent of its speed $v$.

a) Given that $F$ is the driving force in Newtons, write down an expression for $F$ in terms of $v$ and $P$. [1 mark]

Answer: ______________________________

______________________________

b) (i) Explain in words why the kinetic energy of the car increases at a linear rate. [2 marks]

Answer: ______________________________

______________________________

111 In the real thing, there would be many lines for your working after each 'Answer:'

(ii) Using an expression for the kinetic energy of the car, calculate $v$ as a function of $t$, $P$, and $M$. [3 marks]

Answer: ____________________

____________________

(iii) Hence, calculate the acceleration $a$ as a function of $t$. [3 marks]

Answer: ____________________

____________________

(iv) Verify that your answers from (ii) and (iii) satisfy the relationship you stated in (a). [2 marks]

Answer: ____________________

____________________

c) Using your answers from (b), calculate the distance travelled $d$ as a function of $t$. [6 marks]

Answer: ____________________

____________________

d) Describe in words the motion of the car over a long period of time. [3 marks]

Answer: ____________________

____________________

The biology and chemistry questions are very similar in format.

**Q Where can I find more details about the NSAA?**

**A** For more details about the NSAA, check out our free guidebook at oxbridgeformula.co.uk/nsaa

**Did You Know?**

*Your score for each multiple-choice part of Section 1 of the NSAA is converted into a scaled score between 1 and 9, with 9 being the best. In 2017, of those applicants who scored 9 in the Advanced Maths and Physics Part, 1 in 3 still scored 7 or below in Part A, which contains what might be thought of as 'easier' maths. Make sure you check your work thoroughly and proceed methodically, even in the 'easier' questions.*

# 17.4: How should you prepare for PAT/ ENGAA/NSAA?

## When should you start preparing?

For all of these tests, it's vital to make the most of the summer between Years 12 and 13, because free time will be a scarce resource in Year 13. Once the summer holiday ends, you'll be busy studying for A Levels, writing your personal statement and completing your UCAS application! Preparing for your admissions test at the last minute simply isn't an option. In fact, it's best to start preparing around May or June of Year 12 after your school exams, to clarify what topics need the most effort over the summer. This isn't to say you should stop preparing once term starts again in September—you'll need to maintain and improve your readiness all the way up to the exam.

## What should you do to prepare?

There are numerous ways you can prepare for your admissions tests. Many of the preparation tips apply to more than one test, which is why we put together this handy table:

| PAT | ENGAA | NSAA | Preparation tip |
|---|---|---|---|
| ✓ | ✓ | ✓ | **Look over the syllabus**<br>For all three tests, familiarise yourself with all the content covered. Although you'll probably have studied much of the content in your A Levels, you could be tested on |

| PAT | ENGAA | NSAA | Preparation tip |
|---|---|---|---|
| | | | topics you haven't yet learnt; being caught out in the exam means missing marks![112] |
| ✓ | ✓ | ✓ | **Review past papers**<br>There are lots of past papers available, and doing these is the best way to prepare. The questions are of a slightly different and more involved style compared to your A Levels. It's important to do a good amount of practice—ideally, all of the papers. This is a great way to understand the reasoning behind the questions and develop your own methods for solving them.<br><br>*"Practice is the most important thing for the PAT, ENGAA or NSAA, so make sure you do lots of timed papers! Initially, do some papers without timing yourself so that you can get to grips with the structure and style of the questions. However, as you get closer to the exam, it's vital to practise in timed conditions."*<br><br>PAT past papers: |

112 If you need help with this, the Oxbridge Formula Physics Admissions Summer School covers all the topics you'll need for PAT, ENGAA and NSAA—and our guidebooks give a detailed breakdown of all the content needed. Head to oxbridgeformula.co.uk for more information.

| PAT | ENGAA | NSAA | Preparation tip |
|---|---|---|---|
| | | | ENGAA past papers:<br><br>NSAA past papers: |
| ✓ | ✓ | ✓ | **Do extra problems**<br>There is a bank of past papers for each test available, but if you run out, you can find questions of a similar style to practise with. *Professor Povey's Perplexing Problems* includes plenty of these, as does the Physics Olympiad. We also offer extra past-paper-style questions/mock papers with worked video solutions. In our Physics Problem Solving course,[113] tutors will guide you through mock paper questions and help you hone the skills required to succeed in the exam. |
| ✓ | ✓ | ✓ | **Work to time constraints**<br>All three papers are time-pressured, so it's important to practise putting yourself under time constraints. Try and answer individual questions in short amounts of time, |

113 Details of this course can be found at oxbridgeformula.co.uk.

| PAT | ENGAA | NSAA | Preparation tip |
|---|---|---|---|
| | | | and practise moving through the multiple-choice questions as fast as you can.<br><br>Remember: with the multiple-choice questions, you don't always have to find the *exact* answer. You can also use deduction and rule out the answers you know are wrong. We also have a Physics and Maths Time-Saving Tricks course to help you work quickly with physical science and maths questions.[114] |
| ✓ | ✓ | ✓ | **Prepare your maths**<br>A large part of every test is focused on maths, and it's important to practise your maths alongside your science subjects. Make sure you revise your A-Level maths syllabus, and practise more problem-solving in maths; the UKMT papers are a good resource here. We run a course on problem-solving in mathematics, a skill that is invaluable for both the physics and maths elements.[115] |
| ✓ | ✓ | ✓ | **Do other multiple-choice questions**<br>You can use other papers to help prepare for the mathematical multiple-choice questions. Some examples are:<br><br>■ MAT multiple-choice questions<br>■ TMUA Paper 1<br>■ Other physical science tests (such as ENGAA) to help with PAT and vice versa, and the Mathematics section of the NSAA.<br><br>For even more advice on preparing for maths multiple-choice questions, see the multiple-choice advice on page 88. |

114 Details of this course can be found at oxbridgeformula.co.uk; the course takes place in October, so check the website a few months before to book your place.
115 See further details at oxbridgeformula.co.uk/pat.

| PAT | ENGAA | NSAA | Preparation tip |
|---|---|---|---|
| ✓ | | ✓ | **Practise long-answer questions**<br>These questions are more developed than the short answer questions. They are more likely to involve both subject knowledge and maths skills, and require a little more time and thought than the short-answer questions. To prepare, you need to practise as many questions as you can, and also make sure you're completely familiar with the content so that you can apply it in more complex situations. |
| | | ✓ | **Tackle all of the harder questions**<br>In Section 2 of the NSAA, you have a choice of questions to answer. It's worth practising the questions you wouldn't naturally choose in an exam. For example, if you're intending to answer one physics question and one chemistry question in Section 2, make sure you practise *both* of the chemistry and physics questions when preparing.<br><br>Even if you're hoping to answer questions on only one science, if you study another subject at A Level, it would be worth preparing for those questions too, in case the questions in your preferred science turn out to be horribly difficult. |

**Top Tip**

*ENGAA and NSAA past papers only go back to 2016, so you need to do more practice than simply review past papers. If you're looking for **extra practice**, you can find mock papers and video solutions as part of our online resources.*[116]

116 See oxbridgeformula.co.uk/engaa for mock papers and more!

# 17.5: Exam techniques for PAT/ENGAA/NSAA

When the day of the test finally arrives, you need to make sure you perform at your best. You've done all the preparation, but what specific things can you do while sitting in the exam hall to make sure that all of your hard work doesn't go to waste?

Below, we look at some specific 'exam techniques' that you should start practising during your preparation, so that nerves don't get the better of you during the real thing and you can show the admissions tutors exactly why you're worth bringing to interview!

| PAT | ENGAA | NSAA | Examination technique |
|---|---|---|---|
| ✓ | | ✓ | **Tips for the long-answer questions**<br>■ **Marks:** The long-answer questions are worth more marks, so make sure you set aside enough time for them.<br>■ **Order:** Some students benefit from not doing questions in the order they're set and instead doing questions they like the look of first. This isn't for everyone, but it might build up your confidence for questions you're less comfortable with.<br>■ **Move on if needed:** Remember, you can leave out later parts, or earlier parts if there's a 'show that' question whose result you can use for the next part of the question. Make sure you have a good go, but it's not the end of the world if you can't get every answer. It's better not to waste time on a question you're making no progress with. Unlike the multiple-choice section, there are marks available for working in the long-answer section. In fact, this is exactly what they want to see—your reasoning. |
| ✓ | | ✓ | **Sketch out possible solutions**<br>■ **Facts and formulae:**[117] When you get to the longer questions, it's a good idea to write down a list of relevant facts and equations that you may need. That |

117 Since there's no formula booklet given, you should aim to memorise and understand formulae as you learn them in class. This will help you with admissions tests as well as your A Levels.

| PAT | ENGAA | NSAA | Examination technique |
|---|---|---|---|
| | | | way, when you're working through the question you'll have a reference point and something already written down, which may gain you some marks.<br>■ **Tell the examiner what you *would* do:** If you're running out of time but you can see how to solve the question, sketch out a rough solution. Try to write down the relevant calculations, as this will hopefully still get you some marks. |
| ✓ | ✓ | ✓ | **Eliminate answers that are clearly wrong**<br>Sometimes, in a multiple-choice question, although the algebra/numbers you're manipulating may seem complicated, some of the options are clearly wrong. For example, you may be able to see that the answer will be in surd form, and so you can eliminate those options that are rational. Or some answers may be unreasonably large or small, or have the wrong units.[118]<br><br>Even if you don't have time to reach a final solution, eliminating those answers you can see are clearly wrong will narrow down the options from which to make an educated guess, meaning you're more likely to get the correct answer.<br><br>Some question styles naturally lend themselves to this elimination method. For example, you may get a question that has a list of statements, and you have to decide which is true. Here, eliminating the obviously false statements is the way to go. |
| ✓ | ✓ | ✓ | **Make estimates**<br>With *some* multiple-choice questions, it's possible to estimate. For example, if you're comparing complicated expressions, you can round them and hope only one of the options will be in the ballpark. This won't work for |

118 For instance, if $h$ is a height and $t$ is a time, $\frac{2h}{t}$ could be the correct expression for a speed because it's distance/time, but $\frac{2t}{h}$ can't be because it's time/distance.

| PAT | ENGAA | NSAA | Examination technique |
|---|---|---|---|
| | | | every question, but remember: there are no marks for working, so it doesn't matter *how* you reach the answer. Precision isn't *always* necessary!<br><br>With some of the questions, especially those on physics, you may be given options that are all of different orders of magnitude (as in: have different powers of 10 in standard form). For such questions, estimation of the sizes of the numbers given is a great way to quickly select the correct answer. |
| ✓ | ✓ | ✓ | **Take a guess**<br>If you can't answer a multiple-choice question and you're running out of time, just guess—there's no harm in it. Ideally, take a moment to rule out some of the obviously wrong answers, as this can improve the odds of you guessing the right answer from, say, 1 in 5 to 1 in 3. |

## PAT time management

- ❑ **Multiple-choice/long-answer split:** You get 2 hours for the PAT, and there are about 12 multiple-choice questions and 10-12 long-answer questions. Around 75% of the marks will be in the latter section, so this is where you want to spend most of your time.
- ❑ **Number of minutes per section:** You have 6 minutes for every 5 marks, or 72 seconds per mark, but you may be able to race through the multiple-choice questions; ideally you'll spend no more than 2 minutes on each. A good time-split might be 20 minutes on the multiple-choice questions and 1 hour 40 minutes on the long-answer questions.
- ❑ **Rationing your time:** It might also be worth aiming to spend less time per mark on the earlier long-answer questions, as the later questions are harder and you may need more time to get those extra marks.

## ENGAA time management

Both sections of the ENGAA are very time-pressured. Many candidates won't complete all of the questions, leaving some to guesswork. You have

60 minutes to do 40 questions in Section 1, which works out as 90 seconds per question—but you should probably aim for closer to 80 seconds or less in Part A, and 100+ seconds in Part B. In Section 2, you have more time per question (3 minutes), but the questions are more complex and require multiple steps.

## NSAA time management

### Section 1

In this section, you're expected to answer 54 multiple-choice questions in 80 minutes, so that's 89 seconds per question. Therefore, it's vital not to spend lots of time weighing up a question as it will affect your chances of finishing the section. If you're doing Part E (advanced maths and physics), it will be more difficult than Parts A to D, so try to leave at least 30–35 minutes for it. That means spending about 80 seconds per question in the Parts you choose out of Parts A to D—only a small speed increase.

### Section 2

Section 2 is more difficult than Section 1 because it requires longer answers. You need to answer 2 questions in 40 minutes. Unlike in Section 1, where you'll likely go in knowing which 3 of the 5 parts you'll answer, which questions you end up doing will probably depend on the questions themselves.

That's why it's worth taking a couple of minutes to read the questions thoroughly, including *all* the parts of any question you might realistically pick. A question may seem more appealing at first but later become very complicated, so you need to read the questions carefully to inform your judgment.

Having reviewed and selected your two questions, you'll probably have about 17 minutes remaining per question. The questions are quite involved, so the minutes will fly by. Try to be as quick as you can in the earlier parts of each question. You want to bag these marks before the question becomes more complicated and you might need to dedicate more time. This is where knowing the A-Level syllabus like the back of your hand will really help

Remember, in Section 2 you want your working to be clear and scientifically justified. Managing your time doesn't mean neglecting your working, because it's actually a source of marks here. Make sure you write down all the formulae you use and include scientific justification for any steps you take. The examiners want to see your scientific understanding, and this section is really your opportunity to show that off.

Generally, for *both sections* of the NSAA, it's worth starting in your comfort zone. First, complete the questions you're most comfortable with to bag early marks and boost your confidence and reserve the rest of your time to deal with the trickier questions.

# Chapter 18: Interviews

Interviews are an essential part of the Oxbridge admissions process. They are daunting, shrouded in mystery and the subject of many a myth—so it's difficult to know what to expect. This chapter aims to bust some of those myths and give you advice about how to prepare for your interviews. We've even included example interview transcripts based on the real experiences of current Oxbridge students.

Why not also check out our interview with real Oxbridge interviewers on page 143?

## 18.1: What will your interview be like?

Your Oxbridge physical science interviews are likely to centre upon a series of scientific and mathematical problems. You'll have anywhere between two and four interviewers, and you'll be expected to solve a problem in conversation with them—either on a whiteboard or a piece of paper.

The single most important thing in interviews is to speak your thoughts out loud rather than working your solution out in your head, even (especially) if you don't know the answer yet. You need to explain your plans, questions, worries and reasons. Otherwise, the interviewers can't tell what you're thinking about and won't have any way to evaluate you.

> *"The single most important thing in interviews is to speak your thoughts out loud."*

### Will you be asked about your personal statement?

If there's something that particularly interests the interviewers, or that needs clarifying, they may ask you questions about your personal statement—so be sure you can answer a question on anything you have mentioned. It's definitely worth reading through your personal statement beforehand and asking yourself questions on every section (or getting someone else to quiz you). However, your personal statement won't be the focal point of your interviews—they will be predominantly subject-based. It's unlikely you'll be asked many personal questions unrelated to science or your motivations behind studying the subject.

*"I wrote about high-temperature superconductors in my personal statement. In my interview at St Catherine's College, I was interviewed by a world expert in that exact subject!"* –Inigo, Materials Science, Oxford

*"We don't always ask questions about the personal statement and, if we do, it's usually to warm the candidate up. We don't tend to use the answers to these questions when scoring the applicant out of 10."* –Interviewer, Physics, Oxford

## Will you have to do lots of mental maths?

The interviewers aren't testing how quickly you can do subtraction or long division, and although these skills are important, don't worry about them too much. Even if your mental maths slips up, they are far more interested in seeing your thought process and scientific reasoning. Don't spend a disproportionate of time in the interview double checking or even triple checking your calculations—this isn't what the interviewers are testing!

## Should you take a calculator?

No. The interviewers will provide any resources you need, and it's unlikely you'll require a calculator.

## Will they discuss your admissions test?

It's unlikely, but possible, that your interview will touch upon your admissions test. If it does, it may be to correct an issue you previously had with a problem, or to continue developing a question that was on the admissions test. At Cambridge, you may also have a test when you arrive, and the interviewers are likely to go through the questions from this with you at interview. Some colleges may give you material to read and understand at home ahead of the interview.

## Will the interviewers help you?

Remember: although the interviews will be tough, you won't find yourself in a 'sink or swim' situation. The interviewers want you to find the questions challenging and will give you advice to guide you through, as this allows them to see how 'teachable' you are and how quickly you can grasp new ideas. Seeing how you respond to their tips and guidance is part of the process. Make sure you listen to them—they will never try to throw you off with a trick question or hint!

## How do Oxford and Cambridge interviews differ?

**Oxford**

At Oxford, you'll nearly always have two or more interviews. These will incorporate science and mathematical questions, and be based on (but extend) your existing knowledge. Students often get one maths question and one relevant science question in an interview, and each may have multiple parts. Your interviews may also be at different colleges.

**Did You Know?**

*In 2019, there were over 70 Physics and Engineering applicants at Oxford who scored at least 3 points more in their second Oxford interview than their first (interviews are scored out of 10). That's potentially the difference between a very mediocre day and a very good day—and one good performance can be sufficient to get you your offer, so don't give up if you don't feel your first interview went well!*

**Cambridge**

At Cambridge, you'll have at least one interview in which you'll go through problems with a tutor. You may have a separate general interview about your other interests and subjects, unlike not at Oxford. At Cambridge, you may hear questions such as: 'What engineering have you been researching recently?' or 'What are you particularly enjoying about physics at the moment?', but it's unlikely that any question will diverge significantly from the topics of physics, chemistry and maths.

Some colleges are very transparent about how they interview, so it can be worth phoning up and asking if there are any peculiarities about the interview at a particular college. The Engineering Director of Studies at a Cambridge college told us:

> *"We always ask students one mechanics question and one circuits question in the interview, and we don't ask about anything else."* –Director of Studies, Engineering, Cambridge

## How long will your interview take?

An interview is typically 25–30 minutes.

## What will the interview questions be about?

It's likely that the first question will be fairly simple, and that the interviewers will extend and develop the question as you progress through it. Some examples of preliminary questions you may receive are:

- Name the Group 1 metals. (Chemistry)
- Give a definition of the cosine function. (Maths)
- Explain Newton's law of universal gravitation. (Physics)

> *"Going into the interviews, I was expecting more of a general chat. Instead, it was very much, 'Do this problem. Now, do this problem.' which I've come to realise is quite common for Natural Sciences interviews."* –Harry, Natural Sciences, Cambridge

**Physics**

Although the interviewers are more interested in *how you apply* your knowledge than *what you know*, the PAT syllabus, including advanced calculus will be presupposed—and the questions you get may begin by asking you factual questions about this content. Mechanics and circuits questions are especially common.

**Engineering**

As you're unlikely to have studied engineering before, your interviews will probably be a combination of physics and maths. You may see some standalone maths questions, but these are likely to be applied to a physics problem. Graph sketching is a common starting point for engineering interview questions. You may also be presented with diagrams of systems and machines and be expected to apply your knowledge of physics to analyse how they work.

## Chemistry

In your chemistry interview, you may be introduced to new compounds and different types of reactions and be expected to apply your chemistry understanding to this unfamiliar scenario. However, the interviewers won't expect you to have memorised lists of reactions or the periodic table; information like this will be given to you!

## Materials Science

Oxford Materials Science interviews include both mathematical and materials concepts. The materials concepts are likely to be based on A-Level Physics and Chemistry.

> *"In my first Oxford Materials Science interview, I was greeted with a few pages on phase diagrams (something I did not know about beforehand) and was asked to read and digest it for 5 minutes before coming in for the interview. The first question was based on that sheet, and involved deriving an equation for the fractions of different phases. I found this a struggle and the question took me around 30 minutes to complete."* –Inigo, Materials Science, Oxford

You're also likely to get some mathematical questions. Be especially prepared for graph sketching, differentiation and integration, and trigonometry.

Other types of questions that you may come across in your interview include:

- Analysing a material presented to you (What material is it? How do you know? How could you test that? How could you make that?)
- A maths problem involving mechanics or some 3D geometry. For example: How many hexagons are there in a buckyball?[119]

## Physical Natural Sciences

You'll typically have two interviews. Before the interview, you may be asked which of the first-year Natural Sciences options interest you (see page 205). If you've only focused on two sciences, you'll tend to have one interview on each; if you've focused on three, they should all crop up across the two interviews. A maths question may be incorporated into the

119 AKA Buckminsterfullerene.

start of any physical science question. For example, you may be asked to draw a graph, and later asked to analyse what it would mean if this was the graphical representation of the results of a certain experiment.

Even if you're interested in studying Materials Science or Earth Sciences as part of your Natural Sciences degree, your interviews will most likely start with the sciences you're studying at A Level. You might be given hints to extend your scientific knowledge to Materials Science or Earth Sciences if you've stated your interest in them, which is where your technical scientific skills will be combined with any wider reading you have done in these fields.

### Physical science interview myth busting

- **The interviewers will NOT try to catch you out.** They will offer you advice and tips for solving the questions—don't ignore these. They want to see how you listen and react to guidance.
- **You will NOT get asked questions on sciences you haven't studied.** If you haven't done Chemistry A Level, you're unlikely to be faced with questions that can only be done with Chemistry A-Level knowledge. Remember, the tutors aren't monsters!
- **The questions WILL be answerable.** Although they will be taxing and more involved than A-Level questions, the tutors want you to feel able to solve them. They aren't going to make the questions so hard that they are impossible!
- **At the vast majority (if not all) colleges, your interviews ARE marked.** The system is simple; the tutors in your interview will each mark you out of 10 in answer to one question: 'Can I picture this student studying here next year?'

## 18.2: How to prepare for your physical science interviews

### When should you start preparing?

It can be tempting to wait to prepare for your interview until you're certain you've got one. Unfortunately, both Oxford and Cambridge have been leaving it later and later to invite students to interview. In 2019, some applicants only received their interview invitation letter a mere 6 *days* before the interview date.

By preparing for your admissions tests, you'll have already made a start on interview preparation. You'll have built up your problem-solving abilities and will be secure in your subject knowledge. After the tests are over, don't let this slip—start on interview preparation right away! Challenge yourself with tougher and tougher problems and start talking through them out loud.

## How should you prepare for your interviews?

The point of the interviews is to keep you on your toes and ask you questions that take you out of your comfort zone. The interviewers want to see how you cope with new and complicated material—but there's still a lot you can do to prepare for your physical science interviews.

### 1) Practise speaking and writing your thoughts Potential

The interviewers will want to know your thought process and observe your reasoning skills. A good way to practise this is to explain scientific concepts to your friends and family, and discuss questions with your friends who are also interested in science. Alternatively, talk through concepts by yourself instead of simply writing down the solution on paper.

> *"The absolute worst thing a student can do in an interview is to stay quiet."* –Interviewer, Physics, Oxford

Find somebody to ask you questions about topics that interest you so that you have to go into depth to examine and analyse your reasoning. The more comfortable you are discussing the subject content, the more prepared you'll feel for your interviews.

In your interviews, you may be asked to work through questions on a whiteboard at the front of the room. It's worth practising this, as you may feel more exposed than when you're writing on paper. Ask your teacher if you can practise on their whiteboard at school!

### 2) Make sure you have a good sense of estimation Ability

Many interview questions will require you to estimate. For example, your calculations may require you to estimate the volume of the room or the length of an average car. The interviewers won't be expecting a perfect estimate, but make sure you're familiar with rough estimations, as this will allow you to simplify assumptions or make useful analogies.

A typical estimation problem might be:

*Estimate the mass of an average house.*

A good student might respond to this problem with something along the lines of:

"I think most of the mass will be in the outer walls and roof, as wood and plaster and so on are less dense than bricks and tiles. This tea cup is made of a similar material to brick and tile – a ceramic – and I think the ratio of the thickness of its walls to its volume is similar to a house. It's also a similar enough shape if I turn it upside down. The tea cup is about 100g and 10cm across. A house is about 10m across, which is 100 times more. So the mass should be 100g x $100^3$, which is $10^5$kg or 100 tonnes.

Hmm that sounds like quite a lot. Let me try something else...

A brick weighs about 1kg and is about 20cm long and 5cm high. If a house has 4 walls that are 10m long, 5m high and 2 bricks thick, that's 50 x 100 x 2 = $10^4$ bricks. That means $10^4$kg. There will be a bit more for the roof and internal walls, but it probably won't exceed 2 x $10^4$ kg. I think that's my final answer. I might have overestimated the thickness of the walls compared to the tea cup the first time."

The student won't get to the exact answer, because they'll need to guess at some of the details: Do houses have only two rows of brick for walls? Are their size estimates reasonable? Do the foundations count? But they explained their reasoning well, which matters much more than the answer.

Why not see if you can find another approach to estimating the mass of a house?

It's also a good idea to practise working with and converting between units. Make sure you know the units that correspond to different quantities. Checking units is a good way of ensuring that each equation you write is correct; if the quantities on either side have different units, you'll know you must have made a mistake somewhere.

**Top Tip**

*Can you use equations you know to show that the joule ($J$) is equivalent to $m^2kgs^{-2}$ in SI units? This is the type of exercise you can do in your head at any point to become fluent with* ***manipulating units****.*

## 3) Learn equations and basics from A-Level content Ability

*Although the interviews aren't a memory test, you'll be expected to be familiar with all of the formulae and equations from A Level, and you should have many of these memorised.*[120]

## 4) Broaden your A-Level understanding Ability Potential

The most important thing the interviewers are looking for during your interview is not how much you know, but how much you *understand*. They are looking to see solid intuition, an ability to connect ideas from different topics, and logical thinking. Make sure you always take the time to understand what is going on.

It's also worth reviewing other A-Level syllabi. There may be a topic that is more prominent in another syllabus, in which case it may be worth studying independently. If it comes up in your interview, at least you'll have a grasp of what's going on!

*"If you're applying for Engineering*[121] *or Materials Science, a good way to extend what you learned at A Level is by researching* ***material processing****. You don't need to know every type of process, because if you think about steel, glass, concrete, carbon fibre—they're all made in really different ways. But it helps to see a few examples to get an idea of what you might need to think about when processing different materials."* –Student, Materials Science, Oxford

120 At least for your admissions tests, if not also for A Level, which we highly recommend.

121 Especially Chemical Engineering.

**Material processing** covers all the steps involved in turning raw materials into artificial materials, and in combining or altering materials to make new ones.

## 5) Take care over your diagrams Ability

It's really important to draw diagrams in your interviews, as not only will they help you with the question, they will help the interviewers see what you're thinking. If you draw a big, clear diagram, you'll find it easier to visualise the situation, and the interviewer will be able to successfully gauge and guide your thought process.

Definitely practise drawing some diagrams from worked problems or exercises in your A-Level textbooks, and try and draw some large, detailed diagrams to visualise topics you have studied. For example, in preparation for a physics interview, you could practise drawing a force diagram for a suspension bridge, or for pencils resting in a pot. Or you could draw a diagram of light refracting through different glass shapes, such as a cylinder and a tetrahedron.

Take care to label your diagrams accurately, and choose appropriate letters to label your variables. So that you can keep track of all of your variables, you might want to write down a 'key'.

## 6) Work on your maths Ability Potential

In some interviews, you may get an exclusively mathematical question. It might be a complicated derivative or a problem related to geometry. Although your science subjects should be your focus when you're preparing for interviews, it's vital to practise mathematical techniques. Maths forms an integral part of every physical science course, and interviewers will naturally want to gauge your ability in it.

*"In my interview, I was asked to draw $e^{x^3}$ and to differentiate it. Next, I was asked to draw the graph of $e^{-x^2}$. They asked me if I knew what the function was; I didn't (it's a Gaussian), but they didn't seem to mind."* –Michał, Chemistry, Oxford

## 7) Sketch some graphs! Ability

Being asked to draw a graph is a common starting point for a physical science interview because it tests your mathematical abilities.

Some examples of the graphs you may be asked to sketch are:

- $\sin(e^x)$
- $\cos(\frac{1}{x})$
- $e^{\frac{1}{x}}$.

(Why not try sketching these and comparing your graphs to our answers, which we've provided in our bonus chapter online[122] so that you're not tempted to copy!)

When you're sketching, remember to consider:

- The behaviour of the graph close to the y-axis
- Where the graph crosses the x-axis
- How to differentiate the function
- The behaviour of its derivative, especially where it is 0 (stationary points) and where the derivative gets arbitrarily large (where the graph steeply increases or decreases)
- Any asymptotes of the graph
- What happens to the graph as x goes to +/- infinity.

**Top Tip**

*Look at **l'Hôpital's rule**[123] for functions such as $\frac{\sin x}{x}$, in which both the numerator and denominator tend to 0 (here, as x tends to 0). This will impress interviewers and could also help you out in a sticky situation!*

*"In my first interview at Mansfield College, I was asked to draw graphs from the equations they gave me. The hardest equation they gave me was an equation for the path of a moving point in 3D space, so that was tricky to draw!"* –Sophie, Engineering, Oxford

122 See oxbridgeformula.co.uk/bonus-chapter.

123 Want more info on l'Hôpital's rule? See oxbridgeformula.co.uk/bonus-chapter.

## 8) Learn approximate physical values Ability

It's worth familiarising yourself with these quantities and also their orders of magnitude (e.g. that 'nano' means $10^{-9}$).

| Name of quantity | Value | Particularly useful for... |
|---|---|---|
| Density of water | $1{,}000\ \mathrm{kg/m^3}$ | Physics and Engineering |
| Density of air | $1\ \mathrm{kg/m^3}$ | Physics and Engineering |
| The speed of light | $3 \times 10^8\ \mathrm{m/s}$ | Physics |
| Avogadro's number | $6 \times 10^{23}\ \mathrm{mol^{-1}}$ | Chemistry, Physics and Materials Science |
| Charge of an electron | $1.6 \times 10^{-19}\ \mathrm{C}$ | Physics and Chemistry |
| Mass of an electron | $10^{-30}\ \mathrm{kg}$ | Physics and Chemistry |
| Atomic mass unit | $1.7 \times 10^{-27}\ \mathrm{kg}$ | Physics and Chemistry |
| Acceleration due to gravity | $10\ \mathrm{ms^{-2}}$ (In an interview, there's no need for more precision than this) | Physics and Engineering |
| Typical values for resistors and capacitors in circuits | Useful to know that $1$ Farad is large, but $1$ Ohm is small | Physics and Engineering |
| Young's modulus | Values will be on the order of $1\text{–}1{,}000\ \mathrm{GPa}$; you should try to gain a rough sense of which materials have a larger Young's modulus and which a smaller. | Physics, Engineering and Materials Science |
| Yield stress and ultimate tensile strength | These values mostly fall in the range $10\text{–}1{,}000\ \mathrm{MPa}$. | Physics, Engineering and Materials Science |

## 9) Do extra problems Passion Potential

The more you practise solving interview-style questions, the better. Here are some websites with great resources[124] to help you prepare for your interviews:

- Advanced Extension Award papers
- Nrich maths (for Maths-style questions)
- Chemistry Olympiad past papers
- Royal Society of Chemistry's Problem Solving Tutor
- I-want-to-study-engineering.org
- UKMT Maths challenge past papers
- The Oxbridge Formula website.

## 10) Practise PAT, ENGAA and NSAA questions out loud Ability Potential

Your interviews may feature questions that start at the level of your admissions test and eventually go beyond that. Therefore, these questions are a good place to start in terms of interview practice. The PAT is the best test to use for practice, whether or not you have to take it for your chosen course, because the long questions from it are unfamiliar and unstructured in a way that resembles interview problems. Practise working through the questions out loud, so that you're able to express your ideas with confidence.

> *"The most substantial difference is that, unlike the ENGAA (in which you have to think fast to reach answers rapidly), in an interview you need to explain your thought processes and methods clearly."*

You may also have to complete another short test before the interview, and bring your written answers along to discuss them—reviewing your admissions test will also help here.

## 11) Don't prepare alone Potential

Although you can certainly develop your problem-solving skills by working on your own, you'll definitely need to practise communicating about science and maths out loud (which means both speaking and listening).

124 Links to all of these resources can be found at oxbridgeformula.co.uk/bonus-chapter.

This is something you probably don't practise much at A Level, and even if you think you're a good conversationalist, speaking through calculations and physical intuitions requires a new set of skills.

We run interview courses[125] to help students with multiple subjects because we know how essential face-to-face practice is. We also know how important it is to practise under pressure; our methodology includes a mock interview, with an expert tutor, in which you're watched by up to nine other applicants (and you get to watch their interviews in turn, and attempt the questions they've been set too). Our students tell us that feeling other people's eyes on them puts the pressure on—to the extent that the course made their real interviews feel decidedly easy in comparison!

Whenever you have a practice interview, it's also important you receive detailed feedback from the interviewer so you can improve next time. This is something we make a point of in our courses: giving detailed individual feedback to each student.

See page 143 for an interview with real Oxbridge interviewers.

## 18.3: A script of an Oxbridge Physics interview

In this section, we'll present three different physics interview questions with a scripted model interaction between the interviewer and the student working through the solution. These are relevant for a student applying to Physics, Natural Sciences and Engineering, but put together probably most resemble a Physics interview. Some of the maths questions starting on page 114 will also be helpful for you to look over. Each question will touch upon a different topic, giving you a feel for the wide variety of questions you may get asked in an interview.

What you should note when reading these interview scripts is the constant interaction between the student and tutor and how the student tackles the question, even when they aren't completely sure what to do next.

### Physics interview question 1 (Electrostatics/Graph Sketching)

**Question: Suppose you have two neutral molecules. How do they interact as the distance between them varies?**

125 Details of our physics and engineering interview course can be found at oxbridgeformula.co.uk/physics-interview.

## Model interview

**Student:** Well, I know there are four fundamental forces in physics: the weak force, the strong force, the electromagnetic force and the gravitational force. The weak force and strong force are only relevant at extremely small distances; would it be okay if I discount them?

You'll often have to start by figuring out what is relevant. Your interviewer is less interested in whether you can do the calculations (though this matters) and more interested in how you figure out what calculations to do.

**Tutor:** Yes, please ignore those forces for the purposes of this question.

**Student:** Okay, so now I only need to consider the effects of the gravitational and electromagnetic force, which have an infinite range...

**Tutor:** Let me interrupt you there. Why do you think we should include the gravitational force in our model?

**Student:** Well, initially I thought it would be relevant because gravity acts over all distance scales. *(Pause.)* But having thought it over, I realise now that the Coulomb force is a lot stronger than the gravitational force, so I guess it would be sensible to ignore gravity for this question.

It's important to be able to reconsider, if you can explain why.

*(Tutor nods in agreement.)*

**Student:** Okay, in that case, let's just consider the electrostatic force acting between these molecules. I know that molecules consist of protons and neutrons surrounded by an orbiting electron cloud. Even though each individual molecule is neutral overall, I know there can be attractive van der Waals forces between the two molecules. But I don't know how to calculate how large they are.

**Tutor:** That doesn't matter for now. What about the forces between the nuclei?

**Student:** Well, the protons are both positively charged, so there will be a repulsive force between them.

**Tutor:** Now, going back to the original question: how does the interaction vary with distance in this scenario?

**Student:** Well... if they're really far apart, the repulsion between the nuclei and the van der Waals forces are both essentially 0. The forces will increase as we bring them closer, but the first is much smaller because the electrons kind of shield the charges of the nuclei from each other.

**Tutor:** Yes—I'm interested in the *net* force though.

**Student:** Okay. It starts off near 0 when they're far apart. Then it's positive and increasing as we bring them closer together because the electrostatic force between the nuclei is basically 0 and the van der Waals force is attractive. I'm guessing the force starts decreasing again at some point – otherwise all molecules would just stick together – but I'm not sure when.

**Tutor:** Will the repulsion between the nuclei be 0 for even smaller distances?

**Student:** (*Pauses.*) I suppose that when the molecules are sufficiently close together, the electron clouds begin to overlap, therefore it won't be 0 anymore.

**Tutor:** Exactly. The van der Waals force also decreases to 0 once the molecules start to overlap, though it doesn't matter why. And the electrons of the two molecules will repel each other too. So can you describe qualitatively what happens to the net force as the distance varies?

**Student:** It still starts off at 0 when they're far apart. Then it becomes more positive, i.e. attractive. Then it goes negative once the molecules overlap, so there must be a turning point in between.

**Tutor:** <u>And if we imagine we can push the distance all the way to 0?</u>

You'll often have to be prompted a few times to get a complete answer, and that's fine! It's how you respond to prompts that the interviewer wants to see.

**Student:** The electrostatic force would tend towards positive infinity.

**Tutor:** Okay great, let's move on. The mathematical equation for the electric potential energy in the situation you described is called the Lennard-Jones potential, and is given by the following *(begins writing an equation on paper)*:

$$V(r) = \varepsilon\left[\left(\frac{a}{r}\right)^{12} - 2\left(\frac{a}{r}\right)^{6}\right]$$

<u>Could you please sketch this on a set of axes for me?</u>

This might seem like a tough graph to draw from the equation, but the fact that you've discussed the theory and what happens qualitatively for different values of r should help you sketch the graph. Remember to verbalise your thoughts, and go through the standard graph sketching procedure, i.e. behaviour as $r \to \infty$, $r \to 0$, stationary points etc. Sketching is a vital skill for physicists!

**Student:** I'm guessing $V$ stands for potential energy and that $r$ is distance. Can I check that $\varepsilon$ and $\alpha$ are constants?

**Tutor:** Yes, that's right.

**Student:** In that case, I can see it goes to positive infinity as $r \to 0$ and to 0 as $r \to \infty$

To see if there are any turning points, I need to differentiate and set the derivative equal to 0:

Here, you could also complete the square.

$$\frac{dV}{dr} = \varepsilon\left[\frac{-12a^{12}}{r^{13}} + \frac{12a^6}{r^7}\right] = 0$$

I can factorise and divide through by $12\varepsilon a^6/r^7$.

Hence, $\frac{-a^6}{r^6} + 1 = 0$, meaning that the only turning point is at $r = a$. And it must be a minimum, because for a maximum there'd need to be another turning point between the maximum and where the graph goes to positive infinity. So I think the graph looks like this:

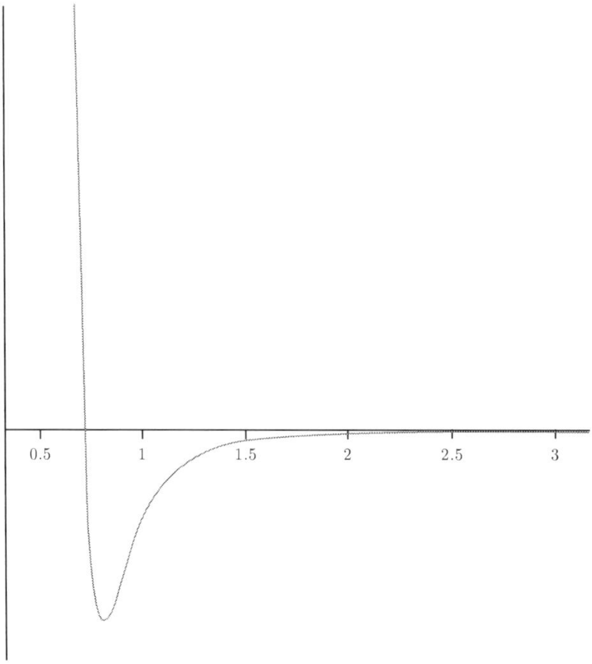


**Tutor:** And what's the net force at $r = a$?

**Student:** Well... I know the force reaches a maximum before it turns around and becomes repulsive. So maybe the maximum of the force is also here? No, wait—the minimum potential energy is where the system is stable. So the force must be 0—it's the point where it goes from attractive to repulsive.

**Tutor:** Great, thank you. Let's move on.

## Further hints

The tutor might ask what forces hold molecules close to each other in solids and liquids, to see if you've heard of van der Waals forces. If you haven't, they will simply tell you that these are an attractive force between molecules and let you work from there.[126]

If you have missed any part of the sketch, they might ask what happens as $r \to \infty$ and $r \to 0$, and what that means for the rest of the graph. If you start, they will probably let you differentiate twice to find the turning point is a minimum, rather than use the student's argument.

## Extending the question

The question could be extended to discuss the relationship between the balance of forces between the molecules and simple harmonic motion:

- Why do the two molecules oscillate when they start at rest with $r$ slightly larger or smaller than $a$?
- Oscillations about $r = a$ would release EM energy. In what region of the EM spectrum would you expect to observe the energy emitted?

## What is the question testing?

This is a long question—in fact it's a few questions strung together, which is something you may or may not experience in your interview. It tests your understanding of electrostatic forces, your ability to give an intuitive and qualitative description of how varying a parameter (distance) will change how a system behaves, as well as your mathematical skills of graph sketching and differentiation (although seeing you could complete the square at the end would be just as good).

## Related topics from university

Examining the relationship between force and potential energy is a major part of uni physics. In particular, you'll study electromagnetic potentials in your first year Electromagnetism course at Oxford, or the Fields course at Cambridge.

126 To find out more about van der Waals forces, see oxbridgeformula.co.uk/bonus-chapter.

## Physics interview question 2 (Estimation and EM Radiation)

**Question: Look at the desk lamp on the other side of the room. How many photons from the lamp are entering your eye each second?**

### Model interview

**Student:** I think this question is to do with power and intensity, and I'll probably need to make some simplifying assumptions. (*Pauses.*) First, I need to know the power of the bulb in the lamp. Do you mind if I get up and have a look at the power rating of the bulb?

Identifying what information you need – and saying what it is out loud, or asking for it – is a key skill.

**Tutor:** *(Gestures towards the lamp.)* By all means, go ahead.

**Student:** *(Checks lamp and returns to seat.)* The power rating of this incandescent bulb is 60W. *(Pauses to think.)* I'm going to divide this question into two stages: the first step will be to find the number of photons being emitted by the bulb, and the second will be to find the number of those photons that are entering my eye. So, first I need to find an equation connecting the power of the lamp and the number of photons being emitted by the bulb... Let me try and derive one on this piece of paper.

Getting a plan together is much better than ploughing through the question without a clear direction.

**Tutor:** Sure thing. Do you mind turning the piece of paper towards us so we can see what you're writing?

**Student:** Yes, of course. *(Pauses to write equations.)* I've come up with the following:

Consider giving verbal commentary to the interviewers as you write these equations, but only if doing so doesn't hinder your thought process.

$$Power = \frac{Total\ Energy}{Time}$$

$$Efficiency \times Power = \frac{Light\ Energy}{Time}$$

$$Efficiency \times Power = \frac{No.\ Photons\ Emitted\ By\ Bulb \times Photon\ Energy}{Time}$$

$$Efficiency \times Power = \frac{No.\ photons\ emitted\ by\ bulb \times Planck's\ Contstant}{Wavelength\ of\ Photon \times Time}$$

**Student:** I'm going to simplify all of this with symbols instead of words. Let $\eta$ = efficiency; $P$ = Power; $N$ = Number photons emitted by bulb; $E$ = Photon Energy; $\lambda$ = Wavelength of photon, $h$ = Planck's Constant; $t$ = Time; $c$ = Speed of light. Given $E = hc/\lambda$ and rearranging for $N/t$:

$$\frac{N}{t} = \frac{\eta P}{E} = \frac{\eta P\lambda}{hc}$$

**Student:** Incandescent bulbs are approximately 10% efficient, and the wavelength of the yellow light this bulb is emitting is approximately 600nm. Planck's constant is $7 \times 10^{-34}$ to 1.s.f.

Hence:

$$\frac{N}{t} = \frac{0.1 \times 60 \times 600 \times 10^{-9}}{3 \times 10^{8} \times 7 \times 10^{-34}} \approx 2 \times 10^{19}\, photons/second$$

You only need a reasonable estimation here.

You won't have a calculator in an interview, and you ought to memorise approximate values of important constants. However, don't be afraid to ask the interviewer if you're unsure.

The easiest way to simplify is to cancel powers of 10 first; the other numbers cancel to 12/7, and the closest integer to that is 2. No need for any more precision than that!

**Student:** Now for the second stage: finding the fraction of these photons that enter my eye, $f$. This fraction is equal to the surface area occupied by my eye, which I'll call $A$, divided by the surface area of a sphere $S$ with a radius equal to the distance between me and the lamp, $d$. *(Looks over to lamp.)* I'd estimate that $d$ is approximately $1m$, and I'll assume that my eye has an area of about $1cm^2$.

**Tutor:** In fact, any light you observe must enter through your pupil, which only has a radius of, let's say, $2\text{mm}$.

**Student:** You're right. In that case I'll try and amend my value of $A$ accordingly:

$$f = \frac{A}{S} = \frac{\pi \times (2 \times 10^{-3})^2}{\pi \times 1^2}$$

**Tutor:** Okay. What did you say $S$ represented again?

**Student:** The area of a sphere of radius $1\text{m}$.

**Tutor:** What's the formula for the surface area of a sphere?

**Student:** Ah yes, it's $4\pi r^2$, not $\pi r^2$

So I get:

$$f = \frac{A}{S} = \frac{\pi \times (2 \times 10^{-3})^2}{4\pi \times 1^2} = 10^{-6}$$

Putting it all together, the number of photons entering my eye per second is $\frac{fN}{t}$, which is about $2 \times 10^{13}$ photons per second.

**Tutor:** Thank you. Well done.

## Further hints

This student was pretty good at knowing what to do, but if you were stuck the interviewer could ask you the following questions as hints:

- What do you know about the average photon coming from the lamp?
- How much energy does each photon carry?
- Think about all the photons emitted in a short period of time. How are they distributed at the moment some of them start to enter your eye? (This question would be to get you to think of the photons as spread out over the surface of a sphere.)
- How could you figure out how much of the light emitted is entering your eye?

## Extending the question

An estimation question can be extended by asking you to consider further details or by changing one detail and asking what else changes:

- Does the light that's reflected from all the surfaces in the room significantly add to the number of photons entering your eye?
- Suppose that, sensibly, you don't stare directly at the lamp, so the light enters your pupil from an angle instead of straight ahead. How would your answer change?
- Suppose that, foolishly, you stared directly at the Sun instead of a lamp. How much larger would your answer be?

## What is the question testing?

This question is a classic Fermi estimation problem[127] that tests your ability to make sensible physical and numerical approximations. The interviewer is not expecting an exact answer, merely an answer of the correct order of magnitude.

Note how both the student and tutor choose powers of 10 and small integers for their estimates. Being overly precise will actually reflect badly on you—it suggests you don't recognise that the margin for error exceeds the

127 For more information and resources on Fermi estimation, see oxbridgeformula.co.uk/bonus-chapter

precision of your estimate and that you aren't good at identifying how to simplify a problem for yourself.

Estimation is not only a skill in its own right, but also an opportunity to demonstrate other useful skills: considering possible sources of data, producing a simple model of a physical scenario, and handling large orders of magnitude in calculations.

### Related topics from university

Although the physics content of this question will be familiar from A Level, the skills required to answer it quickly and confidently, such as identifying relevant factors and creating a simplified physical model, are essential in every part of university physics.

## Physics interview question 3 (Gravity and Potential Energy)

*(The interviewer has a diagram pre-drawn on the whiteboard.)*

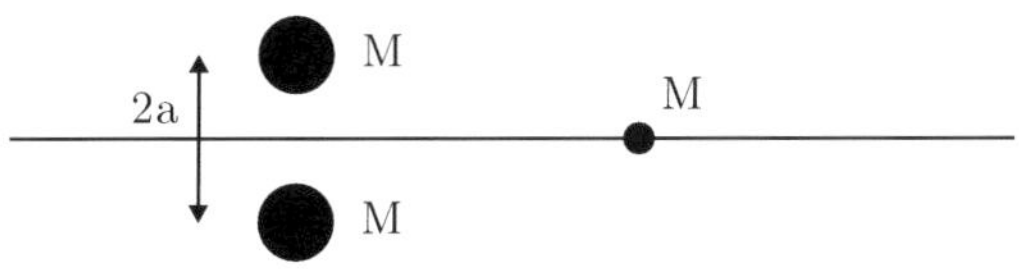


**Question: Two identical masses $M$ are fixed a distance $2a$ apart. Another mass $m$ is placed along the axis bisecting the line joining the two other masses. How does the force on mass $m$ vary as a function of distance along the axis?**

### Model interview

**Student:** So... Newton's law of gravitation is:

$$F = \frac{Gm_1m_2}{r^2}$$

We need to use this to find the resultant force acting on m from both of the masses of mass $M$.
*(Pauses to think.)* Well, by symmetry, the resultant force due to gravity in the vertical direction must cancel out. So we only need to consider the forces acting in the horizontal direction, i.e. along the axis. (*Pauses.*)

Looking for symmetries will greatly simplify many problems for you, especially if they have a geometrical aspect. One way to learn to see them is to watch out for terms that cancel when you're doing practice questions, and go back and see if you could explain the cancelling in terms of a symmetry in the question.

Using symmetry again, we know this resultant force is simply twice the horizontal component of the force on $m$ due to one of the masses of mass $M$.

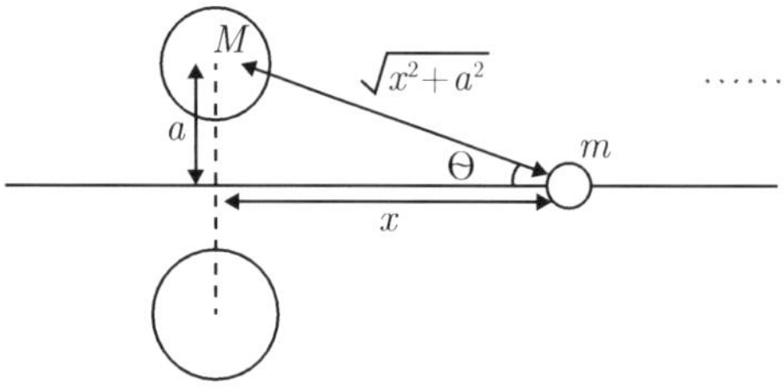


Always try to form right angle triangles if you can!

I'm going to define the positive $x$ direction as going towards the right, with '0' in between the two large masses. Since the gravitational force on $m$ always acts to pull it towards the centre:

$$F(x) = -\frac{2GMm}{x^2 + a^2}\cos(\theta)$$

Substituting: $\cos(\theta) = \dfrac{x}{(x^2 + a^2)^{\frac{1}{2}}}$:

$$F(x) = -\frac{2GMmx}{(x^2 + a^2)^{\frac{3}{2}}}$$

**Tutor:** Could you find an expression for the gravitational potential energy from the expression for $F$?

**Student:** I know the GPE at $x$ is meant to be the work done by gravity in moving a unit mass from infinity to $x$. Here, Work equals Force times Distance. But the force is changing and the distance from infinity...doesn't make sense.

It's fine to say when you haven't seen the details of something, but it's much better to identify exactly what information you're missing, or what aspect you don't understand, as the student does here.

**Tutor:** That equation for work done only applies if the force is constant. If the force varies with distance, how do you think we might change it?

This is something to watch out for in interview questions—for instance, SUVAT only describes motion when acceleration is constant—so if you have a varying acceleration, you'll have to use $a = \dfrac{dv}{dt}$ and $v = \dfrac{dx}{dt}$ and apply your knowledge of calculus to the problem instead.

**Student:** Find some type of average force, maybe? I'm not sure.

This idea doesn't help here, but it's not a bad guess.

**Tutor:** What if I rephrase your equation as *Force = work done per unit distance*?

**Student:** That makes me think of a derivative.

**Tutor:** Yes, exactly.

**Student:** So we could say $\text{Force} = \frac{d}{dx}(\textit{work done})$?

**Tutor:** Yes. That way, it can be a function of $x$ instead of a constant. I'd also suggest we use a variable $V$ for the potential.

**Student:** Okay, so I get:

$$V(x) = \int_x^\infty F(s)ds$$

$$= \int_x^\infty -\frac{2GMms}{(s^2 + a^2)^{\frac{3}{2}}} ds$$

I'll substitute $u = s^2 + a^2$, so $du = 2sds$.

In which case:

$$V(x) = \int_{x^2+a^2}^\infty -\frac{GMm}{u^{\frac{3}{2}}} du$$

$$= \left[ 2\frac{GMm}{u^{\frac{1}{2}}} \right]_{x^2+a^2}^\infty$$

$$= -2\frac{GMm}{(x^2 + a^2)^{\frac{1}{2}}}$$

Don't be afraid to manipulate new expressions, but do recognise how they relate to what you know. In this case, the student hasn't seen non-constant forces before, but what they have here is an integral, so they can switch their brain to thinking about it like any other integral they've seen in A-Level Maths.

The student uses '$s$' as the variable in the integral to avoid giving '$x$' two meanings.

**Tutor:** Is a negative expression appropriate?

**Student:** (*Thinks.*) Yes—or least that the convention I've seen. I think it's because the potential is 0 at infinity, and it should be lower closer to the middle, because objects gain kinetic energy as the fall towards the middle, and that means they must lose potential energy.

**Tutor:** Great, thank you. That's all from me.

## Further hints

If the student started calculating the force from each mass $M$ individually, the tutor would likely ask whether that was necessary, to try to get them to think about symmetry. They might draw the vertical from each mass $M$ to prompt the student to find the distance to $m$ using Pythagoras.

They might also prompt the student to add the angle $\theta$ to the diagram, or to recognise what $\cos(\theta)$ is. If the student didn't know about the relationship between potential energy and force, they would be given it (and this wouldn't count against them).

## Extending the question

The tutor could either ask you to go deeper into the mathematics or what happens when some details are changed. For example, they might say:

- Could you sketch $F(x)$ and $V(x)$ as functions of $x$?
- How would this question change if we replaced all the masses with positive electric charges? How would the graphs of $F(x)$ and $V(x)$ be different?
- How do the graphs change as we vary $a$ and $M$?

## What is the question testing?

Remembering the formula for gravitational force shouldn't be too hard. Instead, this question is testing the student's geometry and integration skills. It also gives them a chance to investigate the relationship between force and energy, which was only touched upon in the first question.

## Related topics from university

The differential and integral forms of the relationship between force and potential energy will be taught in your first year Mechanics course. At Oxford, you'll mostly learn about their application to fields when you learn about electromagnetism rather than gravity. At Cambridge, you'll see both in your first-year Fields course. In either case, you won't learn anything you can't derive from Newton's law of gravitation, because the next step is a very hard one— general relativity, taught as an optional course in later years at both universities.

# Some other examples of physics interview questions to practise:

- How many nuclei are there in the Sun?

- A merchant is travelling through a desert to a city in the savannah. He can move twice as quickly on the savannah compared to the desert. What is the fastest way for the merchant to reach the city? Can you show us why?

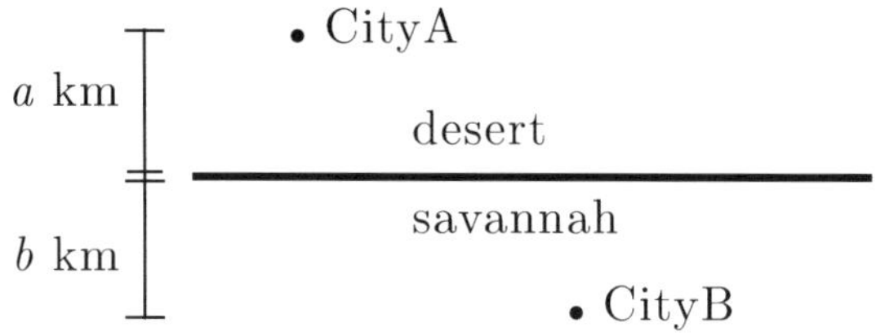


- How far should you move the Earth away from the Sun for it to cool down, on average, by 1 degree Celsius?

- Provided we can power a washing machine with the solar energy falling on an umbrella, how much mass is the Sun losing per hour?[128]

You can also find more physics interview questions in the engineering interview question examples in the next section.

**Top Tip**

*A Cambridge science interviewer told us the* ***three keys to a good interview*** *are:*

- *Showing enthusiasm*
- *Listening to and following the interviewer's cues*
- *Being willing to go beyond your comfort zone.*

# 18.4: A script of an Oxbridge Engineering interview

Here's an example script of a good engineering interview. The first and third questions are more physics-based, and the second is more maths-based. These questions are very relevant for Physics, Physical Natural Sciences and Materials Science applicants too.

## Engineering interview question 1 (Mechanics)

**Question: A cart is travelling along a horizontal track at a constant velocity. What would happen to the velocity of the cart if it started**

128 There are loads of interesting questions (and absurd hypotheticals) such as this in Randall Monroe's 'What if?'

**raining? Assume that the rain droplets fall perfectly vertically into the cart.**

## Model interview

**Student:** Firstly, I have two clarifying questions. <u>Can I ignore the effects of friction between the cart and the track and air resistance acting on the cart? Also, can I assume the rate of rain falling in the cart to be constant?</u>

Attempting a physics question often requires making the correct simplifying assumptions. It's best to spell them out at the start and give your motivations for making them if you can.

**Tutor:** You may ignore friction, but the second assumption is unnecessary.

**Student:** Hmm... My intuition is telling me that the cart will slow down as it fills with rain if no other external forces are acting on the cart. (*Pauses to think.*) But let me verify that using momentum conservation in the direction of the cart. I'm going to call the mass of the cart $m$ and the speed of the cart $v$. A small interval of time $\delta t$ later, the speed of the cart is $v + \delta v$ and its total mass is $m + \delta m$.

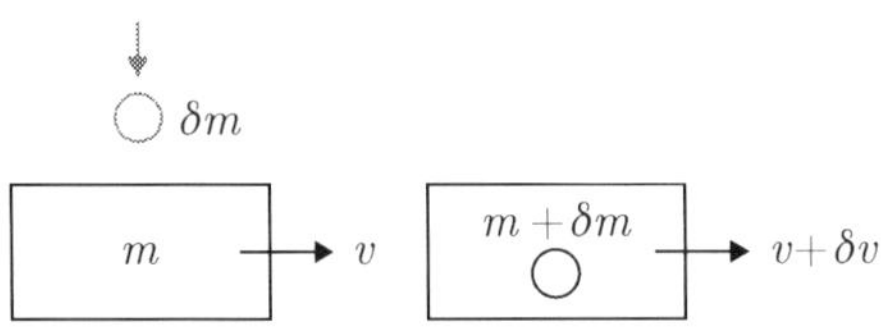


*(Student writes)* Momentum conservation (→) to track:

$mv = (m + \delta m)(v + \delta v)$

$\cancel{mv} = \cancel{mv} + m\delta v + \delta m v + \cancel{\delta m \delta v}$ ⟵ ignore since small

$\Rightarrow \delta m v + m\delta v = 0$

Since I defined $\delta m$ as a positive quantity, $\delta v$ must be a negative quantity. As a result, the cart has to slow down.

If you haven't seen '$\delta m$' and '$\delta v$' used in this way before, check out our bonus chapter online for more information: oxbridgeformula.co.uk/bonus-chapter.

**Tutor:** Okay, you've used a momentum description to explain why the cart slows down. Could you explain why the cart slows down in terms of forces?

**Student:** (*Pauses to think*) Let me answer that by considering the fact that $Impulse = \Delta momentum$. I'm going to consider the momentum of the rain droplet and cart separately during the collision:

the rain droplet gains momentum in the forwards direction and the cart loses momentum in the forwards direction. This means that the rain droplet exerts a force backwards to the left on the cart and the cart exerts a force forwards on the rain droplet. Physically, I think this occurs when the rain 'sloshes' into the back of the cart.

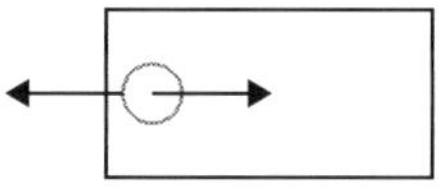

**Tutor:** Can you be more precise about this 'sloshing'?

**Student:** *(Pauses.)* Well, the rain impacts the cart with no horizontal velocity. From here, two things can happen: it is accelerated from rest to the new speed of the cart by a horizontal friction force acting forwards, which according to Newton's third law means the cart experiences a similar friction force in the opposite direction acting backwards. Alternatively, the rain could simply hit the back of the cart and exert a backwards impulse on the cart.

This might seem straightforward, but you're being asked to explain something from basics without being distracted by details (such as the fact the water is liquid rather than solid). The clarity of your explanations matters because it reflects the degree of your understanding.

**Tutor:** Thank you. That's all on that question.

## Further hints

If you're struggling with the fact that rain is continuously falling into the cart, the tutor might suggest something such as: 'Suppose we think about what happens to one raindrop...' (You can often analyse the behaviour of a fluid by thinking about each small part of it as a simple particle.)

They might also draw a diagram for you if you're completely stuck to give you something to guide your thoughts.

To get you started, the tutor might ask 'What quantities are conserved when a raindrop hits the cart?' or 'What force does a raindrop experience when it hits the cart?' To give less away, they could instead ask something such as 'If you're sitting in the cart, what do you see happen when a raindrop falls into it?'—inviting you to think about either the forces involved, or the 'before' and 'after' states of the raindrop.

### Extending the question

To extend the question, you could be asked to find an equation for the velocity of the cart as a function of time, given that the rain falls at a constant rate (hint: if you take the equation $(\delta m)v + m(\delta v) = 0$ and send $\delta m$ and $\delta v$ to 0, you get $\frac{dv}{dm} = -\frac{v}{m}$, where $v$ and $M$ are both functions of time.)

The scenario could also be altered in several ways:

- The rain falls at an angle
- The cart starts full of water, which leaks out of a hole at the bottom
- The cart starts full of water, which leaks out of a hole at the back.

### What is the question testing?

This question is primarily designed to assess your physical intuition and whether you can connect that intuition to physical principles such as conservation of momentum.

Many students will be confused as to whether momentum is indeed conserved. To deal with this problem, it's important to specify exactly what *system* you're dealing with, and to make sure you don't change that system halfway through. For example, you can either define your system as the cart itself, in which case momentum is *not* conserved, or you can define your system as the cart plus rain droplet, in which case momentum *is* conserved.

### Related topics from university

This question is an example of a collision problem in mechanics; the study of collisions comprises a large portion of a first-year Mechanics course.

## Engineering interview question 2 (Differential Equations)

Some interviewers will test you on your maths skills using a physics question, but others will test you on these separately. Graph sketching and calculus are common themes in Engineering maths questions.

**Question:** ***(The interviewer verbally explains, aided by pen and paper.)***
**A differential equation of the form $\frac{dy}{dx} = f\left(\frac{y}{x}\right)$ can often be more easily solved using a substitution of the form $y = u(x)x$ (i.e. $u(x) = \frac{y}{x}$), where $u$ is a function of $x$.**

**Let's take a simple example: $x\frac{dy}{dx} = y$. Differentiating the substitution $y = u(x)x$ yields $\frac{dy}{dx} = u + x\frac{du}{dx}$, but dividing both sides of our initial equation $x\frac{dy}{dx} = y$ by $x$ gives us $\frac{dy}{dx} = u$, so we get $u + x\frac{du}{dx} = u$. Then either $x$ is $0$ (which is a trivial solution) or $\frac{du}{dx}$ is $0$. So, the non-trivial solution is: $y = cx$.**

<u>**Please could you use this method to solve $(x+2y)\frac{dy}{dx} = -x - y$?**</u>

Some interview questions will be of this form, in which the interviewer shows you a technique, gives you an example, and asks you to apply that technique to a more difficult question.

## Model interview

**Student:** Okay, I see how in your example we have $x\frac{du}{dx} = 0$, but <u>I'm not sure how you got from there to $y = cx$.</u>

Always ask when you're unsure!

**Tutor:** Well, if $\frac{du}{dx} = 0$, $u$ is simply a constant $c$.

**Student:** Ah, I see now, so substituting $y = u(x)x$ gives $y = cx$.

**Tutor:** Great! So how about this new equation I've given you?

**Student:** I don't immediately see where I will get a $\frac{y}{x}$ from, but I think I should divide through by $x + 2y$ to give me $\frac{dy}{dx} = -\frac{x+y}{x+2y}$.
*(Pauses to think.)*
Maybe I could divide the numerator and denominator by $x$. That would give me $\frac{dy}{dx} = -\frac{\frac{x}{x}+\frac{y}{x}}{\frac{x}{x}+2\frac{y}{x}}$.
Ah yes, and substituting in $u$ I'll get: $u + x\frac{du}{dx} = -\frac{1+u}{1+2u}$.

I suppose that I want to group the $u$'s together, so I should get: $x\frac{du}{dx} = -\frac{2u^2+2u+1}{1+2u}$. However, I'm not sure if I know how to solve this?

**Tutor:** What form do you want it to be in to be able to solve it?

**Student:** *(Thinks.)* Some function of $u$ times $\frac{du}{dx}$ = some function of $x$?

**Tutor:** Or...?

**Student:** Some function of $x$ times $\frac{dx}{du}$ = some function of $u$? Oh, I see I can do that. I think I should have $\frac{1}{x}\frac{dx}{du} = -\frac{1+2u}{1+2u+2u^2}$, which I think I should be able to integrate... *(pauses.)* I'm not sure how I would deal with $-\frac{1+2u}{1+2u+2u^2}$, though?

**Tutor:** What does the numerator look like? Look at the denominator.

**Student:** (*Pauses for a few seconds.*) Oh yes, the numerator is like the denominator differentiated, so I must get: $\ln(x) = -\frac{1}{2}\ln(1+2u+2u^2)+c$, and I can rearrange and substitute to get...

**Tutor:** That's good, we can leave that there; I think you understand how to get to an answer.

If you substitute for $u$ and rearrange, you'll get to the equation $x^2 + 2xy + 2y^2 = k$, for $k$ a positive constant. However, interviewers will sometimes move on if they've seen you do the most interesting or difficult part of the question.

## Further hints

If you've not seen something such as $-\frac{x+y}{x+2y}$ before, you might not recognise that both the numerator and denominator are made up of terms of the same degree, which means that it can be written in terms of $\frac{y}{x}$. For example if $u = \frac{y}{x}$, then $\frac{x^3+2x^2y+4y^3}{3x^2y+xy^2} = \frac{1+2u+4u^3}{3u+u^2}$. The interviewer could prompt you by saying something such as: '*How would you get a $\frac{y}{x}$ in there?*' or '*How could you rearrange that fraction?*'

Hopefully, you'll be familiar with taking reciprocals in a differential equation from the A-Level Maths syllabus. If not, the interviewer could prompt you with: 'Would it be easier if the variables were switched around?', or 'Would it be easier to integrate $-\frac{1+2u}{1+2u+2u^2}$?'

## Extending the question

A question such as this can be easily extended by thinking of more difficult examples of applying the same technique. (Can you think of your own?) An interesting extension may be a question such as: 'Solve $x\frac{dy}{dx} = y + x^2 + y^2$', which requires you to recall the derivative of $\arctan(x)$.

## What is the question testing?

This question is testing your calculus skills, but more broadly your ability to spot patterns (e.g. opportunities to get $\frac{y}{x}$ terms) and to apply a new technique to a case you haven't seen before. This is an important skill because one of the differences between university and A Level is that often you receive only a couple of examples of a technique in lectures, and other important examples are introduced via problem/example sheets, so you have to figure out how they work on your own.

## Related topics from university

Techniques for solving differential equations are taught in the Mathematics module in the Oxford Engineering course and the Mathematical Methods module at Cambridge. Differential equations crop up naturally in everything from circuit theory to fluid dynamics, so having a full toolbox of techniques to solve them is essential.

# Engineering interview question 3 (Circuits)

**Question: What is the potential difference over each resistor in this circuit, if they all have the same resistance?**

# Model interview

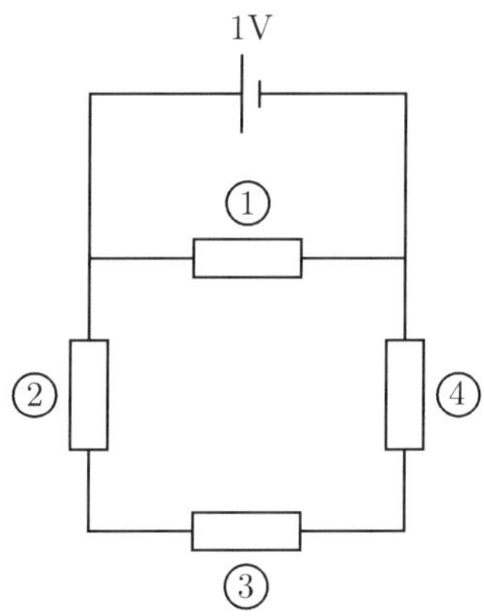


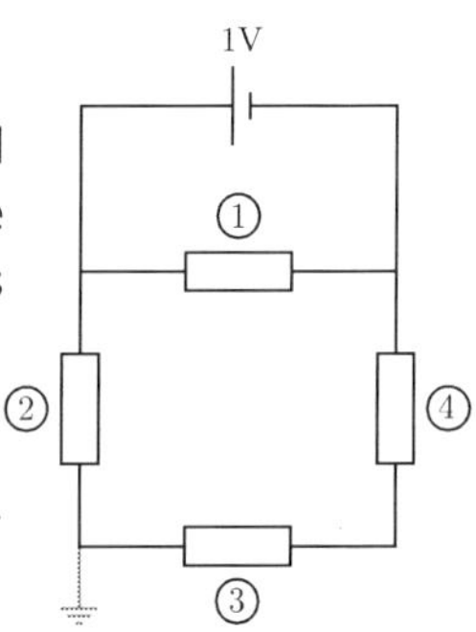


**Student:** Over resistor 1, it will be $1\text{V}$. The total potential difference over the other three will be $1\text{V}$, and they're all the same, so it's $\frac{1}{3\text{V}}$ over each of them.

**Tutor:** Okay. Suppose I add this symbol to the circuit? Do you know what that means?

**Student:** It's a ground. I don't really know what it does to the circuit though. I don't think it can have a resistance, or produce an emf.

More precisely spelling out the limits of your knowledge is better than just saying you don't know what to do.

**Tutor:** In this case, we'll think of it as setting the potential of the point it attaches to 0—the same as the negative terminal of the cell. Does that make sense?

**Student:** I think so.

**Tutor:** In that case, if I attach it as shown, what is the potential difference over each resistor now?

**Student:** I think resistor 1 is $1\text{V}$ because it's the same as before. And the potential difference over the other three also should still be $1\text{V}$, 'because they form a loop with resistor 1.

It's common to face questions in which the tutor changes the situation you're analysing to make it harder; one great way to reply is to identify what hasn't changed.

**Tutor:** Yes, exactly.

**Student:** But now I'm not sure what happens. Can a current even flow through that part of the circuit if it's grounded?

**Tutor:** Yes there can be current in that part of the circuit. Do you think that will help you find the potential differences?

**Student:** I was thinking I could use Ohm's law, but I don't really know about the current either. I think I should at least start with resistor 2 because the other two will follow from it. Is there another rule I could use?

Even when you're unsure, you can try to come up with plans and useful questions.

**Tutor:** Here's one way of thinking about it: the bottom end of resistor 2 is connected directly to ground. What is the other end connected to?

**Student:** Resistor 1 and the cell.

**Tutor:** Which part of the cell?

**Student:** The positive terminal. Okay, so it's similar to going from $1\text{V}$ to $0\text{V}$. So the potential difference over resistor 2 is $1\text{V}$. And that means the potential difference over the other two has to be 0... is that right?

**Tutor:** Does it make sense for the other two to be 0?

**Student:** Actually, yes, because it's as though the potential is 0V at both ends.

**Tutor:** Exactly. Let's expand a little bit. Where else could I attach the ground to the circuit, and what would the potential difference over each resistor be in each case?

**Student:** I think you can attach it in these ways...

A.

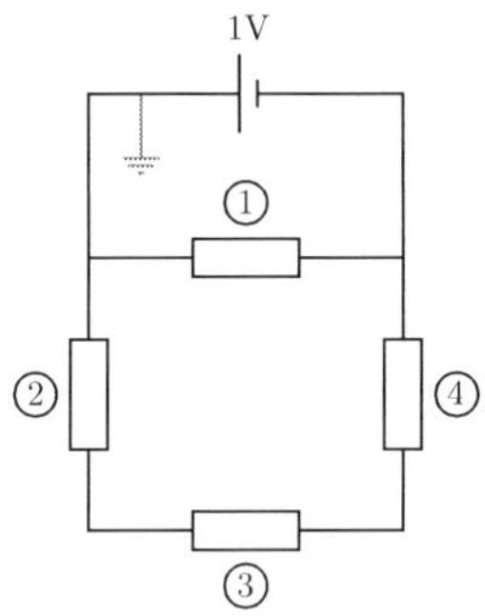


B.

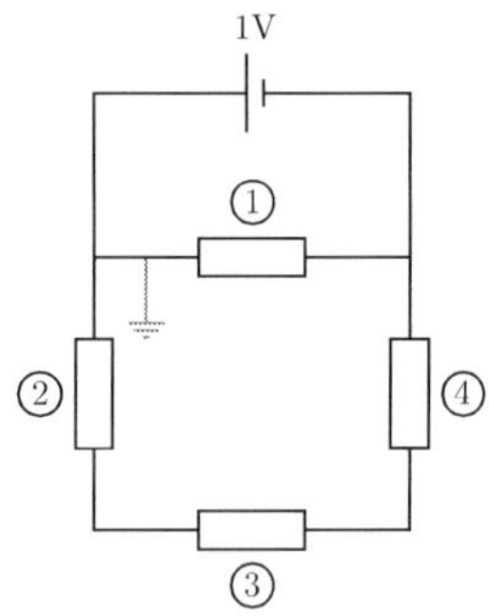


C.

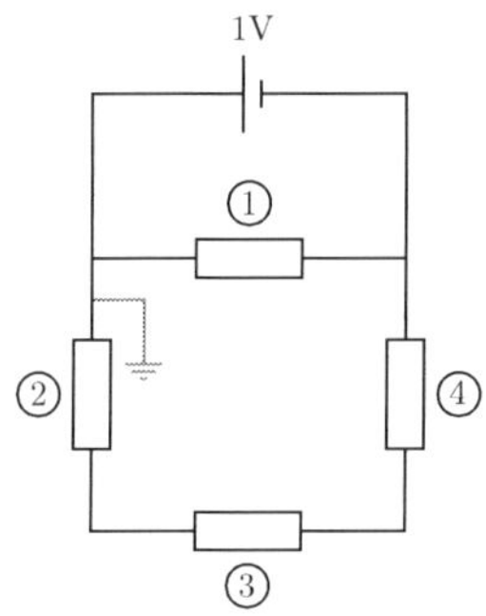


D.

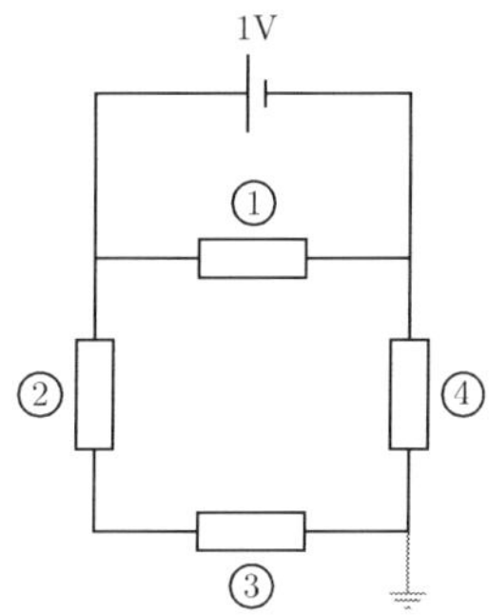


E.

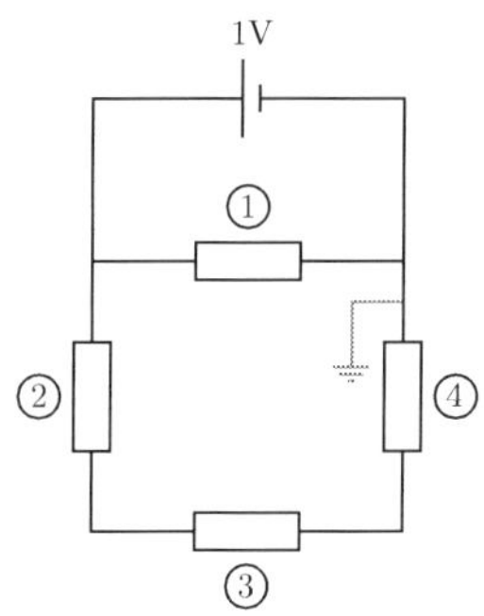


F.

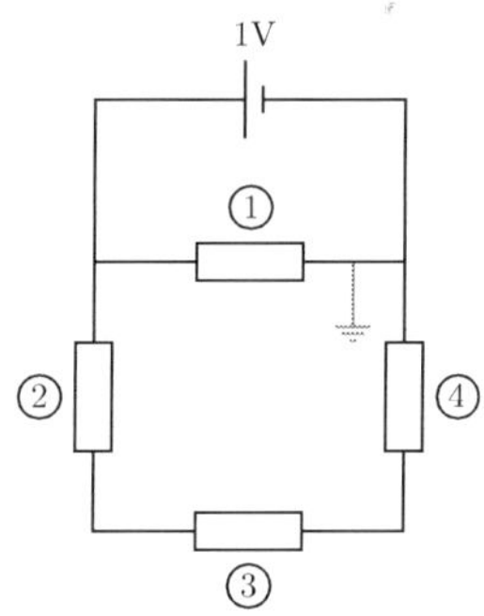


G.

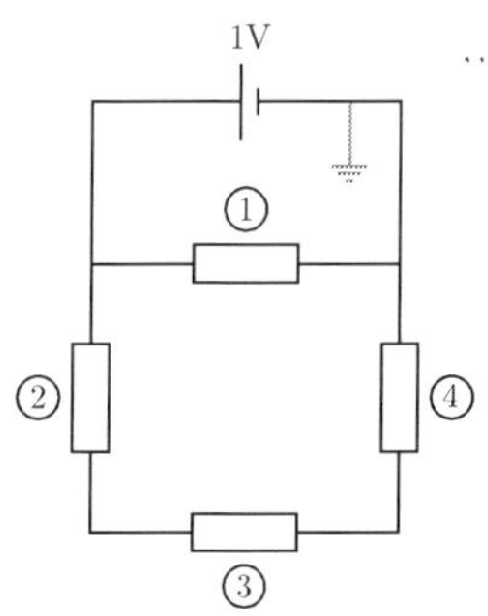


These pictures are for illustration only—in practice, you should indicate by pointing to the tutor's diagram rather than waste time redrawing the circuit.

**Student:** Wait, actually A, B and C are the same, and E, F and G are also the same, because where the junctions are doesn't affect the potential. So there are only three more ways.

**Tutor:** Okay, and what happens for each resistor?

**Student:** In E, F and G, nothing changes from when there was no ground. And in A, B and C, I think the potential difference over any of them is 0, because it's 0 either side. I suppose I have to calculate what happens in D. Let's see: resistor 1 will still get $1\text{V}$. Resistor 4 will get $0\text{V}$. And the other two are the same, so they both get $0.5\text{V}$. Is that right?

**Tutor:** Yes, that's right. Let's look at a final example. *(Draws a new diagram)*

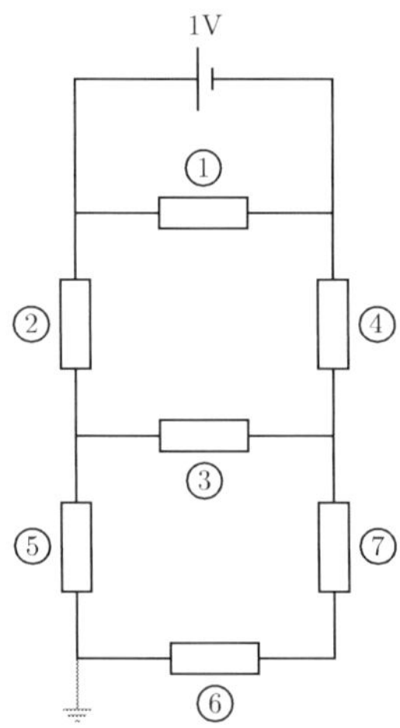


**Tutor:** Please could you find the potential difference over each resistor again? They are still all identical.

**Student:** Okay. Resistor 1 still gets $1\text{V}$. I think that 4, 6 and 7 all get $0\text{V}$ because the potential at either end is 0—wait, no. There's a path through 2, 3 and 4 to the cell, and a path through 2, 3, 7 and 6 to ground. Can I say the total potential difference over 2 and 5 is $1\text{V}$, and they're the same, so they get half each?

**Tutor:** The total potential difference is $1\text{V}$, but they are positioned differently with respect to the rest of the circuit, so we can't conclude they get half each.

**Student:** *(Annotating the diagram.)* Okay, so let's say it's $V_2$ for resistor 2 and $1—V_2$ for resistor 5. And let's write resistances $V_3$ and $V_4$ for resistors 3 and 4.

Don't be afraid to introduce your own notation

Well, $V_4$ is $1 - V_2 - V_3$, so I can simply use that. And resistors 6 and 7 both get half of $V_3 - (1 - V_2)$ because the bottom 3 are in parallel with resistor 3.

And I can try to count the potential differences around different loops to get some equations... Hm, actually, I think I used all the loops already.

It's much better to announce your next step and analyse why it failed, than to attempt it in your head and have nothing to say when it doesn't work.

**Tutor:** What other rules about potential differences have you considered?

**Student:** I thought about Ohm's law before. Maybe I could use that again, because there's a separate rule for splitting currents at a junction. But it means I have to work out all the currents.

**Tutor:** Let's look at one junction—which might be useful?

**Student:** The one between resistors 1 and 2... No, that doesn't work because I don't know the total current. I could work it out by finding the total resistance.

**Tutor:** That would work, but can we find a quicker way?

**Student:** I could look at the junction between resistors 2 and 5. Using the current rule, I get: $\frac{V_2}{R} = \frac{V_3}{R} + \frac{1 - V_2}{R}$.

That means $V_3$ is $2V_2 - 1$, so $V_4$ is $2 - 3V_2$.

And looking at the junction between 4 and 7, I get: $\frac{V_4}{R} = \frac{V_3}{R} + \frac{V_3 - (1 - V_2)}{2R}$.

Plugging in the values of $V_3$ and $V_4$, I have $2 - 3V_2 = 2V_2 - 1 + ½ (3V_2 - 2)$.

*(Does some working out on paper.)* And that means $V_2 = \frac{8}{13}$.

And I can get the rest using that...

**Tutor:** Okay, well done. No need to do all the algebra. Let's leave it there.

## Further hints

The tutor may demonstrate how to calculate potential differences in the presence of a ground if the student is struggling at first. They also may prompt you to recall Kirchhoff's laws for voltage and current.

In the last part, they might ask you 'What paths can current follow?' or 'What paths are there that join the positive terminal of the cell to points of zero potential?'

### Extending the question

The tutor might opt to extend this question in several ways:

- The ground could be moved around the last circuit in the same way it was moved around the first one.
- For one of the circuits, you could be asked to find the current through any resistor or the cell, or the power dissipated in any resistor or the whole circuit.
- You could be asked a more conceptual question about what a ground is and why it might be added to a circuit, especially if you have seen it used before.

### What is the question testing?

The question aims to assess whether you know and can apply Kirchhoff's laws—as well as whether you can be systematic in the way you process information to avoid becoming lost. It helps to be able to fluently and implicitly use the laws rather than write out an equation each time. Finally, you're being tested on your ability to handle the presence of an unfamiliar component (the ground).

### Related topics from university

Circuits and electronics are an essential part of the first-year courses at both Oxford and Cambridge. You'll also be able to specialise in electrical engineering later in your degree if you wish.

The concept of 'ground' occurs in slightly different ways in DC and AC systems. You'll see the latter a lot more at uni than at A Level, because handling varying voltages and currents introduces several complications, and because AC systems appear in so many important applications.

## 18.5: A script of an Oxbridge Chemistry interview

Here are three scripted examples of Oxford Chemistry interview questions with strong, successful candidates.

If you're interested in **Natural Sciences** or **Materials Science**, you may be interested in this section, and the interview scripts for Physics (page 281) and Engineering (page 293).

## Chemistry interview question 1 (Stereoisomers)

**Question: What happens when you react bromine and E-but-2-ene?**

### Model interview

**Student:** The bromine approaches side on to the C = C double bond and a carbocation is formed as an intermediate. Let me draw the mechanism:

Don't wait to be prompted to draw a diagram if it will help illustrate what you're saying.

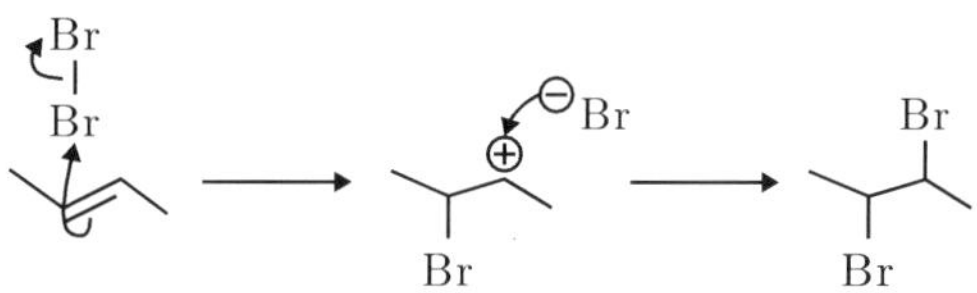


**Tutor:** Very good. And what stereoisomer is that final dibromoalkane?

**Student:** In this case it could be any stereoisomer, as the carbocation is planar, and so nucleophilic attack can occur from either side.

**Tutor:** Now let's consider the carbon atoms, which are both chiral, in 3D, with tetrahedral structures. Can you draw all the stereoisomers that this molecule can have?

**Student:** Yes. *(Draws.)*

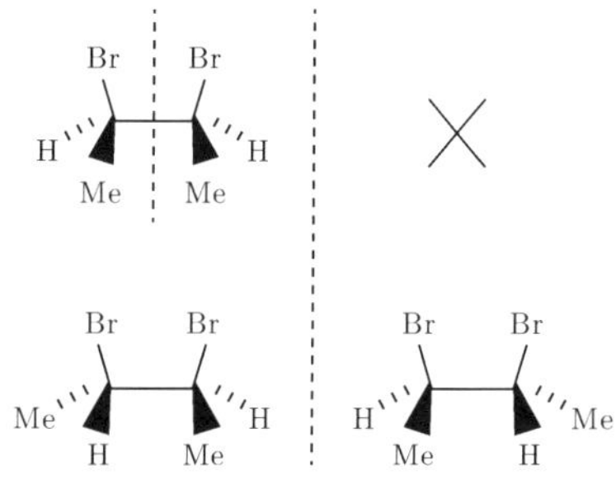


**Tutor:** <u>Why are there only three stereoisomers despite there being two chiral centres?</u>

If you get four enantiomers in the above section, the interviewer will change the question to help you get to the correct number.

**Student:** The first isomer has a plane of symmetry, so it doesn't have an enantiomer—if we drew it the other way it would be just like looking at what I've drawn from the other side of the molecule.

**Tutor:** Yes, and we call this type of compound a meso compound. Now, in reality, only the meso compound is formed in this reaction. Can you think of a mechanism which that might cause that to happen?

This part is difficult if you haven't seen it before. Persevere!

**Student:** That would mean that we have to have a mechanism without a planar intermediate and there would have to be a mechanism which leads to the formation of just one compound. But I'm not sure what that would look like.

Even if you have no idea, talk about what you know that might be relevant!

**Tutor:** Right, so what about if you formed some sort of ring intermediate by using the extra lone pairs of bromine? This results in the bromine atom making up one atom in a 3-membered ring, all atoms in the same plane.

**Student:** Okay, so if we form a three-membered ring, then the second step could be an SN2 reaction because that retains the chirality, like this:

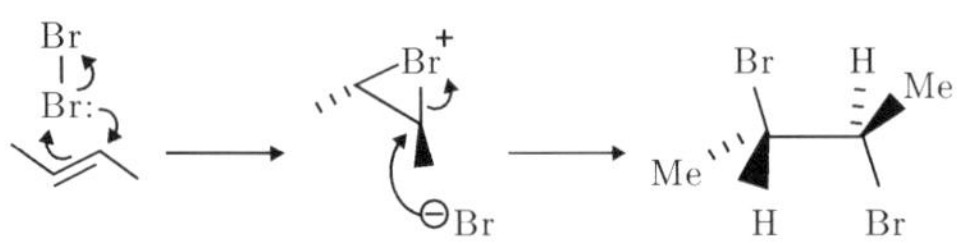


**Tutor:** Okay, thank you. Let's move on to the next question.

## Further hints

If you try to describe the whole process out loud, or don't give enough detail, the tutor might say something such as '"Why don't you try drawing out the mechanism you think is responsible?' A question such as that doesn't mean you've got something wrong—they might want a diagram to help you out in the next part of the question, or to test you really do understand all the details.

If you start the question by incorrectly assuming the bromine molecule splits into radicals, the tutor might ask: 'What conditions would you need to produce radicals?'

If you draw four stereoisomers instead of three, the interviewer might ask: "Are any of these equivalents?"

### Extending the question

The tutor might extend the question by asking about similar reactions; one way to set this up is to replace an element with another from the same group. For instance, they might ask you:

- Would you expect the same reaction to occur with fluorine?
- What about iodine?

They could also ask a question that is broader in scope, such as:

- How do you think the reactivity of bromonium substances compares to epoxides?

### What is the question testing?

The question is testing your ability to think about problems that may seem familiar but that go past your existing knowledge. In particular, it draws on and extends your skills in organic chemistry and identifying mechanisms.

### Related topics from university

This question relates to the first-year Organic Chemistry course. There's a module on unsaturated carbon reactivity, and also stereochemistry (a topic that you'll study in all three years and that is particularly vital in pharmacology and pharmaceutical chemistry).

## Chemistry interview question 2 (Identifying Powders)

**Question: Imagine that you're given the following substances as powders:**

$$KCl,\ KNO_3,\ NaCl,\ CuSO_4,\ glucose,\ Na_2CO_3,\ BaO$$

**Explain how you would differentiate between them. You can use any reagents and lab equipment you like.**

This is a very broad question that has many solutions. Remember to be succinct and provide as complete an answer as you can without getting lost in the detail.

### Model interview

**Student:** We can first see that only one of the substances is an organic compound. We can try to heat all the substances—one test tube where caramelisation occurs contains glucose.

**Tutor:** That is a good start, but would you heat the whole of each sample?

**Student:** No, we take only a part of each sample for each test so that we have pure samples for further tests. We can start testing the inorganic substances by trying to make a solution. Copper (II) sulphate should be the only compound that makes a blue solution.

**Tutor:** That's a very good idea—can you think of any test that can assure you that the two substances you identified are really glucose and $CuSO_4$?

Don't worry if you don't immediately recall where you've seen this pair before—tutors understand that interview is a stressful situation.

**Student:** Well, we can conduct either Trommer's test or Fehling's test to test that glucose reduces copper (II)—

**Tutor:** Exactly! What about the five remaining samples?

**Student:** We can test the pH of all the solutions. $BaO$ is the only strong base, so an indicator paper should turn blue. If we add sulfuric acid, $BaSO_4$ will precipitate and we should see white crystals appearing.

**Tutor:** How about adding sulfuric acid to other solutions?

**Student:** That can help identify carbonate. We should be able to see bubbles of carbon dioxide. *(Pause.)*

**Tutor:** We are left with $KCl$, $NaCl$ and $KNO_3$. Let's test them by adding some silver nitrate.

**Student:** Almost all nitrates are soluble in water, but silver chloride is a white, darkening precipitate. We should see that in two test tubes, so the third one is potassium nitrate. It's hard to differentiate between sodium and potassium cations as they are both metals from group 1. We can try the flame test; sodium will colour the flame bright yellow and potassium will give a lilac colour. Now all the samples are identified.

This is the hardest part of the question and it's likely you won't be able to solve some part of it. All questions are designed to push you to the limits of your knowledge and skills.

## Further hints

There are many other tests you can use. Don't worry—tutors are likely to give hints if you're stuck, or even suggest reagents and ask you to write down some reactions. If you struggle, go back to basics. Think about colours, solubility and characteristic reactions. If you manage to identify four or five substances, but forgot about the flame test or other ways to differentiate between last two samples (e.g. use cation-selective electrodes or precipitate with $ClO_4^-$), it's still a very good answer.

### Extending the question

The interviewer is likely to explore whether you know any other ways to differentiate compounds (think about e.g. the reaction of copper(II) with ammonia, or how to confirm that the gas is carbon dioxide), throw in additional samples (think about $saccharose$, $ZnCl_2$ or $(NH_4)_2SO_4$) or ask about the benefits of a given test (think about the cost, toxicity, time, selectivity, etc.).

### What is the question testing?

This question is designed to test your practical skills, inorganic chemistry knowledge, and creativity in qualitative analysis. It will help to have a good understanding of how each of the tests you have learned about works so that you can more easily see how it can be applied in unfamiliar circumstances.

### Related topics from university

In the first three years of the Oxford Chemistry course, you'll have plenty of practice hours in a real lab. During your first year, you'll also explore the thermodynamics of liquids and solutions and reasons why substances precipitate or not. There's also a Transition Metals course in which you'll examine where the colour of solutions come from.

**Top Tip**

*It's hard to predict whether an unfamiliar substance will **be soluble or precipitate**. Besides the obvious factor of concentration, you could think about intermolecular forces. With simple salts, compare the crystallisation energy of the salt with the interaction between water molecules. Try thinking about the trends of solubility of salts of metals from group 1 and halogens, and look out for the sizes of ions.*

## Chemistry interview question 3 (Estimation and Gases)

**Question: Estimate how heavy the air in this room is. Would you be able to lift it if it were a barbell?**

## Model interview

**Student:** Well, first I need to know the size of this room, the pressure, the temperature...

This question tests your ability to estimate, not your precision. You're not given a calculator or a periodic table.

**Tutor:** Try to estimate them.

**Student:** Let's say the room is $4m \cdot 3m \cdot 2.5m = 30m^3$. I assume that the temperature is 298K and the pressure is 1atm.

**Tutor:** For ease of mental calculations, let's round it up to 300K and round it down to 1 bar.

**Student:** Well, we want to first calculate the number of moles of gas in this room. We know from the ideal gas equation that $PV = nRT$ so $n = \frac{PV}{RT}$. If we round the gas constant to 8, we get

$$n \approx \frac{10^5 Pa \cdot 30m^3}{8\frac{J}{mol \cdot K} \cdot 300K} = 1250\ moles$$

Now we need to estimate the molar mass of air. Air is about 80% nitrogen and 20% oxygen.

You're only given pen and paper. Use them to write down the equations that illustrate what you're talking about. Make sure you explain your entire thought process.

**Tutor:** To side-track for a moment: what else forms air?

**Student:** Depending on location there's some water vapour and carbon dioxide—probably quite a lot in this room, as people breathe them out. There are also some noble gases, but they make up 1% or less.

**Tutor:** Very well, carry on. You can use any molar mass in between those of nitrogen and oxygen.

**Student:** The molar masses of $N_2$ and $O_2$ are $28g/mol$ and $32g/mol$. Let's use $30g/mol$ for easier calculations. The mass of air in this room will be $m = 1250mol \cdot 30g/mol = 37500g \approx 40kg$.

Always simplify the numbers in your estimates where you can. After all, the difference between 30g/mol and the true average will be much less than 10%, and you've already introduced errors bigger than that.

**Tutor:** So would you be able to lift that?

**Student:** Yes, I think so!

**Tutor:** Now imagine the room is filled with iodine vapour instead. Besides the facts that we would be unable to breathe and the iodine would probably crystallise, how does the mass change?

**Student:** Well, the number of moles stays the same because it's not dependent on the substance, only on pressure, temperature and volume. I need to know the molar mass of iodine...

Identifying what doesn't change in the new scenario, and what further information you need are two key steps in many estimation questions.

**Tutor:** Estimate it, thinking about periodic table.

**Student:** I know that molar mass of fluorine is 19 and chlorine is 35.5. In the same group we have bromine and iodine directly underneath. Bromine should have a molar mass around 80, as now there's an addition of first-row transition metals between bromine and chlorine, so let's say iodine molar mass is 130 g/mol.

**Tutor:** Very good! It's 126.9 g/mol, so that is an excellent estimate. Continue.

**Student:** If we consider that iodine is a diatomic gas, we get $m = 1250mol \cdot 260g/mol \approx 300kg$. I definitely wouldn't be able to lift that!

## Further hints

The tutor might give you the molar mass of iodine gas if you're stuck, but they could instead give you further hints for estimating it. You don't have to learn the periodic table by heart—but do memorise the positions of the most common elements. You can think of the periodic table as a city map: if you know the general shape of the map, important landmarks (the common elements) and street names (the groups), you'll be able to find almost any address. Knowing the precise values of numbers such as molar masses isn't essential. If you're not sure of a value, always try to estimate—explaining where your estimate came from.

## Extending the question

The question could develop into why balloons filled with helium fly up, or how hot-air balloons work. Always go back to basics—the ideal gas equation. Other questions that explore similar calculations are: '*How many atoms does this jelly bean contain?*' or '*How many times does water expand on vaporisation?*'

## What is the question testing?

Besides testing whether you can intuitively estimate physical quantities and whether you understand units, it tests some basic physical chemistry/thermodynamics.

## Related topics from university

This type of calculation is the cornerstone of topics such as thermodynamics or kinetics, which are explored in detail in the first year as part of the 'Physical Chemistry' paper. You'll also learn where the ***ideal gas law*** comes from.

> In case you haven't come across it at school yet, the **ideal gas law** describes the relationship between pressure, volume, and temperature in an idealised model of a gas ($PV = nRT$) and is one of the most useful tools in physical chemistry. It was first derived empirically, but can also be understood within the kinetic theory of gases, i.e. by thinking about the velocities of the individual gas molecules.

# 18.6: More examples of physical science interview questions

Here are some more examples of questions on some common topics. If you're applying for Natural Sciences or Materials Science, you will probably benefit from all of these. If you're applying for Physics, check out the engineering questions too, and vice versa. You might also want to have a look at some of the maths questions on page 134.

## More examples of physics interview questions

- If we didn't know the value of the gas constant *R*, what's an experiment we could do to find it? What do you think the main sources of error would be, and how could the errors be minimised?
- Find the kinetic energy of a toppling ladder as a function of the angle it makes with the vertical.
- Suppose you jump up and down on a set of scales. Sketch the reading on the scales as a function of time.
- Sketch $y = \frac{\ln x}{x^2}$. Is the area between the curve and the x-axis from $x = 1$ to infinity finite or infinite?
- Solve $\frac{dy}{dx} = ay - by^2$ for $a$ and $b$ positive constants and sketch $x$ against $y$. What happens as $a$ and $b$ change? What happens if either or both become negative?

*"There was very little chit-chat and it was straight down to pen and paper. I was asked to find* $\cos\left(\frac{\pi}{12}\right)$ *in surd form and then to prove that integration and differentiation are inverses of each other from first principles. I was also asked a mechanics question about an object on a plane that could be tilted up and down. It was a twist on a familiar problem and I needed some help but eventually arrived at the answer."*
–Student, Natural Sciences, Cambridge

## More examples of engineering interview questions

- A cylindrical pipe is required to deliver $1m^3$ of water per second. What's the relationship between the velocity of the water and the radius of the pipe? What does this mean for the pump that is used to get the water up to speed?
- Two wires have the same length and volume and are made of the same material. One has a circular cross section and the other has a square cross section. Which gets hotter when current passes through it?
- Draw a bike frame. When you sit on the bike, which parts are under compression and which are under tension? How might the forces change as you speed up, slow down, or go over bumps?
- What challenges might there be in managing the temperature inside a space station?

*"In both my interviews, I was asked a graph sketching question. Then the two physics questions were on how a bungee-jumper's velocity varied with time, and on the gravitational forces between a hoop and an object passing through it. I was very nervous for the first interview, but the interviewers were very nice and would prompt me when I needed some help. I was a lot more relaxed for my second interview, as I knew how it would go."* –Student, Engineering, Oxford

## More examples of chemistry interview questions

- Explain how you would extract, store, and use each of the major components of air.
- Gunpowder is made from charcoal, sulphur, and potassium nitrate. Suggest how the reaction might proceed when it burns. Many explosives are nitrate chemicals—why?

- Starting with $n = 2$ and proceeding to higher values of $n$, discuss how many compounds can be formed using only $n$ carbon atoms and as many hydrogen atoms as you like.
- You are transported back to the mid-18th century, just before the first scientific recognition of gases like hydrogen and oxygen in their pure forms. How do you become world famous by isolating these elements and demonstrating some of their useful or unique properties? Can you 'discover' any other elements? What else can you demonstrate to the world about chemistry?
- Tell me something about the chemistry of cooking.
- What might be some significant effects of changes in pressure on chemical processes in a deep-sea diver's body?

> *"There were separate interviews for inorganic, organic and physical chemistry. In the inorganic one I was asked to sketch the periodic table and write out the first row as best I could... my mind went pretty much completely blank! Then the tutor asked me which element was below carbon and I replied 'I'm sorry I have no idea'. He gave me a clue, saying it begins with 's', and yet all I could think was 'sodium?'! He finally told me it was silicon and I had an embarrassing eureka moment: I had been asked that question because I had talked about silica in my personal statement. My organic interview involved going through nucleophilic addition mechanisms and my physical chemistry one was on separating gases."* –Student, Chemistry, Oxford

# Part II C: Before Your Degree

# Chapter 19:
# A packing list of skills to bring from school to your degree

Most of the subjects involved in an Oxbridge physical science degree follow on from your A Levels, so you need to retain a good understanding of the relevant school content.

Furthermore, all physical sciences rely on a firm foundation of maths. The skills you learnt in A-Level Maths (and Further Maths if applicable) will be hugely useful throughout a science degree—not simply from a theoretical angle, but also for practical analysis. After labs, you'll be expected to write detailed lab reports using lots of statistical techniques to analyse your data.

Many other skills from your science A Levels will apply to your science degree. Even the subjects that don't directly follow on from an A Level, such as Earth Sciences and Material Sciences, will have roots in skills you learnt at school. Some useful transferable skills include:

- ❑ **Clear methods:** Often the most interesting part of university science is the working-out phase. It's important to present your methodology as clearly as possible, so practise organising your thinking and working at school.
- ❑ **Precision and accuracy:** Whether in measuring results or applying formulae, precision is an important part of both science A Levels and a science degree. Making sure your working is correct, neat and precise will ensure you reach the correct answers.
- ❑ **General scientific understanding:** One of the aims of your science A Levels is to provide you with a general understanding of scientific techniques. These include how to prepare and conduct an experiment, write a risk assessment, and write up your analysis. You also learn how to present your findings and construct hypotheses and theories about the results. These skills form an important foundation for your university studies.
- ❑ **Self-study:** Although at school your teachers carefully guide you through the content, self-study is required to solidify concepts and prepare for the next lesson. This skill will be invaluable in your degree, as most of your learning takes place through self-study. The contact hours

in a physical science degree are high, but you need to learn to prepare well and make the most of them—and fill in the blanks independently. Self-study will include things such as:

- Reading around the subject in textbooks
- Revisiting lecture notes[129] and re-watching them online (if possible)
- Watching videos on YouTube explaining key concepts
- Working through problems on your set problem/example sheets and extra problems in textbooks.

## A word on gap years for physical science applicants

Taking a gap year won't harm your application in itself, and you can even use it to develop useful skills, but it's by no means a requirement, and you need to make sure you spend at least some of your time keeping up your maths and science skills.

> *"Sponsorship schemes offering a year's work experience in a physics-related field may be excellent, but some activities are less useful. An athlete who does not train for a year will be pretty rusty. Likewise a physics (or maths) student who does not use his or her brain for a year will also be pretty rusty and this is the danger of a gap year!*
>
> *The Institute of Physics has contacts with over 300 companies and may be able to assist with suitable activities for a gap year.*
>
> *Some of the activities we hear suggested for the gap year could be done during the long vacation between the first and second years. Or you may like to consider taking a gap year after your degree."* –Oxford

See also the advice on page 139 for maintaining your maths skills during a gap year.

129 Unlike in many arts subjects, lectures are the bread and butter of the learning process for physical sciences, so not attending them isn't an option!

# Chapter 20:
# What should you do over the summer before your degree?

## A-Level/Higher Level Maths

A great way to prepare for your physical science degree is to revise your A-Level Maths content. Moreover, if you didn't study Further Maths (or if you did, but didn't do all the further pure content), it's certainly worth teaching yourself some topics. Not only will practising your self-study skills help you with university work, but the content is crucial to physical science degrees at Oxford and Cambridge (particularly Physics and Engineering).

In the first few weeks of university, you'll race through all of the Further Maths pure content—but if you haven't seen or studied it before, your lessons will feel extremely fast and incomplete. It's definitely worth acquiring a textbook and teaching yourself some of the subject matter so that it's not a complete shock in week 1!

> *"Depending on how much maths you've done at school, in the first term of first year you might see a considerable amount of overlap with school maths. They do go through the material at a pretty quick pace at university, though. I saw an entire Further Maths A Level fly by in two weeks!"* –Nicki, Physics, Oxford

## Preliminary work

Your college tutors are likely to set preliminary college holiday work—make sure you complete it! Not only would it be embarrassing to rock up to your first week having left the holiday work email fermenting at the bottom of your inbox while you celebrated all summer, but completing the work will prove really helpful. It's designed to ensure that everyone starts the degree on a level playing field.

## Reading

Although you're unlikely to receive an extensive reading list, your understanding of the subject and your enthusiasm for it (which may wane during the inhumane process of A-Level revision) will soar if you read around a bit. Refer back to the lists on page 223 for some useful books relating to your subject.

## Equipment

This is more of a practical tip, but make sure you have all the equipment you'll need. You'll be glued to your scientific calculator throughout your degree, and you'll need lots of drawing equipment (such as a 30cm ruler and a protractor). For Chemistry, you'll also need a molecular model kit. Arriving prepared will alleviate a bit of stress and allow you to focus on more important things.

# Part III:

# Economics

# Part III A: The Courses

In this part, we'll cover the different courses at Oxford and Cambridge that involve economics in some form. At Cambridge, you can study:

- Economics
- Land Economy.

At Oxford, economics is instead offered as part of several joint honours courses:

- Economics & Management (E&M)
- Philosophy, Politics & Economics (PPE)
- History & Economics.

# Chapter 21:
# Economics at Cambridge

## 21.1: Why Economics at Cambridge?

Economics is an influential and thriving discipline; its mathematical roots, practical nature and range of applications in business and government might make it an attractive subject if you have a quantitative mind but also a broad set of interests.

The economy forms an essential part of current affairs. Are you looking for something fast-paced and critical to modern society? Are you interested in problems such as finding the best approach to taxation or adapting the economy to avoid climate change? If so, perhaps this degree has piqued your interest already. But to see if it's really for you, ask yourself how many of the following apply to you:

- ❑ **You love economics:** You may or may not be studying Economics at school. But either way, if you're going to study it at uni, you'll need to convince the admissions tutors (and yourself) that you can see yourself pursuing nothing else for three years. If you're fascinated by economics in the news, or particular economic ideas like game theory, then you might be in a position to do just that.
- ❑ **You don't just use maths, you enjoy it:** We're sure you're aware that economics is a mathematical subject, but you might still be surprised by just how much advanced maths there is in the Economics degree, particularly at Cambridge. You'll need to be able to give rigorous mathematical proofs, not just do a few calculations (and even the calculations can require a lot of creatively-applied mathematical knowledge). If that's something you'd relish rather than dread, an Economics degree might be for you.
- ❑ **You can support your arguments with evidence:** Economics isn't just about mathematical theories—you'll also have to make arguments, and importantly, to back those arguments up with evidence that you have to extract yourself from books or sets of data. If that's something you already enjoy doing, perhaps in debates or essay-based subjects at school, you might find the Economics course is right up your street.

- ❑ **Your writing skills are up to scratch:** Another important facet of making strong arguments is being able to write clearly and persuasively. Economics is very much a degree for students who have both quantitative and writing skills. However, if you don't want to be writing essays forever, you can choose to specialise in the mathematical/data-driven side of the degree after your first year, if you apply for a straight Economics degree. You're unlikely to get that option if you apply for any of the joint courses.
- ❑ **You're interested in the role of economics in politics and history:** Perhaps your interest in economics comes from your interest in politics or history, since it heavily influences both. You'll find both of those interests represented in the Cambridge degree. Even though it doesn't contain Politics or History as discrete subjects to the same extent as PPE and History & Economics at Oxford, there are courses relating to both in your first year and thereafter.

## Economics at Cambridge: The details

The Cambridge Economics degree is a three-year course and you leave with a BA. The course is very diverse, offering a wide choice of ***pure*** and ***applied*** modules. It will give you an overview of the role economics plays in society, as well as an advanced understanding of economic theory.

What is the difference between pure, applied and historical economics modules?

**Pure economics** modules focus on economic theories that can be applied time and again to different phenomena. You'll study topics such as game theory, utility functions and graphical techniques.

**Applied and historical economics** modules look at how the economy has existed at different times. You'll probably be given an area and a time period, and you'll use the skills from pure economics to examine the state of the economy at this point.

# 21.2: How do you apply for Economics at Cambridge?

The offer for Economics at Cambridge is usually A*A*A at A Level, or 40–42 points in the IB with 776 at Higher Level. On average, 1 out of 7 applicants is successful.

Maths is a compulsory prerequisite A Level/Higher Level subject for this course, and you're usually required to have an A* at A Level or 7 in the IB.

You have to sit the ECAA (Economics Admissions Assessment) if you're applying to study Economics at Cambridge. See page 383 for more information.

**Did You Know?**

*In 2016, the average number of predicted A*s among Cambridge Economics offer-holders was 3.5. That means that, most likely, at least half of these students were not only taking more than 3 A Levels, but were predicted A*s in more than 3.*

## What A Level/IB Higher Level subjects are useful for Economics at Cambridge?

We have to emphasise that Economics at Cambridge is a highly mathematical degree. Throughout the course, you'll be expected to apply mathematical techniques to analyse functions and graphs, evaluate sums and integrals, and present and analyse data. Here's a list of some of the maths you can expect to study as part of the Economics degree that follows from what you learnt at school:

- Differentiation and integration
- Summing arithmetic and geometric sequences
- Formulating systems of equations from information about a situation and solving them using matrices
- Exponential growth and decay
- Probability and statistics.

In your first year, your Mathematical Methods course will teach you all the techniques required for an Economics degree. However, the mathematics will be taught as a subject in its own right and won't necessarily be applied immediately to economics. This means having studied Further Maths and Maths at A Level will put you at an advantage.

Studying Economics at A Level/Higher Level isn't quite as important as Maths, but it will still make your first year easier.

> *"Interestingly, Economics A Level isn't compulsory, but it's useful because it introduces you to the basic economic concepts that are retaught mathematically from first principles. It also provides an introduction to thinking about the benefits and disadvantages of economic policies."* –Paaras, Economics, Cambridge

> *"I only knew a handful of students on my course who didn't study A-Level Economics or equivalent, and most of these were international students who didn't have the opportunity."* –Maya, Economics, Cambridge

Additionally, although History and Politics aren't compulsory subjects, they can give you useful background knowledge for the Economics degree. History plays a significant role in applied economics modules. In studying the economy of a particular period, you'll study the other social, political and technological forces of that time and how they impacted on the economy.

## 21.3: Doing a Cambridge Economics degree: What's it really like?

The fact that economics is a social science and yet relies heavily on advanced maths means that the content you'll cover and the style of teaching will be very diverse. To give you a taste of what this combination looks like, here are the five modules you'll study in your first year at Cambridge:

### Microeconomics

Microeconomics is about firms, individuals, markets and market failures (think supply and demand graphs, monopolies, competitive markets, consumer choice and game theory). In your first year, Microeconomics involves a lot more maths than A-Level Economics.

Here's an example of a question you might get in an early first-year **Microeconomics** problem sheet:

*Show graphically the effects of each of the following events in the market for a cup of coffee on the demand curve, the supply curve, the equilibrium price, and the quantity supplied:*

1. *The cost of coffee beans increases*
2. *Caffeine is shown to have a new positive health effect*
3. *The price of tea increases worldwide.*

## Macroeconomics

Macroeconomics is about things that affect the country's economy as a whole, including growth, unemployment, inflation, trade and currency. You'll learn about economic shocks, the Euro crisis, the 2008 financial crisis, and the drivers of economic growth. Macroeconomics touches upon politics because it involves evaluating government policies, such as government taxation and spending (fiscal policy) or decisions by the central bank that affect the supply of money, including interest rate adjustments and quantitative easing (monetary policy). As with Microeconomics, this course will involve a good deal of maths.

## Quantitative Methods in Economics

This course comprises two sections: Mathematics and Statistics. It includes a recap of the mathematics techniques You'll learn in A Level, and introduces linear algebra[130] because the use of matrices is incredibly useful in economic theory for solving systems of equations. In the Statistics course, you'll cover probability theory, distributions, and regression and correlation.[131]

## Stata

You'll learn to use a piece of software called Stata for organising and analysing data. It will allow you to find the statistical relationship between economic variables – e.g. the prices of gold and silver in the 19th century – and to perform simulations of model economies.

130 Linear algebra is the study of vectors, matrices and transformations of vectors. It's called 'linear' because of its connection to linear equations.

131 Regression and correlation are introduced in A-Level Maths.

## Political and Social Aspects of Economics

This is an applied economics course that examines how politics and economics are intertwined. You'll study this interaction at both a theoretical and historical level. For example, you'll study the politics of British governments since 1945, including our integration into the European Union.

## British Economic History

This course focuses on the British economy from 1750 to 1939. You'll examine historical economic data to study how economic phenomena have manifested in various ways in the past. You'll study the British Industrial Revolution, the late Victorian period, and the interwar economic scene.

An example **British Economic History** essay question is:

*'Discuss what anthropometric evidence tells us about living standards during the Industrial Revolution.'*

*"Anthropometric evidence relates to the measurements and proportions of people's bodies. When writing this essay, I examined how height differences between urban and rural workers suggested that city workers faced lower standards of living in spite of their higher incomes."* –Student, Economics, Cambridge

## After first year

A major component of the Economics course that is introduced after your first year is *Econometrics*—the application of statistics to economics data sets to draw economic conclusions. In particular, a substantial part of your second-year mark will come from a short (but mathematically intensive) project on an econometric question.

*"I wrote my Econometrics project on the relationship between school funding and student test scores. I had to statistically analyse a data set and then write up my findings"* –Paaras, Economics, Cambridge

In your third year, you'll write a longer dissertation, which can be either in a quantitative or qualitative field.

## A typical work week

In your first year studying Economics at Cambridge, you'll have 10–15 lectures per week and approximately 3 supervisions. You'll have problem sets for the more quantitative topics, and essays for the historical and political ones. A supervision is typically 3–6 students, with a tutor who will review the answers to problem sets, discuss your essays and introduce further relevant material.

# Chapter 22:
# Land Economy

## 22.1: What is Land Economy?

Land Economy is a three-year degree offered at Cambridge. You leave with a BA. The degree combines economics and law to study how we use the spaces around us—both in towns and cities, and in rural or wild areas. Besides economics and law, it has connections to finance, international development, environmental regulation, business regulation, and city planning.

Land Economy asks questions like:

- Who has rights to this space, and what rights do they have?
- What is this space worth?
- How could this space be improved?
- How does this space need to be protected?
- What laws apply to this space, and are they fit for purpose?
- What are the social and environmental consequences of our use of this space?

This degree might be for you if:

- ❑ **You're fascinated by the human environment:** If you're the kind of person who walks through a city and is curious about all the little places you pass, wondering about their histories, the details of the buildings, and what they are used for, then you might find Land Economy a fascinating subject too. Likewise, if you're interested by the history of the landscape, how it is used and maintained, and how it can be protected in the future, you might find what you're looking for in this degree.
- ❑ **You have an eye for detail:** The major academic components of Land Economy are economics and law. Both of them are fields in which small differences can really matter, and you have to be very careful about how your evidence leads to your conclusion. If you're a precise and analytical thinker, you might find it's a good use of your skills.

- ❑ **You care about social and environmental causes:** Land Economy has a significant overlap with public policy—i.e. making decisions and laws that affect society and society's footprint on the world. That encompasses issues like poverty, pollution, and development of cities and whole countries. Sustainable economics and sustainable development in particular are key themes of the Cambridge course, so if these are issues that matter a lot to you, it might be the course for you.
- ❑ **You'd love to work in law or surveying:** Land Economy can lead to many careers, including business or public service. But if you do enjoy the idea of going into law, especially as it relates to property or the environment, Land Economy will be an especially good stepping stone because it can count part of the way towards the CPE (Common Professional Examination—a qualification for becoming a lawyer). The course also gives you the accreditation to become a chartered surveyor and work in property.

## 22.2: How do you apply for Land Economy at Cambridge?

The typical A-Level offer for Land Economy is A*AA, or 40–42 points in the IB with 776 at Higher Level. 1 applicant is successful for every 6 candidates that apply.

You'll have to sit Section 1 of the TSA (Thinking Skills Assessment)—see page 373 for more information about this. Some colleges may also ask you to provide written work as part of your application.

There are no compulsory A-Level or Higher Level IB subjects for this degree, but Maths and Economics are both recommended. Geography may also be useful if you need to submit written work, or to give you ideas to discuss in your personal statement and interview. Human geography topics (e.g. urbanisation and development) are more likely to be relevant than physical ones.

## 22.3: What's it like to study Land Economy?

In your first year, you'll study **microeconomics** and **macroeconomics** just as Cambridge Economics students do. See page 327 for more details of these topics. In addition, you'll study **welfare economics**, which investigates the way markets meet or fail to meet the needs of everyone across society, including concepts like ***externalities*** and ***moral hazard***.

An **externality** occurs when an exchange between two people (or two organisations, or a person and an organisation) has costs or benefits for people who don't directly participate in the exchange. A typical example is that, when someone buys an environmentally harmful product, it has costs for everyone, not just the buyer and seller. See the interview script on page 418 for more discussion of externalities.

**Moral hazard** occurs when a person or organisation changes their behaviour because they know another party will bear some of the costs instead of them. For instance, a business has less incentive to invest in preventing fires if it is insured against damage caused by fires.

You'll also take the following courses specific to Land Economy:

- ❑ **The Public Sector:** an introduction to public law, i.e. laws relating to the powers and responsibilities of local and national governments.
- ❑ **Quantitative and Legal Methods for Land Economists:** you'll be taught the quantitative and computing skills you need for economics in a similar way to Economics students - see page 328. However, you'll also be shown methods for analysing legal cases and presenting legal arguments.
- ❑ **Land Economy, Development, and Sustainability:** a mostly essay-based course on social and environmental issues arising from the use of land, such as housing and environmental crises.

A unique feature of the Land Economy degree is the ability to attend weekly **seminars** on various subjects, which aren't examined but do serve to expand your understanding of the topics you're studying. They are often presented by visiting speakers, and frequently introduce issues affecting countries outside the UK. Past seminar topics include:

- firefighting policies in the Amazon rainforest
- the prospects for development of geothermal energy in the Pacific
- the environmental responsibilities of companies that extract minerals from the sea floor.

In later years, you'll be able to specialise in fields like law, public policy, planning and construction, and environmental economics. In particular, the more law courses you take, the closer you'll be to the CPE qualification, though you would still need to study at least some further law (e.g. criminal law) after your degree to complete it.

# Chapter 23: Economics & Management

## 23.1: Why Economics & Management?

> *"Maths was always my strongest subject at school, but I also loved writing and enjoyed my essay subjects the most. Economics was first offered to me at A Level, and I absolutely loved it. It required both the logical reasoning of a science subject and the critical thinking of a humanities subject. I also loved being able to see its applications in the real world. Economics is so central to current affairs—it's what everyone was talking about! When searching for economics-related degrees, I saw that Oxford offers a joint honours course with management. I didn't quite know what management was before I started, but I loved the look of the course and all the modules I could choose."* –Helen Lily, Economics and Management, Oxford

Economics & Management (E&M) is a degree offered at Oxford that combines the highly mathematical discipline of economics with the more qualitative, comparative and case-based discipline of management. You study the same economics content as PPE and History & Economics students (plus the extra management courses). It's a three-year course and you leave with a BA.

### What is management?

The words 'manager' and 'management' might not have particularly exciting connotations in English, but don't be deceived. The management courses at Oxford aren't about turning you into a character from *The Office*. Instead, they're about studying *organisations* – many of which are highly important and influential – and theories of optimal decision-making and planning.

Whereas politics studies one *type* of organisation (governments), management considers all the other organisations that are essential to society (if less visible in the media).

For instance, manufacturing an aircraft means predicting what the world will look like decades into the future, designing the aircraft under a huge number of constraints, sourcing materials (some very high-tech, and some in astronomical quantities), creating a production line for a machine 100 times bigger than any car, maintaining near-perfect quality (even a 0.1% failure rate on an aircraft is a big problem), and selling the product on the global market.

More broadly, management is *the study of the distribution and coordination of labour and materials within an organisation* (typically a business, but the same ideas could be applied to a university, hospital, civil service, charity or military). This includes:

- How the organisation is divided into parts and how those parts coordinate
- How it coordinates or competes with other organisations
- How it predicts and plans for the future
- Who has authority and how decisions are made
- How it collects and acts on data
- How it sources materials and labour
- How it plans for and responds to shortages and setbacks.

This might be the degree for you if:

- ❑ **You can think both qualitatively and quantitatively:** If you have the quantitative skills and mathematical knowledge needed to study economics, that's fantastic. But Economics & Management might suit you *even better* if you also have the qualitative skills for the management side: if you love to critically analyse ideas you read and construct arguments of your own in writing.
- ❑ **You want to study the big players in the economy:** Economics can sometimes seem a bit abstract. If you're also interested in the details of how individual business and industries function – details that shape much of our lives but aren't seen in the news or popular culture in most circumstances – you might find that Economics & Management gives you a way to discover that side of the economy too.
- ❑ **You're fascinated by how big decisions are made:** Decision making is a vital skill—how do you estimate the costs and benefits, and weigh up all the risks you face? If decision making sounds like something you'd enjoy studying, especially in an economic, financial, or business context, both halves of the Economics & Management degree will give you complementary skills to do so, and also expose you to a breadth of case studies of decision making in action.

- ❑ **You can absorb a lot of new information at once:** Management isn't a subject that's studied at school, so if you're interested in it, you'll have a lot of reading to do once you're at uni. You'll be really well suited to this degree if you can absorb several books and articles in a week to get a grounding in a new topic. It can require a lot of discipline!

One thing E&M definitely *isn't* is an MBA or business degree. It involves the *academic* study of businesses, their economic context and their decision making, rather than vocational training for a career in business.

> *"Management might at first sound like an easy option, but its study at Oxford is highly academic and theoretical."* –Danial, E&M, Oxford

## 23.2: How do you apply for Economics & Management?

Economics & Management is the *most competitive* Oxford course of all: only 1 applicant out of 17 is successful. The average A Level offer is A*AA, or 39 points in the IB with 766 at Higher Level. Maths is a compulsory pre-requisite A-Level/Higher Level subject and must be at A or A* grade (6/7 in the IB).

You'll have to take the TSA (Thinking Skills Assessment) if you apply for Economics & Management. See page 373 for more information.

### What A-Level/IB Higher Level subjects are useful for Economics & Management?

As discussed, Maths is essential, due to the economics component of the degree. Further Maths is not compulsory but could be useful to strengthen your mathematical skills and for specific topics such as matrices and differential equations, which will crop up frequently in your first year.

Likewise, as for Economics and PPE, A-Level/Higher Level Economics is not required but can be helpful in your interview and is likely to make the first term of your degree easier. Business Studies is less important, as the management side of the degree will essentially be taught from scratch, and the style will be very different to that of A-Level Business Studies.

No particular essay-based subject is a prerequisite, but having at least one would be sensible since your application will need to demonstrate your potential for studying an essay-based subject at degree level.

## 23.3: What's it like to study Economics & Management?

*"A perk of studying E&M is that we get to use the Saïd Business School. The facilities are among the best at the university, reflecting the fact that it was built recently and is primarily used for teaching business executives and MBA students. E&M students get full access to business school facilities, including the spacious library, (subsidised!) café and gardens. I particularly love the (very expensive) sofas."* –Student, E&M, Oxford

Here's an overview of the first-year content, to give you an understanding of what it's like to study E&M. The courses studied over the first year are examined in three papers:

1. **Introductory Economics:** This paper examines Microeconomics, Mathematics for Economics, and Macroeconomics. These extend the microeconomics and macroeconomics content of the Economics A Level. The A Level is not a prerequisite because the course starts from a foundational level, although getting an economics textbook and reviewing the key topics and terms will be extremely helpful. A comfortable understanding of core Maths A-Level material is useful. A typical week will include a sheet containing a mix of problems and short essay questions.

   The topics dealt with in the Oxford Microeconomics and Macroeconomics courses are similar to the corresponding Cambridge courses—see page 327.

An example **Introductory Macroeconomics** essay question is:

*What are the strengths and weaknesses of GDP as a measure of welfare?*

An example Introductory Microeconomics problem sheet question is:

*Suppose a worker's **utility function** is given by $U(x, t) = x^2(15 - t)$, where their daily income is $x$ and $t$ is their hours worked per day, with $0 < t < 15$. Find the hours they would choose to work if their hourly wage is £20 and they have no other source of income. How would their hours worked and total income change if they received £60 per day in passive income?*

A **utility function** represents how satisfied a person (or company) is with different possible outcomes. For example: suppose $u(c, s)$ is your utility function, where inputs $c$ and $s$ represent the amount of Coco Pops and Shreddies you eat respectively. If you like Coco Pops but not Shreddies, $u(c, s)$ will increase when $c$ increases but decrease when $s$ increases.

For further insight into the Introductory Macroeconomics course, check out the course textbook (*Macroeconomics*, C. Jones).

2. **General Management:** This is made up of 16 topics, taught one per week over the first two terms. Every week, you'll have a reading list and write an essay on a given question. Topics include:
   - Firms and big business
   - Strategic management
   - Marketing
   - Organisational behaviour
   - Technology and operations.

Some example **General Management** essay questions are:

- *Are entrepreneurs any more important than bureaucrats for economic growth?*
- *Should a company's strategy be based primarily on market position?*
- *What challenges in managing frontline service workers arise from the fact that they engage in emotional as well as physical labour?*

*"I loved seeing real examples of how the principles we learnt are applied. We toured the Oxford Mini[132] factory and had finance execs from London come to give seminars."* –Student, E&M, Oxford

3. **Financial Management:** This course covers financial reporting and financial analysis. Financial reporting includes accounting basics (balance sheets, regulations, etc.) and financial analysis uses formulae and metrics to analyse profitability, turnover, etc. A good grip on mathematical principles is useful but A-Level knowledge is not essential for this particular course, as all the skills needed are introduced as part of the course.

   Topics include:

   - Accounting
   - Budgeting
   - Sources of funds
   - ***Discounting***
   - Asset pricing
   - Investment appraisal
   - Measuring risk.

'**Discounting**' doesn't mean selling something at a discount. It's figuring out how much future income counts for in your accounts. For instance, suppose someone has promised to pay you £1000 later. That debt goes into your accounts as an asset, but in real terms it's worth less than having £1000 *now* because it can't be reinvested, and because inflation will decrease its real value over time. Thus, in your accounts, it should be discounted to less than £1000.

Oxford also runs a non-examined course on statistics to help prepare you for your second and third years.

## After first year

In your second and third years, it's compulsory two take at least two economics courses out of Microeconomics, Macroeconomics, Quantitative

132 Mini, as in the car.

Economics, and Development of the World Economy Since 1800. Taking the first three is necessary for many of the other economics options. In particular, Quantitative Economics gives you the necessary background to study Econometrics—see page 339 for more on this). The rest of your options are open, but you must take at least two management options. That means you can specialise to some extent, but you'll always study both sides of the degree.

The economics options include:

- Behavioural Economics
- Econometrics
- Economics of Developing Countries
- Game Theory
- Labour Economics
- Money and Banking

The management options include:

- Entrepreneurship and Innovation
- Finance
- Global Business History
- Marketing
- Strategic Management
- Technology and Operations Management

## A typical work week

For each of the three constituent papers in the first year, there will be 2–3 hours of lectures, a 1-hour tutorial, and one essay/problem set per week. For some courses, there will be additional maths classes to supplement the tutorials. However, the rest of the learning is independent study: reading books, answering extra questions in textbooks, and consolidating and revisiting your lecture notes.

> *"At first, most people find it difficult to complete the whole management reading list, but you'll quickly learn techniques to read efficiently and will breeze through it!"* –Helen Lily, E&M, Oxford

# Chapter 24:
# Philosophy, Politics & Economics (PPE)

## 24.1: Why PPE?

PPE is a diverse course that allows you to cover three broad and tightly-interlinked subjects. It's a great course if you're looking for the opportunity to dabble in lots of different subjects.

The degree takes three years and you leave with a BA. In your first year, you study all three disciplines. Later, you either continue with all three (the tripartite option) or choose to specialise in two (the bipartite option). You study the same economics content as History & Economics and E&M students (not counting management courses).

This might be the degree for you if:

- ❑ **You're a logical and critical thinker:** Constructing strong arguments, and spotting weaknesses and fallacies in arguments you read, is a key skill for a PPE student. If you enjoy picking apart books or debating your friends, you might have the analytical skills that are necessary in all three parts of the degree.
- ❑ **You don't mind having to think mathematically:** Although you'll be introduced to the maths techniques you need for economics during the course, this is a course for people who are already comfortable with calculations and analysing problems mathematically, both in economics and the 'logic' part of philosophy. And if you want to study politics to any serious degree, you'll need to be ready to handle data. You can make any fancy argument you like, but if you can't back it up with more quantitative evidence, you're unlikely to get very far.
- ❑ **You can move easily between different topics:** If you don't like to be too chained to any one topic at a time, a degree that allows you to flit between three subjects in any one week might just be for you! In fact, you need to be the type of person who can apply their mind to many different problems in turn to cope with a PPE degree.
- ❑ **You want to study the ideas that shape the world:** If you're interested in current affairs, then the economics and politics aspects of PPE might appeal to you. But at the same time, the degree highly theoretical—

investigating the ideas that shape events, not just the events themselves. In particular, the philosophy component allows you to address the philosophical foundations of politics and economics.

- ❑ **You like to leave the future open:** PPE is often stereotyped as the doorway into British politics, but in reality its breadth means it can lead to a range of exciting and varied careers, from finance to journalism to social work. And if you're not quite sure whether you'll actually enjoy all three constituent subjects, that's no problem: you'll also have a lot of freedom to choose your path through the degree, and you'll have several dozen course options after your first year.

**Did You Know?**

*Politics is a popular destination for PPE graduates, but PPE graduates also find themselves taking different career paths including law, journalism, civil service and academia.*

*"I applied for PPE because I didn't know what to specialise in and wanted a mix of discursive and quantitative subjects. I'm very happy with my choice. It gave me variety at a time when I didn't know what I wanted to do. It basically let me make up my own degree, as there was so much to choose from."* –Raj, PPE, Oxford

## 24.2: How do you apply for PPE at Oxford?

The usual A-Level offer for PPE is AAA. For the IB it is 39 points with 766 at Higher Level. There are no compulsory prerequisites, although Maths and History are both recommended.

You'll have to take the TSA (Thinking Skills Assessment) if you apply for PPE. See page 373 for more information.

Of those who apply to study PPE, fewer than 1 in 8 candidates is successful.

### What A-Level/IB Higher Level subjects are useful for PPE?

Unlike for Economics & Management, A-Level Maths isn't technically a prerequisite, but a good grasp of maths is essential to the economics element.

Although all of the necessary maths content will be covered at the beginning of your first year, you'll find it much easier if you aren't learning it from scratch. Knowledge from A-Level Maths may also come in handy if you're asked an economics interview question with a more quantitative component.

Studying any of Philosophy, Politics and Economics at A Level can provide useful background knowledge, but none of those subjects is essential—particularly the first two. History is almost as helpful, because it's so relevant the study of politics and economics.

> *"Not having studied any politics, philosophy, or economics at A Level didn't put me at a particular disadvantage, but other students who didn't have A-Level Maths had to work much harder to catch up."*
> –Graduate, PPE, Oxford

## 24.3: Studying PPE: What's it really like?

Here's a breakdown of the first year PPE course, so you can get a feel for what you would be studying:

### Politics

***Theory of Politics:*** This course covers the essential background for the study of politics. It's divided into two parts: political thinkers, and core topics in politics. Examples of political thinkers you will cover are Locke, Marx and Rousseau. The other half of the course will focus on examining, justifying, and critiquing political concepts such as power, democracy and liberty.

> Example essay questions from the **Theory of Politics** course:
>
> - *'In what sense are citizens free in Rousseau's state?'*
> - *'What is the point of democracy?'*

***The Practice of Politics:*** This course is largely about comparing different political systems, and especially democratic systems. For example, you'll study:

- State strength (i.e. what constitutional or practical constraints are there on the state?)
- State institutions (e.g. legislatures and court systems)
- Definitions of democracy (see the interview script on page 430 for a discussion of this)
- Causes of democracy (e.g. are there cultural, legal, or economic prerequisites for a state to become and remain a democracy?)
- Party systems (e.g. are there two big parties, or lots of little ones?)
- Voter behaviour (e.g. does the electoral system incentivise tactical voting, and if so, do voters actually act on those incentives?)

***Political Analysis:*** This is the mathematical side of politics. You'll learn to use RStudio (a programming tool) to do statistical analysis on a large data set[133] in a series of computer lab sessions. You'll be given data from six different democracies, and you'll write an extended essay using the statistical evidence gathered from your work in RStudio.

An example of a Political Analysis question is:

*'Do **consensus democracies** have better economic outcomes than **majoritarian** ones?'*

A **majoritarian democracy** is one in which any party or proposal that gets more than 50% of the vote always wins, so minority opinions don't have much sway. In a **consensus democracy**, there are mechanisms to allow minority opinions to have more influence, like delegating some decisions to assemblies that can't act until all, or at least a very large proportion, of their members agree on what to do.

## Philosophy

**Moral Philosophy:** This course explores ***utilitarianism***, specifically focusing on John Stuart Mill's influential text of the same name. Each week, you'll study a different element, such as the definition of ***hedonism***, or the differences between Mill's hedonism and that of other utilitarians such as Jeremy Bentham. Another important element is the issue of ***act utilitarianism*** versus ***rule utilitarianism***.

133 Ah, now we (sort of) understand why they decided to put a large data set into the Maths A Level.

**Utilitarianism:** A family of ethical theories that identifies acting morally with trying to maximise the happiness produced by your actions.

**Hedonism:** The theory that happiness is nothing more than experiencing pleasure and avoiding pain/displeasure. Pleasure can take different forms. Mill values intellectual pleasure very highly, for instance.

**Act utilitarianism:** Argues that every individual act should aim to maximise happiness.

**Rule utilitarianism:** Argues that what matters is living by rules that maximise happiness, rather than evaluating the happiness produced by each act individually.

An *act* utilitarian would argue that we should be prepared to tell a lie in those cases where doing so will produce more good than harm. In contrast, a *rule* utilitarian would argue that having a rule against lying has its own benefits, so we should follow that rule even when breaking it just this one time would do more good than not breaking it.

This early focus on utilitarianism isn't an indication that Oxford thinks it's the best ethical theory—it's to introduce you to the methods of philosophy through a specific example. You can study other ethical theories in your second or third year.

**General Philosophy:** This course gives you an overall introduction to key philosophers, concepts and arguments.

An example **General Philosophy** essay question is:

*'What is the difference between knowledge and justified true belief?'*

**Elementary Logic:** This is the more mathematical part of the philosophy course. You learn first-order predicate logic, a logical language in which you can formalise arguments to assess their validity.

See page 45 for more information about General Philosophy and logic.

## Economics

**Microeconomics:** Microeconomics is taught in lectures in the first term, and the weekly assignments are problem sheets. It's a course about the behaviour of firms and individuals within the market.

**Macroeconomics:** Macroeconomics is taught in lectures in the second term, and the weekly assignments are problem sheets. It's a course about the economy at a national and international level.

For more information on microeconomics and macroeconomics, see page 327.

**Mathematical techniques used in economics:** This is an independent study module that is completed through a workbook given to every PPE student. Most of the maths covered is of A-Level standard, so it is not too taxing if you already have A-Level Maths[134], but you'll also study some new material such as maximising and minimising functions of more than one variable (for example, to work out the optimal price at which to sell a product).

> An example **optimisation question** is:
>
> *Find the minimum value of the function* $f(x, y) = 2x^2 + 3x + 2y^2 + 3y - xy + 3$, *where* $x$ *and* $y$ *range over all real numbers.*

## After first year

In your second and third years, you'll have compulsory modules for the subjects you choose to continue with:

- **For Philosophy:** Ethics and either 'Knowledge and Reality' (covering metaphysics and epistemology[135]) or one out of a selection of modules on ancient Greek philosophy
- **For Politics:** At least two out of a selection of five core Politics modules
- **For Economics:** At least one out of Microeconomics, Macroeconomics, and Quantitative Economics (the latter introduces theory needed to study Econometrics later—see page 339 for more on Econometrics). If you continue with all three component subjects of PPE, you can opt for an economic history module instead.

134 There are supplementary lectures for those students who haven't studied Maths at A Level.

135 Epistemology is the study of knowledge: what it is, and whether it is possible

Besides your compulsory modules, you can choose from a gargantuan range of additional options across the three subjects (provided you meet the prerequisites). In particular, the Economics options are mostly the same as for E&M (starting on page 339).

> *"I'd say the most important thing I learnt from each of the three subjects was:*
>
> ***Philosophy:*** *Logic gives you accuracy in the use of language and the ability to sense when you're being taken for a ride.*
>
> ***Politics:*** *Finding frameworks for evaluating systems. For example, do we value democracy because of the decision-making process itself or because of the outcomes it produces?*
>
> ***Economics:*** *The value of modelling, and understanding how complex systems can be reduced to tractable and insightful models."* –Student, PPE, Oxford

## A typical work week

Your weekly workload will vary throughout your PPE degree. The average is one essay or problem sheet per module per week, but you might have one in a fortnight or two in a week, depending on the module and the time of year. There are ten hours of lectures per week, but most people don't go to all of them because sometimes they are repeats and they don't always correspond to the essays your tutors set. For each essay or problem sheet, you'll have a tutorial in college—usually only two of you. There are also maths classes, logic classes and RStudio classes at times throughout the year.

Note the time that you spend working independently is just as significant as the time you spend in lectures and tutorials (if not more so).

**Did You Know?**

*Lectures play a smaller role in a PPE degree than in mathematical, computational or physical science degrees—especially in the philosophical and political elements of PPE. The bulk of your learning will happen though independent reading, which is the basis on which you write essays. Tutorials will be spent (seemingly) tearing your essay to shreds, a process that ultimately makes you a clear and critical thinker who can analyse and put forward a cohesive argument. In short, if you don't like reading, this degree probably isn't for you.*

That might be the working week, but what does it amount to per day? To illustrate, here's a day in the life of Leah, a first-year PPE student at Oxford:

| | |
|---|---|
| 9.00 a.m. | Wake up, eat breakfast, use slides to fill gaps in yesterday's lecture notes |
| 9.50 a.m. | Leave college with other PPE students for politics lecture |
| 10.05 a.m. | Politics lecture on Rousseau's 'social contract' |
| 11.05 a.m. | Microeconomics lecture on firms and production |
| 12.05 p.m. | General Philosophy lecture on Cartesian scepticism |
| 1.00 p.m. | Return to college for lunch |
| 2.00 p.m. | Return to the library to read philosophy articles and make notes |
| 5.00 p.m. | Go to sports training/drama/music rehearsal |
| 6.00 p.m. | Dinner in college |
| 7.00 p.m. | Return to library, plan philosophy essay |
| 9.00 p.m. | Go to debating event/speaker event, and go out afterwards or go to bed. |

# Chapter 25:
# History & Economics

## 25.1: Why History & Economics?

History & Economics is the third course at Oxford that incorporates economics. It's a three-year degree and you leave with a BA. This course gives you the ability to apply economic theories and concepts through a historical lens, and likewise to study historical events through an economic lens, opening up a unique insight into society in the past.

Some examples of important historical economic events include:

- The Wall Street crash of 1929
- The stock market crash of 1987
- The tequila crisis of 1994
- The global financial crisis of 2007.

You study the same economics content as PPE and E&M students (not counting management courses).

This might be the degree for you if:

- ❑ **You want to study where the modern world came from:** If you're really interested in history as a source of insight into the contemporary world, well, that's exactly what Oxford describes the History & Economics degree as being. Economic forces and events from the industrial revolution on influence our lives now in a very direct way, which is a major focus of the course. If that sounds exciting to you, History & Economics might be what you're looking for.
- ❑ **You're fascinated by the lives of everyday people in the past:** History isn't all about national or international-scale events. Many history students also love to learn about what everyday life was like in the past—the work people did, where they lived, what they ate, and so on. These are all things that relate to economics too, and evidence about how people lived can tell us more about what the economy was like and vice versa.

- ❑ **You're a critical reader:** If you have the kind of analytical mind that's essential for economics, you also might find it's something you rely on when thinking critically about historical sources and arguments. In particular, you'll need to think about people's reasons, motivations, and biases when studying both subjects. Likewise, you'll need to have a keen eye for what the evidence *really* suggests, and where it might be misleading.
- ❑ **You want to study economics, not just economic events:** Almost any history student will have to *learn about* some events with economic components, like recessions, political movements, and the development of new industries. But if you want to really *understand* them and study them through an economic lens, including through heavy use of data and economic theory, then History & Economics might be for you.

## 25.2: How do you apply for History & Economics

The usual A Level offer for History & Economics is AAA, or 38 points in the IB with 666 at Higher Level. About 1 in 9 applicants is successful. You must also submit a piece of written work as part of your application.

You'll have to take the TSA (Thinking Skills Assessment) *and* the HAT (History Aptitude Test) if you apply for History & Economics. See page 373 for more information.

There are no compulsory A-Level/IB Higher Level courses—not even History! However, both Maths and History are highly recommended.

### What A-Level/IB Higher Level subjects are useful for History & Economics?

Though A-Level History isn't formally required, if you aren't studying it, you'll have to work hard to motivate your application for this degree and prove that you have the necessary skills (e.g. to understand and criticise sources). Moreover, you need to take the HAT and submit written work on a historical topic—both of which will be much easier for those doing the History A Level.

The Ancient History A Level is a potential alternative if your school offers it—but bear in mind that you won't be able to specialise entirely in ancient history in the History & Economics degree.

As with PPE, Maths isn't *required* for History & Economics, but having it will make your interviews and first year easier. Likewise, Economics isn't required but will be helpful.

## 25.3: What's it like to study History & Economics?

So, what's it like to study these two subjects alongside and in conversation with one other? To give you some insight, we'll look at the four courses you study in your first year.

### Introductory Economics

Covers all the essentials of economics, including macroeconomics, microeconomics, and the quantitative methods behind them. See page 327 for more details.

### European and World History

In this course, you choose to focus on one of the following options:

- ❑ **Transformation of the Ancient World (370–900):** Studies the successors of the Roman Empire in Europe and Asia, with example topics being the papacy, interactions between Christianity and Islam in Spain, and the introduction of the Cyrillic script.
- ❑ **Medieval Christendom and its Neighbours (1000–1300):** You can choose to focus on Western Europe, via topics such as knighthood, monasticism, and the growth of universities, but you can also choose to study other parts of the world, from West Africa to China.
- ❑ **Renaissance, Recovery and Reform (1400–1650):** Studies the renaissance and the rise of humanism as Europe, together with events like the colonisation of the New World and the reformation and counter-reformation, and themes like the changing role of monarchs in society.
- ❑ **Society, Nation and Empire (1815–1914):** Looks at the whole of Europe, with themes including social class, scientific and economic development, and nationalism.

You'll study the period and location that you choose through a variety of themes, including 'the state' and 'the economy', but also 'culture', 'gender', and 'religion'.

### Historical Methods

This course covers the skills needed to study history rather than a specific period in time. It incorporates a wide range of options, including:

- **Quantification in history:** statistical analysis of historical problems
- **Approaches to history:** interdisciplinary work in history, including examples of economics applied to the study of history
- **Historiography: Tacitus to Weber:** examines changes in the way history has been written about via a series of notable historians

You can also choose to study history as written about in a particular language other than English, provided you have the required language skills. Options include Greek, Latin, French, German, Spanish, and Russian.

### Industrialisation in Britain and France (1750–1870)

This course allows you to appreciate the rich intersection between history and economics. You'll study events through a historical lens, but address how these events impacted the economy and different classes within society. The impact that industrialisation had on the British and French economies, and the differences between the two countries, are central to this course.

This course has a special focus on the use of primary sources. In fact, while the History department strongly recommends that History & Economics students take this course, you may be able to replace it with another history option that also involves the use of primary sources.

> An example question from **Industrialisation in Britain and France** is:
>
> *'Was the growth of railways a more important factor for economic development in Britain than it was in France?'*

## After first year

Over your second and third years, you have to take the following courses:

- The History of the World Economy Since 1800, and at least one more history option

- At least one out of Microeconomics, Macroeconomics, and Quantitative Economics, and at least three economics options in total (these are the same courses offered to E&M students—see page 339 for more information and examples)
- Two more options, chosen from out of all of the history and economics options
- A module in which you write a **thesis**, typically on economic history

History options tend to fall into one of two classes. The first is 'outline' papers focused on a fairly specific period and region, such as:

- The Late Medieval British Isles, 1330-1550
- Liberty, Commerce, and Power, 1685-1830
- Power, Politics, and the People, 1815-1924

The second is 'theme' papers, which tend to cover societal changes over longer time periods and broader geographical regions. Some examples are:

- Masculinity and its Discontents, 200-2000
- Global Networks of Innovation, 1000-1700
- Waging War in Eurasia, 1200-1945

All of your options will be examined at the end of your third year.

## A typical work week

In your first year, you'll have about five lectures per week and write at least one essay per week, but typically two or more. Each essay will be followed by a tutorial in which the tutor will dissect and explore your argument, allowing you to improve your understanding of the topic. Tutorials will typically be with one other student. You'll also have some classes (with slightly larger groups) in which you'll go through the economics problem sheets from your Introductory Economics module.

# Chapter 26:
# Economics applicant profiles

What makes for a successful Oxbridge applicant for a degree involving economics? To help you get a better idea, we've included profiles of three applicants, with a discussion of their strengths and weaknesses.

If you're not familiar with any of the steps of the application process that are mentioned here, see Part B (page 358).

## Applicant 1: Nala, 18 (E&M, Oxford)

**Before interview:**

- Nala is studying Economics, History and Maths and is predicted A*A*A.
- She prepares for both the TSA and her interviews by reading books and articles about economics, politics and business.
- She writes about all of this extra reading in her personal statement, explaining what she has learnt from each book. She also lists the many lectures and debates she has attended in London.
- She struggles with Section 1 of the TSA because her economics knowledge hasn't prepared her for the problem-solving questions. However, she does well in Section 2 because she is a strong essay writer and has a lot of examples to draw on from her economics reading.
- Before her interviews, Nala makes sure she is prepared to talk about everything she has read. She also prepares answers for questions such as 'Why did you apply to Oxford?'

**In her interviews:**

- Nala finds she has a lot to say in her first interview, in which she is asked to read and discuss a passage from a book on management and answer some qualitative questions on economic policy. She finds the reading she has done helpful here. However, she is surprised that she never has to answer the question as to why she applied to Oxford.

- In each of her second and third interviews, Nala is given a very mathematical question. One is on exponential graphs, and the other is on maximising a utility function with two inputs. She isn't well prepared for the maths involved and doesn't make much headway with either question.

## Applicant 2: Jayden, 17 (Economics, Cambridge)

**Before interview:**

- Jayden is predicted AAA in Economics, Maths and Physics. He wanted to study Further Maths, but his school didn't offer it so he is studying some of the modules on his own.
- He enjoys doing ECAA past papers because they remind him of the maths puzzles he does in his spare time. He also practises some MAT and TMUA questions, using Oxbridge Formula Academy videos to clarify where he is stuck.
- In his personal statement, Jayden explains the extra maths he's done and the skills he's learnt. There aren't many lectures, debates, or other events held nearby for him to attend. However, he does discuss the EPQ he's written on game theory.
- Jayden does very well in the problem-solving and maths parts of the ECAA, though he drops a couple of marks for arithmetic errors—a problem he also has in A-Level papers. He finds Section 2 hard but not as bad as some past papers—he writes a decent essay.
- He starts preparing for his interviews even before he knows he will be invited. His school finds a retired economics teacher to give him a mock interview. Jayden finds this very helpful because he is taught not to worry too much about small mistakes and instead speak through his thoughts.

**In his interviews:**

- In his general interview (which comes first), Jayden is very nervous, but the conversation is mostly about himself and the Cambridge course, so there isn't much opportunity to make a mistake. It ends with a problem on winning strategies in a card game, which reminds him of a topic he read about for his EPQ.
- In his subject interview, the interviewers begin by giving Jayden a series of short maths questions and a longer economics question that he realises requires solving an integral. He is initially worried about making a mistake, but remembering his practice improves his confidence and he gets the answers with the tutors' support.

## Applicant 3: Lucas, 17 (PPE, Oxford)

**Before interview:**

- Lucas is predicted AAA in Economics, History and Politics.
- He loves politics, and dreams of having an editorial column in a major newspaper—something he mentions in his personal statement. He listens to several current affairs programmes and enjoys debates, which he thinks will allow him to excel at the TSA.
- Lucas has been preparing for his Oxford interview since he started Year 12. He has had multiple mock interviews with family friends, in which he always has a lot to say.
- When he takes the TSA, Lucas is unprepared for the time pressure in Section 1. The problem-solving questions are completely unfamiliar to him, and the style of the critical-thinking questions is unique enough that his debating skills don't help him as much as he expected. He has a lot of ideas for the Section 2 essay, but doesn't plan well and runs out of time before completing it.
- Lucas is not invited to interview.

**Who is the best candidate?**

Jayden is the best candidate here.

**What did Nala do wrong?**

✘ Ability Nala didn't perform as well on the TSA as she should have because her sole focus on economics reading meant that she didn't practise for the problem-solving part of the test as much as she should have. Her predicted A in Maths suggests she should have been capable of doing better if she had practised more.

✘ Potential Nala's interview preparation focused too little on the mathematical side of economics. Being able to talk through what's on your personal statement is important, but it's not what earns you an offer. Instead, the tutors are looking for your potential to tackle undergraduate-style problems (with guidance).

**What did Lucas do wrong?**

✘ Ability Potential Lucas did not prepare adequately for the TSA. It's vital to familiarise yourself with the style of question and practise attempting them under realistic timed conditions.

✘ Ability Passion The admissions tutors were already concerned that Lucas hadn't studied any mathematical subjects at A Level and hadn't described any interest in the components of PPE apart from Politics. His poor TSA score confirmed their fears that he was not suited to the technical demands of PPE, which explains why he was not invited to interview.

**What did Jayden do right?**

✓ Ability Jayden prepared well for the ECAA. He was already in a good position for Section 1 due to his problem-solving skills and practised enough past papers to become familiar with the test. Being able to do almost every question will have made up for his occasional errors. His past paper practice also helped him with the essay, which he found harder.

✓ Passion Potential His personal statement showed he had a genuine interest in economics and the skills required for the degree. His extra maths practice will have reassured the admissions tutors if they were worried about his lack of predicted A*s, though they already look at those predictions *in the context of* how much support a student's school can give.

✓ Ability Potential Jayden did enough interview practice to overcome his nerves and his worries about arithmetic errors, which aren't what interviewers are concerned about in any case. This meant that he could demonstrate his mathematical skills, which are essential for the Cambridge Economics course.

# Part III B: The Application Process

Each Oxbridge economics degree course has its own admissions requirements—this is partly due to the differences between Oxford and Cambridge and partly due to the fact that each course involves a different combination of subjects. In this chapter, we'll walk through the key steps in detail: how to write your personal statement, how to achieve the maximum possible score in your admissions test, and how to ace your interviews.

# Chapter 27:
# Personal statements

## 27.1: What to include in your economics personal statement

The personal statement is a more important for an economics degree than for degrees in the mathematical, computational or physical sciences—it's highly likely that you will be quizzed about what you've written in it.

To check how effective your personal statement is, you can evaluate each sentence in it by asking yourself the following question:

> **"Does this sentence help the admissions tutors see why they should accept me to study *this* subject at *this* university?"**

Remember, your personal statement should provide evidence for:

- Your **ability** in skills related to economics (and other parts of the joint course, if you're applying for one)
- Your **passion** for economics and related subjects, as well as for knowledge and debate
- Your **potential** as an Oxbridge student (i.e. for engaging with tutors and academic literature) and capacity for learning through self-study

Here are some suggestions on how to articulate these three intangible elements of your Oxbridge application:

### 1) Reading Passion Potential

Reading (or listening to audiobooks) is the best way to explore a subject beyond the syllabus. To impress the admissions tutors, you want to show that you've not only *read* a few economics books, but you've also *understood* and *thought about* them. Don't just name-drop random titles; describe why you enjoyed the book, what you learnt, where you disagreed, what you did to follow up on the interest the book sparked, and why all of this makes you want to study economics at uni. Top candidates engage critically with the concepts explored in a book and link them to concepts they have learnt as part of their A Levels and beyond. See page 362 for some books you can read to make your personal statement stand out.

## 2) News Passion

It's vital to show engagement with current economic affairs. If you can present a recent economic event or controversy that particularly interests you, it shows you're switched on and interested in the applications of economics to society. However, make sure you're always linking the news stories you mention back to economics and *why you* want to study it. Your enthusiasm for and ability in the subject are the most important things to get across! Reading sources like *The Economist*, *The Financial Times* or *Entrepreneur Magazine* will allow you to keep up to date with the latest economic trends and events.

## 3) Lectures, podcasts, online videos Passion Potential

There are lots of free economics lectures across the country that you can attend to explore the field further. Two organisations that host fantastic events are the Royal Society of Arts and the New Economics Foundation. Furthermore, there are lots of online lectures, podcasts and videos[136] that might interest you. Some examples are:

- Freakonomics
- Planet Money
- EconTalk
- Jacob Clifford's YouTube channel.

## 4) Debates Ability Passion Potential

Attending or listening to debates on economics – or even in a related subject, such as politics – is another great way to feed your passion for your subject in a way you can concretely describe in your personal statement. Some places to find or take part in debates include:

- Debating societies at school
- Online debates between academics. Some good sources are the New Putney Debates and iai.tv
- Podcasts dedicated to intellectual discussion and debate, such as Intelligence Squared
- Topical TV and radio shows such as Question Time

136 See oxbridgeformula.co.uk/bonus-chapter for more recommendations.

- Debates in (digital) print, such as at theweek.com
- Nearby universities (check their 'events' page)
- MUN (Model United Nations).

If you can form your own opinion, or actively take one side of the debate, this will impress the admissions tutors. And if your opinion was changed by watching the debate, explain why! They want to see not only that you're ticking the boxes of preparing for economics, but that you're thinking for yourself and developing your own understanding.

To gain the most benefit, watch for when a speaker/writer introduces their position by describing and criticising a position they oppose. Provided they are being fair in their description and criticism, it's like seeing half of an additional debate that you could research later. And if they aren't being fair, you can practise figuring out how.

### 5) Academic extracurricular achievements Ability Passion Potential

You might take part in maths competitions to improve your problem-solving skills, or enter essay-writing competitions to extend your skills beyond A Level. If you've performed well in any of these, your ability will shine through. Typically, your A-Level achievements will be included in your teacher reference, so there's no need to mention them in detail in your personal statement.

### 6) Work experience Passion Potential

Having some relevant work experience under your belt will definitely boost your personal statement and your overall application. It isn't always easy to find, but if you're applying for PPE you could write to your local MP, council or newspaper to ask if you could work-shadow for a day. Don't be afraid to look further afield—for instance by interning at a think-tank or a journal. If you have a specific career in mind, find work experience in that area. For example, if you're interested in continuing in the field of economics after your degree, then getting work experience in a bank will hold you in good stead. Alternatively, if you're interested in pursuing law, you might find try to look for work experience at a solicitor's firm or shadowing a barrister at court. Whatever you choose, you'll need to actively search for opportunities. Don't just expect them to land on your lap!

Although it's not technically work experience, if your school offers schemes such as Young Enterprise, this would be very relevant to an Economics & Management degree.

# 27.2: Books to read if you're interested in economics and related subjects Passion

It's vital to show in your personal statement that you've read around the subject. This is how the admissions tutors will know that you're engaged and willing to expand your understanding of the subject. Here's a list of books to get you started:[137]

## General economics books

**McMillan: *Reinventing the Bazaar***

This book is a clear introduction to the functioning of markets, covering key terms and concepts in an understandable, jargon-free way. It draws on both modern examples and famous historical ones to highlight how economics plays a large part in society. The concepts it covers include:

- Sustainability
- Incentives
- Trust
- Competition
- Auctions
- Property
- Intellectual property
- Corruption and collusion.

**Hazlitt: *Economics in One Lesson***

This is a famous introduction to classical economics that introduces many of the key theoretical elements of economics, such as free trade and price controls. The lesson that drives the book is stated in part one:

> *"The art of economics consists in looking not merely at the immediate but at the longer effects of any act or policy; it consists in tracing the consequences of that policy not merely for one group but all groups."*

137 See oxbridgeformula.co.uk/bonus-chapter for links to these books and more.

This introduction is quite technical, giving the reader a comprehensive insight into pre-war economic theory, but is something that will impress admissions tutors if you're able to discuss it on your personal statement.

### Raworth: *Doughnut Economics*

This book is an argument as to what economics should aim to achieve as a discipline, as well as a critique of economic ideas that stand in the way. Raworth takes the goal of economics to be *meeting everyone's needs*, from food to education, without causing catastrophic ecological damage in the process. It's a broad discussion of the philosophy and politics behind economics, although it does also discuss some ways in which the ideas might be put into practice.

### Banerjee and Duflo: *Poor Economics*

Poor Economics answers many questions surrounding the contentious issue of poverty, by exploring the economics behind it. It provides an insightful view of a life lived on 99 cents a day, and allows the reader to understand the daily decisions facing those that live in poverty. It is powerful and moving, but still provides a useful bank of information and knowledge about how the economy impacts the poor.

### Levitt and Dubner: *Freakonomics*

This book is a collection of strange and outlandish questions whose answers are rooted in economics such as 'How does a child's name influence their career?' It's an entertaining read, but also provides useful discussions of many questions in the style you may have in your interview. The open-ended nature of many of the questions may also lead you to further research, so it's a great place to start when looking for topics to cover in your personal statement.

You could also check out the Freakonomics website[138] for its excellent podcasts; these will be useful preparation for writing your personal statement and for interviews.

**Harford: *The Undercover Economist***

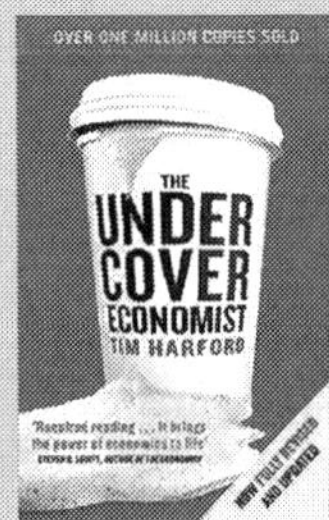


This is an introduction to economic ideas through everyday experiences—a notable example is what determines the cost of a coffee, and where the money goes after you buy one. This book also deals with some economic ideas on a larger scale than you'll see in *Freakonomics* or *Reinventing the Bazaar*, such as international trade and immigration. Harford has also written a follow-up – *The Undercover Economist Strikes Back* – that is even more focused on macroeconomic concepts like these.

**Chang: Economics: The User's Guide**

Ha-Joon Chang is the lecturer for the first-year Cambridge Economics module Political and Social Aspects of Economics, and this book is a non-technical look at the subject. He presents economics as being made up of several schools of thought that have changed through history, with political ideas sometimes giving rise to economic ones—so this book is a great introduction to a variety of economic ideas. It also asks fundamental questions such as 'Is economics a science?' and 'How do we decide what things are allowed to be bought and sold?'

## Books to read if you're applying for Land Economy

For this degree, it's very useful to read about development, environmental, and urban economics, and also (and especially) law. However, these are also valuable topics to read up on if you're studying for other degrees, especially PPE. The following are all recommended by Cambridge for Land Economy.

138 Find this and more at oxbridgeformula.co.uk/bonus-chapter.

### Twining and Miers: *How to Do Things With Rules*

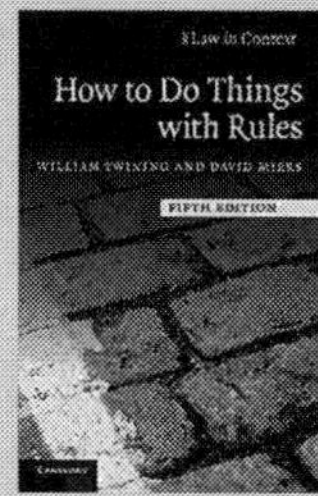


An introduction to legal methodology, such as how laws are made and interpreted. It even includes a large number of exercises, so it's a great way to prepare for studying law at uni even if you've had no exposure to it before. Just doing the exercises in one or two chapters would be something great to talk about in your personal statement. You could also read Barnett's *Understanding Public Law*, which is a textbook, but is a great way to just get a handle on some of the key ideas and terminology—you don't have to read it cover to cover. Hutchinson's *Is Eating People Wrong?* is a very different approach to getting a first exposure to law—it covers a series of entertaining yet instructive historical legal cases to introduce legal concepts.

### Hall: *Cities of Tomorrow*

A history of urban planning that addresses the social and economic effects of both good and bad planning. It presents a variety of fascinating examples from all over the world. Land use in cities is a very complex but important topic—how do we make sure there is space for everyone to live, provide infrastructure like transport networks, and avoid the kind of inequality demonstrated by the existence of slums around modern cities? Another book you might try, which highlights the benefits of urbanisation, is Glaeser's *Triumph of the City*.

### Monbiot: *Feral*

An introduction to the idea of 'rewilding' parts of the landscape, i.e. allowing nature to undo the effects of human cultivation or exploitation of the land. This is an increasingly important idea in environmental studies, and the author gives plenty of examples of how it can be achieved in practice. It's a topic that is especially relevant to the management of land outside of towns and cities, so it complements *Cities of Tomorrow* well. Other books on the land outside of urban areas include Rackham's *Woodlands* and Shrubsole's *Who Owns England?*

## Books to read if you're applying for E&M

Many of the books listed here will also interest applicants to other economics degrees.

**Biographies**

Since you aren't expected to have any particular knowledge of management as a subject when you apply, it's enough to show a broader interest in analysing examples of leadership and business decisions. Having particular notable examples of successful companies and leaders to draw on will be handy in your interview; it's always better to give an example than to speak in generalities.

An example is **Walter Isaacson's official biography of Steve Jobs**, covering his long and highly impactful career with Apple (among others), and both his successes and failures. Other significant figures with biographies include **James Dyson, Sophia Amoruso, Karen Brady, Elon Musk, Jack Ma, Mary Kay Ash, John H. Johnson** and **Phil Knight.**

**Sandberg: *Lean In***

Written by a female Facebook executive, this notorious book analysing the challenges for women in business and giving advice for overcoming them has sparked a lot of discussion over the last few years. For that reason, you'll be able to find plenty of further reading connected to it, giving you all the more to discuss in your personal statement and interview. The role of gender in the workplace is an increasingly important topic in management.

**Martin and Osberg: *Getting Beyond Better***

A guide to social enterprise, including how to found and run an organisation that pursues social goals using the mechanism of the marketplace. That might mean a non-profit organisation such as a charity or NGO, but also a for-profit corporation that aims to produce a particular social change, for instance by selling only sustainably-produced food. It covers a diverse set of examples, and focuses on key topics such as how to scale a business—making it highly relevant for management applicants.

### Christensen: *The Innovator's Dilemma*

Christensen is known for his work on concept of technological disruption, and this book considers how small and large companies need to approach innovation, research and growth differently. Since it's all about business strategy and the way companies should use resources and make plans (giving examples along the way), it's highly relevant to the study of management. A similar book exploring what makes some companies succeed and others fail or stagnate is ***Good to Great*** by Jim Collins.

### Boyce: *The Development of Modern Business*

This book is on the Oxford E&M reading list and provides an enjoyable and highly readable insight into the concerns and style of the academic study of management. It focuses specifically on the internal workings of businesses rather than on the history of the whole economy, and provides plenty of examples of management in action.

### Schneider: *Everything for Everyone*

An example of a study of organisations (rather than companies *per se*), this book covers the history and theory of cooperatives and analyses many examples of human organisation, from monasteries to grocery stores to Bitcoin. It may be especially useful as a complement to one of the other books listed here, since it will allow you to contrast cooperatives with other forms of organisation.

See page 441 for a Philosophy reading list. For a reading list for Politics, check out oxbridgeformula.co.uk/bonus-chapter.

# 27.3: Example Cambridge Economics personal statement

To give you an idea of what you should be aiming for in your personal statement, we've included exemplar statements from successful Cambridge Economics and Oxford PPE applicants. Look at every paragraph and evaluate whether they would answer the following questions in the admissions tutor's mind:

- *'Why should I accept this student to study this subject at university?'*
- *'Can I see concrete evidence of ability, passion and potential here?'*

It's the interdisciplinary nature of Economics that I find particularly attractive. On the one hand, it's a rigorous science that is characterised by theories that can be expressed with mathematical precision. Yet so too is it a social science that must wrestle with the unpredictability of human behaviour.

> Yes! It's great that this candidate goes right in with why they want to study the subject.

This latter dimension is nowhere more obvious than in the field of behavioural economics. My interest in this field was initially sparked by reading Thaler and Sunstein's book 'Nudge'. I was surprised by the amount of inherent cognitive bias in human decision-making it exposed, because this is so contrary to the assumption of rationality upon which neo-classical economics is based. I was even more intrigued to discover that governments have begun to politically exploit this behavioural insight, a practice known as 'nudging'. A lecture by David Halpern of the government's 'Nudge Unit' highlighted to me how subtle changes in the way a possible decision is presented to the public can have a major impact on the number of people willing to take it. Nudging, it seems, is an efficient, low-cost way of encouraging us to make the right choices about everything from organ donation to loft insulation. Such psychological incentives are certainly very different to those that inform Adam Smith's theory of the 'invisible hand' of the market.

> **Potential** Showing a willingness to take new concepts, recognise contradictions and rethink what they have previously learnt.

> **Passion** **Potential** Explaining what they learnt shows they were genuinely interested and can handle both theory and application.

Statistical modelling offers economists another way to predict collective human behaviour. A lecture by the Chief Home Office Scientist, Bernard Silverman, gave me my first insight into how such methods are used to inform policy on issues such as migration. However, I only fully appreciated their usefulness when I heard Kristin Forbes speak at the LSE about her use of modelling at the Bank of England to analyse the likely trends in the UK's current phase of 'lowflation'. She cogently demonstrated how a simple modification of the standard Phillips curve equation could remove the effects of exchange rate movements and oil prices from forecasts of headline inflation.

Be prepared to remember and explain this in the interview, if asked. As it's a new theory, the interviewer may be genuinely interested in knowing more! Perhaps the student could have linked it to why they want to study economics.

I get a lot of personal enjoyment from supplementing my A-Level Mathematics with more demanding problem-solving, such as the monthly British Mathematical Olympiad Mentoring questions, which I discuss weekly with my peers. In addition to the stimulating debate this offers, I value the challenge of explaining my reasoning coherently and constructing elegant proofs, for instance in the Olympiad itself. I recently won a prize for an essay on the mathematics of fractals, a topic I chose because I am fascinated by the potential of chaos theory to describe seemingly random patterns, whether these are found in nature or the stock market.

**Ability** Doing more mathematical problem-solving is highly recommended for any student applying for a maths-related course at Oxbridge, and Olympiad questions are a great resource.

I also enjoyed success in the ICAEW BASE Competition, winning the regional finals. This allowed me to develop my presentational skills, and prepared me for the demanding accountancy audit I had to conduct in the national final. I believe I also have leadership potential, evidenced by my role as the Managing Director of a successful Young Enterprise company.

My enduring passion for aviation and desire to conduct some research of my own motivated me to submit an essay to the annual RES essay competition on the economic case for extra airport capacity in the south-east of England. After thorough research and methodical analysis, I concluded that building a new runway at Heathrow would be the most prudent decision, due to the greater potential for future trade with developing nations, and Heathrow's vastly superior hub-and-spoke system. Although it was gratifying to learn that the essay was highly commended,[139] I decided to focus an EPQ on investigating this complex issue in further detail by considering the social and environmental factors as well. So far, this experience has strengthened my ability to conduct independent research, be organised and correctly reference my work—all attributes that will stand me in good stead for studying Economics at a higher level.

**Ability** **Passion**
Essay competitions are an excellent way to show your initiative in wanting to explore concepts outside of the A-Level curriculum and, if you do well, it's also evidence of your writing skills and clarity of thought.

**Ability** **Potential**
Doing an EPQ is impressive for similar reasons to entering an essay contest, plus it shows you should be able to learn to complete uni-level essays and projects at a high standard.

## 27.4: Example PPE personal statement

Taking part in competitive debating since Year 7, I have had to critique, assess and provide case studies for a range of philosophical, political and economic issues—from foreign policy to poverty. These issues are complex, have wide scope for debate and present an intellectual challenge—yet are concerned with improving and understanding society. This is why I want to study PPE.

Don't worry if you didn't get the chance to start debating in Year 7—focus on how your experiences make you a good fit for PPE. There's always time to start something new if it will help!

**Passion** **Potential**
It's great to state explicitly why you want to study the subject, especially if you show you understand its demands.

Mesquita's 'Dictator's Handbook' and Acemoglu's 'Why Nations Fail' provided me with fascinating political frameworks that now inform my understanding of politics. The former argues that political outcomes depend on how many people leaders need on their side to maintain power. For Acemoglu, economic prosperity depends on how many people form part of political decision-making. Though simplistic, what fascinates me is how far these ideas corroborate much of my reading. For instance,

**Passion** **Potential**
The student shows they are interested enough to keep up with current affairs and have an instinct for attempting to apply ideas in new contexts, which is an essential skill at university.

139 Good ones for potential economists include the RES competition and the Fitzwilliam College Cambridge Land Economy competition.

because of Tunisia's democratic institutions, protesters in 2011 were the same masses needed to keep Ben Ali in power. Once support fell, he could not retain power. That Assad's power base was the Syrian Army meant he could suppress the opposition. Thus, the Arab Spring benefitted Tunisia and not Syria.

However, I found that arguments in favour of institutions more often referred to ideology. To explore this matter further I read books such as 'The Virtue of Selfishness' by Ayn Rand. What struck me was that ideological beliefs often referred to ethics, such as objectivism and Rand's egoism. Inspired by a lecture at the UNIQ summer school exploring whether utilitarianism can be egalitarian, I worked through the Open Yale course 'Moral Foundations of Politics'. I realised I was most interested by how often arguments build on ethics. In the course, I was intrigued by how Sraffa's corn theory of value highlighted a moral basis behind Marx's labour theory of value. Now I can apply this idea to my studies; in my economics lessons the justification of government intervention is that it maximises welfare does appear to be built on a utilitarian stance.

**Passion** **Potential**: Open courses are a great way to show your capacity for independent study and your level of interest.

During these lessons, I am intrigued by the conflict between rational choice theory and my political observations. For example, it is argued that providing information alone solves information gaps. However during the Brexit referendum campaign, I observed that even given the abundance of information, confirmation bias propelled misinformation. Though Hayek, in 'Road to Serfdom', argued that individuals are best-placed to serve their own ends, it seems to me that examples such as rising obesity rates show that social pressures often cause people to act against their interests. However, after reading 'Thinking, Fast and Slow' (Kahneman), behavioural economics provided a framework for these biases. As these biases are psychological, I believe efficient policymaking demands these considerations.

Linking your reading to multiple disciplines, e.g. politics *and* economics, is an effective way to use it.

I developed my research and evaluative skills as a journalist for United Politics and Filibuster UK, the latter of which I also edit. I run the school's Debating Society, give lectures at school societies, and I am Deputy Head Student. Having all of these responsibilities continues to develop my organisational skills. Attending lectures at the LSE, IEA and

**Ability** Linking your extracurricular achievements back to skills that will help you with the course you're applying for is the best way to introduce them.

summer schools has increased my ability to consider ideas that differ from my own. I have won internal and regional awards for debating and public speaking, and I have won an 'outstanding delegate' award at a local MUN conference, demonstrating my communication skills.

During my work experience at Parliament, I attended an oral evidence session in which Jeremy Hunt was challenged on his NHS funding claims. Subsequent media attention led to policy changes. Witnessing how these debates lead to change inspired me to aim for a career in policy. After having an introduction to computational statistics across PPE at a Q-Step Centre, I have seen how studying PPE is not only an opportunity to explore social debates; it also provides an excellent toolkit for a career in tackling these issues. I look forward to studying it.

This is a good use of work experience, as it links clearly into the subject to which the student is applying.

**Passion** The student links everything back to their motivation for studying the subject at the end.

# Chapter 28:
# Admissions tests

What admissions test do you need to take? Find out with our handy table, then read on to get all the details. As a relatively new test, the ECAA is based upon the TSA, so we will discuss the TSA first.

| Course | University | Test | Page Number |
|---|---|---|---|
| Economics | Cambridge | ECAA | Page 383 |
| Land Economy | Cambridge | TSA Section 1 | Page 373 |
| Economics & Management | Oxford | TSA | Page 373 |
| PPE | Oxford | TSA | Page 373 |
| History & Economics | Oxford | TSA Section 1 and HAT[140] | Page 373 |
| (Chemistry) | Oxford | TSA Section 1 | Page 373 |

## 28.1: TSA: The Facts

**Q Who wants the TSA?**

**A** The TSA (Thinking Skills Assessment) is the admissions test used for:

- PPE at Oxford: Both sections of the TSA are required
- E&M at Oxford: Both sections of the TSA are required
- History & Economics at Oxford: Section 1 of the TSA is required, as is the HAT (History Aptitude Test)
- Land Economy at Cambridge: Section 1 of the TSA is required.
- (Chemistry at Oxford: Section 1 of the TSA is required)

140 The HAT (History Aptitude Test) is beyond the scope of this book and we therefore don't expand on it here.

You'll also have to sit the TSA if you're applying to other courses such as for PPL (Philosophy, Psychology and Linguistics) and Human Sciences at Oxford.

**Q When is the TSA sat?**

**A** The TSA is sat in late October or early November.

**Q What is the purpose of the TSA?**

**A** Ability Section 1 (the multiple-choice section) is primarily a test of your ***problem-solving*** and ***critical-thinking*** abilities, which are collectively known as *thinking skills.*[141] These are skills that are imperative to have to be successful in your chosen degree course at Oxbridge. Section 2 (the writing task) tests your ability to construct a line of argument and debate it, and the quality of your written communication. The TSA is used to help decide whether or not you're interviewed, and afterwards whether you get an offer.

**Problem-solving:** Involves understanding problems and finding creative but logical solutions. The questions are often numerical in nature.

**Critical thinking:** Involves analysing arguments and statements, including identifying conclusions, assumptions and flaws.

**Q How long is the TSA?**

**A** Section 1 of the TSA lasts 90 minutes and Section 2 lasts 30 minutes.

**Q How is the TSA structured?**

**A** Section 1 of the TSA consists of 50 multiple-choice thinking-skills questions. For each question there will be a stimulus, a question

141 Hence the name Thinking Skills Assessment!

and 5 options. The stimulus may be a diagram, a table, a graph, or a passage of text. All the questions are worth the same number of marks.

In Section 2, you'll be given four essay titles and you have 30 minutes to write one essay. This will test your ability to organise your thoughts coherently and communicate them effectively.

**Q What is the content of the TSA?**

**A** The TSA does not have a syllabus: there's no list of specific things you have to learn before the exam.

The questions in **Section 1** of the TSA are based on critical thinking and problem-solving.

The 3 types of problem-solving questions are:

- **Relevant selection:** Requires you to analyse a chunk of information (such as a table, graph or chart) and find the part that applies to the question
- **Finding procedures:**[142] You're given a set of rules and/or constraints, that you have to follow to solve a stated problem
- **Identifying similarities:**[143] Involves finding a situation with similarities to the one you were given—for example, spotting patterns, or thinking about how shapes are arranged.

There will also be 7 different types of ***critical-thinking*** questions:[144]

- Summarising the **main conclusion** of the passage
- **Drawing a conclusion** from the passage
- Identifying an **assumption** in the argument
- Seeing if **additional evidence strengthens or weakens** the argument

142 We categorise these as 'maths and logic problems' in our courses.

143 We categorise these as 'spatial reasoning' in our courses.

144 See oxbridgeformula.co.uk/tsa for uniquely formulated techniques to help you tackle each of the 7 styles of critical-thinking question.

- Identifying **flaws** in the argument
- Identifying whether two arguments display **parallel reasoning**, i.e. similar logical structures
- Identifying a **principle** relied upon by the argument.

Each of the above question types calls for a unique set of methods to identify the correct answer. Our online TSA course goes through each method in significant detail.[145]

***Why are critical-thinking skills so important?***

Ability Critical thinking differentiates an active learner from someone who merely accepts information passively.

A critical thinker will meticulously question arguments and assumptions, rather than accepting them as first presented. They will always try to understand whether the evidence, ideas and arguments paint the full picture or whether there are missing pieces.

Critical thinkers solve problems analytically and don't rely on intuition, instinct or emotion.

In a degree with a significant essay-writing component, critical-thinking skills are vital for communicating your argument in a non-ambiguous way. They ensure that you pick the most appropriate and concise words, phrases and paragraphs to get your message across powerfully. All of these skills are vital to subjects such as PPE and E&M and are hence tested in the TSA.

In **Section 2** of the TSA, the essay titles aren't designed to test content you have covered in any of your A Levels, but rather your ability to communicate clearly, evaluate ideas critically and argue convincingly.

145 We would love to include them here, but we would need to include a lot of examples, which we think is much better done with videos. See oxbridgeformula.co.uk/tsa for more details.

**Q Are the multiple-choice questions in Section 1 in a specific order?**

**A** In Section 1, the questions appear roughly in order of difficulty, but the problem-solving and critical-thinking questions are mixed throughout. It's very time-pressured. You only have 108 seconds per question—many student don't manage to complete all 50.

Often, the candidates who do not complete everything are those who get bogged down on one question. Each question has an equal weighting throughout the section, so there's no point spending a disproportionate amount of time on a question.

**Q What score do I need?**

**A** The TSA Section 1 is scored out of roughly 100 (varying slightly each year). This is a standardised score that takes into account the difficulty of the paper.

Here's the 2018 TSA score conversion:[146]

| Raw Mark | 0 | 1 | 2 | 3 | 4 | 5 | 6 |
|---|---|---|---|---|---|---|---|
| Standardised Score | 8.1 | 15.3 | 22.6 | 27.0 | 30.3 | 32.9 | 35.1 |

| Raw Mark | 7 | 8 | 9 | 10 | 11 | 12 | 13 |
|---|---|---|---|---|---|---|---|
| Standardised Score | 37.1 | 38.8 | 40.4 | 41.9 | 43.3 | 44.6 | 45.8 |

| Raw Mark | 14 | 15 | 16 | 17 | 18 | 19 | 20 |
|---|---|---|---|---|---|---|---|
| Standardised Score | 47.0 | 48.1 | 49.2 | 50.3 | 51.3 | 52.3 | 53.3 |

146 You can find the TSA score conversions for all years at oxbridgeformula.co.uk/tsa.

| **Raw Mark** | 21 | 22 | 23 | 24 | 25 | 26 | 27 |
|---|---|---|---|---|---|---|---|
| **Standardised Score** | 54.3 | 55.3 | 56.2 | 57.2 | 58.1 | 59.1 | 60.0 |

| **Raw Mark** | 28 | 29 | 30 | 31 | 32 | 33 | 34 |
|---|---|---|---|---|---|---|---|
| **Standardised Score** | 61.0 | 62.0 | 62.9 | 63.9 | 64.9 | 66.0 | 67.0 |

| **Raw Mark** | 35 | 36 | 37 | 38 | 39 | 40 | 41 |
|---|---|---|---|---|---|---|---|
| **Standardised Score** | 68.1 | 69.2 | 70.4 | 71.6 | 72.9 | 74.3 | 75.7 |

| **Raw Mark** | 42 | 43 | 44 | 45 | 46 | 47 | 48 |
|---|---|---|---|---|---|---|---|
| **Standardised Score** | 77.3 | 79.0 | 81.0 | 83.2 | 85.8 | 89.0 | 93.5 |

| **Raw Mark** | 49 | 50 |
|---|---|---|
| **Standardised Score** | 100.8 | 107.9 |

Different subjects have different cut-off points to determine who gets an invitation to interview. At Oxford, the average ***interview*** cut-off is about 60. However, it's a lot higher for E&M (68) and is higher for PPE than it is for PPL.

In 2017, the average score for a student getting an ***offer*** for PPE was 71.3 whereas the average score for a student getting an offer for Experimental Psychology was 64.3.

The method of scoring Section 2 varies between different admissions tutors—some will give a number, others a letter, each according to their own scale.

**Q Where can I find TSA past papers?**

**A** Scan this QR code to find TSA past papers:

**Q What's an example of a TSA-style 'relevant selection' question?**

**A** A troll wants to find a new bridge to live under. The troll will be able to extort money from travellers wishing to cross the bridge, but it will have to pay for repairs. Every bridge needs to be repaired once per year. Since bridge repair companies aren't fond of trolls, they will charge a minimum of £400 for repairs regardless of the actual cost, unless the troll has made less than £1,000 since the last repair.

| Location | County | Average extorted per traveller | Average number of crossings per year | Actual repair costs |
|---|---|---|---|---|
| Ashbridge | Wessex | £5 | 100 | £300 |
| Beechbridge | Gressex | £10 | 120 | £300 |
| Duckford | Cressex | £5 | 220 | £450 |
| Larkford | Jessex | £10 | 200 | £1,100 |
| Metalbridge | Thressex | £10 | 280 | £2,000 |
| Oakbridge | Gressex | £5 | 110 | £850 |
| Otterford | Jessex | £5 | 200 | £300 |
| Stonebridge | Thressex | £5 | 160 | £500 |

The troll will move to the location that offers the most profitable bridge in the long term. Which county does the troll end up living in?

**A** Cressex
**B** Gressex
**C** Jessex
**D** Thressex
**E** Wessex

**Q What's an example of a 'finding procedures'/'maths and logic' question?**

**A** In pursuit cycling, cyclists start on opposite sides of a 200m circular track and cycle clockwise, and the race finishes when one of the racers catches the other. Racer A cycles at a constant 40km/hr, and Racer B cycles at 32km/hr. How many laps has Racer A done when the race finishes?

**A** 2.5 **B** 4 **C** 5 **D** 10 **E** 16

**Q What's an example of a TSA-style 'identifying similarities'/'spatial reasoning' question?**

**A** A work of art is made out of identical boxes stacked in nine piles. The view from above and the view from the large circle in that diagram are:

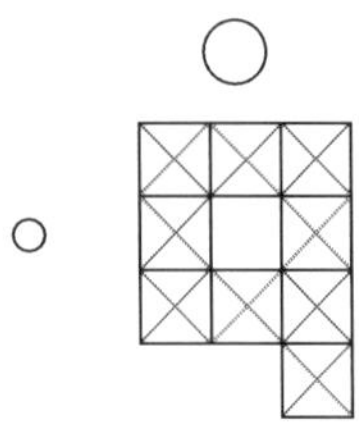

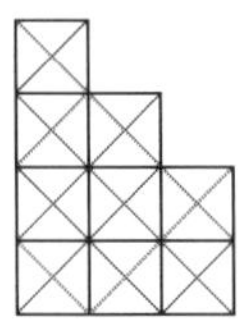

... respectively

Which one of the following could not be the view from the small circle?

**A**

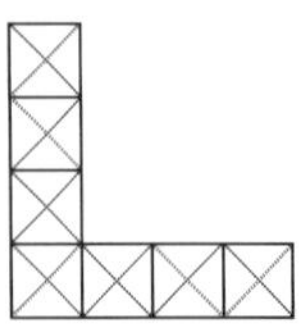

**B**

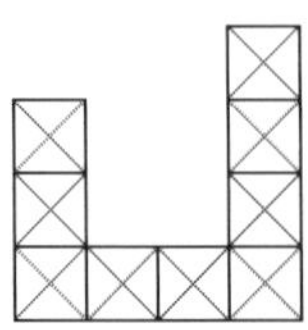

C

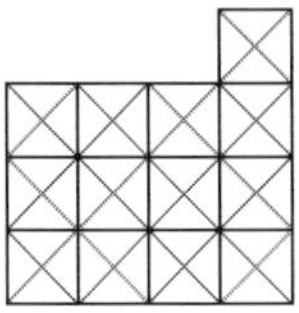

D

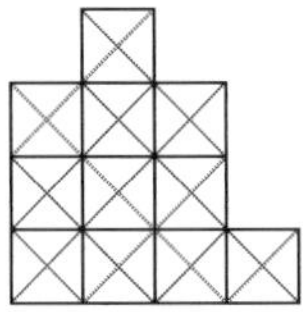

E

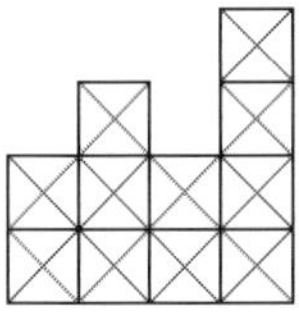

## Q What's an example of a TSA-style critical-thinking question?

**A** Environmental action groups highlight the strains that the meat industry places on the environment and have taken up the vegan cause. Meats and animal products typically need more water to produce than plant-based products. It takes 1,799 gallons of water to produce 1 pound of beef, compared to 219 gallons of water to produce 1 pound of soybeans. It's becoming increasingly clear that, if society does not adopt veganism, we will never achieve the necessary reduction in water consumption. Many people have started to make the switch, starting, for example, with 'meat-free Mondays' and experimenting with alternative milks.

Which of the following, if true, most strengthens the above argument?

**A** Vegans are often concerned with animal welfare as well as the environment.
**B** Alternative milks are healthier than regular milk.
**C** Soybeans are not the most appropriate substitute for beef.
**D** The average person's meat intake accounts for most of the water consumption they are responsible for.
**E** Reducing water consumption is the most important environmental task society faces.

## Q What are some examples of TSA-style Section 2 (writing assessment) questions?

**A**
- Could a robot ever be deemed a human? If so, should it be granted a vote?

- Should we have more artists in positions of political power?
- If someone earns double your income, should they have to pay double what you do for a pint of milk?

**Q Where can I find more details about the TSA?**

**A** For more details of the TSA download our free guidebook at oxbridgeformula.co.uk/tsa

**Did You Know?**

*Oxford uses the following weightings for different parts of the application in deciding who to invite for an interview for PPE:*[147]

| | High | Medium | Low |
|---|---|---|---|
| TSA | x | | |
| GCSEs | x | | |
| Predicted A Levels | x | | |
| UCAS reference | | x | |
| AS modules | | | x |
| Personal statement | | | x |

147 As stated by the University of Oxford.

# 28.2: ECAA: The Facts[148]

**Q Who wants the ECAA?**

**A** The ECAA (Economics Admissions Assessment) is Cambridge's pre-interview test for Economics.

**Q When is the ECAA sat?**

**A** It's sat in late October or early November.

**Q What is the purpose of the ECAA?**

**A** The ECAA is designed to test your aptitude in *mathematics*, *communication* and *problem-solving*—and to gauge how well you'd cope with the taxing Cambridge Economics course. It informs the decision as to whether you're interviewed, and afterwards whether you get an offer.

**Q How long is the ECAA?**

**A** It lasts a total of 2 hours.

**Q How is the ECAA structured?**

**A** **The ECAA is composed of 2 sections:**

**Section 1:** A multiple-choice assessment consisting of 20 problem-solving questions and 16 maths questions. All of the questions in Section 1 are worth 1 mark, and you do not lose any marks for incorrect answers. You have 80 minutes for this section. You might want to spend 40 minutes on the problem-solving questions and 40 minutes on the maths questions—although there are fewer maths questions, they tend to be harder and more involved.

**Section 2:** This section is a written response to a roughly 1000-word economics article or book extract. You have 40 minutes to complete this section.

148 At the time of printing, Cambridge has announced that the ECAA will be changing, but has not released details. Please see oxbridgeformula.co.uk/bonus-chapter for updates.

## Q What is the content of the ECAA?

**A** There's no compulsory economics prerequisite knowledge for the ECAA. The text in Section 2 will be economics-based, but you're not being tested on any specific knowledge. Instead, you're meant to use the information in the passage, plus whatever relevant background knowledge you might have. The only compulsory prerequisite knowledge is Mathematics A Level, based predominantly on the first-year syllabus. However, some of the advanced questions are more challenging—so although it isn't essential to have done Further Maths A Level, having studied more maths will be helpful.[149]

## Q How is the ECAA marked?

**A** The Problem-Solving and Advanced Maths parts of Section 1 are graded on a standardised scale of 1.0–9.0 that is based on the difficulty of the test. Here's the score conversion from 2017:

| Problem Solving | |
|---|---|
| **Raw Mark** | **Score** |
| 0 | 1.0 |
| 1 | 1.0 |
| 2 | 1.0 |
| 3 | 1.0 |
| 4 | 1.0 |
| 5 | 1.0 |
| 6 | 1.0 |
| 7 | 1.5 |
| 8 | 2.0 |
| 9 | 2.5 |
| 10 | 3.0 |

| Problem Solving | |
|---|---|
| **Raw Mark** | **Score** |
| 11 | 3.5 |
| 12 | 4.0 |
| 13 | 4.5 |
| 14 | 5.0 |
| 15 | 5.6 |
| 16 | 6.3 |
| 17 | 7.0 |
| 18 | 8.0 |
| 19 | 9.0 |
| 20 | 9.0 |

149 For a full breakdown of the ECAA syllabus, see our free guidebook at oxbridge-formula.co.uk/ecaa.

| Mathematics | |
|---|---|
| Raw Mark | Score |
| 0 | 1.0 |
| 1 | 1.0 |
| 2 | 1.0 |
| 3 | 1.0 |
| 4 | 1.6 |
| 5 | 2.3 |
| 6 | 2.9 |
| 7 | 3.5 |
| 8 | 4.0 |

| Mathematics | |
|---|---|
| Raw Mark | Score |
| 9 | 4.5 |
| 10 | 5.1 |
| 11 | 5.6 |
| 12 | 6.3 |
| 13 | 7.0 |
| 14 | 7.9 |
| 15 | 9.0 |
| 16 | 9.0 |

The essay section is judged on the following criteria:

- How **well-reasoned** your argument is:
    - Do you have good ideas and use details from the extract to support them?
    - Do you back up the ideas in the extract with logic, economic theory and examples from your own knowledge?
- How **insightful** it is:
    - Don't just quote information from the extract. Use what you know from your Economics A Level and bring in information from wider reading, current affairs or your own research.
- How **logically consistent** it is:
    - Make sure you don't contradict yourself.
    - Have an introduction where you state your argument and a conclusion that reiterates it.
    - Include counterarguments and explain why they don't hold.
- Its **clarity:**
    - Write your ideas in a way that a non-expert could understand. Don't be pretentious.
    - Show all the steps in your argument and define any terms that you use.

- Its **precision:**
  - ➢ Answer the question without going off on a tangent.
  - ➢ Link every paragraph back to the question.
  - ➢ Use economic terms and vocabulary precisely.
  - ➢ Give examples to explain your point.

The essay isn't marked centrally but will be marked by the college you apply to; each college may mark it using a different scoring system.

**Q What score do I need?**

**A** In the Problem Solving part, a score of 6.0 should be considered strong; this is where you want to be to help guarantee an interview. In the Advanced Maths section, most candidates score between 4.0 and 5.0; a score of 5.0 is considered very good.

**Q Where can I find ECAA Sample papers?**

**A** Scan this QR Code to find ECAA past papers.

**Q What's an example of an ECAA-style problem-solving question?**

**A** The ECAA problem-solving questions are identical in style to TSA problem-solving questions, and the majority are actually taken from the same year's TSA paper;[150] see page 373 for examples.

150 Incidentally, this makes the TSA an excellent source of extra practice questions for the ECAA.

### Q What's an example of an ECAA-style advanced maths question?

**A** The function $f(x)$ is defined for all real values of $x$. Which of the following is a sufficient condition such that $\int_{-1}^{2} f(x)dx = 0$?

**A** $f(0) = 0$

**B** $f(x - \frac{1}{2}) = f(\frac{1}{2} - x)$ for all $x$

**C** $f(-1) = \frac{1}{2} f(2)$

**D** $f(x) = -\frac{1}{2} f(-\frac{1}{2} x)$ for all $x \geq 0$

**E** $f(x) = -f(-x)$ for all $x$

ECAA advanced maths questions are very similar to TMUA/CTMUA questions (from both Paper 1 and Paper 2). See page 74 for more examples.

### Q Where can I find more details about the ECAA?

**A** For more details of the ECAA find our free guidebook at oxbridge-formula.co.uk/ecaa.

**Did You Know?**

*In 2016, every Cambridge Economics undergraduate who went on to apply for the Cambridge MPhil in Economics was accepted, so it seems the course gives students a very good foundation for further study.*

## 28.3: Preparing for TSA/ECAA

There are numerous techniques you can use to help you prepare for your admissions tests. Many of these tips apply to multiple papers—so see which columns are ticked to see which admissions test the tip applies to.

| TSA Sec | | ECAA Sec | | Preparation tip |
|---|---|---|---|---|
| 1 | 2 | 1 | 2 | |
| ✓ | ✓ | ✓ | ✓ | **Do past papers**<br>For both the TSA and the ECAA, doing past papers is the best way to prepare. It is important to do at least a couple of past papers in timed conditions, because time management is incredibly important in both exams.<br><br>TSA past papers:<br><br>ECAA past papers: |

| TSA Sec | | ECAA Sec | | Preparation tip |
|---|---|---|---|---|
| 1 | 2 | 1 | 2 | |
| | | | | **Top Tip**<br>*When practising for the multiple-choice section of the TSA or ECAA, you could* ***put a timer on a loop*** *to tell you when you're spending longer on a question than the average time you'll have per question in the exam. That means 108 seconds for TSA Sec1, 2 minutes for ECAA Sec1 problem solving, and 2.5 minutes for ECAA Sec1 maths. That way, you can get an intuitive sense for which types of question tend to take you longer—questions you need to focus on in your preparation.*<br>**TSA and ECAA video solutions**<br>Video solutions are great as you can see the exact thought processes undertaken by the tutors who have successfully navigated the papers. The visualisations usefully illustrate key methods, which is great because written solutions can take as long to understand as the question itself!<br>**TSA video solutions:** |

| TSA Sec 1 | TSA Sec 2 | ECAA Sec 1 | ECAA Sec 2 | Preparation tip |
|---|---|---|---|---|
| | | | | **ECAA video solutions:** |
| ✓ | | | ✓ | **Improve your critical thinking**<br>Critical thinking is a vital skill for Section 1 of the TSA and when you're reading and analysing the passage in Section 2 of the ECAA.<br><br>To improve your critical-thinking skills, read and listen to speeches—for example politicians talking on the news. Reading is more useful because this is what you'll have to do in the test, but you can listen to the news while you're in the car or getting ready for school. Either way: pick out the key argument, ask yourself what ***premises*** were used and try to provide as brief a synopsis as you can. Regular practice at this will serve well as preparation for the TSA.<br><br>The **premises** of an argument are your starting points and the **conclusion** is what you argue towards.<br><br>For instance, in the argument *'Smoking causes unnecessary deaths, and we should ban activities that cause unnecessary* |

| TSA Sec | | ECAA Sec | | Preparation tip |
|---|---|---|---|---|
| 1 | 2 | 1 | 2 | |
| | | | | *deaths, so we should ban smoking'*, the ***premises*** are:<br>■ 'Smoking causes unnecessary deaths'<br>■ 'We should ban activities that cause unnecessary deaths'<br>The ***conclusion*** is: '*We should ban smoking'.*<br><br>A large part of critical thinking is being able to look at flawed arguments and identify the exact spot where they fell through. You could do this by listening to debates between politicians or academics. Look at how the evidence they give shows the weakness in the opposing argument. Look also for where flaws creep into the argument.<br><br>Newspaper editorials are also a good source of practice. For each paragraph, you can ask yourself:<br>■ What the premises and conclusion are<br>■ Whether any assumptions are being made<br>■ What evidence would strengthen or weaken the argument<br>■ What flaws exist in the argument (if any).<br><br>**Top Tip**<br>*See if you can compare and contrast two editorials on the same topics taking* ***opposing views****. See if you can spot how they both use evidence differently and how they point out the flaws in each other's arguments.* |

| TSA Sec | | ECAA Sec | | Preparation tip |
|---|---|---|---|---|
| 1 | 2 | 1 | 2 | |
| | ✓ | | ✓ | **Practise planning and writing perfect essays**<br>Although your exam essay won't be a perfect thesis because of time pressure and nerves, it's worth spending time trying to write perfect ECAA and TSA essays.<br><br>This will help you to hit all the things you want to include in your essay. Also compare your essay to the mark schemes to check you're on the right track.[151]<br><br>TSA essay videos:<br><br>ECAA essay videos: |

151 We have video essay plans that will help you check that you're hitting all the major points! These can be found at oxbridgeformula.co.uk/tsa or oxbridgeformula.co.uk/ecaa.

| TSA Sec | | ECAA Sec | | Preparation tip |
|---|---|---|---|---|
| 1 | 2 | 1 | 2 | |
| | ✓ | | ✓ | **Formulate arguments**<br>For both essay sections, it's useful to read topical articles and news stories and practise forming an opinion about them. The admissions tutors marking the TSA and ECAA are looking for interesting and well-executed lines of argument. You can improve this skill by reading controversial headlines and deciding what you would argue. However, the admissions tutors also want to see that you can have a balanced debate and weigh up both sides of the argument.[152] Try and have debates about pertinent topics such as assisted dying, tax cuts, AI, GM food, private education or private health care with your friends, family and teachers.<br><br>For the second section of the ECAA, it's worth reading some economics-based texts and asking yourself questions about them. You can draw on the books in the reading list on page 362, or simply try and find an economics-based news article. Ask yourself questions such as:<br><br>■ What is the purpose of this text?<br>■ Is this text biased?<br>■ How would I summarise the main argument?<br>■ What are two arguments for and two arguments against the idea being discussed?<br><br>*"For Section 2, I compiled a list of all the questions that had come up in previous years, plus any sample questions I could find online,* |

152 The leaders section of *The Economist* is an excellent example of setting out all sides of the debate before coming to a conclusion.

| TSA Sec 1 | TSA Sec 2 | ECAA Sec 1 | ECAA Sec 2 | Preparation tip |
|---|---|---|---|---|
| | | | | *and drafted outlines for each of them. It helped my confidence a lot to have a vague idea of what I wanted to say for any of the topics that may come up."* –Student, PPE, Oxford |
| ✓ | | ✓ | | **Use other resources**<br>If you run out of questions when preparing for the TSA or the ECAA, or want more to graze on, don't worry. The problem-solving questions from Section 1 of the ECAA are based on the questions from Section 1 of the TSA, so students taking the ECAA can prepare by looking at past TSA papers.<br><br>Meanwhile, Section 1 of the BMAT (a medical admissions test) also contains similar questions, so they are useful whether you're taking the ECAA or the TSA.[153]<br><br>The TMUA/CTMUA[154] is a good source of questions to practise the later questions in the Advanced Maths section of the ECAA. |

153 The BMAT has 15+ years of past papers, and all relevant questions are included in our TSA and ECAA online resources (oxbridgeformula.co.uk/tsa, oxbridgeformula.co.uk/ecaa).
154 To give you extra practice, we've included TMUA/CTMUA and MAT questions and video solutions in our ECAA online resources.

## 28.4: Exam techniques for TSA/ECAA

| TSA Sec | | ECAA Sec | | Examination technique |
|---|---|---|---|---|
| 1 | 2 | 1 | 2 | |
| ✓ | | ✓ | | **Time management**<br>Time management is the most important thing to focus on in Section 1 of the TSA and ECAA. You have 108 seconds to answer each question in the TSA. You have 2 minutes for each ECAA problem-solving question and 2.5 minutes for each maths question.<br><br>All questions are weighted equally, so don't spend a disproportionate amount of time on a question. Even if it's the hardest one, it won't win you any more points with the admissions tutors.<br><br>There are several techniques for approaching the multiple-choice questions, and you'll need to do timed mocks to learn which suit your strengths and weaknesses:<br><br>1. **The 2-step approach:**<br>**Step A:** Go through the whole section, but when you come across a question of a type you know you tend to struggle with, don't even start it—just circle it and move on.<br>**Step B:** After doing all the questions you feel comfortable with, come back to the questions that are circled. Guess if needed, but mark questions with a 'G' if they have been guessed so you can go back if you have time.<br><br>2. **The all-in-one approach:** Go through in order, checking your timing every 5 questions or so. You have an average of 9 minutes for every 5 questions, but you should expect earlier ones to be easier, and should |

| TSA Sec | | ECAA Sec | | Examination technique |
|---|---|---|---|---|
| 1 | 2 | 1 | 2 | |

leave time at the end to check answers and revisit abandoned questions. A suggested split is:

| **No. of TSA questions done** | 5 | 10 | 15 | 20 | 25 |
|---|---|---|---|---|---|
| **No. minutes spent** | 6 | 12 | 18 | 26 | 34 |

| **No. of TSA questions done** | 30 | 35 | 40 | 45 | 50 |
|---|---|---|---|---|---|
| **No. minutes spent** | 42 | 50 | 60 | 72 | 85 |

| **No. of ECAA questions done** | 5 (problem-solving) | 10 (problem-solving) |
|---|---|---|
| **No. minutes spent** | 7 | 15 |

| **No. of ECAA questions done** | 15 (problem-solving) | 20 (problem-solving) |
|---|---|---|
| **No. minutes spent** | 25 | 35 |

| **No. of ECAA questions done** | 5 (maths) | 10 (maths) | 16 (maths) |
|---|---|---|---|
| **No. minutes spent** | 45 | 57 | 75 |

3. **The 50-50 split**: For the TSA, you could do all the problem-solving questions first before tackling the critical-thinking questions, to stay in the right frame of mind for each type of question. It helps to know from experience which type of question takes you longer on average.

These are only loose guidelines—be sensible, and use them in a practical way. If you've spent 108 seconds on a TSA question but you're only 10 seconds from finishing, we're not suggesting you should move on! Also, flitting between questions too frequently can mean you forget the information you've already read, or that you lose concentration. Our biggest piece of advice is to figure out what works best for you ahead of the exam and stick to it.

| TSA Sec | | ECAA Sec | | Examination technique |
|---|---|---|---|---|
| 1 | 2 | 1 | 2 | |
| ✓ | | ✓ | | **Elimination**<br>As Section 1 of both papers is multiple-choice, a good way of answering a lot of the questions is by eliminating the statements you know are definitely false. For example, if you read a piece of writing and have five possible options for what the conclusion is, you can immediately get rid of any options that haven't even been referenced in the argument. You can eliminate some of the answers to the harder questions on the first read-through and come back to them later when you spend some time choosing what you think the correct one might be from the remaining possibilities. |
| ✓ | | ✓ | | **Problem-solving tips**<br>**1.** Get fluent with the following types of basic **maths problem**:<br>■ Fractions, percentages and ratios<br>■ Probabilities<br>■ Money<br>■ Times and dates<br>■ Lengths, areas and volumes<br>■ Speed and distance.<br>**2.** For questions with tables, **scan the headings** before trying to read the data. Take note of **units**, e.g. if a column in a table is 'per 100 people'. Identify parts of the data that are **irrelevant** to the question.<br>**3.** For spatial reasoning questions, **turn the page** if it makes it easier to visualise.<br>**4.** For questions with lots of information, **tick each piece you use** so you don't miss one.<br>**5.** **Check numerical answers** by testing if they satisfy every condition the question gave you. |

| TSA Sec 1 | TSA Sec 2 | ECAA Sec 1 | ECAA Sec 2 | Examination technique |
|---|---|---|---|---|
| | | ✓ | | **ECAA maths questions**<br>For the maths questions of the ECAA, you need to try and work out the answer as quickly as possible. While your working isn't marked, a logical layout can prevent careless errors and lost trains of thought, so it's worth practising laying your work out well when practising for the ECAA maths section.<br><br>**Top Tip**<br>*Ideally, you should aim to write out ALL of your work logically at A-Level* ***so that accuracy becomes second nature*** *to you. That way you won't feel the pressure in an exam situation.* |
| ✓ | | | | **Read the question first—it will tell you how to read the passage (critical thinking)**<br>Before you read the passage, read the question below it, so you know what type of question you're answering. This will determine *how* you read the passage.<br><br>For instance, in a question where you're asked to find the *main conclusion*, *identify a flaw*, *weakness* or *strength* in an argument or *parallel the reasoning*, it's helpful to identify the conclusion of the passage first. One way to do this quickly is to look for words such as 'so', 'therefore' and 'for this reason', though they aren't always present.<br><br>However, in a *draw conclusion* question, the conclusion won't be found in the passage.<br><br>Additionally, in a *flaw* or *assumption* question, you'll be able to read through the passage with the mindset |

| TSA Sec 1 | TSA Sec 2 | ECAA Sec 1 | ECAA Sec 2 | Examination technique |
|---|---|---|---|---|
| | | | | of looking for what's missing, or what doesn't flow logically.<br><br>In a *parallel reasoning* question, you might like to formulate some if-then statements as you read through the passage, so you can compare the logic with the options presented to you.<br><br>In a *principle question*, on the other hand, you'll be thinking about what the principle is, as you read through.<br><br>However, in each case, don't assume what the answer will be without reading the passage carefully.<br><br>**More critical-thinking tips**<br>**1.** Look out for **quantifiers** such as 'all', 'none', 'some' and 'most', as they change how strong a statement is.<br>**2.** You should never need to use your **own knowledge**, only what is discussed in the passage. |
| ✓ | | ✓ | ✓ | **Read carefully**<br>Although the papers are time-pressured, you need to read and comprehend all the stimuli given to you as well as possible. Never skim! A slight misread can lead you to completely the wrong answer. Although moving at a pace is important, there's no point racing through and making silly mistakes. It's better to be slightly more careful and not complete the paper. You need to strike the ideal balance for you, and this can only be found through practice. |

| TSA Sec 1 | TSA Sec 2 | ECAA Sec 1 | ECAA Sec 2 | Examination technique |
|---|---|---|---|---|
| | | | | **Top Tip** *__Underlining__ or __highlighting__ might be helpful with questions with a lot of text. The key to most critical-thinking questions is to find the __conclusion__, so highlighting this once you've found it is useful.* <br><br> Make sure you've read the question before you read the text, or before you scout through a large table for the relevant data. This way you know precisely what you're looking for and are more likely to spot the relevant information faster. |
| | ✓ | | ✓ | **Topic sentences (essays)** <br> When writing, don't go off on a tangent. Your time is precious and every sentence counts. For each paragraph, include a clear topic sentence. This is a sentence at the beginning of the paragraph that sets out what the paragraph is going to achieve (e.g. 'The first reason for X is ...', or 'I agree that Y because ...'). When you're writing each sentence, ask yourself whether it supports the topic sentence. If it doesn't, change it, or add a sentence to tie it back. |
| | ✓ | | ✓ | **Connectives (essays)** <br> Make sure your essay forms a cohesive whole, that each new topic sentence follows from the end of the previous paragraph, and that paragraphs representing a counterargument are clearly signposted with a phrase such as 'however' or 'alternatively, it could be argued'. There are points to be won for your communication in the TSA and ECAA, so make sure your essay reads well. |

| TSA Sec | | ECAA Sec | | Examination technique |
|---|---|---|---|---|
| 1 | 2 | 1 | 2 | |
| | ✓ | | ✓ | **Reasoning (essays)**<br>Making the structure of your reasoning clear is a really important part of the TSA and ECAA essays. For example, consider the statement: 'We should ban smoking'. You want to reason clearly, as exemplified here:<br><br>**1.** Banning smoking would decrease cigarette consumption as people are generally law-abiding citizens<br>**2.** This would decrease the rates of lung cancer as smoking directly causes lung cancer<br>**3.** In turn, this would decrease pressure on the NHS (because it treats lung cancer)<br>**4.** Treating lung cancer would alleviate the funding crisis the NHS is undergoing<br>**5.** Alleviating the crisis would make for an NHS able to treat more people quickly and efficiently, because the crisis is slowing down treatment.<br><br>Not everyone thinks we should ban smoking, but nearly everyone wants a more effective health service. Yet from the initial claim, we provided one clear chain of reasoning that could show why banning smoking would achieve precisely that. Notice too, for each of the five points, there's a 'because', an 'as', or an equivalent. In all, this is a well-justified reason for banning smoking (although not conclusive—there could be other reasons against).<br><br>Everything you say should be both justified and linked to the rest of your argument. This makes your writing more powerful, concise and easy to follow because you won't include irrelevant points.<br><br>In the ECAA, you should also include both economic theory and knowledge from wider reading where possible, but make sure you link both to the extract given. |

| TSA Sec | | ECAA Sec | | Examination technique |
|---|---|---|---|---|
| 1 | 2 | 1 | 2 | |
| | ✓ | | | **Picking which TSA essay to write**<br>In the TSA, you have a choice of essay questions, and choosing the right one is vital. If you're knowledgeable about a topic it can help you understand why that topic is so contentious and what the key points are. There's often a broad selection of questions, making it more likely that you'll have more traction with a few in particular. There's no right way to pick a question, but do choose the one you can clearly see the key arguments for. It may be that you're:<br><br>■ Familiar with the debate<br>■ Familiar with a similar debate<br>■ Knowledgeable about the topic<br><br>Or that you've written a similar essay before. |
| | ✓ | | | **Balanced argument (TSA essay)**<br>The tutors want to see you present a balanced argument that includes paragraphs for and against the topic. A good example of how your TSA essay should be structured is:<br><br>**1.** Introduction<br>**2.** Paragraph against<br>**3.** Paragraph for<br>**4.** Paragraph against<br>**5.** Paragraph for<br>**6.** Paragraph against<br>**7.** Paragraph for<br>**8.** Conclusion.<br><br>Obviously, the number of paragraphs is dictated by how much time you have, but 6–8 is a good number to aim for. |

| TSA Sec | | ECAA Sec | | Examination technique |
|---|---|---|---|---|
| 1 | 2 | 1 | 2 | |
| | | | | Although your argument must be balanced, in the sense that you consider both sides, your essay needs an overall direction. In your introduction and conclusion, you want to show which side of the argument you believe is stronger. Make sure you use counterarguments effectively to weaken the arguments against your eventual conclusion. |

## 28.5: An example TSA essay

To really show you how to ace Section 2 of the TSA, here's an example TSA plan and essay written by an Oxford PPE student. It shows you how to make a brief, structured plan to get enough points for and against your argument into a short essay. Remember: you only have about 30 minutes to write it!

Many of the lessons from this example also apply to the ECAA essay—except that the question in the ECAA will relate to an extended prompt, such as a passage or a set of data. We won't reproduce that here due to the length of the extract required, but you can find more in our online ECAA resources.

### Question

**'Is a referendum a good way to decide a major question facing a country?'**

### Plan

**Conclusion:** Referenda aren't good for deciding major questions

1. **Against conclusion:** More democratic (more people, bypass local representatives, fewer wasted votes, votes better represent population). *Example: Brexit*
2. **For conclusion:** Less democratic (democratic process as an end, yes/no vote of a referendum makes it harder to achieve said end). *Example: Brexit*

3. **Against conclusion:** Greater engagement (more people knowing their vote matters, getting involved, educated population). *Example: Scottish independence referendum*
4. **For conclusion:** Entrenchment (political circumstances and public will change, democratic element of referenda entrench them, becomes counterproductive). *Example: Brexit*

## Essay

**Intro**

Referenda are a poor way of making major decisions as they entrench policies that may go against the ends to which people voted for the policy in the first place. A referendum is a binary 'yes/no' vote decided on by the general population. Referenda can indeed be said to be more democratic and encourage participation. Yet this very strength means people prioritise the unnuanced referendum result above the end voters set out to achieve.

**Argument against conclusion:**

An argument often presented is that referenda are more democratic than decisions made by representatives. Referenda are sent out to the electorate directly, bypassing their local MP. As an MP could vote against a policy their constituent supports, this bypassing means the will of a constituent is always demonstrated. Therefore, a 52% "Leave" vote in the Brexit referendum represented a definite majority. In contrast, under representative democracy, the vote of an MP does not represent the will of everyone in their constituency, so a 52% vote in the House of Commons is not always representative of the will of the majority of voters. As a referendum is a more accurate representation of voter interests, it's more democratic.

**Argument for conclusion:**

However, democracy aims to let people live in a society they want to. Individuals vote on decisions to achieve this end. Therefore, more important than whether the decision is made is whether this end is met, which necessitates nuance and considering multiple options. A yes/no vote neglects other options that may better achieve said end because you are bound to this result, and leads to decisions that are ambiguous and equally fail to meet said end. For example, some voters both for and against Brexit acted in the belief that their choice would lead to better economic growth. It may be the case that optimal economic growth arises out of a settlement that is neither Brexit nor the status quo, or out of some but not all forms of Brexit, depending on the specific negotiations. Yet there were only two options in the referendum question, and there's still no more clarity on what Brexit looks like. So, a referendum narrows the options for people to choose the society they want, making it less democratic.

**Argument against conclusion:**
Another argument often presented is that referenda increase participation, which is more democratic. For the aforementioned reasons, fewer votes are wasted and the overall result is a direct reflection of popular will. As people know this, there's a greater incentive to vote in the first place. As there's a greater incentive to vote, there's a greater incentive to campaign, be educated on the issue, and get involved with politics. In the 2014 Scottish independence referendum, turnout was over 85%, with an unusually high degree of youth involvement. Not only does this directly mean more people's views are represented, but it improves the quality of decision-making by reflecting more people's opinions. As a result, not only is it more directly democratic, but it leads to better outcomes through higher quality decision-making, which can be said to be an aim of democracy.

**Argument for conclusion:**
Though true, the portrayal of referenda as far more democratic makes them far more entrenched than decisions passed under a representative vote. This is to say that, even if there's a change in public opinion or political circumstances, it's difficult for politicians to adopt any policy other than the referendum result. For example, if it becomes clear in the future that Brexit is unlikely to result in optimal economic growth, the democratic aura of the referendum would make any reversal of Article 50 nigh impossible, even though people who voted "Leave" to improve economic growth would prefer that. As referenda offer a binary yes/no choice, the increase in the quality of decision-making is minimal, whereas political circumstances and the public will change frequently, so it's not unlikely that entrenchment leads to policies that a majority of voters oppose. Therefore, referenda are a poor way of making major decisions.

**Conclusion:**
In conclusion, democracy and democratic processes have to be understood as a means to an end and, on average, referenda actively make it harder for this end to be met. The apparent benefits of referenda are counterproductive if they make it less likely that people will end up with the outcome they want. So, on balance, referenda aren't a good way to decide major questions.

You can see how this candidate presents a balanced argument in the sense of examining arguments for and against, but in the conclusion they explain why they think the arguments for their position are stronger than the arguments against.

# Chapter 29: Interviews

## 29.1: What will your interviews be like?

### Will your interviews cover things you haven't studied?

There's variety in how much economics each student will have studied by the time of their interview. Some may have studied a little A-Level Economics, some the whole course, and others none at all. The interviewers will gauge how much you've studied and tailor your interview accordingly. They won't ask unnecessarily complex questions on things you haven't studied. Any new concepts they expect you to work with will be presented and explained.

If you haven't studied Economics at A Level, your economics interviews shouldn't include much technical economic theory. However, you'll be expected to have a grasp of the basic concepts of economics, so you may be asked questions such as:

- Is it possible to measure GDP?
- Should fines be proportionate to the offender's income?
- Is the game Monopoly anything like real life?

Besides GDP (gross domestic product), some other concepts you might want to ensure you're familiar with are:

- Inflation
- Taxation
- Interest rates.

> *"At the beginning of my Economics interview, I was given a piece of card with lots of data and information about a coffee seller on it. I had to analyse it and use different equations to calculate certain things about the economics of their business during my interview."* –Leah, PPE, Oxford

## How many interviews will you have?

At Cambridge, you're likely to be invited to a full day of interviews in which you'll have up to two interviews focused on economics. You may also have a general interview, in which you might be asked questions such as 'Why Cambridge?' (or more indirect versions of the same, like 'Why should we offer you a place and not the next candidate?') to check that you understand what the course and Cambridge style of teaching will require from you. The 'general' part of your general interview could still end up leading into questions on your subject.

At Oxford, if you're applying to a course that incorporates economics, you're likely to have an interview focusing on economics. However, with a course such as PPE (in which the subjects are closely intertwined) your questions may relate to two subjects at once—your interviews won't necessarily be segregated by subject.

At Oxford, you'll also be interviewed at a second college. You might find the interview style differs between the two colleges.

## Will there be lots of maths in your interviews?

As maths is an essential part of economics, there will likely be a quantitative element to your economics interview. For example, you may need to use calculus (differentiation and integration) to analyse a utility function. If you're asked to use mathematical skills, the maths will likely be put within a context so it's essential you know what each mathematical skill *actually means*, not simply *how to do it*. For example, if $P$ is a production function, $\frac{dP}{dt}$ measures how fast it's increasing or decreasing, but its derivative with respect to the number of workers employed (say, $\frac{dP}{dw}$) measures (or estimates) how much extra would be produced if another worker were employed.

Some colleges might also choose to ask more problem-based questions and brainteasers that may not have just one correct answer—they do this to observe your thought processes and how you engage with the problem. Some examples are:

- Alice, Bob and Charlie are armed with guns and are in a three-way standoff. What might decide who shoots first and who they try to target?
- How many doctors do you think there are in the UK?

- Suppose all taxis in a city are owned by a single firm. How should the firm assign passengers to taxis?
- You and 99 other people each pick a number between 1 and 100. You win a prize if you pick a number no one else picks, but you can't confer. What number do you pick?

## Will the questions be too hard to answer?

### NO!

The interviewers haven't invited you to interview to ask you obscenely hard questions that belong in postgraduate study so they can laugh at your failings and shortcomings. You have been invited to interview so they can gauge how *teachable* and *intellectually curious* you are, so they will present you with questions that you can understand and get stuck into.

In an economics interview, it is possible that you will be introduced to new concepts or complex ideas.

> *"In my interview, I was introduced to the idea of* ***game theory*** *and asked to apply it in a basic form to an auction."* –Mary, Economics, Cambridge

> In a nutshell, **game theory** analyses the behaviour of two or more participants in situations involving rewards or punishments. All the players know the rules of the 'game'[155] and we assume they all act rationally.

However, the interviewers will guide you through understanding any new material and help you when you get stuck. They want to see how engaged and switched on you are, not whether you already know the first-year material!

As in any Oxbridge interview, it's best to talk through as many of your ideas as possible—even if they are sometimes off base. However, don't worry if you need to pause to think for a couple of seconds before speaking.

155 It doesn't have to be an actual game, such as a board game. Game theory can model competition, bargaining, auctions, voting theory and more!

## Joint honours courses at Oxford

**E&M:** For Economics & Management, you'll probably have joint interviews because the two are closely linked—and because management is not a subject you'll have studied already. You may have interview questions solely based on economics, such as: 'How can we measure GDP and how accurate are our methods?', or questions on management such as: 'What differences can you see between management and leadership?'

**PPE:** Although the process is different at every college, for PPE you'll typically have two interviews, and one interview that combines two subjects. For example, you might have a philosophy and politics interview in which you're asked distinct philosophy and politics questions, but also some overlapping ones (possibly focusing on ethics). An example question you might get here is: 'What does it mean to be free?'

**History & Economics:** If you're applying to History and Economics, you'll have separate interviews for each subject, though some questions may touch upon the links between them.

**Did You Know?**

*If you apply for Economics or Land Economy at Cambridge, depending on the college you apply to, you may be asked to submit written work (which has been marked by your teachers) before your interviews. Your interviewers may then discuss your essays with you for part of the interview.*

**Did You Know?**

*Oxford PPE tutors score interviewees on the qualities above using the following scale:*

| Interview Score | Qualitative Grade | Meaning |
|---|---|---|
| *70–100* | *Excellent* | *Scoring this indicates to tutors that you should be given an offer.* |
| *65–69* | *Positive* | *It's hard to get an offer scoring less than this on average.* |

| Interview Score | Qualitative Grade | Meaning |
|---|---|---|
| *60–64* | *Neutral* | *Scoring this in one interview isn't the end of the world; scoring it on average usually isn't good enough.* |
| *50–59* | *Weak* | *Score this and it will count against you.* |
| *0–49* | *Very poor* | *Scoring this indicates to tutors that you aren't suited to an Oxford PPE degree.* |

*"In selecting for PPE we look for evidence that candidates can listen effectively and can present reasoned arguments orally and on paper, that they can understand and analyse text, that they are sufficiently numerate to undertake advanced study of economics, and that they have a high level of self-motivation."* –Mansfield College, Oxford

## 29.2: How to prepare for your economics interviews

Here's a list of top tips to prepare for your Economics interviews:

### 1) Read widely on the subject Passion Potential

All the books recommended on the reading lists starting on page 362 are useful preparation for interviews. The best way to get a grasp of economics is to read around the subject and explore key concepts. This will improve your ability to answer questions because you'll have a wider understanding of the subject, and you may also get asked questions about what you have been reading recently.

Another way to use reading to prepare for your interviews is to practise vocalising the concepts you learn. For example, if you read an informative chapter in a book about supply and demand, try to summarise the points and explain them to someone. Ask them to ask you follow-up questions to test your understanding.

## 2) Read the news Passion Potential

You may also be asked questions inspired by current economic news, so ensuring you're up-to-date is important. Many newspapers and news websites have a business section, and some have a long-read section covering current affairs and important political and social issues in depth (including economics). More specialised sources of economic news, like The Economist and the Financial Times, will also be worth looking at.

**Top Tip**

*To practise discussing topical issues, why not form a* ***reading group*** *with some friends? Agree to read particular magazines or papers and get together to argue (constructively) over the most important topics. It's especially useful to be able to source contrasting views on the same issue from at least two publications, so you can see how both sides are presented. The Week magazine tends to offer opposing views on current issues too.*

## 3) A mock interview Ability Passion Potential

If you can find someone to give you a mock interview, this is really useful preparation. It's difficult to clearly vocalise your thoughts and practice is key! Even if you don't have a teacher who specialises in economics, you can find lots of economics interview questions starting on on page 413, as well as online, and simply asking your friends or parents to pose some and debate the answers with you will start to make you more comfortable with the demands of an academic interview.

It's great practice to attempt as many economics interview questions as possible. This will give you an indication of the areas that tutors tend to focus on and the concepts to familiarise yourself with before your interviews.

*"I compiled a long list of all the questions I thought they could ask. Even though you'll inevitably be asked something you haven't prepared, it helped my confidence to know that I'd prepared as thoroughly as possible!"* –Helen Lily, E&M, Oxford

## 4) Review your personal statement

Your personal statement is the only information interviewers have about your interests. It will give them an idea of the parts of economics that interest you and what you have done to explore this interest. Therefore, some of the questions they give you may follow on from things mentioned in your personal statement. Make sure you can answer questions on every sentence of your personal statement. Read through it out loud, elaborating on every point, to ensure you're fully comfortable talking about all of it.

## 5) Graph reading Ability

In your interviews you may be given a graph that represents the changes in some sort of economic variable. If you haven't done Maths A Level (it's not a compulsory prerequisite for all the Oxford courses), you may not have had recent practice interpreting graphs. Look over some graphs that show economic trends and try to analyse them. Some good places to look for economic graphs are the websites of the UK Office of National Statistics and World Bank Open Data.[156] Make sure you're familiar with details such as:

- For supply and demand graphs, the independent variable goes on the vertical axis and dependent variable goes on this horizontal axis (opposite to maths graphs, and some other types of economics graphs)
- If the independent variable is time, you *might* be able to ignore the quadrants where it's negative
- You may need to estimate the gradient of the graph rather than measure or calculate it.

To practise graph reading, ask yourself questions such as:

- Why are the peaks and troughs where they are?
- What does the gradient represent, how is the gradient changing and why?
- Can you predict what is likely to happen to the dependent variable as the independent variable continues to increase/decrease?

**Top Tip**

***Supply and demand graphs** are a staple of Oxbridge economics interviews. Make sure you're familiar with reading, analysing and them—it's not unlikely you'll get a question on one.*

156 See oxbridgeformula.co.uk/bonus-chapter for more info.

> *"For the Economics interview, candidates were given a brief pre-interview reading related to topics in game theory or broader economic principles, and were asked to work through the problem logically and quantitatively during the interview. For the Management interview, candidates were set a brief pre-interview reading from a broadsheet that assessed interest in Management and the ability to identify and discuss issues from a general management perspective.*
>
> *Most candidates were reasonably well-prepared for the interviews and were able to discuss both management and economics topics knowledgeably and fluently. Good candidates were able to revise their arguments to take account of new information, to provide examples and counter-arguments and to defend their conclusions. Weaker candidates did not display an ability to analyse businesses and organisations from a managerial perspective (nor a sufficiently keen interest in doing so), or they performed poorly in general quantitative analysis and reasoning."*
>
> –Merton College, Oxford

# 29.3: A script of an Oxbridge economics interview

To give you a feel for an economics interview, here are three model interview dialogues. Read through each one, noting the interaction between the student and the tutor, how the student asks for clarification and takes on board the advice and hints of the tutor.

## Economics interview question 1 (Inflation)

Tutor: To begin, please could you explain in a sentence or two what the CPI is?

Sometimes the interviewer will start by asking you for a relatively simple definition or explanation, to get you comfortable and motivate further questions.

### Model interview

**Student:** It's the Consumer Price Index, a measure of inflation. It starts with a survey of what goods and services households buy and how much of their income they spend on them. This is used to construct a 'basket' of the most commonly consumed items. A second survey records their prices. From these, a weighted price index is created.

**Tutor:** Great, thanks. Now for a more involved question. In the UK, the target rate of inflation is 2%. Why isn't it 0%, or 10%?

**Student:** (*Pauses*) The reason it isn't 0% and the reason it isn't 10% will be different, so I think I should answer them separately.

Laying out a plan for approaching the question is a good way to show you understand it and simultaneously collect and order your thoughts.

**Tutor:** That seems like a sensible approach.

**Student:** So, why not target a rate of inflation greater than 2%? Hmm... Well, if people's incomes don't rise at the same rate as prices, it's as if they're actually earning less. Some people who receive fixed incomes, such as pensioners, would really suffer under rapid inflation.

**Tutor:** That's true. Who else loses out under a high inflation rate?

**Student:** (*Thinks.*) People who have savings.

**Tutor:** Please explain?

**Student:** I suppose any savings held would buy less. Suppose that I put £100 in a bank account today and want to withdraw it tomorrow—for example, to buy cheese. The price of a wheel of cheese today is £10. So, I can buy 10 wheels of cheese today. Overnight, there's inflation at a rate of 100%. A wheel of cheese now costs £20. I can only afford 5 of them. So I'm worse off.

Numerical examples are generally helpful because they demonstrate mathematical competence and clarify your meaning.

**Tutor:** And who gains from inflation?

**Student:** Mostly those who are in debt. If I have taken out a mortgage on a house of, say, £100,000, as prices rise I effectively owe less. If annual inflation is 100%, £1 at the beginning of the year will be worth 50p at the end of the year. So my mortgage will essentially have fallen to £50,000 and it'll be easier to repay. (*Thinks.*) Well, that's assuming my income increases at least as fast as the inflation rate.

Again, elaborating on the answer with a numerical demonstration.

**Tutor:** Right. And why might we not want to redistribute wealth from savers to borrowers?

**Student:** I guess because it disincentivises saving, and you'd need to know more about the economic climate to say whether you want to encourage people to save or to spend.

**Tutor:** Can you think of any other reasons?

**Student:** (*Pauses.*) A large portion of savers are older people. As they retire, they depend on maintaining the value of their savings. So penalising them would be unethical.

**Tutor:** And what about the reasons for avoiding inflation below 2%?

**Student:** Well, I know the reasons for avoiding inflation below 0%.

> Addressing only a part or aspect of the question is much better than holding back because you don't know the full answer.

**Tutor:** Go on.

**Student:** The deflation trap. If there's deflation during a recession, it disincentives people from spending. Also, we try to end the recession by lowering the real interest rate, which stimulates consumption and investment. But if deflation happens, it means you can buy more with your money, but the cost of your debt also goes up, which makes the recession worse because companies don't want to invest. And that causes the inflation rate to fall further, so it leads to a vicious cycle. So having deflation in the first place is risky, even if it doesn't lead to a massive recession straight away.

**Tutor:** And what's a reason not to have inflation at 0%?

**Student:** Perhaps so we don't accidentally fall into deflation? There will always be random movements in prices.

**Tutor:** That's true, but there are other reasons too. For instance, do you know of a connection between inflation and sticky wages?

**Student:** (*Pause.*) <u>I don't think so, but I know the idea of sticky wages is that wages don't always change in the same way as other prices.</u> For instance, it can be hard to reduce nominal wages for personal or social reasons, even if there's less demand for labour.

> Again, say what you *do* know about a topic, even if you don't have an answer to the question. But make sure it really is relevant—don't waffle or pretend to know more than you do.

**Tutor:** What does that mean if unemployment increases?

**Student:** Well, that is a drop in demand for labour. If wages can't decrease, that means labour is still too expensive in some sense, so there will be more unemployment than if wages could decrease instead.

**Tutor:** And what effect does inflation have?

**Student:** Is this like the case of people on fixed incomes?

**Tutor:** In what way?

**Student:** If wages are sticky, it can be like they're fixed, so the workers would suffer under high inflation as pensioners would.

**Tutor:** That's true if inflation is too high, though we hope it won't be so high if unemployment is high too. But we're thinking about the difference between 0% inflation and small positive inflation. If there's any positive inflation, are the wages truly fixed?

Don't worry if the tutor has to prompt you a few times before you give a completely satisfactory answer—that's expected, as they ask questions that will test how you react to new ideas and arguments.

**Student:** I suppose in real terms they're falling. Does that mean it will prevent unemployment from being as high as if they were fixed in real terms?

**Tutor:** Yes—it will help prevent very high unemployment.

**Student:** It's at the expense of the people who do end up unemployed, though, because they'll rely on saving or benefits, which aren't likely to rise at the rate of inflation.

Don't be afraid to point out what you think are further aspects or consequences of the phenomenon you're discussing—it demonstrates your interest and curiosity.

**Tutor:** Yes, exactly. Unfortunately, there is a trade-off. One more thing: we've argued inflation shouldn't be 0% or negative, but it seems 1% would be okay. So why is the *target* 2%?

**Student:** Is it the issue of random movements of prices I mentioned before?

**Tutor:** Similar, perhaps. Can we actually know what inflation is?

**Student:** No, we can't record the price of every product. We have proxy measures for it, such as CPI. So is the point that our measures might be inaccurate by more than 1 percentage point, so if our target was 1%, we might still fall into deflation without realising it?

**Tutor:** Yes, exactly. Does CPI tend to overestimate or underestimate inflation?

**Student:** It overestimates it. The weights are fixed for a year, which means that there's a substitution bias. If the price of bananas is rising much faster than the price of apples, for instance, then consumers will buy fewer bananas and more apples. But this behavioural response isn't taken into account in the CPI. So it tends to overstate inflation. So that would give us more reason to want a target above 1% to give us a buffer.

Note how the student not only answers the specific question about CPI, but ties it back to the topic of inflation targets.

**Tutor:** Yes, 2% is safer.

**Student:** It's kind of arbitrary, though.

**Tutor:** You're right, we could always have picked 1.8% or 2.5% instead. But 2% is a nice round number that seems to lead to decent outcomes so far. Let's look at something else...

## Further hints

As a way of 'buying time' to think when first asked the question, you might like to offer a definition of inflation and reason from there.

The student answering the question sees straight away that an effective approach would be to consider separately why the inflation target isn't raised and why it isn't lowered. The interviewer might suggest doing this for another student who was less sure of how best to answer the question.

The interviewer would be happy to introduce concepts such as the deflation trap and sticky wages if you weren't already familiar with them.

## Extending the question

You might be asked why inflation rather than the money supply is targeted. To support your answer, try to draw a diagram depicting the market for money and what happens in it when there are shocks.

The interviewer could also prompt you to consider ways the situation might be more complicated than at first glance. For instance:

- 'How does the relationship between inflation and unemployment depend on the bargaining power of workers? What would change if more workers became self-employed?'
- 'Are all savers harmed equally by high inflation, and do all borrowers benefit equally?'
- 'Is there a difference between the ideal inflation rates for the short term and the long term?'

## What is the question testing?

This question is testing your knowledge of inflation, interest rates and unemployment – some of the most fundamental macroeconomic concepts

– and your ability to relate them to policy. And especially important skill in this context is to be able to talk through the step-by-step details of how a change (e.g. increased or decreased inflation) leads to certain effects.

### Related topics from university

You'll study macroeconomics in multiple courses across your university career, including your first year, even if you're studying a joint degree. Monetary policy, including inflation targets, is typically studied within the IS-PC-MR/AS-AD model.[157]

## Economics interview question 2 (Taxes and Externalities)

**Question: Would you advise the UK government to tax palm oil?**

### Model interview

**Student:** I would. The production of palm oil contributes to deforestation and climate change because growing the palms requires destroying rainforests that would otherwise absorb carbon dioxide.

> Nothing wrong with a definite answer, if it's backed up.

**Tutor:** That's true. How does it relate to the decision of whether or not palm oil ought to be taxed, though?

**Student:** Well, it's a negative externality. The price of palm oil doesn't take into account the costs to third parties of the damage to the environment. The price is determined only by what the buyer and seller want. So too much palm oil is produced, from the point of view of society. Taxing it will reduce the amount produced.

> It's great to define a term you introduce when you introduce it and explain its relevance, rather than wait to be prompted.

**Tutor:** Okay, so we have an example of a negative externality. What would be an example of a positive externality?

**Student:** If a shop spends money on putting up lights at Christmas, then the festive atmosphere for passers-by might encourage them to buy more at neighbouring shops too.

> Most applicants have their interviews in December, so Christmas-themed examples are common(!)

157 Investment Savings, Phillips Curve, Interest Rate-Based Monetary Policy Rule / Aggregate Supply, Aggregate Demand.

**Tutor:** Great, thank you. So, going back a step, how exactly would a tax correct the market failure in the case of palm oil?

**Student:** Would the tax be paid by those people who buy products that use the oil? Or would it be paid by firms who use that oil as an input?

If you're unsure what's intended, ask a question!

**Tutor:** Does it matter?

**Student:** I suppose not. All that matters is the effective incidence, as opposed to the actual incidence. If we tax the producers, it might be that they can raise their prices, so in fact the consumers are still paying a part of the increased cost. And if we tax the buyers so they can afford to buy less palm oil, it might be that the producers have to lower their prices, and then they will be paying part of the cost too.

**Tutor:** That's right. The burden of an indirect tax is shared by the consumer and the producer. But what determines how large a share of the burden each faces?

**Student:** The relative price elasticities.

**Tutor:** Could you define these for me on this whiteboard?

Don't be surprised to be asked to write.

**Student:** Sure. The elasticity of demand is $\frac{\frac{\Delta Q}{Q}}{\frac{\Delta P}{P}}$, where $Q$ is the quantity demanded and $P$ is the price. And the elasticity of supply is similar, but with supply instead of demand. The more elastic demand is relative to supply, the less consumers will shoulder of any sort of sales tax and vice versa.

**Tutor:** So going back to how the tax would correct the market failure...

**Student:** Well, now at the new price, anyone who buys palm oil is paying not only the cost to the producer of growing and harvesting the crop—but also a slice of the marginal additional cost to society of the negative impact on the planet of these activities. So in deciding how much palm oil to use, people are considering the effect on the environment.

**Tutor:** Thank you.

## Further hints

If you aren't sure why palm oil is a relevant target for a new tax, the tutor might ask questions like 'Why might we want people to use less palm oil?'

and 'Are there any important societal costs to producing palm oil?' You could even be given a sheet of information on the economic issues surrounding palm oil to read before you go into the interview.

If you aren't familiar with the concept of the effective incidence of a tax, the tutor might introduce it by asking how palm oil producers might react if they were taxed, and how they might react if their customers were taxed.

In this case, the tutor asks the student for a definition of price elasticity because the student already knows that term, but they could explain it for you if needed.

## Extending the question

Taxes are a common source of questions because they force you to think about the effects on different groups and the benefits and drawbacks of the tax. Some further tax-related questions that could follow this one include:

- What would be the effect of a tax on palm oil on the market for other vegetable oils? What might be the environmental impact of these secondary effects?
- Should we tax causes of poor health, such as foods that are high in sugar?
- What are some possible arguments against taxing palm oil?

## What is the question testing?

This question is assessing the student's understanding of the basic supply and demand model, either from their intuition or formal studies—plus the more advanced concepts of price elasticity, tax incidence and externalities. These are all concepts from microeconomics. If you haven't studied A-Level Economics, the tutor might instead start by explaining some of these concepts to you and ask you to apply them to the case of palm oil.

## Related topics from university

In your first year at Oxford or Cambridge, you'll study microeconomics. You'll start by covering methodology and move on to willingness-to-pay (i.e. demand) and willingness-to-accept (i.e. supply). Later, you'll learn about taxes and subsidies. All of this is quite mathematical, in that you'll be expected to differentiate demand and supply functions and calculate the ***deadweight loss*** of certain policy interventions.

**Deadweight loss** is the total cost to consumers and producers created by a market inefficiency.

## Economics interview question 3 (Monopolies and Optimisation)

**Question: Should a merger between rival firms be prevented from happening?**

### Model interview

**Student:** Hmm... Only if banning the proposed merger would be better in terms of maximising welfare than allowing it to go ahead.

**Tutor:** Would this usually be the case?
**Student:** Yes, I think so.

**Tutor:** Why?
**Student:** Because after merging, the market becomes more monopolistic. So the resulting entity can get away with raising its price by restricting its output.

**Tutor:** Okay, let's consider the case of a duopoly. Do you know what the term 'duopoly' means?
**Student:** I think so. A duopoly is where there are just two firms competing.

**Tutor:** Exactly. Call the firms 1 and 2. Firms 1 and 2 produce homogenous goods, say, hydrochloric acid for use in laboratory experiments. *(Writes definitions and equations.)* Firm 1 produces $q_1$ litres of hydrochloric acid and Firm 2 produces $q_2$ litres, which makes total supply $Q = q_1 + q_2$. Suppose an expression for the price is $P = a - bQ$. Firms 1 and 2 use the same production technology, meaning they have the same constant marginal cost, $c$. They compete on quantity, with neither firm acting as a leader or a follower. Given all this information, could you derive an expression for each firm's price and output before their merger?
**Student:** Gosh... I suppose I can. But I'm not sure where to start, to be honest.

It would be better to be able to find a start, even if it's just asking a relevant question, but the interviewer will sort you out if you don't have a clue. They expect that to happen a couple of times in an interview, so don't panic if it happens to you.

**Tutor:** That's okay. How about considering each firm's objective?
**Student:** Each firm wants to maximise its profit. That suggests that I'm going to need to do some differentiation. But I don't know what I need to differentiate... oh, a function giving the firm's profit!

**Tutor:** Good. What determines a firm's profit?
**Student:** Its revenue less its costs. I know the firm's revenue function: price multiplied by output. So Firm 1's revenue is...

**Tutor:** I'm going to suggest that, because Firm 1 and Firm 2 are identical, you solve the profit maximisation problem you're tackling here for an arbitrary firm, call it Firm $i$. You can refer to the other firm as Firm $j$.
**Student:** Okay, thanks, I'll do that. So Firm $i$'s revenue is: $Pq_i$, and that means its revenue function is $q_i(a - bq_i - bq_j)$, since $P = a - bq_i - bq_j$. Now, to get its profit function I need to subtract its cost function from this... which is $cq_j$, because you've told me that its marginal cost is $c$.

If the tutor suggests some notation or simplification, it doesn't mean you're wrong, they're simply choosing what will make the whole interview run smoothly. Do listen to them, and try to figure out why they might have made that choice.

**Tutor:** Very good.
**Student:** I want to find the maximum point of the function $q_i(a - bq_i - bq_j) - cq_j$, so I differentiate it with respect to $q_i$. Right... so, the derivative I've found is this, $a - 2bq_i - bq_j - c$, which I want to set to 0. I'm a bit stuck now though. How does this help me work out the price and output of Firms 1 and 2?

Note we're assuming $q_1$ and $q_2$ are independent, or else there would be a term involving $\frac{dq_j}{dq_i}$. Independence is a very good approximation over short timescales, as the firms can't respond to each other's prices immediately, so it's what we use here as each firm is trying to optimise its profit *right now*.

**Tutor:** Well, you've got *one* equation...
**Student:** Okay, so I can do the same for the other firm. And I have two simultaneous equations. If I start from the beginning... No, actually, I can swap the $i$ and $j$ in $a - 2bq_i - bq_j - c = 0$ to get $a - 2bq_j - bq_i - c = 0$, because that's the same as taking the point of view of the other firm.

Always be on the lookout for symmetries.

**Tutor:** Yes, fantastic.
**Student:** So I can multiply the second equation by 2 and subtract it from the first...

Try to narrate what you're doing as much as possible.

That gives me $q_i = q_j = \frac{a-c}{3b}$...

And I get $P = a - b(\frac{2(a-c)}{3b})$, which is $\frac{a+2c}{3}$.

**Tutor:** Thanks, that was the tricky bit. If the firms now merge, what will the price of their product be, and how much of it will be produced?

**Student:** Well, now there's only one firm, which is a monopoly.

**Tutor:** Yes. What is the monopoly trying to do?

**Student:** Maximise its profit.

**Tutor:** So...

**Student:** So the monopoly wants to find the maximum point of the function... $(a - bQ)Q - cQ$.
That's the same as $-bQ^2 + (a - c)Q$, and I can see completing the square (does some working) will give me $Q = \frac{a-c}{2b}$ for the maximum. <u>That's less than before</u>: because each half is now only supplying $\frac{a-c}{4b}$ as opposed to $\frac{a-c}{3b}$.

Don't stop when you get an answer—explain what it means for the question.

**Tutor:** And what will the price be?

**Student:** Um... the level of output makes the price $a - b(\frac{a-c}{2b})$, which simplifies to $\frac{a+c}{2}$. I don't know if that's more than before.

**Tutor:** It will be if $c$ is small enough. Let's assume it is. What can we conclude about the impact of the merger?

**Student:** Well it will definitely make consumers worse off. They're now paying a higher price and enjoying less of the product.

**Tutor:** Precisely. Now you mentioned that there might be exceptional cases where a merger doesn't have this impact. Can you say a bit more about what these might be?

It's common for a question to go from quantitative to qualitative, or vice versa, to test a range of skills.

**Student:** Sure. If one of the firms involved in the merger is much more efficient than the other. Post-merger, the cost of production falls. That makes it likely that the price charged to consumers will fall and that output will be stepped up in light of increased demand at the lower price.

**Tutor:** And are there any other circumstances under which a merger might benefit consumers?

**Student:** Mmm... I can't think of any, no.

**Tutor:** Well what about if Firm 1 makes engines for cars and Firm 2 makes car bodies? And each of these firms is a monopoly?

**Student:** Ah... that's a vertical monopoly, rather than a horizontal one. I think this would be similar to the efficiency case, in that costs will fall.

**Tutor:** Why?

**Student:** Because now the firm making car engines isn't selling them at a mark-up to the firm that makes the bodies. So the consumer no longer faces a double mark-up.

**Tutor:** Thank you, that's all.

## Further hints

This is a tricky technical question, but for students who don't have a mathematical background, more help would be given with the derivation.

Even without a maths background, you could start by saying the monopolist's supply curve is above/to the left of that of a firm facing competition and explain the consequences for the consumer. You won't have shown why it shifts, or by how much, but the interviewer can lead you through that more gently, or move onto something else.

## Extending the question

The interviewer could ask a more qualitative question next, to test a range of skills. For instance, 'Is there an optimal number of firms to have in a market?'

If they want to keep testing your technical skills, perhaps because you were already very comfortable with the maths in this question, they might change some details and ask you what follows. For instance:

- In the duopoly case, how would the impact of the merger differ if the firms in it compete on price, not quantity?
- In the duopoly case, what would happen if Firm 1 sets its output and, after observing this, Firm 2 sets its output?
- What happens when two firms merge to create a monopsony?

### What is the question testing?

It's important for economists to also be good mathematicians. Much of what is taught in the economics courses at Oxbridge relies on students being able to do calculus and work with matrices and sets of simultaneous equations.

This question is also testing your ability to carry out calculations that are new to you, since you're unlikely to have done this type of optimisation before.

### Related topics from university

The maths in the question is similar to that expected in answering a question on duopoly from a problem sheet or first-year exam paper. Duopolies are the simplest possible model of competition, so studying them allows you to develop techniques and intuition that can later be applied to larger markets.

A few different models of duopoly are covered at first-year level: Cournot, Bertrand and Stackelberg.

## 29.4: Example interview question for students without A-Level Economics

If you haven't studied Economics at school, and especially if you're applying for an Oxford joint course, you could be asked a more conceptual question that doesn't rely on any particular background knowledge. Here's an example of such an interview with a student who shows potential for studying economics at university.

**Question: Does anything have no value?**

### Model interview

**Student:** I suppose something intangible such as happiness? Seeing as how we use 'cost' as a shorthand for 'value', it makes sense it would have no value.

**Tutor:** Can't people purchase things that give them happiness?

In answering these conceptual questions, you need to come up with ideas, but give a reason when you do, as this student does.

**Student:** Yeah I suppose they can. Strictly speaking, it's whatever they're purchasing that has value, but I suppose it only derives its value from its ability to generate happiness. So yeah, happiness does have value.

You'll also often have to revise your ideas! But see how the student explains exactly why and how they are changing their mind.

**Tutor:** So what does it mean for something to have value? And does that help us figure out if anything has *no* value?

**Student:** Well, having value is being considered in some positive regard. That means intangibility isn't the right criterion to use. And it's not about price either, because even if something is priceless, is that really different from having infinite value? I suppose the only things that can have no value are truly worthless things.

**Tutor:** Such as?

**Student:** Air? Even then that's untrue, there's a sense in which any finite object has value. Yeah, I'd argue that nothing truly has no value.

**Tutor:** Let's go back to happiness. Some countries, in response to growing criticisms over GDP, have introduced the measure of 'Gross National Happiness'. Do you think this could ever be a good measure?

The interviewer might go off on a tangent to test how you think about different types of problems.

**Student:** Does that mean as an alternative to GDP, or in itself?

The question you get might deliberately be ambiguous, to require you to think about the different possible interpretations. Asking which interpretation to answer is a good response.

**Tutor:** Let's say as an alternative to GDP.

**Student:** It depends on the criteria for being a good measure. It would probably be inaccurate in the sense of capturing the things that GDP directly captures, such as production, because people's personal sense of contentment is only loosely connected to their wealth. Various other factors such as family, the news, the weather and political turmoil would all affect it. However, those are all quantifiable things that GDP doesn't capture. Considering that GDP is also used as a measure of wellbeing, it seems it's missing a bunch of relevant factors, so in that respect it's not as good a measure.

**Tutor:** Okay, let's talk a little bit more about value now. What explains the difference between the value of a house and the value of a tomato?

**Student:** There would be both supply-side and demand-side explanations. Supply-side, houses obviously cost a lot more to build due to scale, workers involved, raw material costs, etc. Demand-side factors would include advertising, how necessary the product is, the price of similar goods and so on. Part of the reason houses cost more could be that houses are a more essential need than tomatoes.

A PPE student says: *"What I missed at first in a similar question was the use of the word 'value' over 'price', which was probably the point the tutor was getting at."* Always watch out for the language used in interview questions!

**Tutor:** Do you think that this price difference means a house is always more valuable than a tomato?

**Student:** Ah, okay. I do think the price is a good measure of how valuable having a particular item is to people who are buying it, but looking at the relative price differences within a market is a limited perspective because it doesn't explain relative prices between different markets.

**Tutor:** So, what does the price in a particular market tell you?

**Student:** I think the supply-side factors will contribute to the difference between the prices, but demand explains more of the difference between markets. And that means a house isn't always more valuable than a tomato, because it's the demand that corresponds to how much people value something. It's like how designer clothes cost a lot more than the cheapest clothes, and that reflects how they're more valuable, but they aren't necessarily much more expensive to make.

Making a clear argument and providing an example. The tutor could pick at the student's position in various ways, but that doesn't mean it's wrong to have a clear position in the first place—just the opposite!

**Tutor:** Okay, let's leave that question there.

# 29.5: More examples of economics interview questions

## Examples of short economics interview questions

Here are some examples of questions that might be used to start an interview and introduce a longer question:

- Is income inequality compatible with perfect social mobility?
- No one wants to be seen buying the cheapest option on the menu. What does that mean for the quality of the second cheapest option?
- When would a demand curve slope up? When would a supply curve slope down?
- Why hasn't the Asian Tiger experience been seen in other regions?
- Would you rather have £1m now, or £50k per year for the rest of your life?
- If Adam Smith arrived in the present, could he tell who was rich?
- Here's a graph of unemployment and GDP for the UK over the last 100 years. Can you discuss some features you think are important?

As with the last example in the list, it's common to be given a source to respond to in your interview. This source might also be a passage of text.

## Examples of maths questions for economists

Short, mathematical questions might be asked as standalones, or there might be a more qualitative follow-up question too. Some example maths questions are:

- Suppose my factory has one input $x \geq 1$ and output $f(x)$, which is a concave increasing function with $f(1) = 0$. Show the output per unit input is maximised when it's equal to $f'(x)$. Prove it both algebraically and graphically, and explain the meaning of its maximum value in an economic context.
- What could go wrong with a voting system in which voters rated all the candidates in an election out of 10 and the highest average rating won?
- I place 3 bets of £1 at 3:1 odds, but the actual chance of each paying out is 1 in 3. What's my expected profit?

You might also be given one or more very short maths problems to test key skills (e.g. applying percentages and re-arranging formulae).

## Examples of Land Economy interview questions

You might get some questions that reflect on law and the natural and built environments. In general, no specific background knowledge is required, unless the question is related to something you've mentioned reading about in your personal statement, or which you've been given a passage about before the interview.

Some example questions are:

- What causes cities to grow? Should a city seek to grow?
- In spite of China's economic growth in recent decades, its rural areas haven't seen as much development as its cities. Do you think that was inevitable?
- Should development of private land ever be subsidised by the government?
- Should I be able to build anything I like on my own property?
- What responsibilities should come with owning farmland?
- Who is going to pay for tackling climate change (or not tackling it, as the case may be)?

## Examples of management questions (also of interest to other economists)

If you're applying for Economics & Management you might get some management-themed questions, though they won't rely on you having studied management previously. They will tend to be less quantitative than other economics questions and focus on decision-making, strategy and finance in the context of large organisations. Example questions include:

- If all workers in a factory were replaced by robots, what else might change? What if the managers were replaced by robots instead?
- Should there be quotas for the number of women in management roles at large companies? How about quotas by age? Race? Political affiliation?
- In an age of globalisation, what determines where a company builds its factory?
- Can you always put a number on risk? How should you proceed if you can't?
- Is good leadership the same in every organisation? Who is the best fictional leader you know?
- What is it immoral to do as a CEO, but not as a private person? What is it moral to do as a CEO, but not as a private person?
- How would you estimate how much this college is worth? Could the richest Oxford college buy the smallest one? Should it want to?

## Examples of economic history questions (also of interest to other economists)

If you're applying for History & Economics, you may or may not get a question related to the overlap between the two subjects. It's more likely you will if you mention something on your personal statement that is related to both, such as the Industrial Revolution (this also applies if you're applying for other degrees too).

The interviewers won't expect you to know about every period of history. Either the question will be related to something you've studied, or the interviewers will deliberately expose you to something new and see how you approach it, but with the understanding that you won't have background knowledge to draw on.

Some examples of economic questions in a historical context include:

- What can you tell me about the start of the first Industrial Revolution in the UK (or a country of your choice)? What do you think would be a good way of defining the start and end points? Why wasn't the Industrial Revolution in the UK centred on London?
- Did fascism and communism in Europe decline for economic reasons? When they were more successful, was that for economic reasons?
- If Germany had imposed mandatory vegetarianism for its people during World War I, how might the outcome of the war have differed?
- Who benefited most and least from economic growth in the 20th century? Before that?
- How would you determine the rate of inflation in a pre-modern society?
- What could I *not* learn about someone if I could only see records of what they bought, sold and owned?
- Here's a picture of a platform at Liverpool Street station from 1890. What does it tell you about the society and economy of the time? What does it not tell you?

Regarding this last example, sources are even more common in History interviews than Economics ones, and you'll need to think about how they came to exist and how they might need to be treated with caution (more so than in an Economics interview). HAT past papers are a good source of relevant practice for thinking about sources like these.

## 29.6: A script of an Oxbridge politics interview

Here's an example of a question that you may receive in a politics interview, to help you out if you're applying for PPE. See page 452 for a script of an Oxbridge philosophy interview.

## Question

**Is there a clear way to distinguish democracies from non-democracies?**

### Model interview

**Student:** No, I don't think that there is. For there to be a 'clear' distinction between democracies and non-democracies, it must be uncontroversial which countries belong to which category. I don't think that this is the case for every country in the world. Some, such as Iran, have elections, but an important part of the government still isn't elected.

Always try to illustrate with examples, but be ready to critique them.

**Tutor:** So you take holding elections to be characteristic of democracies?

**Student:** Yes. Because the word 'democracy' refers to a system of government for a state in which every citizen participates. And this can't be the case if the government is determined by only a few citizens.

**Tutor:** Okay. Can the elections be held in any old way?

**Student:** What do you mean?

**Tutor:** Well, what about if a country held elections, but only candidates recommended by the ruling party could stand in them? Would this country be democratic?

**Student:** No. Elections can be democratic, but they can also be non-democratic. So merely having leaders chosen in an election doesn't make a country a democracy.

**Tutor:** What do you think does make a country democratic?

**Student:** How about this: not only having elections, but having elections in which anyone can be a candidate?

Having to revise your position multiple times is completely normal. The tutor wouldn't ask this question if it was completely straightforward!

**Tutor:** Okay. But imagine a country, where elections involving many candidates have taken place. But the current government tips the contents of the ballot box into an industrial shredder and declares that its candidates have won. Is this country democratic?

**Student:** No. So, elections have to be held, multiple candidates have to stand in them, and votes have to be counted accurately.

**Tutor:** What about if after the votes are counted accurately, the military occupies the government offices and refuse to leave?

**Student:** Again, this would prevent that country from being categorised as a democracy. The outcome of an election must be respected, and the election itself must be conducted freely and fairly.

**Tutor:** How might a system dividing countries into democracies and non-democracies measure whether or not the outcome of an election is respected?

**Student:** I guess whether or not the party that has been elected would be allowed to take power.

**Tutor:** In other words, the turnover test. Can you suggest a case in which this might not be a good measure?

**Student:** I can't see why it wouldn't be, to be honest. If you can change the leaders through an election, that seems to be enough to count as a democracy to me, and, if you can't, it shouldn't count.

**Tutor:** Could it ever be unclear whether the winning party would be allowed to take power?

Look out for conditional or causal statements—they are often a source of potential problems.

**Student:** I suppose if you don't know whether to trust the ruling party?

**Tutor:** Very good. Suppose a country holds elections, but only one party has ever been in power—either because it's a new democracy, or because they're just very popular. Can we rely on the turnover test then?

**Student:** I suppose if power has never changed hands before, we don't know whether the current rulers will actually give it up if they don't like the result. So for a period of time, it runs like a democracy in terms of having elections, but it might not be. Maybe if they actually do hand over power, that retroactively means it was a democracy before...

**Tutor:** Maybe so. Do you know of any real-life cases where this has happened?

**Student:** *(Pauses.)* I'm afraid not.

**Tutor:** Japan used to be such a case. The Liberal Party won the first elections in 1952, and its successors were continuously in power until 1993. But Japan was no less democratic in 1992 than it was in 1993 after the government changed hands. Today, Botswana is an example of this. Since Botswana's independence in 1966, its Democratic Party has never lost an election. Some political scientists argue that it's unfair to classify Botswana as a non-democracy simply because of this. Would you agree with them?

**Student:** Yes, because even though I'm no expert about Botswana, I do know that nobody is excluded from voicing their political opinions.

**Tutor:** Nobody?

**Student:** As far as I'm aware.

Be prepared to have to defend an overly strong claim.

**Tutor:** What about the UK? Would you consider everyone there able to express their preferences over candidates in elections?

**Student:** Yes. Nobody is excluded from voting on the basis of gender, or race, or whatever else.

**Tutor:** But can 16-year-olds vote?

**Student:** No, only people over the age of 18 can vote.

**Tutor:** So, some citizens are excluded after all. What other groups of people are excluded?

**Student:** Prisoners, and those from overseas who lack citizenship.

**Tutor:** So is the UK clearly a democracy?

**Student:** I think it's pretty close to the democratic ideal, but there are a few imperfections, in that there are certain individuals who should be given the right to vote yet aren't.

**Tutor:** Do any countries reach this democratic ideal?

**Student:** Maybe in future. But not yet.

**Tutor:** Ok, thank you. Let's move on.

## Further hints

At the beginning, the tutor might prompt you for a few examples of democracies, non-democracies, and edge cases. For instance, you might also think about countries that are transitioning to democracy, or elected governments that become autocratic.

When you're analysing the turnover test, the tutor could give more hints about why it might not give a determinate answer. For instance: 'Isn't there a difference between what *should* legally happen after an election and what actually *does* happen?'

## Extending the question

The interviewer might ask the student to consider such things as:

- The best way to ensure that elections are conducted freely and fairly
- Whether every country is either democratic or non-democratic, or whether democracy admits of degrees
- Whether democracy is best understood on a 'thin' conception or on a 'thick' conception (where thick conceptions include having things such as liberal values, as well as simply whether and how elections are held)
- Whether a country that has corruption, poor regulation of campaign finance and occasional abuses of human rights can be considered democratic (think of the implications for countries, including the UK, that are generally seen as democratic if these conditions are made very strict)
- Whether the capacity of the government to enforce the law affects a country's claim to be a democracy.

## What is the question testing?

This question is testing several things: an ability to create and test definitions, an awareness of general political trends across the world, and the skills of constructing and undermining arguments.

## Related topics from university

You'll likely study ways of defining and measuring democracy in the Practice of Politics course in your first year of PPE.

# Part III C: Before Your Degree

# Chapter 30:
# A packing list of skills to bring from school to your degree

Many of the skills you learnt at school will be transferable (and essential) to a degree involving economics, so you don't want to lose them over the summer:

- ☐ **Maths**

  Maths is an essential part of economics, so make sure your A-Level Maths is up to scratch.

  The types of maths that are essential to degree-level economics include differentiation and integration, probability, statistics, sequences and systems of equations. All of these skills will be introduced and taught at university level, but the pace is extremely fast and having a strong prior understanding will put you at a huge advantage.

- ☐ **Independent study**

  In your A Levels, you learn how to study more independently than in your GCSEs. These skills are essential to studying economics at university, where much of the content is left to you to dissect and understand. For example, if you study PPE at Oxford, you'll have your own booklet of maths problems to work through, and much of the material the problems focus on will be self-taught.

- ☐ **Essay writing**

  Economics is not all about problem sheets; you'll also be expected to produce clear and concise written answers. If you have done an essay-based A Level, the writing skills you have learnt will be hugely helpful to your degree.

- ☐ **Reading skills**

  Many subjects that overlap with economics (such as management and philosophy) involve long weekly reading lists. You'll also be expected to digest a lot of information from books in the applied economics modules at Cambridge. Therefore, it's important to be able to read efficiently and with focus so you can be as productive as possible.

*"I honestly didn't know what management was before I arrived—I don't think anyone did! Turns out, it's very reading- and essay-based. Every week, we have a reading list to complete, and we write an essay on the given essay title. We all started off slow at reading, and it was intimidating at first to see how many books were on the reading list, but we all quickly developed our reading skills and now I find the reading list the most enjoyable part of my degree."* –Helen Lily, E&M, Oxford

These four skills are of vital importance to an economics-based degree, so retaining them from school is crucial. Furthermore, you can work on them over the summer if you feel one of them is lacking. Buy yourself an A-Level textbook and review it if you're worried about your maths—this will strengthen your independent study skills at the same time. Likewise, reading economics books will very much help you acclimatise to the content and develop your reading skills.

# Part IV:

# Philosophy

# Chapter 31:
# Philosophy (bonus chapter!)

Philosophy is combined in four different ways with quantitative subjects at Oxford:

- Maths & Philosophy
- Computer Science & Philosophy
- Physics & Philosophy
- PPE (discussed in Chapter 24 on page 341)

The first three of these are the main focus of this Chapter, but there is still lots of useful information for students applying to PPE too. See it as a little bonus chapter hiding out in a world of quantitative STEM subjects.

Philosophy is sometimes described as *thinking about thinking,* and the breadth of study may be appealing to you: you get to address a variety of different issues and topics—from knowledge to God to feminism.

## 31.1: Books to read if you're interested in philosophy Passion

If you're thinking of applying to a joint course involving philosophy, reading some books about philosophy, and about its intersection with your second subject, is an excellent way to discover new interests and get a handle on what the joint course will involve. Independent reading in philosophy is also a great thing to include in your personal statement. Below is a list of philosophy books, as well as some touching on the intersections of philosophy with maths, computer science and physics.[158]

158 See oxbridgeformula.co.uk/bonus-chapter for links to these books and more.

## Philosophy books

**Dupré: *50 Philosophy Ideas You Really Need To Know***

If you're new to philosophy, this is a great place to start. Although not particularly academic, it's a brilliant walk-through of many core concepts in the discipline. It presents 50 central philosophical problems in bite-sized chapters full of engaging anecdotes—and leaves lots of open-ended questions for you to consider.

Some examples of ideas this book includes are:

- The brain in a vat problem
- The divine command theory of ethics
- Ethical questions about animal rights, such as 'Do animals feel pain?'

**Blackburn: *Think***

Although a lot more difficult to digest than Dupré's *50 Ideas*, this is a more in-depth explanation of key philosophical issues. *Think* considers six core topics in great detail; the chapter on *God* in particular offers an interesting and thought-provoking debate.

*"Although admissions tutors won't expect you to have formed an opinion on every debate in philosophy, I would recommend spending some time trying to determine whether anything you previously believed has been challenged. Formulate as clearly as possible what the writer's ideas are, what ideas they are responding to, and what **your own** thoughts are in response. This is what will impress interviewers most."* –Student, Maths & Philosophy, Oxford

### Gaarder: *Sophie's World*

*Sophie's World* is a fictional tale of a girl[159] who ends up trapped in a philosophical matrix and negotiates her way through by considering the major doctrines of philosophy. An entertaining first look at philosophy, the novel covers many of the discipline's most contentious issues. It particularly focuses on knowledge, with Sophie concluding that she cannot know that there's an external world at all.

### Descartes: *Meditations*

This is one of the most influential texts in philosophy, and the ideas in it are deep and complex. Although admissions tutors won't expect you to have a full grasp of the text, or understand the concepts in detail, it's a great starting point for philosophy students. It covers a variety of topics, from epistemology (the theory of knowledge: what it is, whether it is possible to possess) to the philosophy of mind and the ***mind-body problem***. Even if you only read the first couple of meditations (there are six in total), Descartes is an influential philosopher whose ideas permeate much of the subject, which makes them very much worth reading.

**The mind-body problem** challenges the idea that we have a material body and an immaterial mind; *if* that's the case, how can the two interact with each other? For example, if I reach for a book, it seems we'd want to say that wanting the book causes my arm to move, and observing the book helps me move it in the right direction, but how do wanting and observing affect physical movements if they take place in an immaterial mind?

159 Called Sophie!

**Russell: *The Problems of Philosophy***

This is another fascinating overview of the fundamental problems of philosophy. As a relatively modern and eminent philosopher, Russell is also a good name to mention in your personal statement or in your interview. This is a short, digestible book that covers a lot of important ground.

## Books useful for Maths & Philosophy or Computer Science & Philosophy

**Shapiro: *Thinking About Mathematics***

This is the most comprehensive pre-university study of the philosophy of mathematics. It covers lots of interesting topics and explores theories of number and the infinite. It's very theoretical at times, so focus first on trying to grasp the main concepts covered in each chapter.

**Courant and Robbins, with Stewart: *What is Mathematics?***

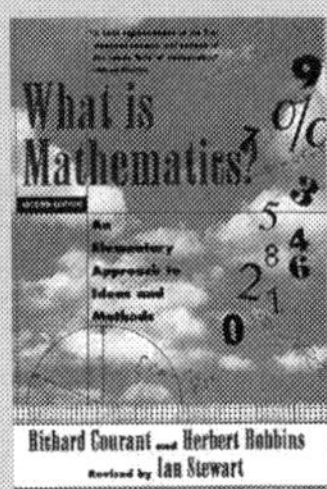


If you're interested in the methods used in mathematics but haven't read much about them, this book is a great place to start—and it could provide an interesting springboard for your personal statement. It also has some really interesting sections on the philosophy of mathematics, questioning what numbers are and how they fit into the wider world.

**Cheng: *Beyond Infinity***

This is a great introduction to concepts of infinity; particularly how it shows the overlap between maths and philosophy. It begins by going through different concepts of infinity and ways of perceiving the infinite before developing applications of infinity in maths, often from a philosophical perspective. Worth a read, even if you only stick to the first few sections.

**Petzold: *The Annotated Turing***

This book expands and comments on the paper in which Turing invented the Turing Machine. The author talks about how the paper relates to Turing's other ideas about computability and artificial intelligence and their influence on the fields of both computer science and philosophy. This book is great preparation for the first year of a Computer Science & Philosophy degree, as you'll take a whole course on Turing and his work.

## Books useful for Physics & Philosophy

**Kuhn: *The Structure of Scientific Revolutions***

This is a landmark text about the history of science, written by the philosopher Thomas Kuhn. It revolutionised the way that both physicists and philosophers view and approach science. It introduced the term 'paradigm shift', which is now fully integrated into everyday speech. The book explores how science has developed over time and explores many of the central discoveries through a philosophical lens. If you don't have the time to read the whole text, it's worth reading a summary, because it contains ideas that are still important in both physics and philosophy today.

**Becker: *What is Real?***

A historical and philosophical discussion of a number of influential approaches to understanding quantum mechanics. This book is highly opinionated in the sense that it criticises commonly-held ideas about quantum mechanics, but it attempts to provide reasons for its criticisms and gives an even-handed overview of other positions without favouring one. A great way to get an insight into the types of debate that quantum mechanics has inspired since its creation.

**Albert: *Time and Chance***

An introduction to the problem of the arrow of time. The 'arrow of time' refers to the fact that some physical processes can be reversed and others can't. For instance, a cake can be put down and picked up again, but it can't be burned and then unburned—burning is irreversible. The problem is that the interactions between the particles that make up the cake and the air around it aren't irreversible, at least not in the same way, and burning is merely a particular rearrangement of those particles, so how do we explain the fact we can't unburn the cake? Albert discusses the relationship of this problem to thermodynamics and probability and attempts to find a solution.

**Other resources**

As well as these books, there is an abundance of useful philosophy resources on the internet.

BBC Radio 4 has released a really interesting series on YouTube that goes through key philosophical concepts.[160] They are very short and accessible—and present lots of different ways to view questions in philosophy.

We'd also recommend any of the *In Our Time* podcasts, which can be found on the BBC Sounds app. Type in keywords (such as philosophy and maths) or the specific concept you're interested in, and you'll find great podcasts that you can listen to wherever you are.

The best way to get good at philosophising is to think! Think about the concepts you've read or heard about. Then try and engage your friends and family in conversation about these topics. This will give you a good indication as to whether or not philosophy is something you would enjoy at university!

## 31.2: How to prepare for a philosophy interview

Preparing for a philosophy interview is very different to preparing for a STEM interview. You'll face a distinct style of interview and will need to display skills that aren't tested in STEM subjects.

160 A link to this and more resources can be found at oxbridgeformula.co.uk/bonus-chapter.

> *"In a Maths or Computer Science interview, tutors are looking to see that you think methodically, employ your natural ability and implement the concepts you've learnt to date. In a philosophy interview, tutors are looking to see how you adapt to new concepts. Although methodical thinking is important so that your thoughts don't become confused, tutors want to see interesting and original thought patterns—ones you can justify."* –Student, Computer Science & Philosophy, Oxford

## When should you start preparing for a philosophy interview?

The summer between Year 12 and Year 13 is a great time to do some reading. However, if the course you're applying to also has an admissions test, make sure you give enough attention to that between the end of the summer term and your test date.

Most students will start their interview preparation as soon as the admissions test is over. Don't waste precious time waiting to see if you've been invited to interview before starting to prepare—otherwise, other applicants will be gaining a huge head start over you.

Don't worry if it seems you have to spend more time preparing for your philosophy interview than the interview for the quantitative part of your subject in order to feel ready—philosophy might be a completely new subject for you and, either way, you'll need to read and reflect a lot to get a sense of it, which takes time.

## What should you do to prepare for a philosophy interview?

Here are our top tips for preparing for a philosophy interview:

### 1) Throw around ideas and examine them critically Ability Potential

The most important part of philosophy is thinking—so try to construct your arguments about a topic and reflect on philosophical theories you've read. Why not start with the following questions:

- Am I the same thing as my body?
- What's the difference between my beliefs about myself and about others?

- Is there a world outside of me? Can I know this?
- Does God exist? Does it matter either way?

> *"My first philosophy interview began with a really abstract question. I was asked 'How do you know the chair you're sitting on is blue?' It really helped that I'd already spent some time thinking about these types of questions in my head and thinking about ways to approach them. I carefully went through why I thought I knew there was a chair underneath me at all and then why I thought it was blue, linking in some ideas I had read in Descartes' Meditations, and also thinking about why it's problematic to just assume the existence of an external world."* –Student, Physics & Philosophy, Oxford

## 2) Talk about philosophy Passion Potential

In the same way that thinking about philosophy is a really important part of developing your philosophical skillset, it's important to practise composing your ideas and formulating them out loud. Ultimately, the interview is your chance to impress your tutors in person, so you need to express yourself concisely and clearly.

Philosophy is complicated, and arguments that seem clear in your head can be difficult to vocalise—so practise this. Over dinner, talk to your parents, your siblings or even your cat.[161] Even if you're only speaking to the mirror, we would definitely recommend spending some time expressing your thoughts about philosophy out loud.

**Top Tip**

*Read a chapter of a book and try to* ***summarise*** *it in under a minute. This will sharpen your communication skills. Although you'd ideally choose a work of philosophy, you can also develop this skill by summarising any other book.*

## 3) Practise constructing your philosophical arguments clearly

Ability Potential

This is much easier said than done—thinking philosophically is hard!

161 Don't expect a response, especially not from your cat. It's about getting confident speaking out loud.

As well as talking through your ideas, spend time writing them down. Get a big piece of paper and draw a flowchart of your thought process—how you move an argument from point A to point B. This will help you check whether you've understood any argument you've read and whether it is valid.

**Example of an argument where you might want to draw a flowchart:** *Agrippa's Trilemma* argues that we can't *prove* any of our beliefs to be true. It's called a 'trilemma' because it argues that any attempt at a proof suffers from one of *three* flaws: assumption, circularity, or infinite regress. One way of setting it out is as follows:

**Assumption for contradiction (A):** Assume for contradiction that I have a *good enough* proof (P) that one of my beliefs (B) is true.
**Definition:** Let S be the set of reasons in P (i.e. further beliefs) that I either use directly to prove B, or to prove something used to prove B, or ..., etc.
**Premise 1:** One of these three things must be true of S and B:

(i) **Assumption:** When we go up the chain of reasons for B, and reasons for reasons, etc., at some point we get to a dead end. In this case, some reasons in S are not themselves proven to be true, i.e. they are merely assumed.
(ii) **Circularity:** When we follow the chain of reasons for B, and reasons for reasons, etc., we eventually get to a reason we've already seen before. That is, eventually some reason gets used in the chain of reasoning that proves itself.
(iii) **Infinite Regress:** The chain of reasons for B, and reasons for reasons, etc. goes on forever without repeating, which means the set S is infinite.

**Premise 2:** A chain of reasoning that starts with unproven assumptions isn't good enough to prove its conclusion to be true.
**Premise 3:** A chain of reasoning that involves circular reasoning isn't good enough to prove its conclusion to be true.
**Premise 4:** It is impossible to complete an infinite chain of reasoning.

**Intermediate Conclusion 1 (drawn from premises 1 and 2):** In case 1(i) (**Assumption**), the 'proof' P isn't good enough, which contradicts (A).
**Intermediate Conclusion 2 (drawn from premises 1 and 3):** In case 1(ii) (**Circularity**), the 'proof' P isn't good enough, which contradicts (A).
**Intermediate Conclusion 3 (drawn from premises 1 and 4):** In case 1(iii) (**Infinite Regress**), the 'proof' P isn't actually possible, which contradicts (A).

**Main Conclusion:** Since we reach a contradiction in every case, our initial assumption (A) must be false, no matter what B is. I.e. none of our beliefs can be proven to be true.

This argument is an interesting example because most people don't want to accept the conclusion, but there is a lot of disagreement on which premise to reject. Try drawing a flowchart for it as we discussed. Think about how you could argue further for some of the premises (which would mean adding more to your flowchart too).

*"Before my philosophy interviews, I bought loads of flashcards. On each one, I wrote a stage of an argument I had read, and stuck them onto a flowchart on my wall. I could visualise the argument moving from A to B, and also review it while I was getting ready for school. I also did this with key philosophical terms, theories and ideas."* –Jess, Maths & Philosophy, Oxford

## 4) Build a bank of interesting concepts and philosophers Passion

This bank doesn't have to be huge—the interviewers won't expect you to know *everything* about philosophy! But it's good to have a general idea of the core topics and philosophers—and how all the different strands of philosophy fit together.

Examples of core philosophy topics include:

- Knowledge and the justification of beliefs
- Ethics
- The nature of the mind and perception
- Causation and scientific explanation
- God and religion
- Political freedom

Examples of core[162] philosophers are:

- Plato
- Descartes

162 These are some particularly influential philosophers, but people have different opinions on which historical philosophers (if any!) are actually important!

- Hume
- Kant

**Top Tip**

*In your interview, be careful not to* ***'name drop'*** *or recite facts you've learned without synthesising or analysing them. Tutors are looking for original thought and engagement with the issues they have raised!*

## Do's and don'ts for your philosophy interview

**Do: Always be ready to clarify**

It's important to keep reflecting on whether you've phrased your thoughts as clearly as you can, and whether you're clear on what the interviewer is saying. Unlike in an ordinary conversation, it's not weird to go back and try to rephrase something even if you think you got the gist across the first time around. It's a good idea to recap what you think the interviewer is saying to clarify before you start responding.

Be sure to have a clear position in the first place. This should go without saying, but it's really easy to start talking without being clear what your overall point is. This also means it's important to take a position (at least some of the time) rather than sitting on the fence.

**Do: Make and observe necessary distinctions**

For instance, the interviewer might ask you: *'Are you justified in believing that the sun will rise tomorrow?'* Perhaps you're tempted to argue that you're justified in assuming that the sun will rise tomorrow for practical reasons (e.g. that it's impossible to make plans otherwise). This isn't necessarily an irrelevant thought, but be careful to observe distinctions in meaning even between uses of the same word. In this case, you've started talking about what is *practically* justified—we have a good reason to *act* as if the sun will rise tomorrow because making plans is important. But the question is really about what's *epistemically* justified—i.e. what we have evidence for or good reason to *believe*.

**Do: Keep it structured**

Lay out the branches of an argument before you start exploring each one. For instance, if you see there are two ways to interpret a statement, or two plausible responses to a problem, say so and briefly describe both before launching into an explanation of the first.

Keep track of what each part of an argument is doing. In particular, it's important to remember which premises[163] of the argument still need to justified. It's also important to keep in mind the difference between proving a claim is false and merely undermining one reason that was offered for it.

**Don't: Be stubborn**

Change your mind if the interviewer gives a good argument against your position—but try to explain *why* you're changing your mind and if you see any other consequences of that change. Figure out if you need to merely *adapt* your position or reject it completely.

Don't just repeat strong opinions. Some students come into a philosophy interview dead set on approaching every topic from a particular angle. This might involve referencing a certain philosopher they've read or taking a strong and wide-reaching position on what philosophy (or even reality) really is (for example, that it's about nothing except linguistic conventions). Even if there are good philosophical reasons to believe your position, merely repeating it, as opposed to engaging with the interviewer's specific examples, isn't very productive.

## 31.3: A script of an Oxbridge philosophy interview

An Oxbridge philosophy interview is the stuff of legend. Have you heard the one about the student who proved the existence of God in their interview? Or the person who walked out of the room when the interviewer asked them what bravery was? Or the interview where the student set the interviewer's desk chair on fire to prove that objects exist outside of the mind? Luckily, these are all myths! Nonetheless, Oxbridge philosophy interviews do have an infamous reputation.

To dispel some of the mystery, here are two mock Oxbridge philosophy interviews. In terms of subject matter, the first is more typical of a Maths/Computer Science/Physics & Philosophy interview, and the second is more typical of a PPE interview. However, the style of question, and the ways in which the tutors test and guide the students, could be seen in an interview for any of those degrees.

You'll notice that the students' answers in these examples aren't flawless, and they aren't expected to be! The interviewers also have to leave some of what the students say unexamined or the conversation would never

163 Think of a premise as a 'reason' which backs up or leads to your conclusion.

end. However, the students do try to spell out their thoughts and interact with the interviewers in a productive way, which is worth observing.

# Question 1

**Question: I want to discuss something called the regularity account of causation. When I clap, a sound is produced. What does it mean to say that my clap *causes* the sound?**

**Well, the *regularity account* of causation says this: Claps *cause* sound because *whenever* someone claps, a sound follows. In other words, the regularity account says that, if one event is always followed by another, then the first event *causes* the second.**

**Do you think this is a good way of explaining what a cause is?**

## Model Interview

**Student:** I'm not sure. It seems pretty plausible to me. It fits nicely with the way we learn about causes and effects. For example, we can only come to know that chickenpox causes red spots after we see several people who have chickenpox who *then* get red spots.

> Although relating the question to what people do or don't *know* means going off at a slight tangent, it's very good that the student tries to identify *why* the idea is plausible, and that they give a concrete example.

**Tutor:** That's true. But there's a distinction between how things truly are and what we *know* about them. Even if we *do* learn about causal[164] relationships by looking for when one event follows another, it might be that there's more to causation than that.

**Student:** That makes sense. But don't I have more reason to believe... this account...what was it called? (*Pauses.*) Oh yeah, the regularity account of causation. Don't I have more reason to believe it if it makes sense of other things, such as how I *learn* about causation?

**Tutor:** Absolutely, you do. But what other factors do you think we might want to consider?

> The interviewer is trying to stretch you, and a way of doing that is to keep asking for ideas to make you think harder.

**Student:** (Thinks.) I suppose it all depends on whether it accounts for what we normally want to say are causes and effects.

> Not quite an answer, but a plan for thinking about the problem further, which is also a great response in an interview.

164 Causal, meaning to do with causation.

**Tutor:** Okay. Great. Let's think about some test cases. I want you to imagine that no-one has ever clapped before. How might that be a relevant scenario in this context?

**Student:** Okay. I suppose the regularity account might say that, when I clap for the first time, the clap isn't the *cause* of the sound because there isn't a regularity yet. And that wouldn't be right, because obviously, the clap would still have been the cause. But I don't see why only events that *already* happened should count towards there being a regularity. If all future claps will be followed by sounds, that should be enough to mean the first clap is the cause of the sound that follows it.

**Tutor:** What if there was only ever one clap and one sound, in the whole history of the world?

**Student:** Ah, okay. I see the point. In that case, there wouldn't be a regularity because there are no other examples of claps followed by sounds.

> Can you see an issue with this based on the original definition provided by the tutor?

**Tutor:** That's not quite what I was getting at. Can you recall what the definition of the regularity account is?

> Always try to use the exact definition given; however, the student won't be marked down a great deal for forgetting it in the heat of the moment—it's how well they understand and use it from now on that matters.

**Student:** I suppose it's that *all* events of the first type are followed by events of the second type. Or, I mean, something such as: A causes B *if* all events of the same type as A are followed by events of the same type as B. Although I'd need to say what makes events the same type...

> Introducing letters can't hurt. The interviewer could have helped by defining this form to begin with, but sometimes they prefer to introduce an idea via a concrete example and only give an abstract definition if the conversation demands it, or prompt you to give it instead.

**Tutor:** Let's leave the issue of what makes events the same type as each other for now, though you're right that it does matter. Let's think about the case where there's only ever one clap and one sound.

**Student:** Alright. I'm not sure what changed from before, though.

**Tutor:** What if you apply the definition you gave?

**Student:** The clap causes the sound if every time someone claps, a sound is produced. Ah, okay. That works: if that one clap is followed by a sound – and they are the only sound and clap that have ever happened – then we are saying that *every* clap has been followed by a sound. So the regularity account would say that the clap is indeed the cause.

Thought experiments often involve examining 'edge' or extreme cases.

**Tutor:** That seems to be a fair analysis of this particular case. But can you see any *problems* arising for the regularity account as a result?

**Student:** I'm not sure what you mean. (*Pauses.*) The regularity account worked in this case.

**Tutor:** This case, yes. But is there maybe something about *why* the regularity account got it right we should worry about?

The interviewer is trying to let the student get the idea by themselves. Can you think of other reasons the regularity account might break down?[165]

**Student:** (*Thinks.*) It got this case right because the clap and the sound only happened *once*, so the sound followed the clap *every* time. Oh, okay. So whenever any pair of events only happens once, one is the cause of the other. For instance, if I clapped and then I sneezed and this was the only time I ever did each one in the history of the universe, the regularity account would say that my clap caused the sneeze, which is clearly absurd.

Providing a concrete example and summing up its consequences for the regularity account—great!

**Tutor:** Some philosophers would certainly conclude that. But they also have *another* reason for reaching this conclusion. I want you to tell me what it is from the situation I'm about to present to you. Whenever a switch is hit, a click is heard and a light comes on.

**Student:** Okay... so if we're sticking to the regularity account, then the click caused the light to come on. Or vice versa. But that isn't true. It was the switch being hit that caused the light to come on, not the click.

**Tutor:** Very good. Situations such as this have led some philosophers to try something else. They point out that, if the switch hadn't been flipped, then the light wouldn't have come on. So we might suggest that for A to cause B means that B wouldn't

165 Possible things to consider: What would happen in a vacuum? What if there were no claps, ever?

have happened if A hadn't happened. This is what's called a 'counterfactual' account of causation. Do you think it does better than the regularity account?

**Student:** With the regularity account, the problem was that it said some things should count as causation that actually shouldn't. So maybe I can make something like that happen here. Is that right?

Again, making a plan is very productive. Don't be afraid to ask to write some of the steps down if you need to.

**Tutor:** What would a counter-example look like in this case?

**Student:** Um... (*Pauses.*) It would mean there are cases where B wouldn't have happened without A, but A doesn't actually *cause* B. (*Pauses.*) But actually, it sounds right to me that if B wouldn't have happened without A, then A does indeed cause B. So I think I should probably look for the other possible type of problem, where A does cause B, but B would still have happened without A. Then the counterfactual account of causation would say A doesn't count as causing B, when it actually does.

Is the student actually correct here? Think of the switch, click and light example above to check. The tutor won't always correct you on earlier points if your later points seem to make sense.

**Tutor:** Great – can you think of an example?

**Student:** I was thinking I could choose B to be something that was always true anyway, such as a mathematical theorem, but in that case, A wouldn't be the cause of it anyway, so that doesn't work. (*Pauses.*) Okay, how about this. I throw a book at the window and it breaks it, but something else would have broken the window anyway, such as a bird that was about to hit it if I hadn't thrown the book.

Don't be afraid to analyse why ideas you had don't work—it's much better than thinking about and rejecting them in silence, because the interviewer can't see into your head.

**Tutor:** Yes, I think that works as a counterexample to the counterfactual account, although there are ways to reformulate it to try to overcome the problem. But we'll leave the question there.

## Further hints

The interviewer might have helped the student by:

- Writing the definitions on paper or a whiteboard and asking the student to apply them to each case step by step (you could even be given

a short passage on one or more accounts of causation to read before the interview)
- Giving the sneezing example (or an equivalent one) and asking the student to identify why it's a problem for the regularity account
- Prompting the student to think about cases where causation occurs but the counterfactual account doesn't recognise it
- Prompting the student to think about cases where there are two potential causes of a window breaking.

## What is the question testing?

No specific background knowledge is required for this question. As with many philosophy questions, it's designed to explore your ability to understand and apply precise definitions and think about all the consequences.

## Extending the question

The discussion might have developed to involve:

- Causation by absences. (For instance, Martha forgets to water her plant on Monday and Tuesday, and by Wednesday it's dead. Did Martha kill her plant? Or did Molly kill it because she didn't mistakenly spill her drink on the plant, which would have given it water to survive?)
- What it means for a counterfactual such as 'B wouldn't have happened' to be true.
- Whether there is, in fact, such a thing as causation at all.

## Related topics from university

Causation isn't covered in the first year of philosophy at Oxford, except perhaps if your tutor chooses to focus on that part of David Hume's thought when he is studied in the General Philosophy module—Hume is the most famous proponent of the regularity account. Causation is, however, a topic that is covered in the Knowledge and Reality course, which is one of the papers offered in the second and third years.

If you want to learn a little more about causation, you might be interested in reading one of the following papers by David Lewis, who is a well-known advocate of the counterfactual approach: 'Causation', 'Causation as Influence' and 'Counterfactual Dependence and Time's Arrow'.

## Question 2

**What makes this apple that I'm eating mine?**[166]

### Model interview

**Student:** Well... I suppose the fact that you're the one eating it already makes it your apple.

**Tutor:** What if I were to offer you a slice and you accepted it? Would my apple be your apple?

**Student:** No. So an apple doesn't just belong to whoever ends up eating it. There must be some other reason that the apple you're eating is yours.

> If you've gone wrong, admit it! Demonstrate to the interviewer that you're aware!

**Tutor:** And what might this be?

**Student:** Maybe that society recognises that you have a right to it.

**Tutor:** Interesting idea. But what do you mean?

> Often interviewers will ask what you mean. A good response will be clear and relate to the discussion. Giving a concrete example is a particularly good way to respond.

**Student:** All I mean is that if someone were to break into your office and steal your apple, you could expect the police to charge the thief and return your apple to you.

**Tutor:** I notice that you've used the words 'steal' and 'thief'. Perhaps you've got things the wrong way round—that society will punish anyone who takes the apple from me *because* it belongs to me?

**Student:** Ah... yes. Anyway, it might be the case that society makes mistakes in deciding who gets a right to what.

> Being able to recognise relevant examples on your own and to criticise your own suggestions are both highly valuable interview skills.

**Tutor:** Good point. Can you give an example?

**Student:** Sure. Well, suppose that I'm a peasant. I've harvested my wheat and it's been requisitioned by the state. If I try and get it back, I'll probably be punished. But the state won't punish itself for taking it in the first place.

**Tutor:** Ok. But what made the wheat yours in the first place?

**Student:** The fact that I harvested it. And planted it.

---

166 The interviewer is unlikely to be rude enough to actually eat in your interview, but they might have an apple as a prop.

**Tutor:** But I didn't plant or harvest the apple I'm eating.
**Student:** True. But you did buy it. Presumably.

**Tutor:** Yes, I bought it from a supermarket.
**Student:** So, you've paid whoever it was who grew it. An exchange has taken place, in that this individual has parted with their ownership of the apple in return for your money. Indirectly, via the supermarket.

**Tutor:** So do you think that what *originally* makes something someone's property, before anything is bought and sold, is their having produced it?
**Student:** Yeah, I reckon that I do.

**Tutor:** Can you go a bit further? What is it about production that creates ownership?
**Student:** (*Thinks.*) I'm not sure what else there is to say.

It's perfectly fine to admit that you don't know the answer to a question. The interviewer will push you and prompt you until you do!

**Tutor:** What are some examples of production? How are they different from other types of action?
**Student:** Well... it depends on what's being produced. Someone might be, I don't know, sewing, or weaving. But it doesn't have to be a craft exactly, because growing an apple isn't like constructing an apple from parts. And, say, composing a song might not even have a tangible physical output.

**Tutor:** What do those activities have in common then?
**Student:** Effort? And time? I suppose effort involves converting time and talent into something else. So I'd say whatever someone puts effort into is theirs.

**Tutor:** Very interesting. Have you read Locke's *Second Treatise?*
**Student:** No, unfortunately I haven't.

Don't pretend to have read something you haven't. There's nothing to gain in doing so.

**Tutor:** Not to worry. The idea there is very similar to the one you've given me.

## Further hints

If you're stuck, you might try developing the question a bit. You can think, 'What makes this apple belong to the interviewer *as opposed to anyone else?*, or 'What makes *this* apple the interviewer's?' Hopefully this discrimination brings to mind factors like having had a hand in the apple's being grown.

Other questions the interviewer might ask to help a student include:

- In general, what do you understand by the idea of right to property?
- Would taking the apple from someone else by force be enough to make it mine?
- If I planted the seed from which the apple grew, would this make me its owner?
- If I own myself, does this mean that I own anything that I make myself?

## Extending the question

The interviewer will likely ask you to consider the opposing point of view, time permitting. For instance, the interview might continue as follows:

**Tutor:** What do you think might be a problem for an account of property similar to Locke's?

**Student:** Well... maybe if two or more people are involved in producing something together. For instance, if a family of farmers are all involved in growing an apple. Which one of them does it belong to?

**Tutor:** Indeed. Any other problems?

**Student:** Yes. I might put in very little, but still some, effort. So I might water a tree once and claim to own all the apples it yields.

The interviewer may further ask you to try to overcome the problems you've mentioned.

## What is the question testing?

The point of the question is to assess your ability to connect and criticise ideas—to give reasons to back up your suggestions and to respond to challenges. The interviewer wants to see you develop a line of argument (or two, or three). You're also being tested on your ability to think of relevant examples, though no specific background knowledge is assumed.

## Related topics from university

Ideas about property and ownership are related to ethics and political philosophy. At Oxford, you can take ethics and political philosophy options in your second or third year. If you study PPE, you'll also take a 'Theory of

Politics' course in your first year, which can either focus on texts (such as Locke's *Second Treatise*) or on themes (such as property).

## 31.4: Doing a Maths/Computer Science/Physics & Philosophy degree (a typical work week)

Studying Maths/Computer Science/Physics & Philosophy, you'll have between 8–12 lectures per week made up of 2–3 philosophy lectures and the rest your other subject. You do about 60–75% of the maths/computer science/physics that the pure mathematicians, computer scientists or physicists do in the first year.

When it comes to philosophy, you'll do one logic problem sheet every week, and you'll write one essay most weeks. Before each essay, you'll be expected to read 5–6 texts from the assigned reading list. This will probably take about 10–12 hours (depending on how quickly you read and the length of the list) and another 4 hours to write the essay.

Overall, Maths/Computer Science/Physics & Philosophy are demanding degrees. The workload is tough but manageable, especially if you enjoy the subjects. The Physics & Philosophy week will probably feel even more packed because you also have to attend labs.

> *"Something I wish I'd known before I started studying Maths & Philosophy is how different university maths is to maths at school. You spend most of your time proving theorems and propositions, as opposed to doing calculations. Also, philosophy isn't just thinking about your own ideas, you really have to spend time analysing and dissecting texts and other people's ideas."* –Anya, Maths & Philosophy, Oxford

## 31.5: Character profiles (spot the successful applicant)

In this section, we'll look at the application journeys of three different students who have applied for joint degrees involving philosophy. For more details about the application process for Maths/Computer Science & Philosophy, see page 52. For Physics & Philosophy, see page 216.

## Applicant 1: Clara, 17 (Maths & Philosophy, Oxford)

**Before interview:**

- Clara is in her final year of school and is predicted 4 A*s in her A Levels. She has 8 GCSEs at level 8/9.
- She studies Philosophy at A Level, as well as Maths, Further Maths and Geography.
- She has read lots of philosophical texts, including all of Descartes' *Meditations* and Hume's *Enquiry.* She has notes on both that she has mostly memorised for her interview preparation.
- She finds mathematics at school quite dull, but is sure she'll enjoy the wider scope of university mathematics.
- She does a lot of preparation for the MAT, making sure she knows all of the content of her A-Level syllabus before sitting the exam.
- Her personal statement includes a couple of exaggerations like:
  - *'You would want me to study at your institution due to my commitment and constant hard-working nature, exemplified by my extraordinary GCSE grades.'*
  - *'I have read most of the major works of philosophy and have explored key proofs in mathematics, such as the Rank-Nullity Theorem in the field of linear algebra.'*

**In her interviews:**

- In her maths interviews, Clara answers the preliminary questions without difficulty, but struggles in the later sections when she has to develop ideas outside of the A-Level syllabus.
- The interviewers also ask her to describe the 'Rank-Nullity Theorem', since she mentioned it on her personal statement. Clara is stuck here: she only read about the Rank-Nullity Theorem once, and can't really remember it anyway.
- She does not enjoy her maths interviews very much.
- In her philosophy interview, the interviewers question Clara's extensive reading. She may have memorised summaries of some key ideas, but when they push her a little further, it turns out she has not explored any of the concepts and is unsure of what they actually mean in practice.

## Applicant 2: Kofi, 19 (Computer Science & Philosophy)

**Before interview:**

- Kofi is currently enjoying his gap year and has a very strong IB score of 42 under his belt. He has 9 GCSEs at level 8/9.
- He was going to apply to study straight Computer Science, but on his gap year he has spent a lot of time thinking about himself and the big questions in life, so he decides to apply for Computer Science & Philosophy instead.
- Kofi has forgotten about the MAT entirely, so he has done next to no preparation for it. He is stumped by the extra questions for Computer Science applicants at the end, which he isn't expecting, and finds the style completely different to anything he had seen before.
- After the MAT, he decides to travel in Europe, thinking there is no point starting to prepare for interviews if he doesn't even know he'll be invited yet.
- His personal statement includes sentences such as:
  - *'When I was finding myself in Bali over the summer at the start of my gap year, I spent a lot of time alone thinking about myself. This introspection made me think I'd enjoy philosophy and probably be really good at it.'*
  - *'I enjoyed Maths at school and believe studying Computer Science with you could reignite and enhance my passion for the subject.'*

**In his interviews:**

- In Kofi's computer science interview, he stumbles a lot on the earlier questions. He has forgotten a lot of his A-Level Maths content and even some of the basics. As the questions get more developed Kofi has good ideas, but he is lacking the foundations required.
- The interviewers ask him what he has been doing on his gap year to improve his understanding of computer science. Kofi hasn't been doing anything.
- He is stumped in his philosophy interview. They ask him some questions about what philosophy he has read. He hasn't done any reading around the subject—he thought philosophy was about thinking?
- When they get to the philosophical questions that require him to think, his thoughts are muddled and confused; he has spent very little time actually exploring philosophical concepts and finds the whole thing a little perplexing.

## Applicant 3: Yi, 18 (Physics & Philosophy)

**Before interview:**

- Yi is in her final year at school and is predicted A*s in Mathematics, Physics and Further Mathematics and an A in History. She has 8 GCSEs at level 8/9.
- She has enjoyed studying history and likes the fact that Physics & Philosophy would allow her to continue writing essays.
- As well as reading a few texts about philosophy, she listens to podcasts, attends lectures and regularly engages her mum in philosophical debate over dinner.
- She does a lot of PAT preparation. She completes past papers, works hard to understand the questions she can't do initially and spends time exploring the skills she will require.
- Her personal statement includes sentences such as:
  - *'I have really enjoyed studying electromagnetism in school. Thinking this is something I would like to explore further, I went to a lecture in London about the uses of electromagnetic induction and tried to answer some challenging problems on it.'*
  - *'I have done some research into logic, watching some videos on YouTube about how to construct truth tables. I was struck by how mathematical this philosophical technique was, and I would like to further explore the technical side of philosophy.'*

**In her interviews:**

- Yi's physics interviews begin solidly. She employs concepts from her A Levels and wider reading. As the questions get harder Yi works slowly, vocalising her thoughts and listening to the advice given by the interviewer. She does not always reach the final answer, but her reasoning is thoughtful and sound.
- In Yi's philosophy interview, she answers the questions methodically, taking alternative positions into account and never sounding too dogmatic. She is grateful for the practice she has had vocalising her philosophical thoughts beforehand.
- She mentions a couple of philosophers and theories she has previously read about but doesn't just mention them for the sake of it. Her references to them are relevant and useful to the discussion.

**How did they all do?**

Despite Clara's thorough preparation, it seems to have been misplaced. Kofi's lack of preparation showed him up in his interviews. However, Yi's preparation was useful, and she performed well in her interviews and wrote a good personal statement, so she is the successful candidate.

**What did Clara do wrong?**

✗ Clara focused too much on reading everything she could that was related to philosophy, instead of focusing on developing and understanding the concepts. This caught her out in her interview when she had to engage with the concepts, as opposed to merely re-stating them.

✗ As she wasn't particularly enjoying mathematics, perhaps she was applying for the wrong course. Remember, Oxbridge is a lot of work and you need to love your subject if you want to succeed at it.

✗ Her preparation for the MAT wasn't particularly useful. It's better to be active in your preparation, such as by doing past papers, attending courses, or using online resources such as those on the Oxbridge Formula website.

✗ She made false claims in her personal statement. For example, she said she understood the Rank-Nullity Theorem and this caught her out in her interviews.

✗ She assumed they would want to accept her for being a hard-working student, which appeared a little arrogant.

**What did Kofi do wrong?**

✗ Kofi failed to keep up his mathematical skills (hugely important for computer science) during his gap year. He assumed he would retain them, which caused an issue in his interview. He should also have actively pursued his love for computer science during this time. He only started preparing for his interview a week before, as that's when he found out he'd been invited, which probably wasn't enough time.

✗ Kofi had little understanding of philosophy and had done nothing to explore the discipline, which meant his personal statement and philosophy interviews were disappointing.

✗ He did no preparation for the MAT, which meant he didn't know the format and likely got a lower score because of it.

✗ Instead of focusing on computer science and philosophy, his personal statement recounted his experiences in Bali.

**What did Yi do right?**

✓ Yi explored the discipline of philosophy by reading widely around the subject.

✓ To prepare for her interview, she spent time thinking about and discussing key philosophical concepts.

✓ Yi prepared well for her PAT, focusing upon past papers and honing the relevant skills for the test.

✓ She performed well in interviews and displayed the 'teachability' that Oxbridge interviewers are looking for.

# Part V:

# Next Steps

# Chapter 32
# How to prepare wisely

## 32.1: What you still need to do

The purpose of this book is to raise your awareness of courses you might enjoy at Oxbridge, inspire you to apply, and give you an overview of exactly what you need to do to get in.

We sincerely hope that you've enjoyed reading this book, have found it inspirational, and have learnt a great deal from it. When we sat down to write this book, our objective was to share with you the vast amount of knowledge we've amassed whilst helping hundreds of students with their Oxbridge applications.

However, while we've taken great care to describe the application process in as much detail as possible, this book only scratches the surface of how we can assist you in gaining your place. If we tried to write down *all* our advice for *every single* test and *every kind* of interview, it would fill several encyclopaedias!

What's more, we genuinely don't believe that a book is the best way to comprehensively relay the nuanced and multi-faceted problem-solving strategies ingrained in the mind of an expert problem solver—exactly what you need to be to impress the admissions tutors.

### Further learning with us[167]

We'd like to share with you details of how we believe we can help you 'zoom in' and develop your understanding on a question-by-question basis. We want to see you through the intricate challenges that you'll face and help make your Oxbridge application journey smoother, more purposeful, and more enjoyable than if you tried to do it on your own.

So, for your information, here is the further training and support we can provide for you. We specialise in helping students prepare for tests

167 We will describe what we offer at the time of writing. However, this is subject to change.

containing maths, science, problem-solving, and critical-thinking components. These are:

Tests involving advanced maths: STEP, MAT, CTMUA, CSAT

Tests involving advanced maths and advanced physics: PAT, ENGAA, NSAA

Tests involving problem solving: TSA, ECAA, GAA*, PBSAA*, BMAT*

Tests involving critical thinking: TSA, GAA*, PBSAA*, BMAT.*

*Not specifically addressed in this book, but covered very thoroughly in our online resources.

## 32.2: Online Oxbridge Academy

Our idea in creating our system of online admissions test resources was to provide an affordable alternative to one-to-one tuition without sacrificing the *effectiveness of the teaching* or the *calibre of the tutors*. We've designed our online resources to address the most common issues students face throughout their preparation:

1. **You might struggle with particular past paper questions:** Our expert tutors have created *video solutions* to every past paper for each admissions test.[168] We use videos so that:
   a) You can watch just enough to get a hint and then hit pause to attempt the question yourself, or skip to the specific part with which you are struggling
   b) You benefit from illustrations, animations and spoken explanations that make solutions easier to follow and don't skip out on any detail.

2. **You understand a solution once you've seen it, but never would have come up with it on your own:** Our tutors don't just talk through the method. Every time they make a decision about how to tackle the next stage of a question, they answer the following: '*Why* did I use this method?' and '*How did I know* to use this method?' We discuss multiple possible approaches where relevant, in case one resonates with you more than another.

168 With the exception of STEP, since the 'back catalogue' is so huge and the older papers don't quite reflect the newer papers in terms of question consistency, so we've created solutions to questions from 2011 onwards (the most recent and relevant papers). We've hand-selected questions from older papers too, in our Platinum STEP Online Bundle.

3. **You've done all the past papers:** Some admissions tests are so new that past papers are scarce—and even for older tests (such as the MAT and PAT), dedicated students will quickly exhaust their supply. We've created and collated hundreds of further practice questions (with video solutions) for each test, so you'll never be short of practice material.

### How to make use of our online resources[169]

You can learn about and sign up to the 24-hour free trial[170] for any of our online resource areas at:
*oxbridgeformula.co.uk/online-courses*

If there are several students in your school taking Oxbridge admissions tests, why not speak to your Head of Higher Education or Head of Sixth Form about signing up for our schools bundle? Send them this link, so they can get a feel for what we provide:
*oxbridgeformula.co.uk/schools-free*

## 32.3: Admissions test courses

We run live (in-person and online) courses throughout the year for tests containing maths, physics, critical thinking and problem-solving components. Typically, we run courses at four key times in the year. Each of our courses is unique—for instance, you can attend all four of our STEP courses and learn completely different material each time. Here's a summary of the courses we run throughout the year:

Summer: STEP, MAT, CTMUA, CSAT, PAT, ENGAA, NSAA, ECAA, TSA

October: STEP, MAT, CTMUA, CSAT, PAT, ENGAA, NSAA, ECAA, TSA

February: STEP

Easter: STEP (with a focus on STEP 3 topics).

These courses are for you if:

**You want to learn clever shortcuts and tricks:** Many Oxbridge admissions tests are highly time-pressured. We'll teach you the most efficient

169 Review this book on Amazon and send us a picture of your review (oxbridgeformula.co.uk/amazon-review) to get £10 off the first payment for any online subscription on our website! ★★★★★

170 The trial is available throughout the year except for two weeks before the test.

and insightful methods, tricks and techniques to maximise your speed in an exam situation, so you'll enter the room brimming with confidence.

**You want to meet your 'competition':** If you're reading this book, you're probably one of the highest achieving students in your school. It's easy to fall under the illusion that you won't have to put in much work to succeed in your Oxbridge application. In our courses, you'll meet your peers who are also at the top of their game, which will motivate you to strive harder and achieve more. Our students often say they appreciate meeting others going through the same process and frequently stay in touch with each other after our courses.

**You want answers to your questions:** Our highly interactive courses are designed by teachers with 10+ years of classroom experience. You won't be attending a lecture and you'll have plenty of time to clear up your individual questions and doubts. We know our students won't all have covered the same material at school yet, so we check prior knowledge and have multiple tutors present to help if you're stuck.

All in all, 99% of students who have attended our live courses say they would recommend them.

### How to join our live admissions test courses

Learn about and sign up to any of our live courses here:
*oxbridgeformula.co.uk/live-courses*

## 32.4: Interview courses

Improving through practice is a recurring theme in this book. This is especially true with interviews—yet finding realistic practice for interviews is even more difficult than for admissions tests, since there are no past papers and knowing how well you're doing is about more than just seeing whether you get to the right answer.

We prepare students for the challenge and pressure of Oxbridge interviews for Maths, Computer Science, Physics and Engineering through our unique, highly specialised courses in which each student receives a full mock interview in front of nine fellow students applying for the same subject. The benefits of these courses include:

**Challenging mock-interview questions:** For the mathematical, computational and physical sciences, many of the questions available on the internet don't replicate the level of challenge faced by real Oxbridge applicants. For highly technical subjects like these, it's vital to be stretched to the correct level—and our courses do exactly that. We don't waste time telling you how to sit, what to wear, or how to answer 'general' questions as many other courses do—these things simply don't hold a lot of weight for quantitative subjects!

**A realistic environment for your mock interview:** Our courses replicate the pressure of a real interview. Although we are a friendly bunch, the pressure of being interviewed by a tutor you don't know, and with other people watching, is immense. But, as a result, all students who have attended these courses have unanimously told us that the real interview felt easy in comparison!

**Expert feedback on your interview performance:** While mock interviews (and other forms of practice discussed in this book) are useful, it's *much* easier to improve when you receive detailed feedback from an expert on what's working and what's not. That's why we provide personalised feedback on ten areas of your performance after your mock interview.

### How to join our in-person interview courses

You can learn about and sign up to our interview courses at:
*oxbridgeformula.co.uk/interview-courses*

## 32.5: Online Oxbridge Academy for schools

If you're a teacher, you may have browsed our online resources (comprising 5500+ videos at the time of writing) and wondered how to sign up all of your Oxbridge hopefuls in Year 12 or 13 (and medical hopefuls: we also offer extensive resources for the BMAT). The good news is that we have massively discounted bundles for schools for this very purpose! If you're a parent or student, please do share this information with your school's head of sixth form, head of careers, head of higher education and academic deputy head.

Some reasons to use the Online Oxbridge Academy in schools include:

**Slashing the time and resources required to provide support for *all* tests:** In our experience, many schools do a fine job of helping students prepare for admissions tests (through extracurricular clubs, for example). But how can students continue to receive the same level of support in the evenings, weekends or holidays (especially that crucial summer between Year 12 and 13)? The solution: our Online Oxbridge Academy. One challenge facing teachers[171] is the fact that each test has its own nuances, and it's impossible to teach students taking different tests at the same time without making compromises somewhere. Our online platform gives students access to material that is specifically geared towards their test, allowing teachers to focus on providing targeted help where students need an extra boost.

**Extra and early preparation for your gifted students:** Stretching your brightest students isn't always easy, and finding a bespoke solution that can be used as a self-study resource might be exactly what you are looking for.

**Case study:** *"We signed up to the Online Oxbridge Academy and use it as a weekly enrichment activity for our Year 12 students who have an interest in applying to Oxbridge or medical school. Once a week, students gather in an ICT room and log in to the Oxbridge Formula website. They each have access to different admissions test areas and work through the resources on their own, watching the video solutions for hints when they get stuck. It works very well for us as a school, as we only need one teacher in the room at any one time, and yet students can get specific help for the tests they are interested in taking."*
–Teacher, King Edward VI Handsworth Grammar School

## How to work with us

You can sign your students up to 50 free Oxbridge and medical admissions test videos here: *oxbridgeformula.co.uk/schools-free*

We are also able to create bespoke versions of any our admissions test or interview courses, to be delivered at your school or school network.

For more info and to book, please call us on 020 7459 4139.

# 32.6: Tuition

We believe our resources and courses completely replace the need for a tutor—and hiring one with the depth of knowledge to address your

171 Especially the maths department, since so many tests have mathematical components, no two of which are identical in level—it's impossible to teach STEP alongside the maths from the ECAA, for example.

weaknesses and really stretch you doesn't come cheap! However, if you're a student or parent looking to invest in specialist Oxbridge entrance tuition, we have a large network of hand-picked tutors and can match you with someone who attended the same university and studied the same subject you want to apply for (including academics and professors!). Our pool of tutors extends beyond the quantitative subjects discussed in this book, covering the entire range of subjects offered at Oxford and Cambridge.

### How to request a tutor

To find out more and speak to our tuition consultant, please see:
*oxbridgeformula.co.uk/tuition*

## 32.7: Keep in touch

### Amazon review

Just a reminder: if you review this book on Amazon and send us a picture of your review (*oxbridgeformula.co.uk/amazon-review*) you'll get £10 off the first payment for any online subscription on our website! ★★★★★

### Contact us

We're always more than happy to answer questions!
You can contact us by:
Email: *support@oxbridgeformula.co.uk*
Phone: 020 7459 4135

### Social Media

If you enjoyed this book, you can get even more tips and tricks, watch interviews with current Oxbridge students, and learn about discounts and offers by following us on social media:

Instagram: *@oxbridgeformula*
Twitter: *@oxbridgeformula*
LinkedIn: *linkedin.com/company/oxbridgeformula*
LinkedIn: *linkedin.com/in/paarulshah*

### YouTube channel

To watch videos of current Oxbridge students talking about their own application journeys, check out our YouTube channel:
*oxbridgeacdemy.co.uk/youtube*

## Suggestions

If you have any ideas of extra things you would have loved to see in this book, please do write to us. We'll see if we can include them in our next edition. We welcome any other comments too.
*oxbridgeformula.co.uk/suggestions*

# 32.8: Final thoughts

A final few pointers from us!

**Aspiration:** If you like the sound of applying to Oxford or Cambridge, go for it! It's only 1 of 5 choices on your UCAS form. And if you're truly invested in getting in, put all your energy behind your application. The courses *are* competitive, but if you don't try—you'll never know whether you would have succeeded!

**Growth mindset:** The academic challenges you'll face during the Oxbridge application process are intense. However, the whole point of a challenge is to overcome it, and grow stronger, brighter and more confident along the way. Challenges are opportunities, and if you approach them with this mindset—you'll go far.

**Persistence:** In quantitative subjects, you'll often spend hours on one problem, mulling it over again and again. This is completely normal—and the best way to strengthen your problem-solving muscles! Don't give up!

We've reached the end of the book. If you're starting to think about applying, we say: go for it! If you're putting together your application, we say: keep at it! If you're looking for last-minute tips before your test or interview, we're sure you'll ace it!

Best wishes for your bright future! We believe in you.

# Thank Yous

A large number of Oxford and Cambridge students and graduates have helped make this book possible by providing insight into their degrees, sharing their personal statements, and giving invaluable tips about the admissions process. A special thank you to:

David Adeboye, Raj Bahra, Peter Belcack, Anna Colley, Jake Cornwall-Scoones, Lizzy Cubitt, Alex Eacott, Joe Etherington, Man Hon Fan, Ben Gade, Joe Gardiner, Rahul Geetala, Leonie Glasson, Alex Gower, Josh Greensmith, Julia Halligan, Amaryllis Hill, Kay Hotchkiss, Inigo Howe, Jacob Jackson, Paaras Kantaria, Conrad Kunadu, Chuqiao Lin, Will Lunt, Dora Marshall, Jacob Mercer, Adam Morris, Redvers Morrissey, Melissa Orr, Claire Otasowie, Akshay Pal, Luke Pitman, Michał Pychtin, Harry Rendell, Eddie Revell, Giacomo Rossetti, Vincent Rustill, Amal Shah, Bijal Shah, Pranay Shah, Sagar Shah, Jamie Slagel, Sophie Smith, Andrew Stapran, Atticus Stonestrom, Anya Swales, Daniel Thomas du Toit, Leah Tillmann-Morris, Emily Townsend, Sam Trevelyan, Nick Trilloe, Jack Virgin, Helen Lily Wang, Alice Wilson, Jack You

This book is dedicated to all of our teachers, mentors and guides. Thank you for sharing your wisdom with us.

# Index

**N**

## S

## T

Printed in Germany
by Amazon Distribution
GmbH, Leipzig

18290308R00315